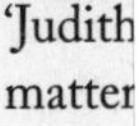

'Judith
matter

'Judith
should remember [Lopokova] . . . writing as fine as one could hope to encounter' *Times Literary Supplement*

'Successfully researched and confidently told' *Independent*

'Admirably researched . . . enthralling' *Dancing Times*

'How shrewd and kind of Mackrell to extricate Lopokova from so many decades as the snubbed alien in Bloomsbury footnotes' *New Statesman*

'Colourful and well-researched' *Tribune*

'Lopokova led a life encompassed by ballet, Russian revolution and the Bloomsbury Group, every disparate strand woven skilfully together in Mackrell's thorough and absorbing biography' *Good Book Guide*

'This biographer is elegant and true about a seminal figure . . . who has long lacked a proper historian-critic. Now, she has found one' *Dance Europe*

'Mackrell has done an excellent job of putting [Lopokova] back in the spotlight again' *Independent on Sunday*

Judith Mackrell has been the *Guardian*'s dance critic since 1995. She has also written for the *Independent*, *Vogue* and the *Literary Review*, among others, and has broadcast regularly on TV and radio. Her publications include: *Out of Line: The Story of British New Dance*; *Reading Dance*; *The Oxford Dictionary of Dance*; and *Life in Dance* (with Darcey Bussell).

Bloomsbury Ballerina

Lydia Lopokova, Imperial Dancer and Mrs John Maynard Keynes

Judith Mackrell

PHOENIX

A PHOENIX PAPERBACK

First published in Great Britain in 2008
by Weidenfeld & Nicolson
This paperback edition published in 2009
by Phoenix,
an imprint of Orion Books Ltd,
Orion House, 5 Upper St Martin's Lane,
London WC2H 9EA

An Hachette UK company

1 3 5 7 9 10 8 6 4 2

A CIP catalogue record for this book
is available from the British Library

ISBN 978-0-7538-2578-5

Typeset by Input Data Services Ltd, Bridgwater, Somerset

Printed and bound in the UK
by CPI Mackays, Chatham ME5 8TD

www.orionbooks.co.uk

For my mother

Lydia, with Frank Dobson's bust.

CONTENTS

ILLUSTRATIONS

Unless otherwise credited, all photos are from the private collection of Milo Keynes.

ACKNOWLEDGEMENTS

In writing this book I have been helped by receipt of an Elizabeth Longford Grant, for which much thanks to Longford's grand-daughter Flora Fraser and her husband Peter Soros, who sponsor the award. I owe an enormous debt of gratitude to my three inspiringly critical readers, Debra Craine, Max Eilenberg and Polly Richards; to Jane Pritchard, who has offered her encyclopaedic knowledge of ballet history, to Geoff Harcourt and Robert Cord, who have corrected my accounts of Keynes's economic theory; to Milo and Stephen Keynes, who have checked and enriched my accounts of the family history; and to Richard and Anne Keynes for their initial support and encouragement. Invaluable help with Russian research and translation has come from Geoff Whitlock, Olga Makarova and Barbara Loughlin. Patricia McGuire at the King's College Archive went way beyond the call of duty. All mistakes are of course my own.

I also want to thank many others who have been very generous with their time, expertise, hospitality, advice or contacts: Robert Skidelsky, Leo Kersley, Henrietta Garnett, Vladimir Lopukhov, Frederick Franklin, Sarah Walton, David Vaughan, Tim Scholl, Christopher Butler, Peter Jones, the late John Drummond, Bob Lockyer, John Barber, John Eatwell, Alison Carter, Igor Stupnikov, Elizabeth Souritz, and the staff of New York Public Library and London's Theatre Museum.

Huge thanks of course go to my editors at Weidenfeld & Nicolson, Helen Garnons-Williams, Francine Brody and Bea Hemming; to my copy editor, Celia Levett, and to my agent, Clare Alexander. My own family have been incredibly patient with me.

My publishers and I are grateful to the following for permission to reproduce quotations. Extracts from the Keynes Papers are reproduced by kind permission of King's College Cambridge © The Provost and Scholars of King's College Cambridge. Extracts from the Lydia Lopokova Keynes papers are reproduced by permission of Keynes family. The letters of Duncan Grant, © The Duncan Grant Estate, are reproduced by permission of Henrietta Garnett and Pandora Smith, and those of Vanessa Bell, © The Vanessa Bell Estate, are by permission of Henrietta Garnett. The letters of Lytton Strachey are reproduced by permission of the Society of Authors as agents of the Strachey Trust. I am grateful to David Higham Associates for permission to quote from *Laughter in the Next Room*, by Osbert Sitwell; to Henrietta Grant for extracts from *Tea at Tilton*; to Thames & Hudson for permission to quote from *Dearest Babushkin: Selected Letters and Diaries of Vera and Igor Stravinsky*, ed. Robert Craft © Robert Craft, 1985; to Virago and the London School of Economics and Political Science for permission to quote from the Diary of Beatrice Webb; to the Society of Authors as the literary representatives of the Estate of Clive Bell for permission to quote from his essay in *New Republic*; to the Society of Authors as literary representatives of the estate of Quentin Bell for permission to quote from *Bloomsbury and Lydia*; and to Rupert Crew Ltd, the literary executor of the late Sir Cecil Beaton for permission to quote from the Diaries of Cecil Beaton. *The Letters of Virginia Woolf* and *The Diaries of Virginia Woolf* are published by Hogarth Press and used by permission of the executors of the Virginia Woolf Estate and the Random House Group; extracts from *Death of a Moth* and *Mrs Dalloway* are reproduced by permission of the Society of Authors as the literary representative of the Estate of Virginia Woolf.

Duncan Grant's portrait of Lydia and Vanessa Bell's *Keynes Keynes* are reproduced by kind permission of the Provost and Scholars of King's College, Cambridge and Henrietta Garnett; Grant's *Scotch Reel* sketch is reproduced by kind permission of Henrietta Grant and Milo Keynes. Grateful thanks must go to Robert Grescovic for permission to reproduce early images of Lydia from his postcard collection of Russian dancers, and also to Milo Keynes, who has been extremely kind in giving me access to the Keynes family archive of pictures.

Mrs Clarissa Heald, the daughter of Vera and Harold Bowen, and her own daughter Henrietta Heald have been generous in giving me access to Harold's diary and giving permission to reproduce the photograph of Vera and her son.

While every effort has been made to contact copyright holders of all material reproduced in this book, if any have inadvertently been overlooked, the publishers will be happy to acknowledge them in future editions.

AUTHOR'S NOTE

Lydia's story falls into two halves. During the first years of her career in which she rose to international fame as a ballerina, her professional life progressed from headline to headline. Her movements were tracked by press reports, and nearly every performance was reviewed. Many daily details of her private life, however, went unrecorded, in part because Lydia kept no diary during this time, and any family letters that she wrote back home to Russia were subsequently scattered or destroyed by looters during the Second World War.

In contrast, the second part of Lydia's career, after she had met John Maynard Keynes, became less active, less adventurous. Yet if her professional life diminished in incident, her day-to-day life became disproportionately well documented. In the self-consciously literary world of Bloomsbury, where she lived with Maynard, Lydia not only became a regular writer of letters but was carefully conscientious about saving those she received.

It is in this second part of her story that Lydia's voice emerges most clearly, and in quoting from her letters I have left the eloquent vagaries of her spelling and grammar uncorrected – just as I have left uncorrected most other quotations from correspondence and diaries.

In the matter of Russian spelling, there is no simple, consistent option. I have updated the transliteration of certain names, for instance the Mariinsky, but with others I have had to make choices between conventional and personal variants, old and new. The standard modern spelling of Diaghilev, for example, feels more natural than Diaghileff although the latter was used by Lydia and by her contemporaries. On the other hand, I have adopted Lydia's spelling of her brother's name, Fedor, despite the fact that the modern transliteration tends to be Fyodor and appears as such in the endnotes and bibliography. As for Lydia's own surname, although she made the decision to Anglicise the spelling and pronunciation in 1914, many critics and members of the public continued to refer to her as Lopukhova, or Lopoukhova, with the stress on the second syllable rather than the third.

In the matter of Russian dating, I have used the Old Style, pre-1918 calendar only for scenes set in Russia. In the matter of money, so crucial an issue to Lydia until she met Maynard, the following may act as a very rough guide to the value of her earnings. Before the First World War, when exchange rates remained relatively stable, 10 Russian roubles was worth approximately £1, $5 or 27 French francs. Lydia's first, basic salary in Russia was 600 roubles per year, which was worth £60, $300 or 1,620 francs respectively. In 1909 St Petersburg she was still benefiting from subsidies and extra income from the Imperial Theatres. To put her earnings in a more modern context, when Lydia was earning a peak weekly wage of $2,000, in the commercial American theatre of 1912–13, the rough equivalent in 2008 money would be £17,000 or $35,000.

INTRODUCTION

On the morning of her wedding, 4 August 1925, Lydia Lopokova dressed with untypical restraint. Ordinarily her attitude towards clothes was vivid, scatty and impatient, her wardrobe veering between bohemian gypsyishness and her own theatrical versions of society fashion. For her appearance at London's St Pancras Registry Office, however, Lydia had taken pains to look neat, even demure. The light woollen suit and simple brown hat in which she had chosen to get married were not a memorable costume for a bride, but that, for Lydia, was the point. In this ensemble she hoped to get through her wedding day as anonymously as possible.

Anonymity was a difficult goal, however, given that in the summer of 1925, Lydia was one of the most famous women in London. As a dancer she had starred with Diaghilev's Ballets Russes, performing at the request of presidents and kings, while the man she was about to marry, John Maynard Keynes, was the most talked-about economist in Britain. Stories of the couple's intriguing engagement, the colourful coupling of an intellectual and a dancer, had already been leaking into the papers and Lydia must have known that the wedding itself was unlikely to pass without comment.

Even so, she wanted to believe the fuss would be minimal. Lydia had suffered from intrusive press attention before, not least over her protracted divorce from her previous husband. And during the three years in which she had been Maynard's mistress, she had suffered still more from the hostile scrutiny of certain of his friends. It had been made clear to Lydia that however courted she might be on the stage, within Maynard's world she was considered an interloper.

The fact that she was a woman hadn't eased her acceptance – the first woman with whom the closeted but contentedly homosexual

Maynard had ever fallen in love. For the whole of his adult life, Maynard had been drawn almost exclusively to other men, and it had taken all of Lydia's erotic ingenuity and emotional determination to break that pattern. Culturally and socially, however, Lydia had appeared still more of an outsider. While Maynard's formidably cerebral world had evolved through Eton, Cambridge, the boardrooms of financial institutions, and the drawing rooms of academics and politicians, Lydia had known nothing but the theatre since she was a child. While he was profoundly rooted in his Englishness, she was a wandering Russian.

Within the privacy of their own relationship, these divisions had often sharpened the couple's pleasure in each other. 'Is there any resemblance between you and me,' Lydia had mused, 'No! so different that it becomes attractive'.[1] And Maynard had felt the same. If he was ever going to fall in love with a woman, one like Lydia, who shone outside his own sphere, was always going to be his instinctive choice. A bluestocking, especially an economist bluestocking, would have been a disaster: 'If she were less than first rate,' commented Maynard's perceptive colleague Austin Robinson, 'he would have despised her. If she had been first rate he would have broken her heart.'[2]

Both at home and in bed Maynard infinitely preferred the poetic quirks of Lydia's analysis. Of his final, great book, *The General Theory of Employment, Interest and Money*, she liked to claim that she found it 'beautiful like Bach'.

Others, as well as Robinson, came to appreciate the chemistry between Lydia and Maynard. To the composer Patrick Hadley the two of them appeared to create 'a most wonderful union … the most wonderful I have ever known',[3] and testimony to their happiness was recorded in the hundreds of letters that they exchanged over the years: 'You do develop my cranium miely Maynarochka,' Lydia wrote, 'and I am so very glad I live with you, and am intimate with your little holes (also cells) your soul your breath and your kisses.'[4] Maynard, equally whimsical in his devotion, sent tributes to his 'dearest darling Lydochka', his 'miele', his 'pupsik'.

But this accord was not what less sympathetic observers had predicted at the time of the wedding. To Establishment grandees like the Earl of Crawford and Balcarres, a ballerina like Lydia was barely distinguishable from a common music-hall dancer, and it was with sniggering disbelief that he had recorded in his diary the news of 'Maynard Keynes marrying a chorus girl'.[5] Among the writers and painters of the Bloomsbury Group, who were Maynard's intimate friends, there was hardly less scepticism over his choice of wife. The qualities that Maynard loved in Lydia – her uninhibited enthusiasms, her extemporising Anglo-Russian chatter and her exotic ballerina ways – seemed to Bloomsbury an affront to seriousness. In the context of their own rarefied society, her charms appeared little more than trivial tricks of personality.

So many subtle snubs and small rudenesses had Lydia experienced from Maynard's circle that it was not surprising she had wanted the wedding kept to themselves. Only two friends had been invited to the short ceremony, along with four members of Maynard's family. But while Lydia could limit the guests, she could not control the curious public, and as she drove with Maynard to the registry office she may have sensed the restless murmur of the crowd awaiting them, before fully registering its size. A mob of reporters, fans and well-wishers had gathered on the pavement; still more were crammed inside the lobby of the office, while curious faces were pressed against the windows of the adjoining buildings. On their arrival cheers broke out, and when Maynard helped Lydia out of the taxi, his tall stooping figure bent down to hers, one woman pointed and shouted, 'Look at her, isn't she tiny.' The couple walked into their 'private' wedding to the accompaniment of laughter and applause.[6]

During the fifteen minutes that it took for the formalities to be completed, more people had joined the crush; and as Lydia hesitated with Maynard on their exit, uncertain how they were to get away, journalists began waving their notebooks and cameras flashed. The photographs that appeared in the press that evening showed Lydia frozen in the public glare, her hands plucking nervously at her clothes, the ghost of an awkward smile on her lips. She could not have looked less deserving of the accompanying headline, describing her as 'one the three great ballerinas of the age'.

Yet even when Lydia was in control of her image, and dancing on stage, she did not conform to type. Small and rounded, with fluffy, mid-brown hair, she bore no resemblance to the finely modelled beauty that had made Anna Pavlova the iconic Swan Princess of her profession. During Lydia's entire career she had never been compared to a swan – only to a sparrow, a canary, or at best a hummingbird. And it had been precisely her lively individuality that had sparked her audiences' devotion. When Lydia danced, her responsive little body appeared to be encountering the music and the choreography for the first time. With the peculiar gift of seeming to deliver herself spontaneously to the moment, she could produce performances that were, as one colleague described, 'more romantic than anyone' yet 'such a romp'.[7]

Over the years, critics around the world had attempted to capture the vivacity of Lydia's stage presence, but it was a bust sculpted by Frank Dobson two years before her wedding that had come closest to evoking it. By casting Lydia in three-quarter profile Dobson had managed to catch the questioning tilt of her head, the wilful curve with which her nose lifted from the solid oval of her face, the wide glance of her eyes. Even in stillness, the grace of her plump arms and the curl of her fingers embodied a musical lilt. As Lydia looked askance at an invisible audience, she seemed caught in a moment of stillness, but very possibly poised on the brink of laughter.

The expressive life concentrated in this little bronze (one copy of which is now in possession of the Keynes family; another in the Arts Council collection) has left some permanent trace of what made Lydia, for a decade, the most popular ballerina in Britain. It is also the portrait of a star whom the world almost forgot. Lydia herself lamented on the death of Pavlova that 'a dancer can leave nothing behind her. Music will not help us to see her again and to feel what she could give us, nor the best words.'[8] And her own career vanished even more completely than most. While her ballerina years were fully documented with photos and press clippings, even with a few clumsy minutes of film, as soon as Lydia retired from the stage she deliberately chose to curtail her celebrity. When Maynard became seriously ill she devoted herself to his care; after he died in 1946, she opted to live out her own last years in the obscurity of her rural Sussex home.

Over the decades, Lydia's name was kept alive by her association with Maynard as well as with the many dancers, choreographers, artists and composers who had been her colleagues and friends. Yet as she flitted through the biographies of Picasso, Stravinsky, Diaghilev, Nijinsky, Cecil Beaton and the inner core of Bloomsbury, the fact that she had been, as Frederick Ashton put it, a 'superstar' in her own right, and the heroine of her own remarkable narrative, became less and less well known.

Piecing together the story of Lydia's life today is partly a matter of tracking the itinerary of her career after she ran away from St Petersburg in 1910, and spent the following two decades dancing across America and Europe. But it also involves making sense of the contradictions in her character. Lydia's paradoxical behaviour on her wedding day, a popular celebrity unnerved by crowds, was rooted in a more complicated wariness. During the course of her nomadic adventures, as she had crossed between continents and dodged the fall-out from revolution and war, Lydia had sometimes had little more than her talent and her luck to sustain her. She had been forced to learn self-reliance, and had also learned to keep guard over her emotions. On stage, and in society, Lydia appeared deliciously accessible, offering up her brimming energy and charm as gifts to her audience, yet on another level these qualities served as a smokescreen behind which she sought to maintain her privacy. Despite the trail of newspaper stories that marked her progress from Tsarist Russia to Broadway and eventually to Maynard's London, there were secrets in Lydia's life that the world did not read about. Even today, gaps remain in her story that have not been explained. Thus, in 1925, as she prepared for her wedding, Lydia's modest bridal suit was in some sense also her camouflage. Her married life with Maynard was yet another new country to which she would need to acclimatise.

Chapter One

THE LOPUKHOV DYNASTY

> When I knelt down by my mother to say my prayers, the only petition I had to send heavenwards was the heart pulsing wish that I might be one of the beautiful angels I had seen at the theatre ... I was going to be a beautiful angel, even if I had to run away from home.
>
> LYDIA LOPOKOVA[1]

When Lydia told the story of her career, she started, as most dancers do, with the first time that she had ever seen a ballet performance, and with the moment of childish epiphany when she had sworn herself, body and soul, to become a part of the stage in front of her. Lydia had been only seven when her father, Vasili Lopukhov, had taken her to St Petersburg's magnificent lyric theatre, the Mariinsky, and to a little girl in 1898 it may have seemed adventure enough simply to cross the immense square in which the theatre was set, dodging the stream of carriages that drove wealthy merchant families to the same performance, enjoying the self-importance of her own specially scrubbed appearance and brushed curls.

But inside, as Lydia and her father were directed to their seats in the gallery, the sense of occasion became still more momentous. Below her the auditorium curved away in a haze of sea-blue drapery and velvet; crystal lamps and gilded mouldings shone under the glitter of an enormous spreading chandelier; the elite of St Petersburg sat ranked across the *bel étage*, diamonds sparking at women's throats, medals gleaming from the uniforms of the men. When the theatre darkened and the dancers began to move across the stage in their mysteriously choreographed patterns, the whole experience could have been overwhelming to a small child. Yet when Lydia later described this event on British radio, her Russian accent swerving through her carefully scripted prose, she remembered herself feeling exuberantly, unabashedly entitled to the whole spectacle:

> Every number thrilled me and I finally found it impossible to keep my feet from moving. When the curtain fell I was standing on my seat and as the music continued I began to dance and do some childish imitations of the poses and some rather bold attempts to lift my leg higher than my head, with the result that I fell from my perch and carried home a fine bump with black and blue decorations just under my curls … My father later told me that I had danced all the way home, keeping it up until bedtime.[2]

Aged seven, Lydia had danced her first comedy role.

But there was another, less innocent story behind the trip, which she didn't choose to relate to her British audience. Vasili Lopukhov was a poor man, the son of peasants, and when he had taken his youngest daughter to the Mariinsky, he had not been offering her an exceptional treat, but embarking on a calculated strategy of grooming her for a life on the stage. He had both financial and professional reasons for planning this, since ballet in turn-of-the-century Russia was still under the protection of the Tsar, and its artists were generously provided for. The Imperial Ballet School, which had originally been founded by the Empress Anna Ivanovna in 1738 to provide dancers for court entertainments, continued to feed, clothe and educate its pupils either for free or at minimal cost. Once students graduated into the adult ballet company, the financial rewards could, to a man of Vasili's class, be fabulous. The most junior dancers were paid a salary of 600 roubles a year, double Vasili's own highest earnings, while a leading ballerina, like Anna Pavlova, could aspire to 3,000 roubles. Even on retirement the dancers were guaranteed a pension, and for certain adroit women the stage was an unparalleled opportunity to acquire wealthy lovers, or 'protectors', as they were discreetly called within the profession.

Mathilde Kschessinska, the diamantine coquette who had been

the Mariinsky's queen ballerina from the early 1890s, had proved just how high a dancer could aim, after she had netted, as her first lover, the young Tsarevich Nicholas. She had then moved on to his uncle, the Grand Duke Sergei, and had finally secured a younger cousin, the Grand Duke Andrei. Even though Kshessinska could not marry into the imperial family (at least, not until after the Revolution), her lovers brought her mounting political influence within the theatre, as well as a magnificent collection of houses, jewellery and clothes. In the world of the Mariinsky, the silks and furs that wrapped Kschessinska's carefully tended body, the diamond earrings that framed her pretty, voracious face, were all graphic images of worldly success; and they must surely have been in Vasili's mind as he manoeuvred little Lydia into embracing her vocation.

Vasili would in fact get four of his five children successfully launched on to the ballet stage. Lydia might be the only one to make her reputation abroad, but her older brother Fedor would become a seminal force in Soviet dance, directing the Mariinsky ballet company in the decade following the Revolution, and choreographing much of its new repertory. In 1965, Fedor's son Vladimir would also become a dancer in the company, and Vladimir in turn would see his own son Fedor follow in the family profession. If Vasili had hoped only to make money by sending his children out to work in ballet, he had ended up founding a minor dynasty.

This represented a dramatic leap of aspiration for a man of his background; yet within the history of Lydia's family it was not entirely without precedent, for on both sides, her father's and her mother's, there had been generations with stories to tell of adventure and upheaval. Years later, when Maynard attempted to map his wife's ancestry, he discovered that in contrast to his own solid line (which could be traced back to an eleventh-century Frenchman, William de Cahagnes, who settled in Britain after the battle of Hastings), Lydia's family tree was so widely scattered that it was often invisible.* Such were the distances travelled by some of her forebears that generations

*Piecing together Lydia's background has been made subsequently more difficult by the fact that none of her immediate family, except Fedor, survived beyond 1947 and that during the 1942–3 siege of Leningrad the family flat was looted and the family's papers and photographs either scattered or destroyed.

of her family had gone unrecorded and the earliest ancestor that Lydia had been able to identify for Maynard had been her maternal great-great-grandfather, born in Scotland during the second half of the eighteenth century.

Lydia had known only his surname, Douglas, and also the fact that as an engineer he had left home to find work in Sweden, possibly inspired by earlier generations of Scots who had crossed the North Sea to hire out their skills for the construction of St Petersburg. The travelling gene had skipped a generation, as Douglas's son Gerhart had remained in Sweden as a tapestry weaver. But it had sent the latter's son Karl (Lydia's grandfather) on a route still further east, sailing to Latvia, where he had found employment as clerk to the Municipal Council of Riga, and where he had also found his future wife, Charlotte Johnson.

Charlotte had been the daughter of an itinerant and unscrupulous Scottish merchant, 'a courageous brigand', according to Lopukhov family lore, 'who always tried to get something for nothing'.[3] But she herself proved a compliant wife and willingly followed her new husband to his next place of work, the Estonian capital Revel (now Tallinn), where in 1860 she gave birth to Lydia's mother, Constanz-Rosalia Karlova Lorvn. In many ways, this little Douglas household was a model of modesty and rectitude, speaking the German language that was native to their district in Revel, and practising a devout Lutheran faith. However, a glimmer of nonconformity shone through their seriousness, for Karl was a keen amateur painter, while Charlotte cut a quixotic figure among the Revel housewives by insisting on dressing in the Scottish fashions of her youth. Their daughter, known by the diminutive Karlusha, was a fair, plump girl with a watchful expression blurring her mild features, but she too had inherited a small spark of Douglas restlessness and Johnson courage. At some point the family moved down to the university town of Derpt, now Tartu, and when Karl died, leaving the family short of money, she overcame her devotion to her mother to travel 200 miles to St Petersburg and take employment as a masseuse.

Barely twenty years old, Karlusha sought security within the city's large German community, where she was at least able to continue speaking her own language. Missing her mother, she clung on to memories of home by wearing the style of tartan cap that Charlotte had always favoured. But by the time she was twenty-three, either work or social contacts had persuaded her to venture further afield, for it was in 1883 that Karlusha met Vasili Fedorovich Lopukhov, a man alarmingly and attractively outside her limited experience.

'Lopukhov' in Russian means burdock or wild plant, and it was a suggestive name for a serf family that had survived as tenaciously as that of Karlusha's new lover. Originally Vasili's forebears had lived and worked in the most north-easterly corner of Russia, on the Mongolia–Buryat border. Yet over the generations, as some of them were sold, gambled or transferred to different estates by aristocratic masters, who until the emancipation decree of 1861 exercised despotic control over peasant lives, the family had migrated down to the central prairies of Russia. For Vasili's father, Fedor Lopukhov, this journey had ended in the Tambov province, around 300 miles south-east of Moscow, in the tiny village of Serpovskaya, and it was here that he met his wife, a woman of Tartar birth whose family had themselves migrated south from Kazan.

Within their closed community this couple seem to have been an active, even exceptional, pair. Fedor was assigned the duties of lay server in the local church; his wife was sought after as a skilled midwife; and their son Vasili, born around 1856, grew up with a lively estimation of his own worth. Having inherited his mother's dark good looks and his father's rich tenor voice, there was no question of him remaining in obscurity in Serpovskaya, and after he had signed up to join the army, Vasili applied for a transfer to the Life Guards of the Moscow regiment, based in distant St Petersburg.

Vasili was almost illiterate – he had barely been able to sign his name on his military papers – yet once in St Petersburg he became something of a barracks hero. He wore his handsomeness with a swagger, growing a closely trimmed beard across his wide cheek-bones; he became leader of the regimental choir; and his gregarious, quick-witted energy made him popular among his peers. His officers too noted his qualities (his final certificate of regimental service commended his 'zealous and excellent conduct'), and when, in 1883, Vasili proposed to Karlusha (having already been briefly married, and then widowed), his companions may have wondered what he saw in this shy Estonian with her halting grasp of Russian. Perhaps Vasili had simply got Karlusha pregnant – their first daughter, Evgenia, was born in 1884. Or perhaps he had seen in Karlusha's more refined background the shape of his own ambitions. Certainly, as he served out his final months in the army, Vasili was imagining for himself a much wider world. He was learning to speak German with his new wife, and when he left his regiment in July 1883 he did not take the obvious route of seeking employment in one of St Petersburg's expanding industries, but instead applied for work as an usher in the city's most prestigious dramatic theatre, the Alexandrinsky.

This was not a skilled job, nor a highly paid one, earning him just 180 roubles a year, yet for Vasili it brought a significant chance to rewrite his prospects. Unlike the mass of the Russian population, who in 1883 still lived and died doing the jobs to which they had been born, employees within the Imperial institutions were given opportunities to rise. Vasili might have begun work at the most menial level, checking in coats at the Alexandrinsky cloakroom, but he had his foot on the first rung of a hierarchy, and he wasted no time in climbing upwards. His personable looks and willing nature soon got him promoted to the job of directing the public to their seats, and, with his growing knowledge of the theatre and his fluent German, Vasili earned himself a reputation as the Alexandrinsky's 'educated usher'. He took meticulous pride in his appearance – one of Lydia's earliest memories was of her father's perfectly manicured nails – and by 1891 he was appointed to some sort of control position among the front-of-house staff. It brought him a taste of power, a salary of 300 roubles and the most prized privilege among the ushers: showing the wealthy boyars to their boxes and earning their generous tips.

Even so, Vasili was not well off. Although he was able to move himself and Karlusha from their first rented apartment on Kabinetskaya to a larger space at 8 Yamskaya,* he had a growing household to support. Two years after the birth of Evgenia, Karlusha gave birth to Fedor, with a second daughter, Anna, following in 1889, Lydia in 1891, and two more sons, Nikolai and Andrei, in 1896 and 1898. With two servants also living in the flat, the family were always

*Now Ulitsa Dostoevskogo.

cramped. Lydia recalled that as a small child she slept on a narrow platform above the kitchen stove, enjoying the warmth but having no kind of privacy. Vasili's earnings were certainly never high enough to protect against any sudden bad luck (it may have been debt that forced him to relocate his family twice in 1895, swapping between different flats within the same building),* and any serious illness or emergency could derail his finances. When two-year-old Anna died from a brain seizure – perhaps meningitis – Vasili had to petition his employers for help with doctor's fees and funeral expenses (he was granted 25 roubles), and in 1896 he again had to plead for emergency funds to treat a recurrent nervous disorder of his own.

The doctor who visited the Lopukhovs wrote in his report that all the family were, at that moment, unwell, and throughout their childhood Lydia and her siblings were lectured by Karlusha about the dangers of illness. St Petersburg's open sewers made the city, at the end of the nineteenth century, one of most disease-ridden capitals of Europe, and while Yamskaya was not located in a slum neighbourhood, each apartment building in the narrow street huddled around a dank courtyard from which rose the stinking fumes of the residents' cesspit. For an anxious mother like Karlusha, contagion lurked in every dark corner, and she was, the children recalled, watchfully vigilant about where and with whom she would allow them to play.

But she was equally alert to the dangers of moral contagion, for it was while the children were still young that Vasili began to pursue what Fedor would euphemistically call in his memoirs 'gypsy freedoms'.[4] Love had been squeezed out of the Lopukhov marriage by the accumulating stress of raising a family; and all the differences in background and temperament that had once made the couple attractive to each other were hardening into suspicion and dislike. Karlusha, at ease with her own family, could be merry and demonstrative, but her shyness with strangers and her strict Lutheran faith made her recoil from the loud drinking companions and boisterous theatre friends whom her husband brought home. Vasili in turn grew impatient with his antisocial wife, who still stubbornly preferred to speak in her native German tongue, and by the time that Lydia was

*They moved from flat no. 11 to no. 6, then to no. 12.

born he was beginning to look for his pleasures elsewhere.

For several years Karlusha struggled to console herself with her religion. Such was her determination to remain true to her marriage vows that she even took temporary care of a baby boy whom Vasili fathered during one of his drinking jaunts. For several years, too, Vasili's excesses were kept under control and away from the eyes of his children, so that their earliest experiences of family life were happy ones. One crucial advantage of his duties at the Alexandrinsky was that they required him to remain inside the auditorium during performances, allowing him to watch every production and learn the craft of the actors. This was the world of culture after which Vasili hankered. Even though he could still barely read, his ear was extraordinarily acute, and he learned chunks of the repertory to recite back home for his wife and family.

These performances remained distinct in the memories of his children, alive with verve and melodrama. When Vasili was at home, the flat rang with the sound of his voice, with his singing, with his constant demands that his family talk and read to him. And clearly the children thrived. A photograph taken when Lydia was about ten shows the five Lopukhovs looking intelligent, grinning, alert. Although they might not get new winter boots, they did always have books in the flat, including, Lydia remembered, a thick anthology of fairy tales that was kept in the sitting room and contained her own favourite story, Hans Christian Andersen's 'The Nightingale'.

From the distance of adulthood Fedor came to believe that their father had been a potentially 'outstanding' person, who in other, more privileged circumstances might have been a distinguished singer or actor.[5] Certainly it was Vasili's theatrical talent that the children all inherited. Yet without any disciplined outlet, this talent became a boorish, dissolute parody of itself. Increasingly restless, increasingly frustrated, Vasili squandered more and more of his free time and money in bars. Five times between 1903 and 1909 he was fined for turning up drunk to work, and his proud professional reputation began to unravel. He was threatened with the sack after abusing a patron who had asked him to pick up a dropped coin, and there were allegations (later dropped) that he had been selling theatre tickets on the black market. Although Vasili's services were twice formally

Lopukhov family photo, back row from left to right: Evgenia, unknown, Lydia; front row from left to right: Fedor, Nikolai, Andrei

recognised – in 1902 he was made a Private Honorary Citizen and in 1906 an Hereditary Honorary Citizen – during his final years at the Alexandrinsky the 'educated usher' had become an embarrassing liability.

At home too he was no longer loved and revered. With his temper blackened by alcohol and his judgement clouded, Vasili became verbally, if not physically, violent towards Karlusha. The children, in defending her, joined ranks against him. Lydia had a photograph of her mother and two younger brothers which she kept by her bed for most of her life. It was taken around 1905, but in it Karlusha looks much older than her forty-five years, a square, anxious woman, her brows knitted tightly as she stares at the camera, her mouth clamped shut.

Of her father, Lydia kept no mementoes.

Yet if Vasili's drinking laid domestic traps and terrors for the future,

Karlusha, with Andrei and Nikolai, St Petersburg, 1900

it was still a reasonably contented household into which Lydia was born on 7 October 1891.* She was baptised Lydia Vasilievna Lopukhova at the Simeonovskaya church on Mokhovaya Street, with the wife of a corporal in the Imperial Guard and a private from the Imperial regiment standing as her godparents. Karlusha, barely recovered from the loss of Anna, may have watched her new baby anxiously, but Lydia grew into a lively toddler, with a wide smile and energetic limbs that tilted boldly at the world. She became her mother's petted child, quick to be entertained by new experiences and always impatient for the family walk on which Karlusha insisted on taking her children every day. During Lydia's early years, her world was mapped by the sights and smells of the different routes her mother took – down the wide Zagorodny Prospekt, whose indoor market was piled with honeycombs, fruit and hams; across to the gleaming Vladimir church with its bronze domes and its crowds of beggars; further off to the park by Vitebsk Station, where Karlusha let

*This is the date under the Old Style Russian calendar. Once Lydia moved to the West and adjusted to the Gregorian calendar, she gave her birth date as 21 October. This deviated by a day from the normal calculation of adding thirteen days to OS dates (twelve days for nineteenth-century dates) but it may have been that Lydia was born late on 7 October and counted from the 8th. Lydia herself was never punctilious about such details, giving different dates of birth on her three passports and, when it suited her professionally, being 'vague' about her age.

her children race alongside the plumes of steam that rose from the trains as they rumbled heavily south towards Kiev and Minsk.

But Lydia's favourite walk was the one that led to her father's theatre, the Alexandrinsky, and to the elegant street that lay in the shadow of its golden stuccoed walls. This was Theatre Street, home of the school where St Petersburg's dancers and actors were apprenticed to serve in the Imperial companies, and where at the age of seven she had vowed her own future would lie.

In Lydia's adult memory it had been the visit to the Mariinsky that had inspired this vow, but in reality the examples of both Evgenia and Fedor must have had some influence on her. Vasili had already secured places at the Theatre School for his two older children, Evgenia in August 1895 and Fedor the following year, and as the pair brought home foreign-sounding chatter of pliés and pirouettes he may have guessed that he would have little trouble convincing his second daughter to follow them. Whether he had Karlusha's wholehearted support is unclear. By 1900 her two eldest children had graduated to boarding status at the school, coming home only at weekends and holidays, and she may have felt some aversion to Lydia, her favourite, being set up to join them. While discipline at the Theatre School was reassuringly strict, its teachers were still preparing the children for a life on stage and, with it, a world of bohemian morals and material dazzle that were disturbingly alien to her own simple Lutheran beliefs. To Karlusha, unlike Vasili, Kschessinska would hardly have been a persuasive role model.*

On the other hand, she was in no position to argue with the privileged care and education that entry to the Theatre School would bring, nor with the fact that these advantages were fiercely sought. Thousands of families petitioned every year simply for the chance to apply to the school, and of the 100 boys and 200 girls given auditions, fewer than twenty were finally accepted. Priority was given to those who had close relatives working as actors or dancers, and Vasili had already had to work his contacts hard to secure Fedor and

*Karlusha kept only one of her children, Nikolai, at home. He later confessed to Fedor that he had 'behaved like a lout' at his audition so that he could go to a regular school and study maths and science. F. Lopukhov, *Sixty Years in the Ballet*, Iskusstvo, Moscow, 1966, p.75.

Evgenia's applications, helped by a dancer at the Mariinsky with whom he was friendly. The two older Lopukhovs had only just scraped a place each, and by May 1901, when it was time for Lydia's own audition, she was feeling the burden of her family's expectation. Even though the school was, officially, only looking for suitable raw material – an attractive face, a pliable personality and graceful build – experience had taught Vasili that many of those petitioning had already acquired some dance training. The competition would be intense, and he had attempted to prepare Lydia with some rudimentary coaching, impressing on her the need to smile prettily at the panel of examiners and explaining to her that when she was asked to run up and down the room for them, she must try to turn out her feet as she did so, like a real ballerina.

It was also Vasili, rather than Karlusha, who took charge of Lydia during the long day of the audition, as they joined the apprehensive line of families filing into the Theatre School. Lydia was familiar with this building from the outside and, wearing a brand-new pair of white silk socks that Karlusha had given her, she may even have felt some chirpy spurt of confidence. But there was little to reassure her, or any of the girls, as they were directed down the echoing hallway and up the marble staircase that led to their waiting room. Even those few precocious applicants who had been preening themselves in grown-up ruffles and jewellery – eclipsing Lydia's pride in her new socks – were cowed by what awaited them in the hall where the first stage of the audition took place.

Twenty-five of the most powerful figures within the world of the Imperial Theatres had been gathered to watch the little girls perform, some of the men wearing the full dress uniform of court, several of the women identifiable as ballerinas by their graceful hauteur. Seated behind a long table, they were an impenetrably august group, terrifying for the nine-year-olds who were being delivered up to their scrutiny. In small groups the girls were first checked over by a ballet master who delivered a dry, professional commentary on their appearance to the examiners and dispassionately weeded out those with physical defects, such as knock knees or flat feet. The girls were then requested to run, one by one, the length of the enormous room, and Lydia could only repeat Vasili's instructions to herself like a mantra: 'I kept on thinking I must point the feet outwards, all the way up the hall.'[6] Her run was evidently correct, however, or perhaps the examiners had simply seen interesting possibilities in her diminutive prettiness and in the determined energy that animated her pert body and grey-blue button eyes. By the end of the day, after a medical examination and an afternoon of academic tests, only thirteen girls remained, and Lydia was among them.

Over the next eight years she and this select band would get to know each other more intimately than sisters, as they were drilled into the mysteries of their new vocation. Only the finest dancers were considered fit for the Tsar, and the Imperial coffers had, historically, paid generously to ensure that they were well trained. The most skilled ballet masters in Europe had been brought over to St Petersburg during the previous century and a half, instilling elements of French elegance, Danish buoyancy and Italian virtuosity into the Russian style. And if the Mariinsky dancers who inspired Lydia now look stolidly limited to us – posing in their photographs like stiff curios from a distant era – they were the outstanding athletes of their day. The women had exploited rapid advances in the technology of pointe shoes to master a scintillating vocabulary of pirouettes and bourrées, of delicate, skimming hops and airy balances. Their male partners, too, were engaged in a heroic conquest of gravity as they pushed their bodies towards more vaulting jumps, and lifted their ballerinas to more daring heights.

As for the ballets they performed, no more spectacular repertory could be seen anywhere in the world. Marius Petipa was their principal architect, a French choreographer who had been employed at the Mariinsky since 1847 and over the years had perfected a formula for combining technically brilliant dancing with theatrical sensation. *La Bayadère* (1877) was a typically opulent product, its stage designers conjuring dazzling illusions such as a castle in the sky and a collapsing Indian temple, its hand-embroidered costumes made from the finest silks, velvets, ermines and Brussels lace. During the second half of the nineteenth century the Imperial purse donated around 80,000 roubles each year to the staging of two such productions; and when these costs were added to the dancers' salaries, to the upkeep of the horses and carriages that drove them to the theatres, as well as to the

Mathilde Kschessinska, Nitri, *The Talisman*; St Petersburg, 1909

wages of teaching staff, dressers and maids, ballet constituted a conspicuous drain on the Tsar's resources.

St Petersburg's intellectuals had tended to be critical of this extravagance, judging that most ballets in the repertory amounted to little more than a parading of pretty legs, designed for the titillation of young soldiers and old men. However, Nicholas II was a serious admirer, and after he came to the throne in 1894, artists at the Mariinsky became still more privileged, petted by the Tsar's family and fêted by the city's dedicated band of balletomanes. Four years after Lydia's audition, during the abortive revolutionary uprisings of 1905, some of the newly politicised dancers began to complain that the drudgery of their life rendered them little better off than serfs. Yet most of Russia's population would regard the dancers' status as rare and fortunate, for the rewards for their daily discipline could be life-changing – not only for themselves but for their families. When little Lydia first prayed to become one of the beautiful dancing angels that she had seen at the Mariinsky, Vasili had had every reason to pray beside her.

Chapter Two

IMPERIAL PROPERTY

> For a year we did nothing but simple exercises holding onto the wall bars and repeating what might seem meaningless movements to the cracked notes of an old piano. First position! Third position! Circle, point, return, circle, point, return.
>
> LYDIA LOPOKOVA[1]

When Lydia next returned to Theatre Street* at the end of August 1901, she was clutching her lunch box and wearing the brown cashmere dress that marked her out as a first-year pupil of the Imperial Theatre School. She was proud of her status and excited by the novelty of wearing a uniform, even though the dress was a hideous garment for a small child – bunchy, old-fashioned and cumbersomely restrictive. It was also, as Lydia was about to discover, entirely apt for her new life, in which rules and regulations would govern every detail of her day.

Whatever colour and drama she had pictured for herself as a future ballet student, it was made immediately clear that the glamour of the stage existed in a separate sphere from the convent-like order of the school. Outside in Theatre Street, there might be actors arriving at the Alexandrinsky, and ballerinas coming to rehearse in the adjacent company studios. Inside, however, all contact with the external world was sternly policed: windows on the ground level were frosted over to prevent anyone looking in, or out; the children were permitted to play only in an inner courtyard; and every minute was punctiliously timetabled.

*Theatre Street is now called Rossi Street after its architect.

From Monday to Saturday the pupils' routine followed an almost identical pattern. After an hour's study period, Lydia and her fellow noviciates were marshalled into a changing room to dress for the morning ballet class, learning how to fix loops of elastic around their pink stockings, adjust their shawls around their starched grey ballet frocks, and tie their shoe ribbons with precisely judged tightness, spitting on the knots for luck. Inside the dance studios, two hours of concentrated physical instruction followed, after which came lunch and a long afternoon of academic lessons. Throughout the school day the children were monitored by a small army of black-gowned governesses referred to universally as the Toads, who not only quelled any stirrings of bad behaviour, but five times a day lined up their charges to be counted. Lydia in retrospect judged this practice to be some antiquated form of stocktaking – 'After all we were Imperial property'[2] – but according to school legend it had been introduced only after a legendarily daring senior pupil had run away with an officer of the Horse Guards. Remembered with shocked admiration as 'lunatic Ann', this romantic rebel had left behind a detailed diary of her love affair scrawled on the wall of a cupboard. She had also bequeathed a punishment to the generations of girls who came after her. Not only were they continually watched by their governesses, they were forbidden to leave the school unaccompanied, and any unnecessary, unscheduled contact with the boy pupils was proscribed.

After the crowded, animated household in which Lydia had grown up, this culture of restraint might have been bewildering to her; as a restless, imaginative, untidy child she might have been destined to suffer. Even though the Tsar's future dancers were never beaten, strict punishments were in place to chastise every lapse of punctuality, every excess of high spirits and every prank. Yet according to Tamara Karsavina – a senior girl who was appointed Lydia's mentor, and would later become her professional rival and friend – this littlest Lopukhova, with 'the face of an earnest cherub', was adopted as the school pet. Even the strictest of the Toads were apparently disarmed by her prettiness and enthusiasm. 'The extreme emphasis she put into her movements was comic to watch in the tiny child,' Karsavina wrote in her memoirs. 'Whether she danced or talked, her whole frame quivered with excitement, she bubbled over. Her personality was manifest from the first, and very loveable.'[3]

As always in Lydia's life, her charm won her special exemptions. Yet her transition into school life may also have been eased by the fact that she was a few months younger than the rest of her class, and became a boarder only in her third year. Lydia was thus allowed to escape her teachers' vigilance at five o'clock each day and be taken back home by Karlusha or one of the servants. Home was now at the far end of Nevsky Prospekt, St Petersburg's largest and busiest boulevard, where Vasili had recently moved the family, and the twenty-minute walk from school plunged Lydia back into the familiar hubbub of the city. On dry spring days she was taken up the side of the Fontanka River with its crowded cargo boats and ferries; otherwise she was walked around the massive walls of the Alexandrinsky, to be caught up in the crowds that jostled along the Prospekt's wide expanse. On dark winter afternoons the snowy pavements were pooled with the light from gas lamps, the frozen air jangling with the traffic of sleighs. During the short, bright summer the Prospekt was clamorous with the noise of iron-wheeled carriages rattling over cobbles, and with the calls of peasant farmers shouting out prices for their milk, honey and eggs.

By the time Lydia neared home, the press of stall holders, shoppers, pedestrians and beggars would have thinned, for number 69 Nevsky Prospekt was located at the quieter, shabbier end of the boulevard. A functional, mid-nineteenth-century apartment building with a cramped courtyard at the back (now used as a welding yard), this was not an address for the wealthy. Yet there were large windows at the front, giving light and air into the flats (the Lopukhovs' was number 24), and during the weekdays, with Fedor and Evgenia away at school, the household felt almost spacious.

In the autumn of 1903, when Lydia was eventually enrolled as a boarder and allowed home only for a day and a half each week, she may have suffered at being further separated from family life, and especially from her mother. She had remained Karlusha's favourite, her naughtiness indulged, her chatter listened to, and it was out of this unconditional sweetness that her confidence had flourished. Lydia herself did not record that the separation made her miserable, beyond quipping that 'even [her] sleep had become regulated';[4] but from a reading of the memoirs of her close contemporaries Tamara Karsavina, Bronislava Nijinska and Alexandra Danilova it is possible to guess that the experience was harder than she acknowledged. These three ballerinas recalled nights of stifled sobbing as they and the other new boarders ached for home, sleeping with fifty other junior girls in a vast, hangar-like dormitory, their individual school numbers hanging repressively over their beds.

If the new boarders went to sleep feeling lonely, they woke to a day even more closely supervised than those they had known as day pupils. A loud bell summoned them to shiver, briefly, under a cold tap and get themselves dressed, the youngest girls still having to be helped by school maids as their chilly fingers struggled to comb, braid and pin their long hair, fasten their cashmere day frocks (now blue, to designate boarding status) and bundle on the black alpaca apron, thick white stockings and black lace-up shoes that completed their uniform.

After prayers and breakfast – tea, a buttered bun and an egg – the day was regulated by the usual lessons until five o'clock, when, instead of going home, the boarders faced a new evening timetable. First came dinner, during which their hushed conversations were dominated by the hissing of a large samovar at one end of the room, and their conduct monitored by a watchful governess. Then came private study, needlework or music practice. It was only on Friday evenings, when they took their weekly baths, that the pupils experienced a small frisson of freedom. The school's wooden bathhouse was tucked away in a small courtyard, which had to be reached by a maze of dark pathways. Not only was the short, unlit walk a licence for private whispering, but in the bathhouse itself, as the pupils were scrubbed to shining pinkness by their maids, they could no longer be observed by the otherwise vigilant Toads. Hidden by scalding clouds of steam, the giggling, near-naked girls came as close to unsupervised anarchy as the school permitted.

Lydia did chafe under the new confinement, even if she did not admit to feeling unhappy. She fantasised, sometimes, that her parents had died and that she was free to run away and join the circus or, just as excitingly, that she might go off and play truant in St Petersburg's zoological gardens, which she considered thrillingly 'low'.[5] Yet if the restraints of Theatre School life could feel oppressive, during morning dance classes there was always the sense that she and her classmates were gaining access to important mysteries. Even during the first year, when ballet had seemed disappointingly remote from the pretty poses of Lydia's imagination, the dry, repetitive exercises took on a new significance when their regular teacher* was replaced by the head of the Girls' Division, Enrico Cecchetti. This fierce, eccentric martinet was renowned for the bullying brilliance of his teaching methods, and any rebuke from him could be devastating. 'His abuse was terrible,' Lydia remembered, 'all of us he would reduce to tears.' Yet she and her friends had yearned for his criticisms as if they were love tokens. Cecchetti was the Maestro, the teacher who could spot, and make, a future ballerina, and all the pupils knew that it was a 'bad sign not to be abused, for that would show that one had no gifts, no possibilities'.[6]

Often Cecchetti's abuse had been directed at Lydia, for however delinquently she dreamed of joining the circus, she had been marked out early as one of her year's talents. Physically she was lucky. Her body adapted itself to the demands being made on it without any damaging stress or injury – her childish muscles strengthening term by term, her tendons gaining in length, her spine and her limbs becoming steadily more flexible. She also seems to have been born with a natural dance intelligence, a physical sixth sense, through which she could hear rhythm with her body and visualise shape, colour and line through her movements.

But almost as crucially, Lydia was gifted with a survivor's temperament. Having been cosseted during her first year, she continued to coast through the school's competitive culture, buoyed up by her father's easy gift for friendship and by her mother's sturdy good sense. Masochism, obsession and narcissism – the psychological perils of her vocation – were not part of Lydia's make-up. The world was too interesting and entertaining for her to get sucked an unhappy, inward battle with her own talent. And when she was

*Lydia's other teacher, Stanislav Gillert, was less terrifying. She recalled him arriving at class 'with a piece of cheese in his hand, as if we were mice'. (See Note 6.)

called to perform on the Imperial stage, as she frequently was, she came to feel that it was her natural space.

Child dancers and actors were extremely popular in Russia at this time, and it was part of the school's training to encourage even the littlest pupils to appear in ballets, operas and plays. Among the boys and girls at the school, these opportunities were hotly coveted. It was an adventure simply to escape from class and be driven to and from the theatre in one of the school's ancient carriages, which, with blinds drawn protectively over their windows, creaking and blinkered through the streets of St Petersburg. But to be on stage was to enter another world, especially if the children were cast to dance in one of the Sunday ballet performances attended by the Tsar. On such occasions the Mariinsky acquired the concentrated glitter of a court event as the city's nobility sat in strict order of rank on either side of the Imperial box, the women lustrous in tiaras and ropes of pearls, the men in the full plumage of their military livery or court dress. For the children, earnestly playing their parts as pages, cupids or flower children, this splendour would register as little more than a blur of wealth and privilege. Yet they might be instinctively aware of how the stage around them was duplicating the hierarchy of the audience, with the ballerina and her prince in centre frame, flanked in descending order of importance by the soloists, the coryphées and corps de ballet. It was an early lesson in professional and social gradation, and an early spur to their own ambitions.

Lydia was chosen for her own first performance very shortly after she entered the school. It was the tiniest of walk-on parts – a baby crow in Gounod's opera *Faust* – but years later she could still relive the momentous sense of initiation it gave her: 'I was shown into a very big dressing room, had my cheeks rouged and a long woollen frock put over me, and taken by the hand onto the stage. It was all very dark. There I saw a terrible monster with red legs and horns who was a doing a sort of Mā-a-a, Mā-a-a in a bass voice. It was Chaliapin as Mephistopheles ... but I thought it *really* was the devil – and fainted.'

She went on, 'This was how they used to accustom us little ones to the brilliance and spaces of the stage.'[7] But even more daunting to her and her classmates were the performances that were staged in

Lydia, *The Fairy Doll*, St Petersburg, 1903

the Tsar's tiny private theatre in the Hermitage. Here they had to dance with the Imperial family sitting in armchairs just feet away from the stage. Lydia was about eleven when she first underwent this ordeal, dancing in the premiere of Nicolas and Sergei Legat's ballet *The Fairy Doll*, and it gave her a profound feeling of unease hearing the Tsar guffawing during one of the ballet's comedy scenes. But the photograph of her in her lace doll's costume suggests the precocious assurance that Lydia was now able to bring to such occasions. The pale oval of her face, framed by ringlets, appears gravely innocent; yet her mouth is tucked into a winsome moue, and she is artfully conscious of the camera as her audience.

By now, Lydia felt herself to be a true professional, for she was not only given regular opportunities to dance on stage, but was also being allocated substantial acting roles.* Out of all the Lopukhov children, she had most obviously inherited Vasili's dramatic talent (the celebrated St Petersburg actress Mlle Komissarzhevskaya had been so

*The children were paid well for these appearances, with each dance role earning a fifty-kopek fee, and speaking roles meriting one rouble and fifty kopeks per performance. These sums were entered into a notebook and paid out to parents at the end of the school year.

impressed by Lydia's performance in a mime class that she had urged the school to switch her studies from ballet to drama) and by the time Lydia was ten she had been cast as Prince Mamillius in *The Winter's Tale* and the following year as Peaseblossom in *A Midsummer Night's Dream*. Lydia was still young enough to be ignorant of who Shakespeare really was (she believed he was a Russian) and was still treated as a child by the rest of the cast. She giggled at the fat comedian playing Bottom, whom she called 'Uncle Kotya'; she took sweets from the actor who was Puck, and developed a crush on the 'blond idol' who was Demetrius. Yet there was nothing childish about the roles she aspired, eventually, to take herself: 'I had ambitions to play Puck or Oberon, these characters had grit for me. I did not want to play Titania, Hermia or that awful bore Helena.'[8]

Lydia's early independence manifested itself, too, on the occasion that she and her friends were offered a lift back from the Mariinsky by the notorious Kschessinska. The snow was falling and the great ballerina had leaned out of her carriage window, wrapped in furs with her trademark diamonds twinkling at her ears, to urge them to drive with her. Lydia had known enough of Kschessinska's gold-digging reputation to be horrified by this invitation and despite the bitter cold had insisted piously to her friends that they must resist: 'Oh no no no, we mustn't go with her. She's a wicked woman.'[9]

Given the school's customary vigilance it is unclear how Lydia could have remembered herself standing in the snow, rather than being whisked immediately back to bed in one of the pupils' carriages. However, the real significance of this anecdote is that it took place after a performance in which Lydia had been dancing Clara,* the child heroine of *The Nutcracker*. This was the most substantial dancing role open to a small girl and by far the most challenging, requiring Lydia to be on stage for most of the ballet's two acts. She was still only about twelve years old, young enough to be awed by her position in the spotlight and fearful of forgetting her steps. But her teachers were in the wings to encourage her, and after the curtain fell Lydia was formally presented to the Tsar. It was the surest possible sign that her star in the school was rising.

---

*Clara is called Marie in Russian productions.

*

Until Lydia was thirteen, her life revolved securely around the twin axes of home and dancing. During her fourth year at school, however, the world shifted.

Since the turn of the century the political mood of Russia had been turning increasingly combative, as middle-class campaigns for democratic reform had been swelled by protests from the growing urban workforce, demanding shorter hours and higher pay. Even the historically compliant peasants had raised their voices against the Tsar, as Russia's bungled war with Japan in 1904 began sending tens of thousands of untrained, ill-equipped men to their slaughter. Yet as St Petersburg had grown more unstable, more agitated, Theatre Street had retained its atmosphere of dedicated, cloistered calm. Talk of politics was suppressed by the governesses, and even the outbreak of war had made little impact on the pupils, beyond the knitting needles that been handed out to the girls after supper, along with orders to knit socks for the troops. However, on 9 January 1905, 150,000 St Petersburg citizens marched on Palace Square, and even the Tsar's fledgling dancers were plunged into the first, violent chapter of the Russian Revolution.

Revolution had not been the marchers' intention – their demands had been only for a basic programme of reform and for an accelerated end to the war, while their mood had been almost supplicatory, with many of them carrying icons and portraits of the Tsar. But mass political assembly was forbidden, and as the unarmed crowd entered Palace Square the jumpy Imperial Guard had opened fire, killing and wounding thousands. The march had disintegrated into a massacre, and this in turn became the tipping point into anarchy. While some of the survivors went on a maddened rampage, calling on the rest of St Petersburg to rise up against 'Nicholas the Bloody', others formed frantic search parties to hunt for the injured and missing. The army, incapable of dealing with the chaos that it had unleashed, reacted with more mindlessly brutal gunfire, generating further waves of violence across the city.

Many of those who were casualties of Bloody Sunday were passive bystanders, many of those who were traumatised by it were children, including Lydia and some of her fellow pupils. Having been sent off to perform in the city's theatres as normal, some were caught up in the day's violence, especially at the Alexandrinsky, where jeering protesters forced a way into the auditorium and brought the performance to a halt. Lydia, in later years, tended not to share her most extreme or personal experiences with the public, and did not include stories of Bloody Sunday in her own broadcast reminiscences. But she did disclose some memory of the event to a student journalist writing for the Cambridge magazine *Granta*, and his apocalyptic description of Lydia having been driven, in a panic flight, back to Theatre Street 'over the bodies of the slain and through the ranks of the still smoking artillery'[10] attests to the terror that she and her friends must have felt as their carriages forced a path through St Petersburg's turbulent crowds.

By early spring the worst of the city's unrest had been contained by ruthless policing. But insurgency remained close to the surface, and in the autumn a strike organised by printers spread through the rest of the workforce, bringing St Petersburg close to breakdown. Public transport was halted, faltering gas supplies left the grey, sleet-slicked streets eerily dark, and many schools, hospitals, shops and theatres were closed. Rumours that a starving rabble would imminently be roaming the streets kept many citizens fearfully behind closed doors, while the political activists were everywhere, hanging red flags from any balcony that they could access and organising impromptu demonstrations.

The school turned in on itself, imposing a strict curfew and guarding the children from contact with the dangers outside. Yet however tightly the curtains were drawn, the authorities could not blank out the spirit of insurrection that was now brewing within the ballet profession itself. During this second wave of political agitation, key members of the Mariinsky began declaring their own radicalised positions, headed by the dancers Mikhail Fokine (who was now also Lydia's teacher at the school), Anna Pavlova and Tamara Karsavina (now a rising ballerina within the company). Strikes were threatened unless the management acceded to a list of changes, which included higher salaries and more democratic policy making; and this unprecedented act of defiance also had a galvanising effect on the pupils. A group of senior boys issued their own set of strike demands (mostly minor issues concerning uniform regulations and the right to smoke), and for weeks the school talked of nothing but politics and protest.

Ostensibly, by spring 1906 the lid was again jammed shut. The authorities in St Petersburg curbed the revolutionaries by instituting a series of repressive measures, sugared by a few conciliatory reforms.* A parallel policy was also enforced among the apostate dancers, with the management pandering to a few of their demands but sacking or demoting those whom they considered dispensable. Rebellion had been heady, however, and even if Fokine, Karsavina, Pavlova and their supporters no longer dared talk openly of political change, they continued to question the aesthetics and practice of their art form.

Ballet was now at a critical moment of transition within the Mariinsky. Marius Petipa, who had for so long held the company within his artistic grip, was an old man, his power broken, his ideas almost exhausted. Fokine's influence, meanwhile, was on the rise, especially among his younger colleagues. With his dark hair swept off his wide poet's forehead, Fokine had initially made his reputation as one of the company's most handsome male dancers. Yet since his appointment in 1902 as head of the Girls' Division at the Theatre School, his ambitions had turned more rigorously towards the reform of ballet instruction, and towards a modernisation of choreography. It was Fokine's conviction that productions at the Mariinsky had become stifled by a combination of over-upholstered spectacle and academic correctness, and he envisioned a future in which new stage conventions and new dance idioms might open up the art form to a fuller, more human range of expression.

Fokine's instinct was to look outside the inbred culture of ballet for his influences, to the uncorrupted vigour of Russian folk tradition, to the psychological realism of Stanislavsky's new Moscow Art Theatre, even to the art and poetry of the ancient Greeks. And at the end of 1904 he was also stirred by the St Petersburg debut of a new and very American dance radical, Isadora Duncan. Duncan was far more

*A newly drafted constitution allowed for freedom of speech and assembly, plus an elected government, but the Tsar's power was barely checked.

strident than Fokine in her condemnation of the prevailing ballet culture as 'sterile' and 'unnatural',[11] and far more absolute in her disdain for the tyranny of the classroom. She had also evolved an alternative concept of movement, impassioned, instinctive, almost naïf, which Fokine and many of his colleagues found profoundly moving. Dancing on a bare stage, with her dark hair loosened and wearing a stylised Greek chiton that left her limbs and feet bare (and later, more scandalously, revealed her naked breasts), Duncan seemed to the meticulously trained Russians to have found a miraculous, resonant simplicity in the way she used her body.

Fokine would defensively rebut any suggestions that his own choreographic innovations had been taken from Duncan, yet it was around the time of the latter's first Russian visit that Lydia and her friends went to Fokine's lessons to find their carefully schooled habits being suddenly challenged. In place of the familiar classroom corrections, they were ordered by their teacher to begin listening to the 'inner music' of their bodies, and to find a new elasticity of line within their everyday exercises. It felt, to Lydia and her friends, close to a revolution: 'We girls had always been taught to hold our bodies tight and stiff in precise poses, any individuality was curbed.'[12] And whilst Fokine's demands for self-expression struck some of the class as incomprehensible, to Lydia they seem to have made exciting sense.* They chimed with her instincts for drama; they quickened her sense of how those years of repetitive exercises might transcend routine and become an individual statement of style. Soon she was advancing so quickly in Fokine's favour that when he came to create his first official piece of choreography, *Acis and Galatea*, he cast her in the solo role of Cupid, or Amour.

Acis, set to music by Andrei Kadletz, was created for the school graduation show of April 1905; and even though Fokine was barred from putting his cast in sandals (the girls were required, at these performances, to demonstrate their facility in pointe work), the ballet did elicit an unusual range of dramatic colour from its young dancers.

*Later Lydia would admit that while Fokine's teaching had been good for 'creating images', it had perhaps been less technically effective than his predecessors. Fyodor Lopukhov, *To the Heart of Choreography*, 2003 edn, p.157.

To embody the antique, pastoral spirit of Ovid's tale, Fokine had worked simple folk rhythms and classical Greek poses into the choreography, and he had tailored each role to maximise a fresh, unfettered vitality of expression. Lydia, as Cupid, was given a solo of light, delicate jumps, which according to her brother made her appear as weightless as 'one of those little angels of quattrocentro painters'.[13] Fedor himself was a poetic Acis, and overshadowing even the Lopukhovs was a sixteen-year-old boy, Vaslav Nijinsky, who was given the tumbling, acrobatic role of the lead faun. Nijinsky's technique, especially his astonishingly high jump, had already become the subject of gossip in the school corridors, but when he appeared in *Acis* his gift was transformed into some more mercurial force. On stage, Nijinsky seemed to concentrate all the light and oxygen into his dancing, and the startled ovation that greeted his performance signalled that Fokine had just launched an extraordinary career.

The critics' reviews were full of Nijinsky, although Lydia did get her own favourable comment in the journal *Slovo* (*The Word*), which noted that the 'little pupil Lopukhova had been "splendid" in the role of Amour'. She herself was now fascinated by Fokine and by the dissident glamour that he represented. In any argument over the merits of Isadora Duncan, she would always champion the American dancer; and she later recalled her thrill when, during a class at school, 'the door opened and in came a tall, statuesque woman in a long white Grecian robe, with her hair in a fillet. It was Isadora Duncan and she and her troupe opened a new world for us with their new, wavy, flowing, rhythmical movements. We girls exchanged chocolates and kisses.'[14] But Lydia was herself becoming very interesting to Fokine, and while it was unusual for non-graduating students to be allocated major solos in school performances, he continued to use her and in 1908 he cast her as the Winter Snowflake in his setting of Tchaikovsky's *Four Seasons*.

Lydia was now sixteen and a half, and beginning to acquire her adult profile as a dancer. She was still very small and the waxy pallor of her skin made her face appear childishly plump, but her prettiness had unusual angles. Fedor, who later wrote an admiring critical study of his sister, described her as 'an elegant little doll, with eyes that shone whenever she performed', and he recorded, too, that she possessed an unexpectedly powerful technique. She was very fast: 'her running on pointes was infectiously gay and light as if she was tripping on air'; while her light, springing jump was almost comparable to Nijinsky's: 'Her leg muscles were remarkable and she could achieve an incredibly big leap, almost masculine in its power, yet at the same time, her flight through the air was as delicate as was her landing. Whereas [Nijinsky's] leap reminded one of the jump and flight of a grasshopper, Lydia's resembled the ... descent of dandelion down.'[15]

Daily life for Lydia was, however, becoming more obdurate and more challenging. At home her father's alcoholism was now a harsh given and there were often brawls to negotiate when she visited the family flat. Viewing the household through more adult eyes, Lydia was forced to share Fedor and Evgenia's concern about the threats to their mother from Vasili's disintegration, and about the danger to the family finances. At school, too, she was under new pressure. The time was fast approaching when her class would be graduating into the Mariinsky, and competition was intensifying as she strove to raise her profile still higher, fighting for the attention and the examination marks that would single her out as a possible future ballerina in the company.

Among her friends and her teachers Lydia may have seemed unchanged, a charmer, a natural comedian, a free spirit whose trajectory through school was buoyed along by the fluky good fortune of her talent and temperament. Yet as an adult Lydia would become adept at putting the fizz of her personality to deliberate use: it enabled her to mask her anxieties or to throw the switch on a difficult situation. It may have been now, as she emerged from protected childhood, that Lydia started to develop that skill.

By this time Lydia had gained the rank of senior pupil, her status denoted by the pink practice dress she wore in the ballet studio and by the few precious boarding privileges that came with it. She was given a bed and private desk in an annexe separated off from the main dormitory, as well as access to the seniors' dressing room, which allowed precious glimpses, through unfrosted windows, of life in the street below. Yet as she and her friends looked down at the hawkers selling food and trinkets, at the carriages carrying actors and dancers to their rehearsals, they felt themselves even more unnaturally confined. Those like Lydia whose ambitions were fixed on the stage were impatient to take their place within the company; those with more worldly aims were waiting for the moment when their dancing might catch the eye of a rich protector. (The older pupils had now grasped that many dancers were kept by lovers at court, and traded information about those who were rumoured to benefit most from the 'secret' passage at the Mariinsky which ran between the Grand Dukes' box and the stage.)

Finally, by the spring of 1909, all that stood between Lydia's class and independence were their two graduation shows. These were the occasions on which their skills would be judged by a professional audience of teachers, critics, dancers and theatre management, and by which they would be ranked according to talent. Only eleven girls remained (the other two class members having been weeded out as unsuitable), and among them Lydia had two clear rivals: willowy Maria Piltz (who in 1913 would create the role of the Chosen One in Nijinsky's avant-garde ballet *The Rite of Spring*) and the technically prodigious Yelena Lukom (who would become one of St Petersburg's leading classical ballerinas).

From the formal graduation photograph that was taken of Lydia around this time, it is hard to get much sense of how she might have impressed her judges. Her pose for the camera is anonymously conventional and it is only in the curling, idiosyncratic placement of her fingers, close to her neck, that a scintilla of personal style appears. However, from a dry review of her first performance, at the school's own theatre on 23 March, it seems likely that Lydia's personality on stage had been striking – almost too striking. The critic of the *St Petersburg Gazette* had ticked off her technical points more or less approvingly: 'a very nice-looking dancer ... good pirouette [if] still undeveloped *pointes* and not entirely correct *port de bras*'; but he had noted warningly that she had displayed a great deal of 'self-confidence' and should 'immediately begin to divert herself from over-emphasised affectation and mannerism'.[16]

The fact that this writer complained of similar flaws in the rest of Lydia's class suggests that he may have been taking a swipe at Fokine's unorthodox teaching methods, but Lydia was evidently chastened. By the second show, a much grander affair, held on 9 April at the Mariinsky, she had smoothed out the quirks of her performance sufficiently for the same critic to congratulate her stiffly on 'a good tone and manner',[17] and a month later she was joining with the others in the graduation ceremony that would mark her final day as a pupil. Dressed for the first, and last, time at school in non-uniform frocks, as vain and excited as young brides, Lydia and her friends were presented at this ceremony with three critical tokens of passage. The first was a grant of 100 roubles to aid their transition to adult independence; the second was their final report (Lydia would have been relieved by hers – she was graded excellent or very good in all of her subjects). The third was official permission for all successful graduates to submit their petitions* for admittance to the Imperial Ballet.

Lydia had passed through the first stage of her professional destiny with distinction, and it was inevitable that when she embarked on her second stage, at the end of August, she would be conscious of a loss of status. At school she had been a privileged child performer, Fokine's show pupil, a beneficiary of the new radical spirit. Even after graduation she had been selected to perform in the short summer season held at Krasnoe Selo, the military camp just outside St Petersburg, for which she not only had been paid extra salary, but was also rewarded with a formal presentation to the Tsar and his wife, and given a gold watch bearing the Imperial crest. At the Mariinsky, however, Lydia was required to become a virtual nobody – an anonymous member of the corps de ballet working exhaustingly hard for minimal applause. During her first season alone, she not only had to learn the choreography for ten evening-length ballets and operas, but had to master the exacting discipline of dancing in line. The collective beauty of the corps de ballet (the massed chorus, or literally the body of the company) depends on thirty-six or forty-eight young women lifting their legs at the same angle, rounding their arms,

*This was a formality. All those who had survived the rigorous training of the Theatre School were acceptable as corps de ballet material. Occasionally, exceptional talents like Pavlova's were admitted into the company at the higher rank of coryphée.

Left: Lydia, friend of Lise (Liza), *La Fille mal gardée* (*Vain Precautions*), St Petersburg, 1909–10. *Right:* Lydia, Polovtsian Girl, *Prince Igor*, St Petersburg, 1909

jumping and even breathing in unison. In Lydia's new working life there was little call for the lively temperament or the piquant appearance that had made her a child star.

Yet if she was physically drained by her new professional duties, she was not crushed by them. Within the humid, gossipy atmosphere of the juniors' dressing room, Lydia's rattling high spirits brought her the same popularity that she had enjoyed at school; and there was another practical way, too, in which she established herself as a ring-leader among her peers. One of the ignominies of dancing at the very bottom of the Mariinsky hierarchy was the meagre allocation of ballet shoes sanctioned by management. Artists of Lydia's rank were required to eke out every pair until their blocked points had turned so soft and crumbling that, as she later claimed, 'we could hardly stand on our toes'.[18] Junior dancers used to look with envy at the senior ballerinas, who enjoyed the luxury of wearing two, even three pairs during a single performance. Anna Pavlova they regarded with particular awe for, as one of the Mariinsky's most fêted stars, she had a devoted following of admirers who kept her supplied with her favourite and very expensively crafted brand of Italian shoes. This collection of treasures was, as Lydia had discovered, stored in a large basket in Pavlova's dressing room, and she had the brainwave of masterminding a small gang of dancers to make raids on it during the ballerina's absence: 'We did, what shall I say, a kind of stealing. We took out hers – never a new pair of course – in exchange for ours – so dreadfully worn out – which we put carefully at the bottom of her basket.'[19] On stage, Pavlova was famous for her fragile lyricism; off stage she had a steely, implacable sense of her own status. To make an enemy of her was extremely dangerous, and Lydia had been entranced by the risk she was running: 'It seemed nothing could have been naughtier.'[20]

Yet just as at school, Lydia was able to deflect attention from her misbehaviour by making model progress in class and on the stage. Determined to dance her way out of the corps at the earliest opportunity, she had signed up for additional study with her former teacher Cecchetti (who had returned from three years as ballet master in Warsaw to set up a private studio in St Petersburg), and her diligence was rewarded with some very small solo roles, including that of Miranda in Mikhail Fokine's baroque supernatural fantasy *Le Pavillon d'Armide*. As the heroine's confidante, Lydia had only a brief moment in the spotlight, but the role did have crucial political significance in re-establishing her as an official protégée of Fokine, and also in aligning her with the faction of dancers who were now regarded as the most dynamic, and magnetically controversial, element within the Mariinsky.

In the wake of the 1905–6 uprisings, the ballet company had split into two opposing camps, and a dancer's future could be strongly affected by where he or she was positioned. At the centre of one camp was Alexander Krupensky, the entrenched conservative who directed the St Petersburg office of the Imperial Theatres and who retained the allegiance of older dancers like Kschessinska. At the centre of the other was Fokine, who wielded far less power but was being tipped as the future choreographic voice of the company.

After *Acis and Galatea*, Fokine had gone on to create a string of new ballets, each of which he had attempted to choreograph in its own distinctive idiom. His 1907 ballet *Eunice* (based on Henryk Sienkiewicz's novel *Quo Vadis*) had featured an Egyptian-styled pas de trois, with flattened profile poses taken from ancient friezes and bas-reliefs; *Chopiniana*, his homage to early nineteenth-century Romanticism, had combined an ethereal ballet vocabulary with rousing folk dance. This quest for authenticity was radical enough for its time, but equally iconoclastic had been Fokine's mission to stage each ballet with a faithful attention to its setting – a notion utterly counter to the St Petersburg tradition, by which ballerinas came dressed in tutus, pointe shoes and jewellery irrespective of whether they were meant to be dancing in an Indian temple, a gothic palace or a Spanish plaza.

When Fokine set out to challenge this convention, he was courting trouble. His refusal to let Kschessinska parade her famous personal diamonds in one of his ballets earned him the ballerina's peevish enmity; his attempts to have the cast of *Eunice* perform with bare legs and feet attracted the disgusted wrath of the management, who reacted as if Fokine had wanted to parade his dancers naked. But Lydia recalled that if 'the old people were staggered and shocked by the new life he gave to the ballet ... we would watch from the wings with glistening eyes'.[21] To be associated with Fokine was, for the younger dancers, to feel themselves at the vanguard of the profession – to be marked out as spirited, original and daring.

For Lydia, Fokine's charisma had been heightened, too, by the unprecedented triumph that he had enjoyed in Paris during the summer of 1909, when a season of his ballets had been performed at the city's Théâtre du Châtelet. For any Russian artist to gain the admiration of Paris was awe-inspiring, but almost as impressive to Lydia had been the fact that the impresario for Fokine's season had been Serge Diaghilev, known to her as one of the most fascinating and dangerous men operating within St Petersburg's cultural circles.

At this time it was hard to define the exact nature of Diaghilev's power. When he had first arrived in St Petersburg, fresh from his family's country estate near Perm, all his dreams had been of becoming a great composer. His talent for music, however, had turned out to be less significant than the encyclopaedic brilliance of his mind, the sureness of his aesthetic instincts and the pushiness of his ambitions. By 1898 he had become co-founder and co-editor of *Mir iskusstva* (*The World of Art*), a magazine promoting new Russian painting and the European avant-garde, and had already established himself as an arbiter of the St Petersburg art scene. Then, as assistant to the director of the Imperial Theatres, he had spread his influence into the heart of the theatrical establishment, where the full extent of his aspirations began to emerge. To the more old-fashioned members of the Imperial Directorate, Diaghilev's whole manner had presented itself as a provocation. Aggressively inquisitive about every aspect of the theatre business, he had turned up uninvited to rehearsals and meetings, where his black, hooded stare had seemed to penetrate unsettlingly into matters that did not concern him. Even his immaculately groomed appearance had been a challenge. Diaghilev was a dandy and, in a city where dress codes were minutely judged, he did not care who condemned him for it, as he twirled his trademark cane and drew elegant attention to the unusual silver streak that ran through his carefully combed and, later, carefully dyed black hair.

After two years these simmering conflicts of style had come to a head when Diaghilev was given control of a new staging of the ballet *Sylvia*. Rather than using the Mariinsky's in-house artists to design the production, he had chosen to commission the young painter Leon Bakst – his colleague on *The World of Art*. This brazen disregard for protocol had led to his dismissal and to an uneasy relationship with key members at court. But Diaghilev now had a bulldog grip on his own advancement. After having curated an historically successful exhibition of Russian portrait painting in St Petersburg, he began to reconfigure himself as a new breed of cultural entrepreneur, selling Russian art to the West.

He had long understood that the market existed: 'Europe needs our youth and our spontaneity,' he had boasted back in 1896; 'we must show our all'.[22] And in October 1906 he had gained permission to mount a huge retrospective of Russian painting at Paris's prestigious Salon d'Automne. The timing and the presentation had been perfect. The exhibition had ranged from old masters and icons to the new generation of painters, Bakst and Alexandre Benois; and to the Parisians it had appeared to distil the vast mysteriousness of Russian culture, its Slavic rituals and Asiatic brightness, its refined melancholy and its barbaric soul. The exhibition was declared a revelation, and over the next three years Diaghilev worked the city expertly. He brought over programmes of Russian music and opera, and in 1909 prepared to expose Paris to the new Russian ballet.

Diaghilev had been introduced to Fokine's work in St Petersburg by Benois and had seen its possibilities, but for Paris he knew it required better marketing. He wanted new sets and costumes designed by serious artists; he wanted ballets created to more challenging music. These ambitions would not come cheap (even allowing for subsidies donated by his Russian patrons, the 1909 season left Diaghilev in debt to his French promoter by 86,000 francs), but he was right to pin his hopes on their creating a sensation. The savage, warrior energy of Fokine's *Polovtsian Dances*, set by the painter Nicholas Roerich against a scorched Russian steppe and burnished sky, accompanied by the frenetic rhythms of Borodin; the hot Egyptian tableaux of *Cléopâtre*; the delicate, romantic poetry of *Les Sylphides* (a reworking of *Chopiniana*). For Paris these amounted to nothing less than a new dance form for the twentieth century.*

The Russian dancers were also greeted as the century's new stars, for Diaghilev and Fokine had chosen their debut company carefully. Their most exotic calling card was the twenty-year-old Vaslav Nijinsky (now Diaghilev's lover), whose marvellous jump, rising and hovering on invisible currents of air, was coupled with a rare gift for translating himself physically and emotionally into each role that he performed. Solidly built, with long, slanted eyes and flaring Slav cheekbones, Nijinsky could appear both feral and secretive, primitive and perfumed, and that summer he was fêted by Parisian critics as a 'prodigy', a 'god of the dance'.

Diaghilev's ballerinas were also mobbed. Pavlova's haunting pallor and musical intelligence were hailed as a reincarnation of the great Romantic dancer Marie Taglioni; Karsavina's eloquently nuanced acting was adored – especially by Robert Brussel, critic of *Le Figaro*, who took to hanging around her, backstage, until Fokine had him

*The Russians created a dramatic contrast to the inert state of French ballet, whose productions had largely deteriorated into a vapid recycling of choreographic formulae cynically designed to showcase the fine bosoms and pretty legs of its female dancers.

thrown out of the theatre. Even the company's mime artist, Ida Rubinstein, was rarely out of the headlines. An electrifying beauty, Rubinstein possessed an infallible instinct for publicity, and that summer was to be seen drinking champagne out of lilies and parading through the city with a panther on a lead. Her panache impressed even Paris, which had as its exemplar the notorious Madame Rachilde, a society hostess who presided over her salons with a pair of rats named Kyrie and Eleison perched on her shoulders.

But the acclaim that Diaghilev and Fokine had won in Paris created trouble for them when they returned to St Petersburg. To the authorities at the Mariinsky, it seemed that the two men were acquiring threatening levels of influence over the company's artists; while among the dancers who had been excluded from the season there was resentment at the glory they had missed. During the following winter, rifts between what were labelled the 'Imperialist camp' and the 'Diaghilev–Fokine camp' turned bitterly political, and they became more so when it emerged that the latter were planning a second summer season, in Berlin, Paris and Brussels.

This was expected to be still more ambitious than the first, with the young composer Igor Stravinsky commissioned to write a new score for Fokine and a dance drama planned to Rimsky-Korsakov's *Schéhérazade*. But the atmosphere surrounding the season's preparations also became correspondingly fraught. Rumours began to fly that the upstart Diaghilev was losing more of his friends among the Grand Dukes, and threats were issued by management that anyone involved in the project would be sacked if it interfered with their scheduled performances at the Mariinsky. The aura of illicit activity only added to the glamour of those who had been summoned by Diaghilev and Fokine, and Lydia, of course, yearned to be one of them. Although she was not among the first group of dancers to be called to rehearsals, in April 1910 word did finally come to her that she was to be included in Diaghilev's corps de ballet.

The money she would earn was enough to make Lydia skittish with triumph. Even though she was to be promoted the next season to the rank of coryphée (midpoint between corps de ballet and solo artist) and would receive an extra 120 roubles a year, her fees for the

Diaghilev season still came close to a full year's salary at the Mariinsky, for just six and a half weeks of work. In addition, she would be going to Paris – a city she had always dreamed of as a Mecca of style, its inhabitants dressed with ineffable chic, its shops stuffed with delicacies. So extreme were Lydia's expectations in fact that, in June, when she eventually stepped out of the train at the Gare du Nord, she fainted with emotion. To Bakst, who rushed to help her, she could only explain that she had been overcome by the 'lovely sight' of the station's soaring iron and glass magnificence.[23]

But another factor that was playing on Lydia's mind was a simple desire to get away from home. The Nevsky Prospekt flat had become additionally crowded since she had returned there from school, for while Fedor had been partially away from home, dancing a season in Moscow, Evgenia had recently married a student from the city's Engineering Institute, and she not only continued to live at home with him but also entertained his friends there. With everyone back in the flat for the holidays, there was no chance of privacy for Lydia, nor any escape from Vasili, whose presence was becoming increasingly hard to tolerate.

Karlusha, even though upset by the prospect of her impressionable daughter heading off to Europe for two months, may have sympathised with Lydia's desire to remove herself and she made no effort to stop her. Perhaps she was reassured by the fact that Evgenia had performed with Diaghilev the previous year and had come to no harm. Perhaps she consoled herself with the knowledge that Fedor would, coincidentally, be performing in Paris at the same time, with a small troupe of Russian dancers led by Nicolas Legat and Julie Sedova. He would surely be able to keep a watchful eye on his little sister and ensure that she returned home safely. In her worst imaginings Karlusha could not possibly have foreseen that when she hugged Lydia goodbye, fifteen years would pass before she would embrace her youngest daughter once more.

Chapter Three

PARIS AND DIAGHILEV

> It was at the Opéra that she made her remarkable leap from the ranks of the corps de ballet to the position of a recognised ballerina who was the talk of the ballet correspondents. Paris was abuzz: a new star had been born.
>
> FEDOR LOPUKHOV[1]

On the day that Lydia left St Petersburg, she had no more reason than her mother to doubt that she would return, and had formed no ambitions beyond enjoying the adventure that lay ahead. She had barely been out of the city before, and the huge cross-continental train on which she was travelling was an engrossing novelty to her, with its leather-embossed walls and brocade seats, its ingeniously compact washrooms and rattling speeds. Outside the windows, she could watch her dream of Europe approaching: dense stretches of fir and silver birch turning into lush, speckled farmland; wooden houses and onion-domed churches being replaced by stone and spires. During the long journey, as Lydia admired the scenery, gossiped with her friends, played cards and imagined the wonders of Paris to come, she was no different from any of the other excited teenagers in the corps. It was only after the company arrived in Berlin that she gained some inkling of how this trip would single her out for a different future.

The dancers had all assumed that the fortnight's season at the Theater des Westens was essentially to be a dress rehearsal for Paris, a period for polishing off the new repertory as well as drilling the company (several of whom had been hired from Moscow) into a coherent ensemble. As they unpacked their trunks, several of Lydia's colleagues were impatient at the delay, longing for the excitement of Paris and dismissive of the suburban charms of Charlottenburg, where their theatre and lodgings were located. Yet for Diaghilev and Fokine there were crucial matters still to arrange in Berlin. Neither Pavlova nor Karsavina was with the company at this point, the former having preferred to organise her own season for the summer, the latter having signed up to dance at London's premier music hall, the Coliseum, for all but the last three weeks of June.* Substitutes had not yet been selected for them (Diaghilev having stubbornly refused to believe that Karsavina could not be disentangled from her London contract). And it was apparently only in Berlin that Fokine suggested Lydia might have sufficient personality and talent to attempt two of the vacant ballerina roles: Columbine, the pert heroine of his new *commedia dell'arte* ballet *Carnaval*, and the Prelude variation in *Les Sylphides*.

To give this sort of preference to an unknown junior was an unusual break with protocol, and for Lydia, who accepted her promotion in 'half a dream',[2] it meant an alarming amount of choreography to learn. The style and character of the two new roles that she had been given were both very different. In *Sylphides*, Lydia was required to become a dreaming embodiment of her accompanying music – Chopin's Prelude in A major; in *Carnaval* (set to Schumann's titular score)† she had to assume the character of a fickle flirt, a party girl who schemes and romances with a group of carnival friends. Yet Fokine had been right to judge that both ballets would fall within her natural range. The choreography of *Sylphides* showcased Lydia's pretty arms and bright bevelled footwork – Karsavina, watching her a few weeks later in Paris, would generously admire the way in which she 'ecstatically and swiftly ran on her toes"[3] – while for Columbine, her temperament as well as her technique proved an exceptional match.

Several years later, the British critic Cyril Beaumont would judge

---

*Karsavina had been ignorant of Diaghilev's plans for a second summer season when she had signed her contract with the Coliseum.

†*Carnaval* was set to an orchestrated version of the 1835 piano score.

that Lydia's 'enticing smile and shaded glance' were perfectly modulated to capture the 'innocent, irresponsible roguish' spirit of Columbine.[4] Yet even in Berlin, a mere eighteen, she seemed fully in command of the role. Viewed from the front, Lydia's round cheeks and wide eyes presented an image of guileless sweetness to her public; in semi-profile, however, the impudent curve of her nose came into focus, as did the sharpness of her glance, so that her features suggested mischief, knowledge, secrets. Physically, Lydia was perfectly formed to dance Columbine, and on 20 May, when she circled the stage on the arm of her Harlequin, Leonide Leontiev, skimming the floor in her white Bo-Peep frock and pantaloons, she claimed the ballet as her own.

Suddenly, the alarming Diaghilev, who rarely acknowledged his junior dancers, was eager to embrace Lydia; and she never forgot her excitement when 'the great, generous big Serge came up to me and gave me a present of three hundred francs', nor the 'new hat and false curls' on which she splurged it all the next day.[5] But it was not only Diaghilev who took notice of this surprising teenager. Leading members of the Ballets Russes's inner council, Bakst and Serge Grigoriev (the company chief administrator or regisseur), also recognised that she had remarkable presence, and it was judged that she should continue performing ballerina roles in Paris even after Karsavina's return.

Two weeks later, Lydia stepped out of the company train at the Gare du Nord and fainted on a pile of luggage.

It would be tempting to paint this moment as an archetypal ballet image – an innocent young woman falling into a magical sleep, out of which she awakes to a transformed world. But the reality of Lydia's first few days in Paris was less dramatic. Certainly there was no more marvellous or terrifying city in which she could be tested as a ballerina. The elaborately decorated Paris Opéra was itself a legend, connected with the lustre of former stars like Marie Taglioni and Fanny Elssler, home to one of the world's most historically demanding audiences, and on 4 June, when Lydia stood in the wings for her first performance, even her youthfully tough nerves would have been jumping. That night the theatre was packed with aristocrats and bankers, with artists and critics as well as with the cream of society

Lydia with Vaslav Nijinsky, *Carnaval*, New York, 1916

hostesses. As Lydia waited for her music she could sense the audience as a collective, waiting entity: making out the pale glimmer of the women's jewellery and lace; smelling the musk of their perfume; and, above all, feeling the expectancy of the crowd, more avid and more predatory than the St Petersburg balletomanes that she was used to, and certainly less indulgent than the good-natured Berliners.

She was dancing *Carnaval* and also a role in *La Princesse enchantée*,* a classical pas de deux from Petipa's *Sleeping Beauty*, which along with several other divertissements had been repackaged into a virtuoso showcase titled *Le Festin*. Petipa's scissor-sharp choreography demanded both precision and stamina, and it was another mark of

*This was the 'Blue Bird' divertissement from Act III. It had been performed the previous year under the title *L'Oiseau de feu*, its change of name necessitated by Fokine's new *Firebird*.

favour for Lydia to be entrusted with it. Yet while she danced well enough for the Italian poet Gabriele D'Annunzio to corner her at the post-performance party, and to declare to the assembled guests that he longed 'to write a dance for your legs, which are as eloquent as Duse's intellect',[6] it was to be a few days before Paris would be 'abuzz' with Lydia's name. Exactly as Diaghilev had planned, the sensation that night was created by *Schéhérazade*, Fokine's latest creation.

The ballet was based on a story from the *Arabian Nights*, and Fokine's choreography had liberated his cast to extremes of physical abandon. Nijinsky, as the doomed Golden Slave, danced with a soft, supple savagery; Rubinstein as his haughty seductress Zobeide moved with a feline voluptuousness, exquisitely carnal even by her standards. But almost as marvellous to the Opéra audience was the vibrant palette of greens, ochres, blues and reds with which Bakst had transformed the stage into an Arabian palace, and the costumes with which he had metamorphosed the performers into a harem of slaves and houris. To the watching Parisians in their formal evening clothes, these Russian dancers appeared like a race of beautiful barbarians. Tunics and harem pants moved like a silken second skin around their bodies; gold ornaments pressed against their naked flesh; thick ropes of pearls bound their wrists and ankles. It was an epiphany as aesthetic as it was sexual, and it generated a cult. Oriental cushions and rugs appeared almost overnight in student attics; within the fashionable drawing rooms of Paris, walls were repainted in an excess of hot primary colour; and the next collection created by the couturier Poiret was modelled on the draped, sinuous lines of Bakst's oriental wardrobe.

Yet if Lydia herself did not appear in *Schéhérazade*, she profited directly from its success, as the Ballets Russes became the main summer attraction of the French capital. Diaghilev was increasing her opportunities almost every day, casting her in two ballets per programme, and adding new roles to her growing repertory. She danced the peasant pas de deux from *Giselle* (Diaghilev's other concession, besides *Festin*, to nineteenth-century tradition) and also the female lead in *Polovtsian Dances*, in which it was rightly judged that her baby face would create a poignant contrast to the muscular primitivism of Fokine's choreography. She was also being marketed hard.

New faces sold newspapers and tickets, and an 'infant prodigy' was especially sellable. Within days, Diaghilev had shaved a year off Lydia's age, presenting her as a seventeen-year-old fresh from school; and Paris, quick to respond, began referring to this latest novelty as La Précose. With *Comoedia Illustré* publishing her photo in its 'Stars of the Russian Ballet' gallery, Lydia began to move tickets almost as fast as Karsavina or Nijinsky; and Brussel, in his reviews in *Figaro*, made a special point of tracking her progress. He was impressed by her stylistic range, praising her 'adorable subtlety of expression' in *Sylphides* (13 June) and the 'vitality and grace' of her variation in *Giselle* (19 June). He also noted that this 'mere child'[7] was receiving demands for encores almost as noisy as those of her seniors.

As the French critics observed this original, little soubrette, they noticed too that her stagecraft was deepened by a wistful streak of poetry. At school Lydia had learned to screen her emotions, internalising any unhappiness she felt at being cooped up by governesses and separated from her mother. On stage in Paris, however, she seems to have found some direct line of access between her performance and her inner self. Impulsive, spirited and piquant as La Précose might be, her dancing was starting to reveal unexpected qualities of dreaming and melancholy.

If the Parisians were beguiled by Lydia, so too were her Russian colleagues. As the youngest member of the company she would normally be expected to observe extreme deference towards her seniors, for even though the Ballets Russes had been set up in opposition to the Mariinsky, it had assumed that institution's absolute hierarchical structure. Towards Diaghilev, the company's self-styled tsar, Lydia should have behaved with awe. Yet as the troupe's baby she seems to have been granted special licence. Flitting around the maze of corridors and studios backstage at the Opéra, visiting the other dancers in their dressing rooms, Lydia was petted and indulged. While other members of the company would rise mutely to their feet whenever Diaghilev entered a room, the men clicking their heels whenever he addressed them, Lydia was treated almost like the impresario's daughter.

She was also encouraged to attend the succession of parties that revolved around the company, mixing with the princesses, the artists and the intellectuals who courted the dancers that summer. Lydia had a healthy appetite, for excitement as well as for food, and it is easy to visualise her in the thick of these soirées, charming her admirers with her schoolgirl French, her upturned face shining with enthusiasm as she was plied with compliments and introduced to distinguished admirers, including her own stage heroine, Sarah Bernhardt. But she must have appeared a curious little thing to the Parisians, for, as she later admitted, she arrived in Europe 'knowing nothing of myself or the world'. In particular she knew nothing about clothes.[8] Like all her friends, Lydia had been desperate to experience the Paris shops, and in this city of fabled fashion houses – Worth, Doucet and Paquin – she was determined to look her best. But the layered, fussily tailored styles of the period muffled rather than flattered her body, and to judge by the photographs from this period, Lydia rarely achieved the glamour to which she aspired.

There is no record of whether she felt overwhelmed by the attention she was receiving, nor whether she regretted being divided from her friends once Diaghilev ordered her to be booked into her own suite at the Grand Hôtel on the Boulevard des Capucines. In public at least, Lydia's sense of the ridiculous and her light, melodious laugh lifted her above the scrutiny of the Parisian hostesses as well as the professional rivalry of her peers. But towards the end of the season she was faced with a challenge before which even her courage wavered. In mid-July, Karsavina was required by her Coliseum contract to return to London, leaving Diaghilev with no ballerina to dance her remaining performances in *L'Oiseau de feu* (*The Firebird*), the third and most radical of Fokine's new works for the summer.

Initially no one thought of Lydia as a possible candidate. Stravinsky's score was unlike any music to which she had danced, its rhythms jangling with a fractured modernity, its orchestration a mosaic of coruscating colours, howling furies and unearthly shimmer. The choreography, too, was an extreme challenge. While telling the simple tale of a young prince, Ivan Tsarevitch, who braves an evil demon for the sake of a kingdom and a beautiful princess, Fokine had experimented with his most eclectic dance palette to date. The demon Kostchei and his crew of enchanted monsters were figures from an expressionist nightmare, pumping and seething with an almost mechanistic energy. The ballerina role was written in flames. This magical bird-woman whom Lydia had to embody did not fall in love with her partner, Ivan Tsarevitch, like any traditional ballet heroine, but was cast first as his proud adversary, eventually as his saviour. And in order to convey the character's independence Fokine had twisted and reimagined classical convention – turning the Firebird's long solos into a concentrated flare of jumps and white-hot stillness, and making her pas de deux with Ivan Tsarevitch into a battle of wills as she beat her arms, arched her body and twisted her head to evade his grasp.

A century later, dancers still find the Firebird a challenge. It requires a technique light and powerful enough to suggest a bird in flight; musicality precise enough to articulate Stravinsky's serrated rhythms; and acting expressive enough to dramatise wildness. When Karsavina had first premièred the role back in June 1910, her performance had seemed definitive, her huge eyes scouring the stage with a feral anger, her arms folded like powerful wings around her face. No other dancer had been permitted to follow her and no one imagined that Lydia, who was anything but fierce or flammable, could do more than scrape through the role. As Serge Grigoriev wrote, 'To learn a part like the Firebird in only a few days was no slight task: and considering Lopokova's extreme youth and inexperience we did not expect her to be perfect.'[9] As for Lydia, when she first thrust herself into the eerie swell of Stravinsky's score she too must have felt that nothing in her short career had prepared her for the moment. In *Carnaval* she had had the comic chemistry of the other characters to sustain her; in *Sylphides* she had been lifted on the gentle pulse of Chopin's music. In *Firebird*, dressed in her elaborate oriental costume and plumed headdress, she was a lone contender and her prime concern must simply have been to harness the adrenalin jolting in her veins, to will her legs not to turn to jelly during her opening jumps, and save sufficient breath for the long, embattled pas de deux.

Yet Grigoriev recalled that Lydia did much more than survive her debut on 20 July. With a 'daring technique, and temperament enough to give an excellent account of herself', she won her own ovations.[10] Although she might never rival Karsavina – Benois later observed that Lydia was always 'more of a delicate humming bird than a flaming phoenix ... more lively, nervous, even perhaps childish'[11] – the role was added to her repertory and she would continue dancing it for the next sixteen years.

However, if *Firebird* clinched Lydia's conquest of Paris, it may also have turned her head, as during the last days of the season foreign theatre agents begun to buzz around the Russians' dressing rooms, making what one Parisian described as 'stupendous offers'.[12] Especially predatory were the agents from America, where the lack of a flourishing native ballet culture meant there was a prime market for foreign 'toe dancers'. Since vivacious La Précoce was at the top of their shopping lists, Lydia found herself flattered by talk of the enormous sums she could earn if she were willing to venture across the Atlantic for a season or two.

It was perhaps only now that Lydia started to picture the future that awaited her once the Paris adventure was over. There was no guarantee that Diaghilev would be able to organise another ballet season like this one. And back in the cramped family flat on the Nevsky Prospekt, all she might ever have to show from this summer would be a new wardrobe and a few newspaper clippings. She could also be certain that her triumphs in Paris would have little purchase on her career back home. A raft of senior ballerinas were blocking her way to significant promotion, and for a few years to come she would still be dancing minor roles at the Mariinsky. In fact, if Lydia was honest with herself, she knew that she was unlikely to reach the prima ballerina status of a Kschessinska or Pavlova. Although she was vivid, fast and strong, her style was not naturally suited to the grand classical roles that still dominated the St Petersburg stage. She might be a captivating instrument for Fokine's poetic imagination, but she was not, and never would be, an ideal Sleeping Beauty or Swan Princess.

Yet if Lydia was aware, suddenly, of what she would lose by returning to St Petersburg, she also knew what a risk she was running if she failed to show up for the start of the Mariinsky season. Dancers who graduated from the Theatre School were legally obliged to perform for a minimum of five years in order to repay the debt of their training, and while a few privileged individuals were able to renegotiate the terms of their contracts, Lydia as a junior would be committing a sackable offence if she took an unofficial sabbatical in America. For a day or so she seems to have dithered miserably, her head spinning with talk of Broadway dollars and fame while her instinct for security argued against the danger of compromising her Russian career. And in this frame of mind she was helpless against the blandishments of the most Mephistophelean of the agents, Josef Mandelkern.

Mandelkern was a fast-talking Russian émigré who wielded his professional powers of flattery as aggressively as he sported his glossy black moustache and 'Yankee' cigar. He was representing one of New York's most eminent producers, Charles Frohman, and on the latter's behalf was offering Lydia an eight-month contract for which she would be paid a monthly salary of 18,000 francs (roughly £13,000 by today's values). This was sixty times more than she had earned during her first Russian season, 1,000 roubles more than Pavlova's annual Mariinsky salary, and if Lydia found it a staggering sum, others were equally incredulous on her behalf. The *St Petersburg Gazette*, reporting on the negotiations, noted that 'Mlle Lopukhova [who is] not famous in St Petersburg at all ... is invited to the USA and offered 4,000 roubles a month',[13] while *Footlights and Life* commented with simple, dumb amazement, 'The USA astonishes us by big fees!'[14]

But Mandelkern had also gilded his offer with two extra incentives. To partner Lydia the agent was proposing to hire Alexandre Volinine, a dancer from Moscow whose equable temperament and handsome technique had made him one of the most popular men in Diaghilev's company. Better still, the agent was also offering a contract to her brother. Genetically and temperamentally, the two Lopukhovs were very much alike. Although Fedor's mind, like his long nose, was sharper, more cutting than his baby sister's, the two siblings were both as fair and round-faced as their mother, and as gregarious as their father. For Lydia to be able to share her American adventure with Fedenka, as the family called him, and to be assured of his experience and protection, was to make the crossing of the Atlantic seem a less intimidating prospect.

It may even have been Fedor who helped to guide Lydia through the final negotiations with Mandelkern, suggesting how she might accept the agent's offer while still keeping her options open at home. Even as the ink was drying on Lydia's contract with Frohman, she was also writing a carefully calculated letter to Alexander Krupensky, her boss back in St Petersburg:

> Much respected Alexander Dmitrievich
>
> Sorry to trouble you again but I am too heavy in my heart. You always treated me well and this is why I can tell you what has happened with me: thanks to my success in Berlin and Paris, different agents began to approach me, inviting me to various cities and countries; some suggestions were very tempting, but I declined all of them, remembering that, after all I have achieved I should be grateful to the School and to you ... money and fame are nothing in comparison with the management's appreciation and my status in the Petersburg Theatre. Try to imagine, I was surrounded by agents and they persuaded me to sign a contract for New York. Next day I changed my mind; I was crying; you know I would give everything to avoid this. I am too distressed I don't want to go anywhere. But the agents are like Cerberuses and the consequences of not observing this contract would be awful. I beg of you to give me a two month holiday from August 15. Give me a document with a statement that I can't be on leave more than two months. It will give me the chance to leave New York and I hope to God I'll be in St Petersburg on October 15 ...
>
> For God's sake carry out my request. I will be grateful.[15]

This letter was written on 22 July, just four days before Lydia was due to set sail, and it is hard to judge the exact degree of duplicity in its contents. Lydia was a long way from home, she was being tempted with life-changing decisions, and part of the distress and confusion she portrayed to Krupensky may have been genuine. But she had also pitched her agony with considerable care, for this letter was designed to gain her two critical advantages. The first, and most obvious, was to obtain official leave of absence from the management, which would allow her to dance in America without fear of reprisals – she would, in fact, be granted leave from the Mariinsky until 21 December. The second was to ensure that she received a written summons from St Petersburg demanding her eventual return. Mandelkern may not have been aware of this, but his adorable new property was already planning to acquire some leverage, should she want to extricate herself from Frohman's contract ahead of time.

Lydia was growing up fast, learning how to manipulate others to get what she wanted, learning about the commercial laws that governed her profession. Krupensky might certainly have been less moved by her piteous protestations if he had known how close she was to leaving for New York; and he might have hardened his heart entirely if he had known that while she had been playing the tragic victim for his benefit, she had been simultaneously conniving with Mandelkern in an entirely different charade. Eager to endow his newly signed toe dancer with a bankable mystique, the agent had begun leaking news to the American press of a rich and aristocratic admirer who had been courting Lydia during the summer. This Polish count had, he alleged, fallen into a jealous rage when it was announced that his little ballerina was about to disappear to America and, in a headline-worthy gesture, he had whisked her away to a secret location. Dramatically, Mandelkern announced that Lydia had been discovered by detectives just hours before eloping to Russia, and the press were told it had only been after heavy persuasion that she had agreed to postpone the wedding until her contract with Frohman was completed.

There is, in fact, some evidence to suggest that Lydia had become romantically involved during her summer in Europe. In among the horde of personal papers that she kept beside her in old age was a photograph of a smartly dressed youth with a flourishing handlebar moustache, dated Paris 1910 and signed 'Cecil'. Even though the pretty woman sitting beside Cecil was not Lydia, the young man himself was evidently important enough for her to keep his picture, and there are reasons to assume that he may indeed have been a Polish count. Years later, the novelist Virginia Woolf would make gossipy reference to the 'Polish princes'[16] in Lydia's sexual past, and in 1927, when Lydia herself was commissioned to write a newspaper article about her favourite food, she would cite an unnamed Polish count as the source of a delicious recipe for pheasant – even though her inability to cook at the age of thirty-six, let alone at eighteen, makes it hard to credit the idea of an aristocratic lover having whispered details of a favourite recipe during his courtship.

Given how similar in style this story was to later PR fictions that Mandelkern span around Lydia's career, most of this escapade could simply have been a melodramatic fantasy. Certainly it was never corroborated by any other anecdotes or press reports. Despite Mandelkern's claim that the count had threatened to pursue Lydia to New York and physically drag her off the stage, there were no stories of any such skirmishes taking place. Nor did Lydia display any overt signs of reluctance when, on 26 July, she travelled with Fedor and Volinine to Cherbourg to board the transatlantic steamship the *Oceanic*. Not yet nineteen, only a year out of school, Lydia appeared ready to sail towards the other side of the world without a backward glance, and ready to take an extraordinary gamble with her fledgling career.

Chapter Four

THE NEW WORLD

> The invasion of the theatres of the Western World by ballet dancers of the Russian opera house is one of the interesting phenomenon of the present day.
>
> (*NEW YORK SUN*, 7 AUGUST 1910)

Lydia was not the first classical dancer to have ventured across the Atlantic in search of money, adventure and fame. As early as 1840 the Austrian ballerina Fanny Elssler had made her debut in Boston and travelled with her troupe as far south as Havana; a decade later, Léon Espinosa had toured an intrepid route down the Mississippi (during which, according to family legend, he had been taken temporarily captive by Indians). By the late nineteenth century several Italian ballerinas had visited America, paving the way for the Danish virtuoso Adeline Genée to triumph on Broadway and for Anna Pavlova to cast her spell over the Metropolitan Opera with what critics admiringly described as her 'motion made fluid loveliness'.[1]

That was in February 1910, and by the time Lydia was due to arrive, America considered itself to have developed a serious enthusiasm for imported ballet. As a nation, however, it still had a tenuous grasp on what it was seeing.* 'Toe dancing', 'ballot' or 'ocular opera' remained a mysterious art to most of the public, and little guidance was provided by reviews in the press. Apart from a few educated

---

*America did produce two distinguished ballerinas: Mary Ann Lee, who starred in her own production of *Giselle* in 1846, and Augusta Maywood, who made a successful career in Europe. But there was little enthusiasm for founding ballet schools and companies in America – perhaps because the art form was still too closely associated with the courts and boudoirs of Europe.

exceptions, such as Carl van Vechten and H. T. Parker, critics rarely stirred themselves to appreciate anything more than a pair of twinkling feet or a pretty face; and most were at their happiest publishing wildly inaccurate 'titbits' of gossip about these dancing foreigners, or inventing comic Anglicised variants of their names. (Pavlova's partner, Mikhail Mordkin, would send a furious telegram to the editor of an Irish-American paper when it was mischievously reported that his name was 'nothing less than a cover up for one Mike O'Mordkin'.)[2]

This breezy irreverence also came with a culture in which dance, in all its forms, was regarded as big business. From the cakewalk dancers and clog dancers who dominated the cheap variety shows, to the scantily clad 'tableaux' artistes in burlesque, to the upmarket vaudeville recitalists like Maud Allan (whose wildly popular *Salomé* routine was little more than a striptease legitimised by high cultural associations), pretty girls with fancy footwork were widely guaranteed to bring in the punters. Certainly Mandelkern had not been lying to Lydia when he had conveyed how much interest she would attract from the American public – only that summer the *New York Tribune* had reported the city to be in the grip of a 'Terpsichorean mania'. Yet the agent would have glossed over how utterly unrecognisable that interest would be from the educated balletomania with which she had grown up in Russia, and how mercilessly it would be driven by the logic of the marketplace. He would also have underplayed how often Lydia would be forced to peddle her talent on vaudeville stages or in the middle of popular musicals, finding herself increasingly isolated as an artist even as the adulation of her American audiences became louder and more adoring.

The five years that Lydia ended up spending in the States are among the least documented in her life: she rarely referred to them afterwards and very little correspondence has survived, so we can only guess at how unsettled she became by the rackety detour her professional path had taken. On the voyage out she certainly had no reason to see beyond the exciting terms of her new contract with Frohman as she, Fedor and Volinine spent nine days cosseted in the luxury of spacious wood-panelled cabins, taking meals in the first-class dining room and enjoying entertainments on the sunny games deck. Lydia, as the youngest of the three, also believed that she was tasting independence for the first time in her life. No longer answerable to Diaghilev and Grigoriev, far from the reach of the Imperial Theatre's authority, she was putting thousands of miles between herself and her past. By the time the *Oceanic* steamed into New York's harbour and the city's soaring skyline came into focus, she was more than impatient to embrace the new experience: 'When I saw New York first,' she later recounted to the press, 'I was on the steamer coming from France. First there was Liberty, the statue. It was wonderful, I had never seen Liberty like that before. And then the big houses, and then – Hurry up. Hurry up. Hurry up.'[3]

If Lydia had already read about New York's famous new skyscrapers, nothing had prepared her for the voraciousness of the city's reporters, who swarmed to greet her as she was escorted down to the dock. Primed by Frohman, several news items had already started to circulate about 'Lydie Lapoukhova', with the *New York Telegraph* reporting, somewhat freely, that '[this] slender little creature of unusual grace is a great favourite at the Russian court and is the only dancer to whom Pavlowa [sic] has shown the least jealousy. The intense rivalry between them is one of the bits of gossips at the St Petersburg court.'[4] Even fresher meat was the story of Lydia's thwarted elopement with her count. Probably few newsmen cared about the truth of this scandal but, just as Mandelkern had planned, it gave her a titillating cachet of Old World sophistication, and everyone wanted to hear 'Lydie's' version of events. Aided by Mandelkern's advice and translation, she seems to have played the press like a pro, refusing to give her lover's name but insisting on his aristocratic status: 'He's wealthy and his family is an old one. Why, they have a real castle in Poland.'[5] As she assured reporters 'with just a suggestion of a pout on her lips', she still planned to marry but she promised that she would not attempt another vanishing act: 'Oh do not be worried. I have a contract with you for 8 months and it will be kept. The presence of my fiancé will have no effect upon my work. I am 16 and can afford to wait.'[6]

It had to be handed to Mandelkern. Not only had he been expertly coaching Lydia on her lines but he had taken the opportunity to drop yet another year from her age. Lydia was close to her nineteenth birthday but she was being sold to America as a child star.

As Lydia ran the gauntlet of the New York press she had her first taste of how strange the city's customs might be. Then as she, Fedor and Volinine were driven around its streets, she realised too how physically foreign this twentieth-century metropolis would feel. Motor cars honked and rattled between the horse-drawn carriages, while subterranean rumbles signalled the presence of the new subway. Tall buildings fifteen or twenty storeys high were being erected everywhere, rising to block out the sun; and on every street corner stood tobacco and candy stands piled high with goods to serve the jabbering crowds of blacks, Asians, Europeans and sharp-talking locals.

Lydia may have felt that she had landed in a city where anything was possible, but almost immediately after her arrival the commercial imperatives of this brave new adventure kicked in. Back in Paris, Mandelkern had assured his Russian properties that they would be given a lavish debut in the Palace, the aristocrat of New York's vaudeville theatres, where Sarah Bernhardt, Ethel Barrymore and Lillian Russell regularly performed. At the last minute, however, Frohman was offered a deal from a rival producer, Charles Dillingham, which was too lucrative for him to turn down. Dillingham needed some Russian dancers for a new production that he was staging, and he was prepared to pay handsomely for them. Without having any say in the matter, Lydia, Volinine and Fedor were demoted from being headlining stars at 'the best Variety House in the world', as the Palace styled itself, to a novelty act in a trivial musical.

This was *The Echo*, written by William Le Baron and Deems Taylor, and the trio's insertion into its cast was a classic instance of Broadway opportunism. While the show had been touring its pre-New York run, it had featured very little dancing, its plot revolving around the running gag of a 'human echo' – actually a songwriter – employed by a country hotel to entertain its guests by repeating every joke or song uttered in his vicinity. As Dillingham had prepared for the show's Broadway première, however, he had been impressed by reports of the Terpsichorean mania sweeping Manhattan and realised that he needed to include some extra dance numbers. New performers were hired, who could break into a clog dance, a hula or a military march as *The Echo*'s flimsy plotline allowed; and the show's female lead was reinvented as a dancing waitress, to be played by the vaudeville star Bessie McCoy. According to Dillingham, it had been McCoy herself who had come up with the idea of introducing ballet into the mix. Watching her first run-through of *The Echo*, she had exclaimed, 'Why, it's a regular dancing tournament. I never knew there were so many styles of dancing. If only you had some Russians now it would be complete.'[7] It had been just at that point that Lydia, Fedor and Alexandre Volinine had sailed into town.

Unfortunately, while Dillingham was prepared to pay generously to acquire the Imperial Russian Dancers, as he would bill the trio, he was not able to offer them generous stage space. Within the crush of *The Echo*'s other acts, there was room for Lydia and Volinine to dance only one pas de deux, a prettily expressive piece that Fedor had choreographed to the Czibulka waltz 'Love's Dream after the Ball', and for Fedor himself to perform a solo 'Danse Russe'. Nor was much space given to their other professional needs. While the Mariinsky maintained a sacred timetable of class and rehearsal, dedicated to drilling the best possible performances out of its artists, working at the Globe was a hustle. Its situation in the commercial heart of the city, between 46th Street and Broadway, meant that the raucousness of the street seemed to leak into the theatre and, with dozens of dancers and singers competing for time and attention, it was difficult for Lydia and her partners to organise their essential daily practice.

And the conditions only got worse. On opening night, 17 August, the Globe's theatre crew were instructed to dampen down the stage before the Russians' slot, in order to make the wooden boards less slippery. In their enthusiasm, however, they slopped twenty or thirty full buckets over the floor, and when Lydia came on to dance with Volinine, she managed to skid through only a few steps before her feet lost their purchase and she crashed to her knees. It was a humiliating way to make a debut, and even though Lydia recovered to finish the pas de deux, she was observed to be 'shaking her head sadly' as she left the stage, with Volinine 'mumbling violent protests' beside her.[8]

The next day's reviews mitigated the pain a little. Even though praise for Fedor and Volinine was largely directed at their manly bearing (the American public having strong views on the subject of limp sissiness in male dancing), Lydia's performance was garlanded with adoring clichés, hailed as 'poetry in motion', 'a song without words'.[9] The *Journal of Commerce* gushed that altogether the Russians' dancing had been 'a revelation, nothing quite like it has been seen here', and there were loud calls for the trio to be given additional numbers in the show. Dillingham, however, did not respond, and as *The Echo* settled into a long summer run, Lydia and her partners began to experience a creeping sense of drudgery. The expansive performing schedules of the Imperial Theatres had not prepared them for the routines of a commercial production in which they had to perform the same two numbers eight times a week. Nor were they used to the heat of a New York summer. Dancing through the torpid humidity, the three of them were apparently unable to conceal their loss of enthusiasm on stage. After three or four weeks, applause for the Russian toe dancers started to decline and by the end of September, when *The Echo* went out on tour, Lydia, Fedor and Volinine were no longer required, their slot to be replaced by McCoy dancing a new comic duet with a 'grizzly bear'. Some mildly unflattering press surrounded their departure, including a humiliating put-down from McCoy herself, who informed the papers that she was planning on making a trip to St Petersburg in order to add classical ballet to her own skills. 'I can't even stand on my toes as yet,' she said carelessly, 'but I hear that the trick can easily be acquired with two months' hard work.'[10]

Lydia, with her long Imperial training, had been put in her place. Yet if she hoped to snub McCoy in return when she made her much-delayed debut at the Palace, Frohman had other plans for her. The remaining six months of the Russians' contract were to be worked out not in New York, but in a travelling vaudeville show scheduled to perform in thirty cities across the length and breadth of America.

According to Fedor, Frohman was not a harsh employer; he tried to 'look after us as a father' even though 'he never lost sight of his own profits'; and initially the trio allowed themselves to hope that the long tour might work to their advantage.[11] They were appearing in some of the nation's prime theatres, including the lavishly built Orpheum circuit, and even within the confines of a vaudeville programme they had been given scope to perform much more varied material – Lydia and Volinine, for instance, added the Valse pas de deux from *Les Sylphides* to their repertory.

Lydia was also being given the full celebrity treatment that Mandelkern had promised. To accompany the trio's week at the Chicago Majestic in mid-October, the *Herald* ran five profiles on her life and career, while the critic of the *Tribune* dedicated long, earnest reviews to communicating the beauties of her technique. 'She is pretty is little Lydia Lapokawa [sic],' wrote Richard Henry Little in a manful attempt to master this new ballet vocabulary;

> all curves and dimples, and what is unusual in a toe dancer, she hasn't the appearance of an athletic spider with large hunks of muscles over-prominently displayed. Little Lydia dances like an Autumn leaf fluttering around the ground ... she whisks this way and that at the caprice of the orchestra ... she dances on the stage or twinkles in the air for a while and lands on the shoulders of Alexander Valienne [sic] of Moscow as light as thistledown.[12]

But Chicago seems to have been the high point. Lydia and the two men had never been on tour before and had certainly never had to take practical charge of their working lives. Rapidly the novelty lost its appeal. Every few days, as they arrived at yet another city, they had to get settled into a new hotel and orient themselves to a new stage, where unknown pitfalls threatened. A rough hard surface or, as Lydia knew to her cost, a slippery floor, carried the risk of strain or injury, while inadequate facilities backstage could make it difficult for them to improvise their daily class. Even Volinine, who was the most stoic of the three, began to rail angrily against the conditions under which they had to perform.

Sixteen years later, when Lydia recalled the hardships of this tour, she claimed that the worst was having to perform with a new orchestra at every venue: 'At the end of a week we would just be beginning to pull together, when we would have to go on to another town, another theatre and another orchestra, faced with the whole business over again after a tiring railway journey of perhaps a thousand miles.'[13] It was all so exhaustingly unlike the Mariinsky, where the conductor and musicians knew every note of the ballet scores and could anticipate the dancers' needs. Yet the more insidious misery of this tour was homesickness. Lydia may once have fantasised about running away to the circus, but it was hard even for her to become accepted by this troupe of acrobats, ventriloquists, comedians and clowns. None of them understood ballet, almost certainly none of them spoke Russian, and although Mandelkern was travelling with them to translate, Lydia and her two partners felt themselves to be among strangers.

They had utterly underestimated how alien this new world would feel, and it would become more so the further west they travelled. The empty American plains and small, straggling towns were barren wilderness compared to the cityscapes of St Petersburg or Moscow. By late November, Lydia seems to have been missing home so badly that she wrote a letter to Krupensky begging him for the official summons that she had requested back in July, which might lever her out of Frohman's grip. There is a possibility that she was again being disingenuous and simply trying to stall Krupensky from sacking her. But compared to the carefully rehearsed complaints of her first letter, there was a ragged edge of desperation to this second plea, which, even in translation from the original Russian, sounds as though she was sincerely dying to return:

> I need to present a document with a statement that the management doesn't give me more than a month's holiday [or] it will threaten me with dismissal. As a human being you'll understand me: it's awful for me to live without my native theatre and people. I wish to God these 4 weeks will pass soon and just then I'll be able to breathe freely and go away.
>
> I'm sorry to trouble you but you are the only person who can help me.
>
> Sincerely L. Lopukhova[14]

Certainly there was nothing faked about the waves of misery that were now emanating from Fedor. Out of the three, he felt most adrift in America, despising its marketplace morality, where 'love, work, business all move in the tune of the devil Lucifer', and especially despising the ever-present Mandelkern, who 'treated the black Americans disgustingly and thought of nothing else than the profits'.[15] A quarter of a century later, Fedor would be able to turn his memories of the tour to creative use, conjuring up a bicycle-riding dog and a transvestite Sylphide for his ballet *The Bright Stream*, which carried comic echoes of American vaudeville. Back in 1910 he could only endure its horrors by drinking heavily and, as he guardedly admitted, 'allowing [himself] all kinds of excess'.[16]

His amused and irritated American colleagues began referring to Fedor as 'the Crazy Russian'. But Lydia, who had witnessed the slow disintegrating tragedy of Vasili's alcoholism, watched her brother's breakdown with real terror. She must have longed for Karlusha's advice and maternal authority, and she was as relieved as she was astonished when they arrived in Oakland to find Anna Pavlova sweeping in to greet them. The ballerina was back in America, touring with Mikhail Mordkin and her own company, and, having heard stories of Fedor's wild behaviour, she had broken her schedule to offer help. She took Fedor off to a park, where she sat with him for several hours, weeping and reminiscing about Russia, and urging him to pull himself together. As he later wrote in grateful amazement, 'I was younger than her and did not really count on her close friendship, yet she came to bring [me] to reason.'[17]

On 21 November, just a few days later, Lydia, Fedor and Volinine were again with Pavlova in San Francisco. Her company were coincidentally performing at the Valencia, while the trio were appearing at the Orpheum, and the local press were buzzing with stories about a potential stand-off between temperamental Russian rivals. (The *San Francisco Chronicle* advised its readers to support Lydia, Fedor and Volinine, who, with 'technique at the tips of their fingers (and toes)' and tickets at a fraction of the price, were considered to offer the better value.[18] For the dancers themselves, however, this second encounter brought only renewed comfort – the solidarity of exiles. And for Lydia it also marked the beginnings of an unexpectedly close friendship with Pavlova.

Their intimacy may have begun with the photo shoot that was arranged for them at San Francisco Zoo, where the two ballerinas were seated, rather precariously, either side of a large walrus carved in stone. As Lydia obeyed the photographer's instructions to link arms with Pavlova across the walrus's head, she must have been conscious that only two years ago she had been an anonymous junior at the Mariinsky, daringly stealing the great dancer's shoes. Even now, dressed in a boxy tweed suit that might have been borrowed from her maiden aunt, Lydia looked more like Pavlova's youthful travelling companion or dresser than her rival star. But the hierarchy of the Mariinsky held little sway in the middle of America, and the affection that was staged for the photograph developed into genuine fondness. During the following years, whenever Lydia and Pavlova were dancing in the same cities, they would always contrive to meet; thirteen years later, Lydia would boast to Maynard that Pavlova loved her, because she was the only person in the world who could reliably make her laugh.

Lydia had only a few days of intimacy with Pavlova, however, before Frohman's itinerary sent them out on the road again. Krupensky had not deigned to answer her letter, and she had no alternative but to dance out the remaining three months of her American contract. Fedor, who would willingly have cut and run back to Russia, also stayed. He was worried about the damage that his defection might do to Lydia and Volinine, perhaps resulting in some stiff financial penalty, and he also felt responsible towards his family back home, who had become reliant on the subsidies that he and Lydia were sending back from their earnings.

So the trio limped on, down the west coast and then on a long-distance loop back up to Minneapolis and Pittsburgh. Photographs of Lydia picking oranges in Los Angeles and riding an ostrich in Pasadena, accompanied by a stream of adulatory reviews, suggest that her career at least was thriving. Yet another, bleaker picture was conveyed by the St Petersburg magazine *Theatre and Art*, which reported that Lydia had become ill 'from overwork' and that she and her partners were complaining bitterly against 'the American order' and once again begging to be allowed home.[19] By mid-March, when the Imperial Russians gave their last performance for Frohman, all three were apparently dancing on their last reserves.

Deliverance from Frohman nevertheless brought fresh dilemmas. Fedor, who alone seems to have successfully negotiated an official leave of absence, had a job to return to at the Mariinsky and wasted no time in booking himself on to the first crossing to Europe. He did not care that it turned out to be a slow, overloaded cargo boat, in which he had to sleep next to a cageful of bears. 'The ship was

Lydia with Anna Pavlova at San Francisco Zoo, 1910

Russian, the captain was Russian. He fed me Russian cabbage soup and drank Russian vodka. I was happy to come home.'[20] Lydia, however, could not leave so easily, however much she might miss her mother, however disillusioned she might feel about her American prospects. Not only was there no work awaiting her back in St Petersburg, but her broken contract at the Mariinsky could be punished by restrictions on her future travel – journeys both inside and out of Russia all requiring the rubber stamp of Imperial permission. Lydia might thus find it hard getting employment in any other part of Russia, even with Diaghilev – if he would have her. Going home could result in her being trapped and jobless in the cramped family flat, a slide into dependence too grim to contemplate.

But Volinine too had been sacked from the Bolshoi,* and if

*It was noted in the diary of Moscow official Vladimir Arkadievich Teliakovsky for 15 September 1910 that Volinine and several other Bolshoi dancers 'have not returned from the summer vacation, and have asked to extend their leave of absence, and having been advised that this has been refused, have sent in sick notes, which I considered impudent'.[21]

he stayed on with Lydia in America she would at least have a partner, as well as a friend. Mandelkern was certainly urging them both to remain, promising that he could find much better opportunities than Frohman had offered and could even double their fees. It was very tempting for Lydia to believe that a future could still be salvaged from this escapade and it may have been as early as March 1911, as she and Volinine were wondering what they should do next, that Mandelkern got wind of a production that would keep them in New York, in style, throughout the summer.

A wealthy revue dancer, Gertrude Hoffmann, had recently embarked on a project to stage a glitzy Broadway imitation of Diaghilev's Russian ballet. She had hired Theodore Koslov (a Moscow dancer who had arrived to make his own American fortune the previous autumn) to help recreate the choreography for three of Fokine's works – *Les Sylphides, Cléopâtre and Schéhérazade* – and at huge expense she was having the costumes and scenery copied from photographs of the Paris productions. For Hoffmann the point of this 'Saison des Ballets Russes' was primarily to provide herself with a European-style showcase in which she could star as Cleopatra and Zobeide – the roles that had brought Ida Rubinstein such renown. But she was canny enough to understand that she needed authentic Russian dancers to give her enterprise credibility, and as soon as she started hiring her cast, Mandelkern had no trouble getting his own clients engaged – while stepping in adroitly to secure himself a job as the season's 'general manager'.

The moment must have been surreal for Lydia when, on 14 June, she and Volinine stepped on stage with Hoffmann's ersatz Russian Ballet. New York's Winter Garden, with its harsh acoustics and lightbulb-studded decor, was nothing like the gilded and marbled Paris Opéra where she had last performed this repertory; and some of the choreography could only be a crude likeness of Fokine, given that Hoffmann's technical limitations required camouflaging under much artful posing. Yet the season retained enough original material for Lydia's talents to shine – so much so that when she made her debut as Ta Hor, the beautiful betrayed slave in *Cléopâtre,* and reprised her variations from *Sylphides*, she ousted Hoffmann from her own expensively purchased limelight.* According to the *New York Review*, Lydia became the undisputed 'darling' of the show, attracting a 'storm of hand clapping' at her every appearance; and within days her name began to overshadow Hoffmann's in the gossip columns and life-story pages of the press.[22]

This was more like the American experience that she had hoped for, even if she had to enjoy it against the background of Hoffmann's jealous displeasure. In New York, as in Paris, it was the unexpected combination of Lydia's Imperial graces and her childlike enthusiasm that the public took to their hearts – she seemed to America like the ballerina equivalent of their own baby-faced sweetheart Mary Pickford. Apparently unspoiled by her Broadway triumph and still looking younger than her actual age, Lydia replicated all of Pickford's unthreatening sweetness and 'lack of side'. Even her dancing had a reassuring bloom. As the journalist May Mackenzie claimed in her column, 'Broadway under a Feminine Microscope', Lydia looked so much more adorably smiling and fresh than the other 'dames' who 'galloped to it' on the ballet stage: 'We can see some distance back of Lydia's teeth,' quipped Mackenzie with laborious approval, 'which somehow seems to make mothers and grandmothers believe in her.'[23] Unsurprisingly, the nickname that America eventually coined for Lydia was 'Little Pet'.

Reports, carefully spun by Mandelkern, began to circulate about Lydia's captivating girlishness. She had a cute taste in food – 'Of all the things which I like here most in America,' she was quoted as saying, 'the ... very most is the short cake strawberry.'[24] She also displayed a cute taste for mischief. One much-repeated story told of a dispute that Lydia had had with a beach official when she had attempted to go swimming in the ocean with bare legs. Astonished to discover that adult women were required to wear stockings to bathe in America, Lydia had apparently plaited her hair, bought a doll and some chewing gum, and then had gone 'lispingly ... to enquire of the president of the beach company why she had to wear stockings when "the other kids don't"'. When the official was

*Publicity photos suggest that Lydia may even have danced Hoffmann's own role in *Schéhérazade*.

confronted with this apparently prepubescent girl, permission for Lydia to show her 'naked calves' had then been granted.[25]

Some of the media coverage, however, turned distinctly cloying. One profile that appeared in the *New York Times* came with the subtitle 'Peter Pan's Sister' and was obsessed by Lydia's youth. Readers were assured that she wore her success with the 'unaffectedness of the best sort of school girl'; it was reported that a teddy bear and a Chantecler* doll were prominently displayed among her clutter of ballet shoes; she was even described as spending half the interview bouncing up and down on her couch and humming music to herself as though she were a hyperactive infant.[26]

Yet Lydia – almost twenty – was now far from being a child. A series of photos from this summer show her at the natural peak of her beauty, dressed offstage in loose white frocks with her hair in an unfussy cloud around her face. She was enjoying a life, too, that was far more materially independent than that of most American women her age. The *Times* interview had been conducted in Lydia's large hotel apartment, which boasted an expensive view over Central Park; and if the reporter chose to see her simple dress as an aspect of her fetching girlishness, she herself regarded it a statement of her freedom from the constricting fashions still in vogue: 'I do not like shoes with heels,' she told the journalist, pointing to her sandals. 'I can dance in these and run in the Park in the mornings. And I will not wear what you call 'rats' [fake hairpieces] and I will not use powder or rouge.'[27]

Just a year earlier, Lydia had been buying herself false curls, courtesy of Diaghilev. Yet during this summer, perhaps inspired by Fedor's rants against capitalist America, or recalling the radical energy that had swirled around Duncan and Fokine back in St Petersburg, she had begun making contact with New York's progressive circles. Amidst all the column inches about strawberry shortcake and dolls, the press were also beginning to quote Lydia's enthusiasm for the women's suffrage movement, and to list her guest appearances at charity benefits for 'liberationist societies'. There was even a report

*The Chantecler doll was one of the many novelty dolls manufactured by a specialist toy company, Louis Amberg & Son. This one, inspired by a popular card game of the same title, featured a conventional doll's head on the body of a rooster.

Lydia in New York, circa 1911

of Lydia declaring her political sympathies to President Taft during an official presentation. According to observers, she had gazed up at the massively built and notoriously reactionary Taft to remark startlingly, 'You are as big as two men but I think I would rather have Mr Roosevelt as President.'[28]

There is no record of how Lydia's candour was received by the stately Taft, nor what inspired her to risk it. She may, idealistically, have been flying the kite of her democratic beliefs, but it was equally likely that she was being deliberately naughty. During the long tour with Frohman, Lydia had been exhausted and scared by what she had undertaken; now, with her confidence restored, her heightened spirits began to channel into misbehaviour. Official events were oppressive to Lydia; their tedium and rigidity a throwback to school, and throughout her life some desperate mixture of boredom and attention seeking would regularly impel her to disrupt them. Lydia was fully aware that her smallness and unblushing directness made it difficult for her victims to take offence, and in the America in 1911 they were also disarmed by the charming Anglo-Russian style with which she now spoke. Since her arrival in New York, Lydia had been taking English lessons, and, having already learned French at school, she was a quick student. The journalist from the *Times* had evidently fallen under the spell of her new vocabulary when she had informed him poetically, 'I love to dance. It is my heart', and even more so when she had sweetly bidden him 'Goodbysky'. Possibly Taft had been just as smitten when Lydia had lobbed her political dart at him.

Settling into New York life and enjoying the uncritical adulation of the press, Lydia had regained the sense of adventure that had brought her to America, the fantasy of unlimited possibility, the frisson of international fame. But at the end of September, when the Winter Garden run came to an end, she was brought up short by new obstacles and constraints. Her life was still dictated by the demands of her contract, she still had to follow wherever the work took her: so when Hoffmann's 'Ballets Russes' left the Winter Garden for its cross-state tour, Lydia was obliged to leave behind her interesting New York life and go with it. Even more frustratingly, just three weeks into the tour a new impresario made a bid to acquire her and Volinine from the Hoffmann troupe. Once again with no control over the deal, Lydia found herself diverted into a much less flattering repertory and subject to the whims of a much more territorially aggressive director.

This was Mikhail Mordkin, who early in the autumn had launched his own company, the Imperial Russian All-Star Ballet. During the final months of his tour with Pavlova, the two celebrity dancers had become locked in a toxic battle over precedence. Pavlova had initially hired the handsome, muscular Mordkin to be a foil for her own refined beauty, and she had not been amused when his vigorous dancing, along with his trademark leopardskin tunic, had started to win him a fervent following among the women of America. The rivalry between them had reached a climax when Pavlova, slipping during a performance, had blamed Mordkin and slapped his face on stage, in mortifying view of the public.

Mordkin, vowing never to dance with Pavlova again, had decided to return to America as director of his own troupe, with his own star status guaranteed. Unluckily, his expectations had been dealt a blow by his appendix, which had become inflamed during the transatlantic crossing, and it was while Mordkin was having to submit to the surgeon's knife that his American impresario, Max Rabinoff, went in search of a substitute to cover his roles. Volinine, with his pure Bolshoi pedigree, was the obvious choice. But since he was bound with Lydia under the same contract, she apparently had to be included in the transaction by which Rabinoff paid $30,000 to Hoffmann's producers, Comstock and Gest, to transfer them to the All-Star Ballet (along with Mandelkern, who managed to get himself on Rabinoff's payroll as Lydia's 'personal manager').*

For Volinine, this move would mark a new phase in his international career, giving him a much wider repertory to dance and eventually the mixed blessing of control over Mordkin's company. For Lydia, too, it ought to have widened her options. When she joined the All-Star Ballet the troupe had only one leading ballerina on its books, Julie Sedova, and there was at least one principal role that Lydia could have danced. This was Swanilda, heroine of the popular nineteenth-century ballet *Coppélia*, whose choreography would have been a sparkling, witty spur to her technique. Yet Mordkin, from his sickbed, was extremely nervous at having this baby celebrity brought into his nest, and apparently stipulated that she be barred from any major roles. Lydia was to be given just two or three small divertissements to dance, along with a brief solo in *Swan Lake* – actually *The Dying Swan* by Fokine, which Mordkin had shoehorned into the second act, along with its Saint-Saëns score.†

As far as the public and the press were concerned, this casting was a mystifying waste of Lydia's talent. When the All-Star Ballet toured up to Canada, the *Montreal Herald* judged that none of the other dancers could equal her 'reckless exuberance of youth and ... un-tramelled extasy [sic] of well being'.[29] Back down in Pittsburgh

*Hoffmann's producers stalled for several days before accepting Rabinoff's offer and were still negotiating for a legal injunction after Lydia and Volinine had joined the company. The two dancers had been sitting in the audience to watch the show when news came through of their formal release, and they were immediately hurried on to the stage.

†Mordkin's production of *Swan Lake* may have been a stylistic hotchpotch, but it had the distinction of being the first staging of the ballet to appear outside Russia.

the *Dispatch* singled her out with even more lyrical approbation, speculating that 'If a beautiful wild thing, an untamed creature utterly unconscious of its own grace were suddenly endowed with human intelligence and human form it is conceivable that it would dance as Mlle Lydia Lopoukowa did.'[30] But for Mordkin, such eulogies damned Lydia further. By November, when he had willed himself back on stage in record time, he apparently began to use every directorial trick not only to limit her appearances, but to sabotage them.

On 10 November the All-Star Ballet was booked to dance at the Teck Theater in Buffalo, where Lydia had been advertised to dance her usual numbers. What the audience saw, however, was not 'Mlle Lapakouwa' in *The Dying Swan* but a very young English dancer, Blanche James, who came on to perform a completely different solo. Lydia's fans presumed that she must have been taken ill, yet as soon as the curtain fell, a near-hysterical Mandelkern stormed into one of the boxes to inform the audience that she had been barred from the stage by a jealous and vengeful Mordkin. 'She is the only one of them all who is any good,' he ranted, 'she is the only one who gets good notices.'[31] This dramatic denunciation then elicited from the public such a sympathetic volley of hisses and boos, that Mandelkern clambered down into the auditorium to continue his harangue. As his accusations grew wilder, Mordkin tried to wrestle him to the floor, and urgent messages had to be sent to the police to separate them.

It cost Mandelkern a $25 fine for disorderly conduct – despite pleading mitigating circumstances of 'a Russian temperament'.[32] But Buffalo had not witnessed such an enjoyable scandal in a long time, and over the next few days he was thrilled to see the incident reported in avid detail, even reaching the papers in New York. With every new report, however, the story shifted. Mandelkern claimed that the 'Czar' Mordkin had used a brutal subterfuge to keep Lydia off the stage, instructing the orchestra to play James's music rather than her own just as she was about to make her entrance. Mordkin flatly contradicted this by insisting that Lydia had not even been scheduled to dance her *Dying Swan* solo that night, that her name in the programme had been a printer's error. Finally, another bizarre twist was added by Rabinoff's statement that the entire drama had been engineered by Mandelkern, who had just been fired from the All-Star company on account of his obnoxious and overbearing behaviour and who had decided to take revenge by keeping Lydia off the stage.

With everyone protesting their innocence, the noise of legal threats added to the confusion. Mandelkern declared that he would be bringing a suit against the All-Star management for breach of contract, and while Rabinoff responded smartly that there had been no breach, and Lydia was welcome in the company just as long as she ditched her manager, Mandelkern instructed his lawyers to ask for $6,500 in damages and unpaid salary for Lydia, plus $2,068 for himself. He also threatened to deliver his injured client straight back to the bosom of her family in St Petersburg, where, he intimated, she would be safe from crooks like Mordkin and Rabinoff. This last threat was pure, headline-grabbing bluster. By now, however, Rabinoff was busy pursuing Comstock and Gest in order to get back some of the money he had paid for Lydia, and at the same time fending off the manager of the Teck, Miss Mia David Smith, who was filing against him for damage to her theatre's business.

Lydia's own role in this farce is impossible to determine. She may have been Mordkin's innocent victim; she may just as easily have been Mandelkern's knowing ally. But either way she was forced to retreat back to New York and confront the possibility that her career had been badly damaged. She had no stage partner, as Volinine had stayed with Mordkin; she had no job to move on to, and weeks of expensive legal wrangling were likely to eat up most of her savings. The apparently passive way in which she had allowed herself to be led by Mandelkern also raises questions about the nature of their relationship. Mandelkern was now creepily styling himself as Lydia's 'foster father', and while there was never a whisper of scandal printed about them, the tone of his language, and Lydia's own curiously biddable behaviour, do suggest that his influence over her had become more complex, and possibly more sexual, than mere professional interest.

The case against Mordkin and Rabinoff was finally heard in New York in the middle of December, and Lydia, doubtless coached by Mandelkern, made a most touching plaintiff. According to the *New*

York Telegraph, she was so exhausted by the court proceedings that she had to lie down on the bench for 'five minutes' repose' and in doing so created a highly effective stir among the watching officials. 'A woman secretary stroked her head and cooed to her while John O'Connor, the chief court attendant, ran down stairs for a glass of water, and sent another attaché to the nearest café for a pair of straws so that the aqua beverage might seem more stylish.' Everyone was said to be mightily relieved when 'after drinking a thimbleful ... Mlle Lopoukowa said she felt much better.'[33] Yet even with this successful assault on the court's sympathy, the case did not pay out the financial dividends that Mandelkern had hoped. At the end of December he and Lydia were awarded unpaid salary but the larger claim for damages dragged on and was eventually dropped, leaving Lydia out of pocket and perhaps less confident in her 'foster father's' professional acumen.

She may have questioned Mandelkern's judgement even more over the engagement that he eventually found for her, dancing in a new revue called *Vera Violetta*, that was opening at the Winter Garden. The work itself was respectable, Al Jolson was starring and Lydia had acquired some new material to dance including a solo, *Xylophone Polka*, whose rhythmic choreography would cause the *New York World* to marvel at her ability to 'play a tune with her toes'.[34] The problem was that the dancer hired to partner her in the rest of her repertory was none other than her recent nemesis, Mordkin.

Getting rid of Lydia had backfired on Mordkin. With his own popularity tarnished, his company had lost any claim to All-Star status, and during December both the press and the box office had turned against him. By the New Year, Mordkin was sickened by the whole project and, giving the company over to Volinine, he decided (along with his wife, Bronislawa Pajitskaya) to put himself and some of his choreography out to hire on the commercial stage. When it turned out that the best-paying opportunity was *Vera Violetta*, he was no more pleased than Lydia. And whilst they were professional enough to conceal their antagonism – the publicity photos show them wreathed in smiles – their performances together in the *Czibulka Waltz* and in Mordkin's own *Bacchanale* were mortifying to them both. Any pleasure that Lydia had in being trumpeted as the

Lydia and Mikhail Mordkin, *Bacchanale*, New York, 1912

'greatest success of the show' was scotched by the awkwardness of having to dance with Mordkin, whose own 'ridiculously affected'[35] manner was being slated in the press. As for Mordkin himself, the humiliation was more than he could bear. After he and Lydia were moved on to a new engagement, where they had to take ignominious second billing to a popular farce, *Baby Mine*, he became so disgusted by America that he and his wife retreated back to Moscow.

Lydia may have been relieved of Mordkin, but her own situation was hardly triumphal, for without him she was again left partnerless. As a lone ballerina she was more difficult to place, and by June the only work that Mandelkern had found for her was a cameo slot in a new light operetta, *The Lady of the Slipper*. Based on the Cinderella story and with a score by Victor Herbert, this self-styled 'musical fantasy' was another production by the indefatigable showman

Charles Dillingham. Following his usual formula Dillingham had hired a crew of acrobats, singers, comics and mimics to pep up the storyline, and in his search for a little additional class he was delighted to engage Lydia to dance her ever-versatile *Dying Swan* solo and to lead a short 'ballet' entertainment.

For Lydia there may have been a troubling flicker of déjà vu as this contract was signed. The musical might promise to be *The Echo* all over again, confining her to the same tiny repertory for the foreseeable future. On the other hand, she could not quarrel with the extraordinary fee that Mandelkern had negotiated for her – $2,000 a week and four times the wage that had first lured her to America. This was riches for Lydia, and even though *The Lady of the Slipper* did indeed turn out to have a gruellingly long run, touring throughout the summer and then playing for nine months on Broadway, she could at least persuade herself she was reaping solid rewards – building up a cushion of savings, sending extra money home to Russia and enjoying the material luxuries of life in New York.

Lydia was working in the city full time between October 1912 and June 1913, and between performances at the Globe she had time to become even more visibly the 'Americanised ballerina'. Her new apartment was in the Hotel Rector, on the corner of Times Square, and all around her were the pick of Broadway premières to attend, as well as films to sample in the nickelodeons and the new movie palaces springing up around Manhattan. There were invitations to dance at the charity galas, parties and fêtes organised by the city's aristocracy – the Astors, the Winthrops and the Havemeyers. There were opportunities for her to make new friends. One of her closest companions was said to be an intimate of the writer George Moore, and according to the gossip columns of *Variety*, Lydia was everywhere becoming the 'toast' of the city's 'social and artistic circles'.[36]

She was certainly enjoying herself enough to let Mandelkern advertise her interest in gaining a more permanent American status. Stories began to circulate in the press that a malevolent Russian ballet master was threatening to kidnap Lydia and force her back on to the St Petersburg stage, and in order to defend herself she urgently needed to be granted US citizenship. This lurid PR fiction was one of Mandelkern's finest inventions, a scenario straight from the silver screen, which portrayed pretty little Lydia caught between a benign America and a wicked foreign despot: 'I do not wish to go back to Russia,'[37] she had pleaded to reporters. 'My only fear is that they will call me back before I am citizen. I want to live in New York always. I want to be like other American women and most of all I want to vote.'[38]

Possibly what Lydia wanted most of all was an American passport – so that she would be free not only to live in the States but to travel in and out of Russia without reference to her former Imperial bosses. Yet she delivered proof of her commitment to American democracy with convincing earnestness, posing for a photograph in *Theater Magazine* while holding a newspaper that had the campaigning headline 'Votes for Women'.

That Lydia had other personal commitments to America is also a possibility. She had obviously formed close ties to Mandelkern – they were seen together at restaurants and parties – and they may even have been lovers. Alternatively, there may now have been other men discreetly involved in her life.

At this early stage in Lydia's career it is difficult to see beyond the precociously talented, free-spirited but essentially virginal young girl being marketed to the American public. Mandelkern had not allowed a breath of newspaper scandal to taint his Little Pet; and Lydia, who had inherited from Karlusha a respect for the appearance of social proprieties, if not a strict adherence to their substance, had complied with his professional discretion. Yet in reality she had begun to outgrow this innocent image immediately after graduating from school. At the Mariinsky an aggressively sexualised culture had operated, by which the Grand Dukes not only selected their ballerina mistresses from the company's ranks, but more casually took their pick of the pretty juniors in the corps de ballet. Aged 17, Lydia may have appeared too childish even for the taste of the predatory Dukes, yet still her curiosity must have been aroused by this newly adult world of gossip and liaisons, and given her impulsive, experimental temperament she may have felt impatient to join it.

In the subsequent disorienting excitement of her Paris season with Diaghilev, she may possibly have allowed the Polish count, whoever he was, to take her to bed. And by the time Lydia had spent two years in America, cut off from her family and living in a world of theatrical nomads, she had inevitably become emotionally and physically tougher than her stage image suggested. Certainly if her private life had outgrown her publicity, so too had her professional expectations. In December she was questioned by a journalist about her time with Diaghilev, and there was an undertow of nostalgic envy in her report of how successfully his company had been scandalising Europe. His latest experiment, *L'Après-midi d'un faune*, choreographed by Nijinsky, 'must have been fine', guessed Lydia, 'for even Paris said that it was beautifully immoral'.[39] By now she was becoming conscious of how little that could be said of her own relentlessly bland material. All the spoils of fame could not compensate her for the trivial way she was squandering her gifts, and a critic reviewing her performances the month before had commented that while she danced 'like a sunbeam', her heart had not been in her performance and her smile had looked 'notably wooden'.[40] By early summer Lydia seems to have been dancing with gritted teeth, for when *The Lady of the Slipper* closed in mid June, she abruptly disappeared. Restless and disenchanted, she not only abandoned Broadway, but also ran away in quest of an alternative career.

Chapter Five

AMERICAN PROJECTS

I wish to be an artiste dramatique Americaine.

LYDIA LOPOKOVA, *NEW YORK TIMES*, 2 MAY 1911

Those who were close to Lydia, or had scrutinised her recent comments in the press, might have anticipated this sudden disappearance. On several occasions she had spoken warmly of two Russian actresses, Bertha Kalich and Alla Nazimova, who had made spectacularly successful careers on the American stage; and their inspiration had become increasingly potent to her as the creativity had drained out of her own ballet prospects. Lydia had always believed she might act one day. It had remained a point of pride to her that at school she had been singled out in drama as well as dance, and that she had performed alongside St Petersburg's most distinguished dramatic artists. Probably she had never imagined herself trying to act in English. Yet with hard work on her accent and diction, she now believed she might attempt it. When *The Lady of the Slipper* closed, she made the decision not to consider any more dancing engagements and, relying on the money that she had saved during her long Broadway run, she cocooned herself away from the stage until she was ready to emerge as an American actress.

To most of the public she had left behind in New York, Lydia's flight remained a mystery. There was some speculation that she might have sailed back to Russia but, otherwise, journalists who had written in gossipy detail about her taste in sweets and shoes had nothing to report about where she had vanished to, or why. This news blackout continued for a full seven months, the longest period that Lydia had been out of the public eye. And even after the story had eventually been leaked that she had gone to the Catskill mountains in order to rest and study for her change of career, the thoroughness with which she had disappeared remained a riddling interlude in her career.

Professionally it had made no sense for Lydia to go so far, since in New York she could have hired the best voice coaches, kept up with the latest plays and made useful contacts in the theatre. Personally, too, she had no history to draw her to the countryside. Even though in later life she would rhapsodise over the power of a beautiful view, writing of 'the feeling of grandeur and rest [that] spreads in one's bosom',[1] back in 1913 Lydia was a creature of the city still. For her to spend seven months in the remote pine-forests of the Catskills, 150 miles from New York and detached from any professional stimulus, was without any precedent.

Equally without precedent was Mandelkern's failure to spin any publicity around this rural fugue. His normal form would have been to bombard the press with titbits of news – comic anecdotes about Lydia's adaptation to country life, tantalising hints of how she planned to make her acting debut – all of which would keep his client in the papers. Yet no such stories appeared, and this peculiar reticence suggests that, beyond Lydia's scheme to metamorphose herself into an actress, other private motives had prompted her flight, which she did not care to disclose.

During the three years in which she had been in America, Lydia had rarely allowed illness or injury to interfere with her performance, or let her 'sunbeam' image slip. Yet she had been working almost non-stop, and the demands of her schedule, coupled with the stress of learning to adapt to a foreign culture, may have strained even her resilient system to near collapse. It is possible that when she exited so absolutely from New York, she was not only running away from dancing but suffering from some emotional or physical breakdown, which she did not want her fans to witness. A more urgent motive could, even, have been the need to deal with an unwanted pregnancy. If Lydia was now sexually active, she would have been protected only by the most primitive forms of contraception,* and this was still an

*Condoms and vaginal diaphragms were available, alongside traditional douches, but were manufactured out of thick and smelly vulcanised rubber, and not surprisingly were unpopular. They were also relatively awkward to buy as, legally, they were available only to those suffering from venereal infections.

era in which unexplained career gaps were very common in the lives of female dancers and actors. It would not be the last occasion on which Lydia herself disappeared from the stage for a suggestive length of time, nor the last occasion on which she would find it necessary to cover her tracks.

But if there was a secret shadowing this period, it did not stop Lydia from pursuing her professional ambitions. As well as trying to improve her English, she was reading widely, scouting for a suitable play in which to make her acting debut. At some point she began advertising for scripts to be sent to her in the Catskills and dozens arrived, which Lydia trawled through hopefully. It was here, however, that her grand plan began to falter. Most of the material turned out to have been written by novices, blindly hoping to attach themselves to the skirts of her own fame. Not one script possessed the literary substance, even the basic theatrical craft, that Lydia believed could launch her in her new career.

By the New Year, Lydia seems to have come close to exhausting both her savings and her optimism, for she was suddenly back in New York and dancing in cabaret at the rooftop ballroom 'Jardin de Danse'. She had been provided with a handsome new partner, Edward Makalif, plus a very handsome weekly fee of $1,500, and despite record blizzards over New York, huge crowds 'of trotters and tangoers' came to see the return of 'the delightful Mlle Lopoukowa'.[2] Such was the success of the season that other ballrooms and hotels began offering Lydia thousand-dollar contracts to dance the same material. Yet she showed no interest in any of them. Disillusionment with her acting ambitions, the long period of solitude in the Catskills, her lengthening absence from home – all these circumstances had apparently brought Lydia to the point of abandoning her American dream. Slipped into the publicity for her final dates at the Jardin de Danse was the claim that these were to be her 'farewell' performances to the States[3] before she left for Russia.

Then, just as suddenly, Lydia's plans changed again. On 23 January 1914 a brief item appeared in *Variety*, announcing that she was excitedly awaiting the completion of a play 'now being written for her to star in'. This late-arriving script was a comedy titled *The Young Idea*, and whilst its authors were an unknown husband and wife team,

Henry Watts and Ethel Watts Mumford, Lydia had seen enough in its first draft to commit herself to it. All talk of Russia was scotched, and Mandelkern, reprieved from losing his lucrative property, went into action to find a producer and director willing to take on the play.

With typical brashness, he took Lydia directly to New York's most powerful theatrical couple, the theatre owner and director Harrison Grey Fiske and his wife, the actress Minnie Fiske. Harrison Fiske was initially inclined to dismiss the whole project as a bored ballerina's caprice – doubting Lydia's ability to act, and unwilling to commit to a pair of novice playwrights. Minnie Fiske, however, was sufficiently intrigued to suggest that Lydia audition for them, suggesting her own signature role of Nora from Ibsen's *A Doll's House*. Other performers of Lydia's stature might have taken this as a snub. She was simply grateful. After closeting herself away with her lines for a month, she turned up dutifully at the Fiskes' Manhattan Theater for her audition, and the performance she delivered evidently won them over. Afterwards Minnie Fiske announced to journalists that she and her husband had found a new protégée. 'I have never seen parts of Nora more beautifully portrayed,' she declared. 'The child has talent and possibly a spark of genius.'[4]

This was a thrilling endorsement, given added authority by Fiske's deep, classically modulated tones and by the penetrating seriousness of her dark eyes. Lydia, giddy with triumph, was quick to inform the press that Minnie and Harrison were 'the most wonderful people she had ever met' and, on the strength of their wonderfulness, she announced that she would henceforth be making a radical break with her past.[5] She would be Americanising her name from Lopukhova to Lopokova;* even more immoderately, she would also be renouncing her ballet career for good. 'I like to originate and do things that are original,' she loftily informed the *New York Tribune*; 'to prove myself an actress ... is the thing I want to do most of everything in the world'.[6]

The wonderful Fiskes may, however, have been making a somewhat cynical gamble with their new discovery. Although Lydia had

*'Lopokova' acceded not only to American spelling, but to American pronunciation, with the stress placed equally on the first and third syllables.

convinced herself that *The Young Idea* was the right vehicle for her, the older, experienced couple must surely have perceived that the play betrayed all of its writers' inexperience. As most reviewers would subsequently point out, its plot was formulaic, its dialogue artless and Lydia's own role as Euphemia Kendal a transparent tissue of clichés.

Essentially the action of the play revolved around Euphemia's return home to America after ten years' education in Germany, and the clash that inevitably ensued between her hilariously 'new-fangled' European notions and the conservative world of her family, especially that of her snobbish stepmother. Swearing allegiance to free speech, sensible dressing and democratic principles, prone to breaking into extravagantly emotional 'interpretative' dances, which she had learned from an Isadora Duncan-inspired teacher in Munich, Euphemia was a whirlwind of earnest comic defiance, and never more so than when she embarked on a love affair with a man she believed to be a chauffeur, but who was, in reality, the son of a local millionaire.

On a crude level, the Wattses had tailored their material very conveniently to their star client. Having given Euphemia a long European education, they had provided some plausible explanation for Lydia's own Russian accent – which was still marked, despite her diligence in the Catskills. Having made Euphemia an acolyte of a foreign dance teacher, they had provided every excuse for Lydia to perform the kind of crowd-pleasing dance numbers that her fans would still demand. As for Lydia herself, who so badly wanted to 'originate' a new role, the gratification of having an entire play created around her made it easy to trust blindly in its merit.

For several months no one disillusioned her, certainly not Minnie Fiske, who was coaching Lydia intensively in her new role, nor Mandelkern, who was still doggedly attached to her side. When *The Young Idea* opened in Pittsfield, Massachusetts, on 20 July, Lydia looked nervous and even opted to make her debut under the coy stage name Vera Tula. But she was greeted with loud affection by a capacity audience and, as the play travelled on to Buffalo, Syracuse, Boston and Atlantic City, that affection seemed to follow her. The verdict of the *Boston Christian Science Monitor*, that Lydia was proving herself an actor of 'charm and distinction',[7] was echoed from critic to critic, and the goodwill that she had accumulated during her earlier dancing tours continued to swell her audiences.

It was only five months later, when the play opened on Broadway at the Playhouse on 23 December, that Lydia was shocked out of her faith in the project. Some efforts had been made to improve the Wattses' script during the tour – its dialogue tightened, its jokes increased and, ironically for Lydia, extra dancing included. Even the title had been altered, to the marginally less vapid *Just Herself.* But unlike the regional critics, who had soft-pedalled their attacks on the play out of deference to Lydia, the New York journalists left her in no doubt of their contempt. With the kindest of them laughing it off as 'silly' and the harshest reviling it as a 'hack job', the *New York Times* claimed that it was impossible to give an objective assessment of Lydia's new career in such worthless material: 'How good an actress she is or may become it would be monstrously unfair to judge.'[8]

Most of the New York critics were fond of Lydia and their judgements of her own performance were more gallantly moderated, with the *New York Telegraph* claiming that 'so many attractive elements unite in the charming personality of pretty little LL ... that any appraisal of her that does not sound enthusiastic must needs sound crabbed and ill-natured'.[9] Yet even so, Lydia was forced to confront the truth: that her acting had not impressed. The most generous-seeming reviews contained some excruciating caveat about her lack of experience, and there was even criticism of her narrow emotional range. While *The Herald* reproved Lydia mildly for a certain 'monotony of manner' in portraying Euphemia,[10] George Jean Nathan, in the *Cleveland Leader*, spelled out her failings with pitiless directness. Her gestures had been 'artificial', her deportment 'stilted' and her voice 'tuned to remind one of a clock persistently chiming twelve'.[11]

This level of abuse was completely new to Lydia and it upset her badly. It did not help that the main target of Nathan's review was actually Minnie Fiske, against whose power and celebrity the influential young critic was currently waging a political campaign. Nor did it help to be told that the flaws Nathan had so ruthlessly detailed in her performance, such as 'italicising the meaning of her speeches with strange maneuvers of the neck',[12] were, in his judgement, tics of the Fiske acting style which had been imposed on Lydia. Even if

Lydia could be persuaded that there had been an alternative agenda to Nathan's hatchet job, nothing could have drawn the sting of his vicious conclusion that 'this otherwise delectable young person cannot at present act worth a hang'.

Nor could anything limit the damage that Nathan's review inflicted on the production as a whole. Broadway gave no slack to failure, and only a week into the run, when the cast arrived at seven o'clock to prepare for the evening performance, they found the theatre had been locked against them, with notices announcing that the Fiskes had closed the play down. Mandelkern had at least managed to spare Lydia this public humiliation, having brought her the news before she left her apartment; but the sudden deflation of her ambitions was no less horrible, and a report in the *New York Times* that she was 'completely overcome by disappointment' and was remaining 'secluded and upset' at home was not exaggerated.[13] Lydia had been promised that her own standing would guarantee a reasonable New York run, yet as soon as the Fiskes had scented financial problems, the 'most wonderful people in the world' had turned their backs on her and left town.

In the bleak period that followed, Lydia had neither the heart nor the courage to make light of her failure. A whole stage enterprise had been staked on her name, and its debacle had called into question her reputation as well as her prospects. The press were again speculating about what her next move might be, and at this point Lydia may have yearned to act on her impulse of the previous winter and simply go back to Russia. Thoughts of Karlusha and home may have come crowding back, and they may have been made more compelling by the fact of her father's death years before. In August 1912 Vasili had been delivered to the St Petersburg Palace Hospital in a 'helpless condition' and had died within days. The official report had cited 'pneumonia with a swelling of his lung',[14] but it was clear that alcohol has hastened his death. Whether Lydia had felt some guilty impulse of relief on hearing the news we don't know, but the removal of her father was now another incentive for her to return. Perhaps she fantasised that sufficient time had passed for her to wheedle a reconciliation with the Mariinsky. Perhaps she dreamed of re-engaging with Diaghilev, especially since an overture had already come from him eighteen months previously. His company, now known internationally as Les Ballets Russes, had been on a tour of South America, and she had been offered the chance to guest with it. Yet if Lydia was dreaming of home, she had lost her moment. By January 1915, much of Europe was locked into war. With borders closed, and Atlantic crossings commandeered for troops and military supplies, travel for a single young woman had become precarious. Getting back to Russia was close to impossible.

Back in August 1914, when Lydia had been deep in the professional dramas of *Just Herself*, she had probably registered the outbreak of war as casually as most Americans. The battles were being fought thousands of miles away, over issues that few understood; the papers were confidently predicting that peace would be brokered by Christmas. She also knew that at least two of her brothers were safe, Russian dancers having been exempted from military call-up. But as the New Year turned, the fighting became more entrenched and Lydia had little choice but to stay in America and try to rescue her career. Since her contract with the Fiskes had been so abruptly terminated, her wages were possibly still unpaid, and her immediate concern had to be money. So reneging on her fine promises that she would never dance again, Lydia took the best-paying job offered her, performing classical solos in cabaret at the luxurious Waldorf Astoria Hotel.

Predictably, the public and press were thrilled. 'Lydia is Just Herself,' trumpeted the *New York Herald*.[15] But she was dancing on sufferance. By early March she had drifted on to the Knicker Bocker Theater, performing ragtime numbers in a much-derided revue called *Fads and Fancies*; and from April she was back on the vaudeville circuit, heading a small chorus in what were pallidly described as 'ballet interludes'. Sharing the stage once more with acts like the performing Loughlin Dogs, and competing with an irritatingly popular group of Isadora Duncan acolytes, Lydia was mired in a scene that she had only recently sworn never to revisit. Her frustration was measurable by the incautious response that she made to some favourable reviews which the rival dance troupe had gained at her expense. With reckless disregard of local pride, Lydia had riposted that not 'one in 50' American girls had the makings of a good dancer, for they were all raised to be so lazy. 'Why they don't know what work is. At home in Russia we are brought up with the idea that to be idle is almost a crime.'[16]

Lydia's rudeness outraged her normally doting press, who grumbled that she was turning out to be as ungrateful and temperamental as every other Russian toe dancer. Yet by now she was scenting a chance for freedom, and could not have been less concerned. A small, semi-professional theatre company, the Washington Players, had recently been gaining attention for their stylish new productions, which according to *New York American* were delivering 'the livest theater in New York right now, possibly the livest in America'.[17] Some time over the summer, Lydia had been put in touch with the Players, and her tentative enquiries about joining them had been enthusiastically received. Even though they performed way off Broadway, at the little Bandbox Theater on East 57th Street and Third Avenue, and could offer only a tiny fraction of her usual pay ($100 a month, compared to $1,500 a week), Lydia was glad to make the sacrifice. Not only did it give her the chance to experiment with serious theatre away from the glare of Broadway, but it would get her away from the insistently commercial management of Mandelkern, which was by now so oppressive to Lydia that it would leave her with the fixed prejudice that theatre agents were all 'vampires'.

Moving to the Players may even have forced the final break from Mandelkern, for his name was never linked to Lydia's again, and when she began rehearsals with the Players, in Percy MacKaye's romantic comedy *The Antick*, she was in a euphoric state. Her new colleagues declared themselves to be 'crazy'[18] about her high spirits – bowled over by her humour, her sweetness, her spontaneity. And even though Lydia had been cast very much to type (her first role, Julie Bonheur, was that of a spirited young woman with a talent for dancing), she had been given very good reason to feel optimistic about her professional progress. After her debut on 4 October, the eminent critic Burns Mantle wrote that of all the cast it had been she who had 'stabbed our interest in the proceedings, and held it, though she danced but little'.[19] Equally encouraging was her follow-up appearance in a revival of Alfred de Musset's 1833 play *Whims of Marianne*. Lydia's role as the experienced tease Marianne, who ends up as a grieving, guilty woman, was easily the most complex she had attempted, and her successful debut on 20 November allowed her to believe that New York was finally ready to let go of her baby ballerina past.

Liberation from Mandelkern and his spin may also have precipitated Lydia's first public affair, for it was literally on her opening night with the Players that she met the man who was to become her American fiancé. His name was Heywood Broun, he was one of the *New York Tribune*'s star journalists, and having come to review Lydia's debut in *The Antick* he fell immediately and uncritically in love with her.

Ironically, Broun had almost missed seeing Lydia, as *The Antick* was the fourth in a long evening of one-act plays and the *Tribune* set tight deadlines for overnight reviews. But Lucy Huffaker, the Players' press representative, had persuaded him to stay, and when Broun's review finally appeared it was nothing less than a love letter to Lydia, out-gushing almost everything that had ever been written about her: 'We regret now every wasted adjective and we pine for every superlative with which we have lightly parted. All words denoting, connecting or appertaining in any way to charm we would bestow on [her] for she did not tread, she did not even walk, she skipped, she danced, she pranced and, like as not, she never touched the stage.'[20]

On a professional level Lydia might not have been entirely pleased with these outpourings. She was seeking recognition as an actor, not as a charming elf, and any reader could spot that Broun's prose was compromisingly loaded with infatuation. His biographer, Dale Kramer, later recorded that even the critic's own mother had judged this notice to be absurd: 'Heywood, if you want to be a reviewer, don't be so mushy,' she had scolded. 'You sound like a little boy watching them dip the strawberry ice cream at a party.'[21]

Yet on a personal level Lydia was intrigued by her new admirer. As Kramer told the story, the dazzled, disconcerted Broun went to pay court in her tiny dressing room and stood twisting his hat in tongue-tied delight as Lydia 'skipped around clearing a space for him to sit'. In a lover's blur he registered the details of her appearance: 'five foot, fair skinned, blue eyes and a mass of dark brown hair,* broad faced,

*A strange glitch in Heywood's memory – Lydia's hair was mid-brown.

mouth turned down at corner, elfin moves and gestures'.[22] Yet once Broun had taken Lydia off to supper at Mouquin's (an expensively fashionable French restaurant, probably chosen in deference to her celebrity), he evidently found his voice. Only twenty-six years old, he had already established himself as an eloquent campaigner, a champion of new theatre and a ferocious critic of censorship, and as such he made a powerful appeal to Lydia's own progressive sympathies. He also appealed to her physically. At that time Broun was a very attractive man – six foot two, as solidly built as an athlete, with a flop of thick brown hair, a loud laugh and a carrying voice. By the end of the meal, Lydia had accepted Heywood as her suitor.

From then on, Heywood took to haunting the wings of the Bandbox Theater, watching Lydia in performance and writing about her in his column as often and as devotedly as he dared. When he was forced to review elsewhere, he took his mother to the theatre, so that if the play was a long one she could fill him in by telephone while he escorted Lydia out to supper – no longer to Mouquin's but Joel's, a popular hang-out for actors and writers on Seventh Avenue. Out on the streets of New York they made an odd couple – Lydia tiny and animated beside Heywood's bearlike frame. But if Lydia's smallness and foreignness fascinated Heywood, she in turn was attracted by the very generous, very American scale of him, potentially far more reassuring to her than Mandelkern. As Lydia allowed herself to be enfolded by Heywood, it cannot have escaped her mind that this new man in her life might also be a ticket to US citizenship. While there is no direct evidence to confirm when the affair became sexual, the gossip handed down through the New York ballet world was that Lydia rapidly accepted her role as Heywood's unofficial fiancée and rapidly moved into his bed.*

She was also introduced to his parents: Heywood Cox Broun, who was part owner of a printing business, and a frequenter of gentlemen's clubs; and Henrietta Brooks, a clever, striving woman prominent within the intellectual societies of New York. These were potentially alarming types for Lydia to meet, and their clipped Manhattan manners may have alerted her to the fact that there was

*See the letter from Lincoln Kerstein to Milo Keynes, 17 July 1981, LLK/8: 'I gather they lived together and that he desperately wanted to marry her.'

an element of rebellion in Heywood's pursuit of her. As a child he had felt rejected by his mother and father, and had grown into a restless, disruptive teenager, wasting most of his Harvard years on the sports field and taking his first job in journalism, as a baseball reporter, in defiance of his parents' milieu. Even after his lively reporting style had established him as New York's leading sportswriter, and even after he had been offered an additional theatre column – making his job suddenly more acceptable to his literary mother – Heywood had continued to trail a certain self-conscious challenge, hanging out in bohemian, left-wing circles and choosing actresses, waitresses and feminists as his mistresses.

Yet Heywood's parents were either won over by Lydia or resigned to their son marrying outside their circle, for by 11 December 1915 the *New York Review* was reporting a rumour that 'the dainty Russian dancer' was 'soon to wed a well known journalist'. By 8 January 1916 that journalist had been publicly identified as Heywood, and immediately there had been a furore of speculation in the press as to how he had succeeded with 'the fair Russian heroine', when no other man had apparently got close.

It was a question, however, that even Heywood was having to ask himself. In the past he had taken his own appeal for granted. His expansive energy, his good looks, his success as a writer had all made him attractive to women and, after a mildly promiscuous fashion, he had broken several hearts. Yet when he had fallen in love with Lydia, he had found himself in an unaccustomed position of uncertainty. While he had been ready to devote himself to her, she showed nothing like the same commitment. As he confided miserably to Lucy Huffaker, 'When Lydia is with me I know she's fond of me. I even think she loves me. But she lives exactly as you said, in the moment. When we're apart I doubt she even knows I exist.'[23]

What Heywood was painfully discovering was that Lydia's butterfly charm did not make her transparent or easy to understand, but was often a form of distracting camouflage. During the long years in which she had been separated from home, Lydia had learned the advantages of focussing on what was around her, on the people and the places that were here and now. Emotions that tugged deeper – nostalgia, hope, desire – might feed into her stage performances, but offstage she still tended to deny them. The habits of secrecy and self-reliance were rooted in her, and flattered, even moved, as she might have been by Heywood's courtship, she did not yet love him enough to open herself up to him.

Her elusiveness inevitably fuelled Heywood's anxiety, and it may have been his desperation to pin her down that prompted him to propose marriage only two months after their meeting. The lovers had been taking their daily constitutional in Central Park, Heywood striding along in his huge raccoon-fur coat, Lydia skipping to keep up, when he had asked her, in a rush, to marry him. According to Kramer's account, Lydia's reactions had hardly been reassuring. She had asked simply, 'And when would this marriage take place?'; and after Heywood had chivalrously replied, 'That would of course be your decision,' she had rattled him further by shrugging cheerfully and saying: 'Alright. If you want it so, we are engaged.'[24]

Even if this romantic scene did not go as Heywood had hoped, he lost no time in leaking it to the gossip columnist Franklin P. Adams, who ran with the story the following day. The rest of the press picked up on it, exactly as Heywood had planned – for he assumed that the more publicity the engagement received, the more tightly Lydia would be bound to it. What he had not taken into account, and could not have expected, was that in under a week a rival would appear on the scene, against whose long-term entitlement his own claims to Lydia's love and loyalty would simply evaporate.

On 11 January, Diaghilev's Ballets Russes docked into New York harbour, ready to make their much-publicised first tour of North America. In the weeks leading up to the company's arrival there had been some discussion of Lydia being hired to dance certain guest performances, discussions that she might or might not have shared with her fiancé. To Heywood's pained astonishment, however, as soon as she met up with the company Lydia gave herself over to Diaghilev and her fellow dancers completely – abandoning not only her professional association with the Players, but all of his own carefully orchestrated plans for their future together.

Most shocking for Heywood was seeing the joy with which Lydia reverted to her former incarnation as a Russian ballerina. During their short association he had completely failed to grasp the kind of divided life she was leading. She had been so deft at exploiting her cultural doubleness, at marketing her quaint American-Russian gestures and speech, that he had not realised that the woman he loved was also a woman in translation. When he saw Lydia swept up in her old professional routine with the Ballets Russes, when he overheard her chattering fluently to her dancing colleagues in Russian, Heywood could hardly recognise the person he had just proposed to. And while he was still desperate to try to hold their engagement together, she seems to have let it go with careless ease.

According to Kramer, not only did Lydia have little time to spare for Heywood once the Ballets Russes were in town, but she began to display a wounding interest in the flirtatious attentions of another man, Diaghilev's business manager, Randolfo Barocchi. Later, his memory distorted by bitterness, Heywood would claim that Lydia and Barocchi had been lovers long ago in Paris, and that they had fallen into bed with each other soon after the company arrived in New York. In reality, Barocchi had only joined Diaghilev in 1915, and even if Lydia had felt an attraction to him it is very unlikely that she acted on it straightaway. She was working too hard to prepare for her reunion debut to cope with the complications of a new affair.

Yet even though Heywood got the timing wrong, he was not mistaken about the final outcome. Shortly after Lydia left New York on the company's cross-state tour, she did indeed become Barocchi's mistress, and by April a stricken Heywood would be informed that she was no longer able to marry him.

It would be misleading to suggest that Heywood never got over Lydia, but her betrayal knocked him badly. He was wretched for months afterwards, drinking heavily and writing a morbid little play about death, which he carried around in a breast pocket, close to his heart. A couple of years later he wrote a mournfully autobiographical novel about a sports writer who falls unhappily in love with a foreign dancer.* This at least was to exorcise Lydia from his life. Heywood

*In the novel the couple marry and have a son, before the dancer eventually sails off to take up her career once more. However, Heywood's choice to end the novel with the son meeting his mother and following her on to the stage implies some kind of forgiveness of Lydia's own willingness to leave him for the Ballets Russes.

went on to marry a former mistress, the feminist journalist Ruth Hale, and professionally there seemed to be no limits to his success. After being appointed sports editor of the *Tribune*, he was given his own personal column, one of the first of its kind, which was syndicated right across America. The combination of Heywood's colourful prose and crusading opinions lifted him to nationwide fame, he was considered a hero of his profession and his column was subsequently ranked as a pioneering contribution to US journalism. Yet in other respects Heywood's life remained vaguely unfulfilled. His marriage to Hale turned sour and his attempt to run for Congress foundered, as his own increasingly radical politics ran counter to the mood of the nation. By the time he died in 1939 his days as an American golden boy were long over. Aged fifty-one, he was a drinker and a mild disgrace.

He had, by this time, been all but forgotten by his former Russian mistress. Lydia would make just one public comment about Heywood, in 1948, probably in response to an enquiry from Kramer during his writing of the biography. She made no reference to her compromising affair with Barocchi, but admitted very coolly that her engagement to Heywood had been a mistake: 'Our brief acquaintance was interrupted by my rejoining the Russian ballet and my professional career involved me in a whirl of excitement. I felt I didn't now want to be tied up to Heywood so I broke it off, hurting him very much at the time I am sorry to say.'[25] Thirty-two years on, Lydia had long consigned the memory of Heywood to a minor footnote in her past.

Chapter Six

THE REUNION

I do not feel one can do the best possible in ballet, unless one lives with the rest of the troupe as a large family.

LYDIA LOPOKOVA, *SUNDAY TIMES*, 17 JULY 1927

If Broun had been winded by Lydia's abrupt desertion to the Ballets Russes, for her it had been a homecoming. The Americanised habits with which she had armed her lone celebrity had fallen away as she found herself back among colleagues who spoke her language and shared her history. Serge Grigoriev, the tall, spare, watchful company administrator who had quietly doted on Lydia in Paris, was quietly delighted to have her back, judging her to be 'hardly changed at all ... just as charming and gay and full of laughter'.[1] Diaghilev greeted her with his usual theatrical flourish, still the immaculate dandy in his pristine starched collar, monocle and rings. But it was Lydia's reunion with Enrico Cecchetti, her former teacher, that came closest to a familial embrace. While the Maestro was stouter and whiter-haired than when she had last seen him, and growling about the 'impossible things'[2] he was asked to do as Diaghilev's principal character dancer, he had lost none of his focus as a ballet master. When Lydia first walked into his class in New York and heard Cecchetti's instructions rapped out to the familiar accompaniment of his cane, she may momentarily have doubted that she had ever been away.

Still, the Ballets Russes was not as Lydia had left it, for the last five and a half years had been marked by fundamental changes in style and personnel. Mikhail Fokine had left and for a while had been superseded as company choreographer by Vaslav Nijinsky, whose primitivist, angular experiments had allowed Diaghilev to push the Ballets Russes towards a more confrontationally modernist agenda. In May 1913, while Lydia was being toasted by New York in the fairy-tale world of *The Lady of the Slipper*, her former colleagues had been fielding a storm of controversy in their performances of Nijinsky's *Rite of Spring*, simultaneously fêted and demonised as the harbingers of a new ballet avant-garde. Nijinsky's moment had not lasted, however, for in the summer of 1913 he had been wooed and married by a young Hungarian fan, Romola de Pulszky, causing a violently wounded Diaghilev to throw him out of the company. Both on stage and in bed, Nijinsky was replaced by Léonide Miassine, a slender nineteen-year-old from Moscow out of whose enormous, black, goblin eyes and mercurial energy Diaghilev hoped to make his next star.

If old loyalties had been breached, the war had effected even more radical change. When hostilities were declared, in August 1914, the dancers had all been scattered for their summer holidays, and as the fighting had spread, Diaghilev had briefly had to face the possibility that the Ballets Russes might be finished. His performance circuit was being disrupted by closed borders and battle fronts, and most of his former sources of money and patronage had become inaccessible. During 1915, however, he had begun negotiating with Otto Kahn, chairman of New York's Metropolitan Opera, the rescue package of a North American tour,* and from the safety of neutral Lausanne the Ballets Russes was reassembled. Several members of Diaghilev's former artistic council were able to join him straightaway, including Igor Stravinsky, who regularly bicycled the ten-mile journey from his home in nearby Morges. The dancers, however, took longer to convene. Completely beyond reach were the Ballets Russes's two biggest names, for Karsavina was now pregnant and unable to travel, and Nijinsky (with whom Diaghilev had agreed to make a temporary, pragmatic truce) was in Budapest, where he was under house arrest as a citizen of an enemy state. Grigoriev, who had been dispatched on a precarious route across Europe to scout for talent, had

*Diaghilev, as the main contractor, was paid $13,500 a week plus half the net profits, from which he had to pay most of the company's salaries and expenses.

not only failed to find substitute stars, but the fifty dancers that he had assembled for the company had been drawn from a variety of different backgrounds, including ballet-backward Britain. The wartime version of Ballets Russes which Lydia met up with in New York seemed both smaller and a little less splendid than the phenomenon that she had remembered.

Particularly vulnerable were the younger dancers. They were unnerved at having travelled so far out of Europe in such dangerous times, and the non-Russians among them were intimidated by the strict internal protocol upon which Diaghilev still insisted – even in 1916, even in New York. One of these juniors was a young British dancer, Hilda Munnings, whom Lydia had briefly encountered four and a half years before, when the latter had been a raw recruit to Mordkin's All-Star troupe. Munnings had her own confusing issues to deal with as Diaghilev attempted to rebrand her as a Russian, initially calling her Munningsova, then elevating her to the more graceful persona of Lydia Sokolova, which became her permanent stage name. Yet Sokolova recalled in her memoirs that the 'heavy atmosphere' which had settled over the company had immediately lifted with the arrival of Lydia, who was not only willing to talk to everyone in her mongrel mix of Russian, English and French but, most amazingly, displayed a fearless intimacy with Diaghilev, whom she dared to address, to his face, as Big Serge.

'On stage, as well as off,' wrote Sokolova,

> Lydia Lopokova was full of surprises. She had not the appearance or physique of a classical dancer but to everyone's astonishment whatever she attempted came off. Few dancers have performed with such assurance or flown through the air as she did ... She had no idea of hairdressing and wore very little make up on the stage – what there was [was] usually still there next morning – but when she stood looking up at Big Serge ... with her screwed up little bun of hair, the tip of her nose quivering and an expression between laughter and tears, I defy anybody to say she wasn't worth her weight in gold.[3]

Diaghilev's affection for Lydia was genuine but, as in Paris, he had compelling financial reasons for embracing her as readily as he did.

Kahn had made difficulties about selling this tour without the head-lining names of Karsavina and Nijinsky, and Lydia, with her buoyant technique and her legions of American fans in tow, had seemed to Diaghilev to offer a most marketable substitute. There were people within the Met's organisation who believed otherwise, writing to warn the impresario that Lydia's previous appearances in vaudeville theatres that charged only a 'dollar and a half', would make it difficult for the public to accept her as 'a five dollar artist' with the Ballets Russes.[4] But Diaghilev had ignored their advice, believing that Lydia's familiarity would be a far more useful commodity than mystique.

All that America had seen of Russian ballet, so far, had been the undemanding mix of nineteenth-century classics and watered-down Fokine that had been variously peddled by Pavlova, Mordkin, Hoffmann and by Lydia herself; and as Diaghilev fretted to Miassine (his name now simplified to Massine for America's benefit), this had left the public assuming that ballet was no more than 'a light entertainment to be enjoyed after a hard day at the office'.[5] The impressionistic paganism of Nijinsky's *L'Après-midi d'un faune* and the discordant energies of Massine's new Futurist-inspired ballet *Le Soleil de nuit* would, he suspected, require a careful marketing campaign, in which Lydia's mollifying image would be key.

In fact what America would find hardest to accommodate would be the sexual content of the repertory, in particular the dreamy, quasi-masturbatory climax of *Faune** (which as Lydia had noticed had shocked even Paris) and the harem revels in *Schéhérazade*. Even though audiences had seen Hoffmann's bowdlerised version of the latter, nothing in that staging could have prepared them for the sensual charge of Fokine's original, and especially for the unsettling eroticism embodied by its male lead, the Golden Slave. When Adolph Bolm first performed this role with the Ballets Russes in New York, his skin darkened with body paint, his supple gestures insinuating a disturbing mixed message of male desire and feminine acquiescence, American sexual and racial sensitivities were muddled

*Inspired by Mallarmé's poem, the ballet portrays a young faun who becomes erotically transfixed by a group of bathing nymphs. Its closing moments show the faun coming to orgasm with an unambiguous motion of his pelvis.

beyond bearing. A wave of hysterical prurience was unleashed, causing the critic Grenville Vernon to remark that Bolm's 'remarkable negro' portrait would be impossible to perform 'South of Mason and Dixon's line', and the Catholic Theater Movement to head demands for the ballet to be banned outright.[6]

On 25 January a legal injunction was passed against both *Schéhérazade* and *Faune*, requiring Diaghilev to lighten the Slave's make-up and restrict the Faun's climax to a mute expression of longing. But even with these changes, censorship continued to plague the company throughout their tour. In Boston the mayor gave instructions that the Russians were permitted to bare only their toes; and in Kansas City, Captain Ennis of the Police Department gave stern notice that no lewdness was permitted on his watch. As he reported proudly to the *Kansas City Star*, 'Dogleaf, or whatever his name is couldn't understand plain English [so] ... I told a fellow [the interpreter] "This is a strictly moral town and we won't stand for any high brow immorality. Put on your show but keep it toned down." I told him we didn't want to make trouble but if the show was too rank I'd come right up on stage and call down the curtain.'[7]

Even if Diaghilev had not anticipated the full fury of American moralists, he had still understood that his repertory would be a difficult sell, and he had seen Lydia performing a critical role as his ambassador. She was known by audiences, she spoke reasonably fluent English, and her lively, demotic charm chimed well with the promotional campaign being organised by Edward L. Bernays from the Met. Gaudy photo shoots at the Bronx Zoo; gossipy life stories in the popular press; fashion features in women's magazines: all these had become natural to Lydia after years of Mandelkern's tutelage, and as soon as she had signed her contract with the Ballets Russes she did the rounds of the press willingly, giving interviews and helping to translate for her colleagues.

But it was ultimately Lydia's dancing on which she would be judged, and she must have been apprehensive as she sweated over her barre with Cecchetti in the week leading up to her reunion debut. She had not danced professionally for over six months and she now had to prove herself against some steely competition – especially the virtuoso technician Xenia Makletsova, whom Grigoriev had hired from Moscow. Lydia may have been privately grateful that her last contracted performance with the Players had meant that she could not appear with the Ballets Russes in their opening gala at the Century Theater on 17 January. Yet two days later, when she danced *Carnaval* on the arm of her new partner, Stanislas Idzikowski – a fiercely gifted Pole, who was barely taller than she was – New York's verdict was unanimous. Lydia's technique looked as winningly intact as if she had never left the company – her jump as elastic, her feet as quick and pretty. Her stage manner, which Sokolova described as combining 'a remarkable sense of sincerity [with] a suspicion of naughtiness', was also artfully deployed.[8] Five years of selling herself in every kind of venue and in every kind of material had refined Lydia's knack of letting something of herself, both intimate and ebullient, spill into her performance, making the choreography look like an impulsive act of expression, the overflow of her pleasure in the moment. According to the *New York Post*, her 'lapse into acting' had merely intensified the 'bewitching and piquant charm' of her dancing.[9]

Double-edged as this compliment may have appeared to Lydia, she was more than recompensed by Diaghilev, who promised to give her back her old roles in *Firebird* and *La Princesse enchantée* and, most gratifyingly, instructed her to start learning the Ballerina Doll in Fokine's 1911 fairground ballet *Petrushka*. Lydia probably did not yet know of her own unwitting part in the history of this work – back in Paris her performances of the coquettish Columbine had lodged in the mind of Igor Stravinsky as he wrote the score for this second ballet, inspiring the music for the Ballerina.* But *Petrushka* was known to her as the most dramatically resonant of all the works in the Ballets Russes's repertory – as she later put it, with 'more flesh and bones than any of the ballets, old or new'.[11] Even though its three principal characters were only puppets, trapped within the most simple of love triangles, Fokine had made their story astonishingly human. For Lydia this ballet represented the kind of rich interpretative challenge that as a dancer she had yearned for, but never yet found.

---

*Fedor commented on this and critic Richard Taruskin concurs, writing that Stravinsky's conception of the Doll as a 'poupée de Hoffmann', a 'personification of the eternal feminine', had originated with Lydia's Columbine.[10]

On the surface, she had only to portray a dancing doll, confined to a language of mechanical, technical tricks, yet she also had to convey the genuine emotions that played around the Ballerina's limited heart – infatuation with the swaggering Moor puppet who seduces her, guilty grief over the death of pathetic Petrushka, whose timid adoration she has spurned. Many who later saw Lydia in the role believed that she made it uniquely her own: the London critic Cyril Beaumont claimed that her transformation into a marionette carried an uncanny conviction, with the strange stiff angle of her head and the 'drollery of her vacant stare';[12] while her brother Fedor* argued that she became 'unbelievably moving' at the ballet's tragic climax, 'her radiant joyful eyes filling with tears of remorse as she realised her error'.[13]

In America it rapidly became one of her signature roles, and conductor Ernest Ansermet's dry assurance to Stravinsky that his muse was acquitting herself 'très bien' was an understatement of the acclaim that she received. One critical voice, Carl van Vechten, dissented, arguing that Lydia appeared out of her depth compared to the performances by Karsavina that he had seen and treasured in Paris. But to all the other Americans, who had no such comparisons, Lydia was one of their own. Patriotic pride and affection swelled their applause so loudly that Makletsova, who had arrived in New York billed as the company's authentic Russian ballerina and expected to be treated as its star attraction, eventually stalked out in disgust.

If Lydia felt any twinge of empathy with Makletsova's attempts to sue Diaghilev for damage to her reputation, just as she had once sued Mordkin, she was too exhilarated to dwell on it. Nor apparently did she give much thought to Heywood when the New York season ended and she left town on the Ballets Russes's two-month tour across the rest of the country. In fact, just as her confused, heart-sore fiancé had predicted, Lydia had barely steamed out of New York in the company's splendid, three-train cavalcade before all her thoughts of her American lover were supplanted by the fluent, distracting attentions of Randolfo Barocchi.

---

*Fedor could not have seen Lydia perform *Petrushka* with Diaghilev, so he must have been reporting on a demonstration that she subsequently gave him in Russia.

Lydia, Ballerina Doll, *Petrushka*, New York, 1916

As Lydia subsequently admitted, Heywood had not stood a chance against the emotional drama of her reunion with the Ballets Russes; and perhaps it was inevitable that, having fallen back in love with her former company, she had become infatuated with one of its personnel. Only later could she perceive how excitement had skewed her powers of judgement. Six months after meeting Barocchi Lydia would find herself attracted to another, far more impressive man. Three years later she would have come to detest Barocchi so thoroughly that she could hardly mention him by name. By this time, too, she would have long understood that the witty, sophisticated veneer that had first attracted her to Diaghilev's little business manager had been a flimsy tissue of self-publicity and lies.

Barocchi was in his mid-thirties when Lydia first met him and, in contrast to the rumpled and passionate Heywood, he appeared to be a glossy man of the world. In reality this image had been only recently acquired, for Barocchi seems to have worked with his family's marble statue business for most of his early adult life, and he had spent little time outside Italy. However, he had a quick ear for

The Ballets Russes leaving Chicago on US tour, 1916. From left to right: Adolph Bolm, Serge Grigoriev, Léonide Massine, Lydia Sokolova, Hilda Buick, Serge Diaghilev, Lydia, Lubov Tchernicheva, Olga Khokhlova, Nicolai Kremnev

language, a genuine interest in the arts and an easy, clubbable temperament; and when, in 1914, he had been hired by an American agent, Henry Russell, to work as general assistant and translator for a US tour of the San Carlo Opera, he had made the transformation into cultured cosmopolitan with speed. Russell had found Barocchi so useful that he had recommended him to Diaghilev for the Ballets Russes's 1916 tour, and, having joined the company, he put himself out to be amenable to everyone. At the same time he took considerable care to censor the truth about his personal life. It may only have been vanity that inclined Barocchi to maintain a careful vagueness about his age, his background and his finances – to some of the dancers he claimed that his extravagant habits were serviced by family money; to others he airily suggested that he lived off credit. However, he had pressing reasons for remaining cryptic about other details. Unknown to anyone in the company, Barocchi had acquired an American wife during his time with the San Carlo Opera tour, a singer called Mary Hargreaves. And unknown to anyone, least of all Lydia, he was, in 1916, still married to her.

If Randolfo Barocchi kept his personal biography a closed book, his outward appearance was never less than assiduously polished. Whatever the state of his finances, he kept his soft, plump body elegantly dressed, his receding black hair and moustache immaculately oiled (it would be a dreadful blow to his image when his whiskers were accidentally shaved off during the tour). What mattered most to his new colleagues, however, was his talent for entertaining. Although Ansermet found Randolfo insincere and pushy in his eagerness to please, many of the dancers sought out his company, drawn by his multilingual stock of theatrical (and occasionally filthy) anecdotes, and by his wicked talent for mimicry – especially his impersonation of Diaghilev. Even in a crisis Randolfo aimed to deliver a comic spin. Years later when he was delegated to sign up a temperamental group of Spanish dancers for the Ballets Russes, he responded to his duties with a bravura sense of the ridiculous; and the good-humoured telegrams that he sent to Diaghilev convey some sense of what Lydia herself had, briefly, been attracted to in his character. Rather than fussing over the chaos that he was enduring, Randolfo encapsulated an endearing sense of soap opera into his missives: 'Have spent entire evening with Marcarona and Ramirez. Do nothing but embrace them entire time.' 'Ramirez has lost wits. Refuses sign unless we engage Rosario who will not come without aunt.' 'They are all repeat all dotty.'[14]

When Randolfo first encountered Lydia in New York he

presumably saw her as a delightfully receptive audience for his jokes, as well as a delightful ally in his role as company entertainer. But as a star ballerina he also saw her as a covetable prize, and once on tour he lost no time in trying to win her. Long, empty hours on the train provided an ideal scenario for his courtship, especially since private travelling compartments had been allocated to all the principal dancers and chief members of staff, giving Randolfo every opportunity to manoeuvre Lydia into quiet spaces and woo her. Hotels provided even better cover. According to a journalist who reported on the Ballets Russes's arrival at Kansas City, the swarming, chattering mass of dancers brought vivid pandemonium in their wake. Bewildered reception staff at hotels, who had 'never seen such luggage, queer hand bags and portmanteaus', were overwhelmed by the tumult that erupted as the company tried to find their rooms and quarrelled over which accommodation they had been assigned.[15] In the middle of the commotion it would have been very simple for Randolfo to secure discreetly adjoining rooms for himself and for Lydia.

Edward Bernays claimed that the collective mood on tour was always extremely volatile, fraught with 'medieval intrigue, illicit love, misdirected passions and aggression'.[16] As in any group confined to each other's company, the dancers' loves, hatreds and irritations were intensified, and as the stresses of travelling accumulated, the Ballets Russes became an emotional pressure cooker. Within such an atmosphere it is understandable that Lydia yielded to Randolfo's attentions as quickly as she did.

Yet she may also have been urged into the affair by Diaghilev, for according to the latter's biographer, Richard Buckle, he was now counting on Lydia's relationship with Randolfo to keep her in the company full time. While it would be extreme to cast Diaghilev as a pimp in the affair, he was a manipulator of subtlety and skill who would not have balked at facilitating the lovers' private meetings, nor even at singing siren praises of Randolfo to Lydia. From Diaghilev's perspective, any strategy for binding Lydia to the company was now acceptable. As the battle lines hardened back in Europe, it was clear to him that America was his key market, and already a second tour was being planned for the autumn. Yet the Ballets Russes had not travelled far from New York before it became clear how hard a campaign still

The Ballets Russes on set with Charlie Chaplin, Hollywood, 1916. Randolfo Barocchi (bearded) is sixth from left; Lydia is on far right in front of Nijinsky and Chaplin

had to be waged for American hearts and dollars. On 16 February the *Chicago Daily Tribune* observed that audiences were not only meagre but difficult to impress, quipping that the orchestra had 'proved a most wonderful accompaniment' for the public's chatter. And if high ticket prices were partly responsible for these disappointing houses, the company's continuing reputation for 'high browed immorality' was an even greater problem. Lydia, who was seemingly known and loved in every state, was the dancer best able to shift this perception. It was around this time that she was deputed to front a series of newspaper articles, in which she reassured the public that Diaghilev's ballets were not as alien as they appeared (having stories and characters 'just like plays'), and in which she vouched for the decency of all her fellow dancers. On stage the Ballets Russes might transform into harem girls or priapic fauns, but in real life they were wholesome, nature-loving folk, just as she herself was. 'I have always found it helpful', Lydia glibly enthused, 'to get out into the big and beautiful world when I could slip away from the theatre ... the fine bracing air, the flowers, the green and growing things, laughing and happy peoples.'[17]

Marketing Lydia's lack of side and her quaint Russian-American idioms was fair game. A follow-up interview, however, which ran in the *Minneapolis Journal* and which was also syndicated throughout the area, revealed another, far queasier aspect of this publicity campaign. Lydia's still-official engagement to Heywood had remained one of the central factors of her appeal, and in this interview she seems to have been encouraged to focus solely on her role as his loving fiancée. While stopping short of claiming that she missed Heywood, she explained to the journalist that she was using their time apart to master the mysteries of her lover's sporting vocabulary. Unblushingly, she gave a demonstration: 'Play ball ... Was that right?'; and even more unblushingly, when quizzed about her future married life, she gave no hint that this might be in doubt. She stressed her excitement at becoming a good American: 'After Mr Broun and I are married I shall be an American citizeness ... I love America, yes I'll be an American citizeness.' She brightly trotted through her plans for combining marriage and career, assuring her public that she would not submit to becoming a housewife but at the same time would restrict her dancing to 'organisations like Diaghileff's which are congenial'. She would also retain her stage name, even though the press never seemed to get it right. With mock severity she challenged her interviewer to try – not 'Coco cola or Look her over' but 'Lopokova' – and when he failed, she offered him an encouraging trade: 'When I come again perhaps you'll be able to say Mrs Broun correctly and I'll know what are the Giants.'[18]

This sparkling exchange presented Lydia at her most winning. Yet with brutal timing, the day that the article appeared on the newsstands she had not only given up all her plans of becoming Mrs Broun, but was on the verge of becoming Mrs Barocchi. When the Ballets Russes rolled into Minneapolis, on the morning of 2 March 1916, Lydia and Randolfo had applied to the City Registry for a wedding licence and shortly afterwards were secretly married.

In fairness to Lydia, the interview may have taken place days, if not weeks, before it was actually published, at a time when she might have partly believed that she was still going to marry Heywood. But the tawdry coincidence in the timing of its appearance makes her abandonment of Heywood look cruelly precipitate; it also implies a guilty furtiveness in the manner that she and Randolfo concealed their wedding from the rest of the world (with the possible exception of Diaghilev). They continued to remain silent until the middle of April, when they invited a few colleagues to attend a short religious consecration in New York. And so expertly had their secret been kept from the rest of the world that when the press finally got wind of Lydia's split from Heywood, journalists could offer no explanation. It was not until early August that news of her marriage to Barocchi was printed.

From Randolfo's position both the delay and the mystery were essential, for in his impatience to secure Lydia he had not got around to organising his divorce from Mary Hargreaves, and when he had signed his name on the wedding certificate in Minneapolis he had actually committed a howling act of bigamy. Naturally he did not care for this 'marriage' to be publicised in the press, at least until he had persuaded Hargreaves to give him his divorce. The longer he could delay the announcement, the safer he would feel from potential prosecution.

In fact his failure to take proper legal advice over the summer would only make his situation worse. In the autumn he finally gained his decree nisi from Hargreaves and, deciding it would be prudent to 'marry' Lydia again, persuaded her to go through a second, civil ceremony in Westchester, New York State. But even this was illegal, for having failed to wait the statutory six months before his decree nisi became absolute, Barocchi had simply made himself a bigamist for a second time.

As for Lydia, she always claimed that she had no knowledge of this bungled farce until she left Randolfo in 1919. In fact she may deliberately have chosen not to enquire into the more puzzling aspects of her new husband's behaviour, for fear of discovering anything that might risk her marital status. By abandoning Heywood she had lost her chances of American citizenship, but by marrying

Randolfo she had gained Italian nationality and she needed his precious papers in order, finally, to travel without interference from the Russian state.

There was also, however, a more honourable explanation for her reticence about publicising the marriage, which was her desire that Heywood hear the news directly from her. Although Lydia's behaviour might appear slippery, even callous, in this episode, she would go to see her ousted lover as soon as she returned to New York in April, meeting him in their old haunt, Joel's, to confess that she had replaced him with Barocchi. While Kramer's biography draws a veil over the actual conversation, we can guess that it was a grim one. Afterwards Lydia ducked out of seeing Heywood' s mother, sending instead a quick guilty note of apology for all 'the upset' she had caused.[19]

In the thick of this emotional upheaval it would have been understandable if Lydia's professional appearances had lost some of their focus, yet now that she was installed as the company's lead ballerina, this tour was proving to be a personal tour de force. From Boston, where the exacting H. T. Parker complimented her glamour and charm, to Albany, where she was judged the troupe's finest asset, down to Kansas City and across to Washington, where she danced for President Wilson and the Russian ambassador, Lydia's performances were fêted. After the company returned to New York for their April season at the Met, the *New York Times* was ready to pronounce that 'Lydia Lopokova may well be classed as one of the great dancers who are supposed to appear at intervals of twenty-five years.'[20]

If there were any stresses to her dancing, they came not from Lydia's private life but from a new presence in the company, Vaslav Nijinsky. Months of heroic string-pulling by Diaghilev and Kahn, involving Queen Alexandra of England, King Alfonso of Spain and even the Pope, had finally secured the dancer's release from Budapest, and on 4 April 1916 he and his family sailed into New York to rejoin the Ballets Russes. Diaghilev, who had not seen his former lover since 1913, went down to the docks for a ceremonious display of conciliation. As journalists swarmed to take Nijinsky's photograph, demanding to feel his muscles, Diaghilev composed a photo-perfect welcome, handing the dancer a lavish bunch of flowers and welcoming his baby daughter, Kyra, with an avuncular embrace.

The star, however, had returned with old scores to settle, claiming that half a million gold francs of unpaid salary was still owed to him, and refusing to set foot on stage until he was paid. This was not the magnificent start to the New York season that Diaghilev had envisaged, and as he and Otto Kahn scrabbled to find a portion of Nijinsky's money, the dancer began to wreak petty damage on the company by slipping defamatory stories about the Ballets Russes to the press. The public meanwhile, who had paid good dollars to see the 'god of the dance', started to demand their money back and, as a wit in Kahn's office quipped, the atmosphere around the company became brittle with apprehension:

> O Mr Nijinsky
> Where have you binsky?
> And if you are here
> Why don't you appear
> And save the ballet from ruinsky?[21]

It was a full week before Nijinsky deigned to make his debut, but it was a measure of his continuing genius that, once he was dancing, his colleagues were prepared to forgive him everything. 'On stage,' Lydia recalled, 'he was a god to all of us',[22] and when she performed alongside him in *Spectre de la rose* on 12 April, she fully acknowledged that the standing ovations, the blizzard of rose petals that floated down from the gallery, were all for him. Yet if she concurred humbly with the *Herald* that Nijinsky was 'a great artist, probably the greatest that the present generation has seen here',[23] there were moments during the rest of the season when she wished that she herself did not have to be partnered by him as regularly as Diaghilev required. Unlike the theatrically agile Massine, who could reliably spark her dancing to greater élan, or Idzikowski, whose lively speed matched her own, Nijinsky did not flatter her as a partner. His charged mystique could make her own vivacity appear shallow, and complaints from Pitts Sanborne of the *Globe* that Lydia was no Pavlova or Karsavina struck a sour note in her otherwise honeyed press.

Nijinsky in turn was not overly delighted by Lydia. She was evidently a rival to be reckoned with, and if he noted with displeasure the swell and fervour of her fans' applause, his ego was further jolted when, at the end of their month-long run in New York, reproachful comments were printed in the press about the problems that he had created for the company, leading to Lydia being singled out as 'the Americanised ballerina'[24] who had averted box office disaster. Nijinsky did not overlook this disparagement, and the undercurrent of rivalry that was stirred between the two dancers that spring would eventually fester into a stage relationship so dysfunctional that Lydia herself would try to walk out on it.

For the summer, however, they would be apart. Nijinsky was staying on in America to choreograph two ballets for the company's return in the autumn. Lydia was setting sail with the rest of the Ballets Russes for Spain, where two short seasons had been organised under the patronage of King Alfonso. This trip promised to be an unusually tranquil interlude, for Spain was one of the few neutral countries left in Europe, and a full two-month holiday had been written into the dancers' schedule. For Lydia, sailing under her new married name of Lydia Barocchi, boarding the *Dante Alighiere* also marked her exit from America, and the fantasy she had so long nurtured of becoming an American artist and an American citizen.

Had she known precisely how the next two years would develop, as she and the Ballets Russes moved closer to war, enduring danger, poverty and bone-aching exhaustion, she might have felt grave doubts about leaving behind her sunny New York apartment, her life of privileged independence and thousand-dollar contracts. Even during the balmy crossing to Cadiz, Lydia was given premonitory warnings about the future she'd chosen. Horses that were being transported to the European battlefronts could be heard screaming from the hold, and among the passengers rumours were spreading of German threats to resume U-boat attacks on Atlantic shipping. What news they heard over the ship's wires remained bleak, as British and French forces counted their losses after the battle of Verdun, and the Russians continued to retreat before the German advance in the Balkans.

But once they docked in Cadiz, and Lydia joined the superstitious rush to kiss the soil in gratitude for their safe arrival, any regrets that she might have been feeling for the safety and riches of America were dispersed in a flush of enthusiasm for Spain. The little port city of Cadiz, with its pretty whitewashed streets, felt a world away from the war; and a few days later when the company arrived in Madrid, Lydia felt even more inured from danger by the shaded elms and fountains outside her window at the Ritz Hotel, and the stately procession of carriages up and down the Paseo del Prado.

At the Teatro Real, where they were appearing from 26 May to 9 June, the audience was also worlds away from the sceptical, chary public whom they had been battling to impress in America. The King was in the royal box for most of their eight performances, leading the applause and sending bouquets to Lydia and her beautiful colleague Luba Tchernicheva, to whom he had taken a particular shine. Filling the expensive seats were a cosmopolitan mixture of war refugees, European aristocracy and wealthy criminals, whilst among the Spaniards themselves were an excitable core of locals who had never, apparently, seen any ballet and were vocally demonstrative in their enthusiasm. Lydia would later claim that a group of Madrid journalists had cornered her backstage, requesting permission to inspect her *Sylphides* costume because they refused to believe that she could jump as high as she did without the aid of a harness and wires – or without the help of the Devil.[25]

It was these Madrileñas whom Lydia and her fellow dancers were most eager to meet. While rich Europeans offered invitations to the Ritz or the Palace Hotel, where they might take tea with the bejewelled opera diva Mara Kuznetsova, or catch glimpses of the now notorious Mata Hari,* Lydia and her friends preferred to find their entertainment away from the Paseo del Prado with the gypsy dancers and musicians who performed all night in the neighbourhood cafés cantantes, and with the spectacular crowds who surged into bullfights, their 'shouts and jeers', according to Lydia, capable of making even 'a baseball crowd feel small'.[26] Lydia fell in love with the layered history

*The exotic dancer and alleged spy would attempt to ingratiate herself with Diaghilev, pleading for work with the company and even showing up in one of the Ballets Russes's trains. Lydia later claimed that she and Hari had slept side by side in the same carriage.

of Madrid and with its elegant, impassioned people, and during the next itinerant years of the war, Spain would come to feel the closest place to home.

Her sightseeing, though, lasted only a few days, for in early June Lydia's attention was diverted by a new arrival, Igor Stravinsky, who had rejoined the company to conduct the Spanish première of *Firebird*. The last time that the two had seen each other had been in Paris, where there had been nothing but professional interest between them. Lydia had been caught up in the whirlwind drama of her new ballerina status and, perhaps, in the romantic attentions of her Polish count; Stravinsky had been happily and faithfully married, to his pious and clever cousin Katya. However, during the intervening six and a half years both of them had changed. Lydia, the teenage muse, was growing into a sexually experienced woman, intelligent, adventurous and fun, Stravinsky meanwhile had become restless and frustrated, and was looking for consolation. The accumulating misery of his long exile from Russia, the struggle to provide for his growing family, and the deteriorating health of Katya had all put his marriage under strain and his later confession to his second wife, Vera, that he had enjoyed a 'flirtation' with Lydia in Madrid was a coded admission of the fact that they had an affair.[27]

According to Stravinsky's biographer Stephen Walsh, Lydia would be the first in a series of mistresses with whom the composer would experiment during the next five years. Stravinsky, it seems, came to Madrid almost primed for adultery, and Lydia presented an immediate object of attraction. What is harder to determine is why she herself responded so readily. She was probably alone in Madrid, since Randolfo had business still to settle for the next American tour, but even so she had been married (or what passed as married) for only four months. It was very early days for her to be disappointed in her new husband. Nor did Stravinsky himself present an obvious image of temptation. He looked both physically older and emotionally less assured than his thirty-four years, and his narrow, nervous body and fanatical air of neatness could match neither Heywood's solid appeal nor Randolfo's ease. Yet Stravinsky was acquiring the reputation of a musical giant, which mattered to Lydia, and, according to Vera, he became a very different man in the company of attractive women, warm, funny and unexpectedly sexy. Flattered at being sought after by this celebrated musician, and interested in flexing her own power, Lydia may have persuaded herself that if she told no one of the affair, it would remain in its own emotional box, separate from her life with Randolfo.

There were other factors, too, that drew her to this new lover. Shared language and years of shared history bound Lydia closely to Stravinsky. He, like Lydia, had grown up around the Mariinsky, where he had regularly attended ballet and opera performances. He, like her, he had been whisked into exile by the all-consuming Diaghilev experiment and was able to sympathise with her own background emotions of homesickness, nostalgia and anxiety. In fact in the heat of Madrid this affair seems to have rapidly become more complicated than a holiday fling. When the rest of the company dispersed for their various holiday destinations, circumstantial evidence suggests that the two of them prolonged their time together. Stravinsky stayed on in Madrid, despite having no professional business or friends to detain him; and since nothing is known of Lydia's whereabouts until she met Randolfo in Paris on 9 August, there is good reason to suppose that she too remained in Madrid.

At the end of August they were united again, as Stravinsky returned to Spain for the Ballets Russes's final performances in Bilbao, on the northern coast. Even though Diaghilev commandeered much of the composer's time – taking him off to bullfights and Chaplin movies – Stravinsky seems to have stayed as close as he dared to Lydia, or Lopushka as he now sentimentally called her. When the Ballets Russes travelled up to Bordeaux to board the *Lafayette* back to New York, he went with them; and at the last minute posed with Lydia for a photograph – one small keepsake – before waving her off from the dockside.

The two lovers had no idea when they would be in the same country again, and during the following years Stravinsky would often use Ernest Ansermet to supply information about his Lopushka's wellbeing.[28] But the affair continued to flicker on and off as circumstances permitted, and even though there was never a question of Stravinsky leaving Katya, one significant, if cloudy, clue to his continuing feelings for Lydia would be the intimate dedication that he signed on one of her ballet scores, in 1921. The music was his own arrangement of a variation for Petipa's *Sleeping Beauty*, and on the right-hand corner of the manuscript he would write 'to Lopushka the Traitress' (in Russian, *Izmennitsa*). This cryptic little phrase meant enough to Lydia for her to frame the score and keep it close to her until she died. Even in 1965, when she met Stravinsky for the last time, it was a far from casual encounter. He was conducting a concert at London's Royal Festival Hall, and when she sought him out back-stage she was observed to burst into tears in his embrace.[29]

What Lydia felt as she sailed away from Stravinsky on 8 September 1917, and towards her husband in New York, we can only imagine. During the summer, she and Randolfo had spent only a very short period together, and for three months she had effectively transferred herself to another man against whom Randolfo's own limitations had been thrown into sudden relief.

There were other issues to unsettle her during this crossing, too. The short summer in Spain had brought Lydia a tantalising step closer to home, and to a more acute sense of the situation that her family were facing. Back in America the occasional letter had reassured her of their personal welfare – Fedor had had a ballet premièred at Petrograd's Theatre of Musical Drama; Andrei had graduated into the Mariinsky – but the news that Lydia had read in the European press, and which she had picked up through Diaghilev's extensive information network, told her that Russia itself was under threat, with food shortages and soaring casualty figures from the front lines brewing political unrest right across the country.

These were potentially dangerous times for her family, and if Lydia had mixed feelings about putting 3,500 miles of ocean between herself and them, there was little about the crossing to improve her mood. A violent storm blew up as the *Lafayette* sailed out of Bordeaux, confining many of the seasick dancers to their cabins, while stark notices were posted outside the purser's office warning that enemy attacks had been resumed in the Atlantic and that Allied citizens would be taken as prisoners of war if their ship were intercepted by Germans. Looming even more ominously was the prospect of the tour ahead. Four months of arduous performing and travelling awaited Lydia and her colleagues, after they had barely recovered from the last American marathon. This time too they were having to survive without either Diaghilev or Grigoriev in control.

Tensions between Diaghilev and Nijinsky had continued to fester so badly during the previous spring that the Met feared they would completely destroy the company during a second tour. It had thus been decided that Diaghilev and Grigoriev would remain behind in Europe, while artistic direction of the company would be temporarily handed over to Nijinsky.* Logically, this transfer of power appeared to benefit everyone. Diaghilev (who had an aversion to long-distance travel) planned to go to Italy where he could dedicate himself to the preparation of new repertory, along with Massine, Cecchetti and a tiny group of dancers. The rest of the Ballets Russes, according to the Met, would be free to benefit from the inspired and undistracted leadership of their star.

The dancers were disinclined to share the Met's confidence, however, for if Nijinsky's introvert temperament made him awkward as a colleague, few could imagine him being sufficiently robust to function as a director. Certainly when the company arrived in New York in the middle of September, the signs were not good. Nijinsky should have completed two new ballets by this point, ready for the Ballets Russes's opening at the Manhattan Opera House on 9 October. But hampered by his own near morbid perfectionism, he had finished only half of one work, a setting of Strauss's dramatic tone poem *Till Eulenspiegel*, and to the dancers' consternation it seemed impossible that Nijinsky could finish even that on time. Reunited with them in the studio, he appeared to have grown more socially inert, finding it hard to communicate what he wanted and obsessively picking at his cuticles. At some rehearsals he failed to appear at all and, as the days passed, progress on *Till* was so slow, and the rest of the repertory left so badly unrehearsed, that the agitated dancers staged a 48-hour strike to try to force the Met into making some kind of intervention.

Lydia's own work was not immediately affected, as she had not

*The Met, acting through a subsidiary called the Metropolitan Ballet Company, took charge of the tour's major expenses, including Nijinsky's salary. The sum of $9,000 per week was paid to Diaghilev, which along with his half of the profits was deemed sufficient to cover the rest of the dancers' salaries and expenses.

been cast in *Tyl*, and the only new ballet that she was learning was a revival of Fokine's *Papillons*,* which, like several works in the repertory, had had to be put under the supervision of the senior dancer Adolph Bolm, rather than Nijinsky. But still she was sucked into the histrionics of the situation. Romola had begun to make melodramatic accusations of sabotage, claiming that the dancers were under orders from Diaghilev to undermine her husband's work. Meanwhile, the rehearsal schedule had fallen so badly behind that the opening night had to be delayed by a week, and the repertory reshuffled to cope with the fact that *Tyl*, their highly publicised première, would not be ready until 23 October. What affected Lydia most of all was that her own husband, in Grigoriev's absence, was expected to manage these traumas. The duties that Randolfo had temporarily inherited were onerous, for Grigoriev was almost single-handedly responsible for the practical state of the company's morale. He advised Diaghilev on casting and programming, oversaw the budget, kept a watchful eye on the condition of sets and costumes, and gave detailed notes on every rehearsal and performance. Randolfo, having neither talent nor experience for any of these tasks, was growing hysterical in the attempt to maintain order.

In the middle of this, Randolfo was also having to attend to his incomplete marriage arrangements, and it was on 21 October that he had to persuade Lydia to take a two-day trip to Westchester for a second, legal wedding ceremony. Whatever treacherous passions she had felt for Stravinsky in Spain, she was not ready to threaten her precious travel papers, and apparently she made no objection to postponing her advertised debut in *Papillons*, allowing the press to report vaguely that she was indisposed. However, on 23 October Lydia was back on stage, performing alongside the delayed première of *Tyl*, and, like most of her colleagues, expecting the night to be an excruciating disaster. New York was already out of patience with the company, having suffered so many delays and changes to the advertised programmes, and Nijinsky's new ballet, which had appeared shambolically incomplete at its dress rehearsal, seemed likely to turn

***Papillons* was another of Fokine's *commedia dell'arte* ballets, and a very feeble one. Lydia took the role of a young woman dressed up for a party as a butterfly and mistaken by Pierrot for the real thing.

the public's frustration into outright hostility.* Yet by a fluke of theatrical alchemy, *Tyl* arrived on stage as if fully complete. Inspired by the vigour of Strauss's boisterously figurative score, the cast succeeded in improvising across the remaining gaps in the choreography, while at their centre Nijinsky as the taunting, anarchic Tyl danced like a man possessed.

This eighteen-minute ballet proved to be the success of the season, and if the dancers were forced to scotch their doubts over Nijinsky's effectiveness as a choreographer, they were still more impressed by the sudden surge of confidence with which he tackled his duties as director. Rehearsals became crisp, orderly and productive, and by the time they began their cross-state tour, H. T. Parker claimed that the Russians looked like a different company. In this judgement he included Lydia, observing how the 'white sparks' of Nijinsky's dancing were kindling her to still greater brilliance.[30] Nevertheless, Lydia's own assessment of their partnership remained doubtful. With Massine in Europe she was dancing even more regularly with Nijinsky, in *Sylphides*, *Spectre* and *Carnaval*, and her performances were affected not only by their uncertain stage chemistry, but by her partner's tendency to take extreme, unscheduled risks. Many dancers use the adrenalin of a live performance to push themselves to new levels of technique or expression, but Nijinsky went further than most in abandoning timings that had been set in rehearsal, and forcing lifts and balances to unstable limits.† While thrilling for an audience, these unpremeditated variations could be disconcerting for his ballerina, and most disturbing to Lydia may have been her suspicion that Nijinsky was deliberately contriving to undermine her. Several journalists noticed that an ungallant spirit of rivalry galvanised Nijinsky when he partnered her, and complaints were printed about his ill-mannered treatment of her during curtain calls.

After the Ballets Russes left New York, winding its way down the

*The box office had also suffered from Nijinsky cancelling all his performances in the first week, due to a sprained ankle.

†Sokolova was also partnered by Nijinsky and recalled that his habit of taking his supporting hand away in the middle of an arabesque or throwing her unexpectedly in a lift was 'very frightening'.

eastern coast to Houston and up through the Midwest, Lydia's colleagues also had reason to feel renewed concern. Nijinsky's mood began to fluctuate so that while he was sometimes clumsily eager to ingratiate himself with the other dancers, playing schoolboy pranks and offering them puppyish endearments, at other times he withdrew completely, his slanted gaze unreadable, his behaviour a baffling blank. On one occasion he seemed almost mad. The company were advertised to dance *Sylphides*, for which the dancers, probably including Lydia, were all dressed in their appropriate costumes, but shortly before the curtain was due to rise, Nijinsky suddenly announced that he would prefer to dance *Carnaval*. A panicking Randolfo locked Nijinsky in his dressing room with only his wig and costume for *Sylphides*, and when the star finally emerged, wearing the correct costume, he simply went on stage to dance the advertised ballet as if nothing had happened.

It may have been the pressure of his new duties that was making Nijinsky act so erratically, or, as some dancers would later suspect, he was exhibiting early symptoms of the mental illness that would incapacitate him in 1919. But some of his wilder decisions were also made under the influence of two other dancers in the company, Dmitri Kostrovsky and Nicolas Zverev. These men were evangelical advocates of an austere, Tolstoyan school of socialism, and Nijinsky – religious, superstitious and in many ways unworldly – was a susceptible target. When the two zealots persuaded him that it was his duty to dismantle the hierarchy of the Ballets Russes and restructure it as a collective, he eagerly concurred. Junior dancers found themselves cast in lead roles, while Nijinsky made drastic, disruptive gestures of humility – relinquishing the role of the Golden Slave in *Schéhérazade* to Zverev and himself taking the role of the fat, doddering Eunuch.

At some performances Nijinsky refused to dance at all, and, given the high prices set by the Met, this was considered an outrageous affront by the American public. Even though the first weeks of the tour were critically acclaimed, as the company travelled further south business at the box office started a perilous downward slide. The dancers' own morale declined with it, and towards the end of November it reached rock bottom. The tour's failure to deliver its expected profits* had left Diaghilev short of his own promised cut – and, claiming that he had run out of money, he stopped authorising payments for the company's wages and expenses. Apart from the three dancers who were paid directly by the Met (Nijinsky and the two new ballerinas who had temporarily joined the company from Russia, Olga Spessivtzeva and Margarita Frohman), the company were financially abandoned. The juniors, who were paid only $33 a week and had no savings to fall back on, faced immediate physical hardship.

For the first time in their history the Ballets Russes turned against their leader, and Randolfo, for the first time in his life, displayed masterful qualities of leadership as he fired off stinging cables to Diaghilev, demanding that the wages, including his own, be reinstated. The senior dancers shared out what spare cash they had, but by 11 December, R. G. Herndon, the Met's touring manager, had to report back that 'The company are on their last dollars as Lopokova, Monteux, Revalles, Bolm have given up all the money they have at their command.'[31] Ironically it was Diaghilev's betrayal, rather than Nijinsky's idealism, that brought the company as close as it had ever come to being a collective.

On Lydia this crisis had a lasting impact, for even though money did start to dribble through from Diaghilev, her savings had been badly hit, and with them her financial independence. She was now tied even closer to the Ballets Russes, and the photograph that was taken of the company in Los Angeles soon after Christmas does not indicate that she was enjoying her situation. The Ballets Russes were visiting a film studio as guests of Chaplin, and Lydia, pushed to the front of the group, looks wary and tired, failing to muster a glimmer of her usual smile for the camera. By the final leg of the tour there was still less to smile about as the company toiled through an exhausting string of one- and two-night stands, their lives reduced to a blur of unfamiliar towns, hotels and half-empty theatres, feeling abandoned by Diaghilev in Europe and by the Met organisation in New York. The company's self-esteem was in tatters. But the final

*To make a profit, the tour needed to average $6,000–$7,000 per show. In Fort Worth one performance netted as little as $767, and by the end of the tour the Met had lost $250,000.

insult came after the tour ended in Albany on 24 February when the dancers straggled back to New York to discover that no ship had been booked to take them back to Diaghilev in Italy.

Nijinsky was not among them, the conditions of his release permitting him access only to neutral countries for the duration of the war, but the rest of the company were forced to hang around the port for several days, waiting for whatever crossings became available. Lydia never recorded how she sailed back, but Sokolova recalled that she and many others had ended up on a 'filthy Spanish boat' and had had to subsist on a diet 'of greyish coloured beans'.[32]

It was a chaotic, wretched conclusion to a largely wretched tour. Yet more stress awaited the Russians in the company, as rumours came over the ship's wires of the events unfolding back home. Information was patchy, delayed by news blackouts and poor communications, but by the third week in March, when all of the dancers had finally regrouped in Europe, it had become clear that Russia had undergone convulsive and irrevocable change. On 8 March (24 February OS) there had been mass demonstrations in Petrograd as hungry crowds ransacked the shops for food, sparking wholesale defections from the army and further demonstrations nationwide. The demands of the Russian people had gained an unstoppable momentum, and on 15 March (2 March OS) Nicholas II had been forced to abdicate. Whatever the dancers' individual politics, all those like Lydia who had grown up as part of the Tsar's extended family, trained in his school and performed in his presence felt in some way traumatised by the news. Not only had their pasts been cancelled out by the violent overhaul of Imperial rule, but their futures, like the future of their country, were now an unreadable blank.

Chapter Seven

DANCING THROUGH WAR

> If anyone could dart about the stage as swiftly or neatly as she did, nobody could ever imitate the witty way she used her head and shoulders or the zest with which she threw herself into the action as if every step was improvised on the spur of the moment and every situation was occurring for the first time.
>
> LYDIA SOKOLOVA ON LYDIA LOPOKOVA IN *LES FEMMES DE BONNE HUMEUR*[1]

It was a dispirited, dishevelled group of dancers who were eventually met by Grigoriev and herded across France to be reunited with Diaghilev in Rome. Their director had met them in a foul temper, aggressively rehashing the disasters of the American tour and looking for scapegoats. Yet during the months that followed, as the company faced up to the worsening conditions of war, their morale would also be lifted by some of the great artistic achievements of their history. Europe in 1917 was still a crucible of opportunity for Diaghilev, and only four weeks after the Ballets Russes's fractious reassembling in Rome, Lydia would be standing in the wings of the Teatro Costanzi, poised to première her most scintillating role yet. The stage awaiting her would be an elegant denial of the carnage raging on the battle fronts close by, an eighteenth-century Venetian piazza peopled by powdered and pomaded aristocrats, among whom Lydia as the pretty maidservant Mariuccia would be speeding a trail of adorable, comic havoc.

When Lydia had first been informed of her new role, she could not have understood the impact that it would have on her work. The libretto of Massine's *Les Femmes de bonne humeur* was a standard comedy of manners based on the farce by Carlo Goldoni (*La donne de buon umore*) about a maidservant Mariuccia and her mistress Constanza, whose mission to test the fidelity of the male sex turns into a tangle of deception and misdirected flirtation. From the first step that Lydia learned in rehearsal, however, it was clear to her that Massine, twenty-two years and barely more than a novice, was working this material with an exhilarating, experimental spin. During his six months in Italy with Diaghilev he had become fascinated by the art of the Futurists* and, inspired by their dynamic, subversive embrace of popular culture, he had invented a new vocabulary in which classical steps were wired to the jerky, cartooning body language of the silent screen. The result was, as Lydia understood in her first exhausting session, to be a total disruption of everything she had learned at school, with familiar positions hardened and angled into new lines, and phrases revved to fantastic speeds: 'Our bodies began to ache as never before,' she recalled. 'The knee was always bent and the arms akimbo, the limbs never in a straight line.'[2]

Dressed in Bakst's costume, an ochre and red frock weighted down with the period trappings of wig, padding and farthingale (although not the false nose that the designer had initially proposed), Lydia claimed that Massine's new style was 'torture' to perform, especially her long solo, which, she ungrammatically boasted, 'was the equal to run a mile in four minutes'. 'We felt like rugby football players dressed as eskimos pretending to be the most elegant and dainty females of the eighteenth century. It is easy to forget how we airy fairies sweat and blow and gasp flat on our backs the moment we reach the wings.'[3] Yet despite her protests Lydia understood, completely, that this was the ballet for which she had been waiting. Massine might have choreographed much of her role during her absence in America, but it was her strong little feet, her eloquent hands, her veering speeds and above all her comic élan that had been the physical template for his imagination. As Lydia was propelled across the stage by the staccato gallop of Scarlatti's music (an

*Massine's and Diaghilev's interest in Futurism had begun in 1914, when they had seen its vibrant, antisentimental aesthetic as a way forward from the earnestness of Fokine's naturalism and the remote, interiorised rituals of Nijinsky's modernism.

orchestrated version of twenty harpsichord sonatas) she knew exactly what tilt of the head, what flick of the wrist, what sideways glint would summon up Mariuccia's personality. She knew precisely how to pitch her engagement with the other characters as she mocked the coquetry of Constanza's elderly aunt, whispered nonsense into the speaking trumpet of the amorous old Marquis, and tauntingly elbowed her two admirers, Leonard and Battista, as they competed for her attention.

Later, Lydia would claim she could 'hardly dance because I laugh so much',[4] but it was her visible delight in the role that charged her triumph. She had never been the kind of ballerina whose performances acquired the esoteric quality of ritual. She interpreted the choreography through her own idiosyncrasies and her imperfections, and what made Mariuccia an ideal vehicle for her was that in exploiting her quirks, it opened up a core of freedom for her. She did not have to strain after a classical perfection of line, nor was her personality sugared by sentimentality, as it had been in some of Fokine's ballets. Mariuccia was a modern heroine, active, smart and in charge of her own destiny, and in giving her the role, Massine transformed Lydia into something much more than a lovable, rogue talent. He allowed her to achieve greatness.

The ballet did not just have a transforming effect on Lydia alone. All the cast were inspired by its splintering energies, especially during the climactic dinner party, in which Massine had his dancers riotously beating out Scarlatti's rhythms with their cutlery. The British writer Viola Tree would later describe this as the most immaculately constructed of scenes: 'They clatter their knives, put their elbows on the table, rattle their chairs, yet it is perfect dancing, it is eating, wit, quarrels, gallanteries, drinking, protestations and the apotheosis of gaiety',[5] while the public in Rome found it masterly. The French writer Colette was at the première on 12 April, as was Eleonora Duse, who came on stage afterwards to congratulate the cast. Lydia revered the Italian actress and, after kissing her hand and, embarrassingly, smudging lipstick all over Duse's glove, was overwhelmed by the latter's 'beautiful' reaction, as she assured Lydia that she would keep the ruined glove among her 'treasures'.[6]

Also in the theatre that night was Pablo Picasso, who had joined the company to collaborate with Massine on his next ballet. This was the first time that Lydia had met the painter, and an immediate sympathy developed between them, which would continue for many years. Picasso found Lydia extremely attractive and the sketches he made of her at this time, lightning impressions in green ink, were graphically evocative of their intimacy. One of the best caught her sitting between Diaghilev and Massine, leaning casually against the impresario's bulk, while turning her face towards Massine as if mid-conversation. In the inquisitive thrust of her nose and the eager dilation of her gaze, Picasso had distilled all the artless enthusiasm that had captivated Karsavina so many years ago when Lydia had been an eight-year-old child at the Theatre School.

Working with the Ballets Russes had rekindled Picasso's interest in the human figure – which he had virtually abandoned during his early Cubist years – but it had also kindled an interest in dancers. Lydia watched with amused interest as her new friend fell in love with the auburn-haired, grave-faced Olga Khokhlova, whose serene resistance to the painter's sexual blandishments eventually forced Picasso into proposing marriage. More uncertainly, Lydia may also have watched Stravinsky, who had arrived in Rome to conduct the first staged performance of his symphonic fragment *Fireworks*, but was probably out of bounds to her, given that Randolfo was in daily close attendance and possibly even carrying her off to meet his Italian family and friends. The season in Rome was brief, however, and any emotional conflicts that Lydia may have been experiencing had to be packed away as she and the company travelled on to perform in Naples, Florence and finally in Paris, where Diaghilev was to unveil his next production, provocatively advertised as 'the world's first Cubist ballet'.

This was Massine's *Parade*, and with designs by Picasso, a libretto by Jean Cocteau and music by Erik Satie it was presenting itself as the Ballets Russes's most overtly avant-garde creation yet. Cubism was not in itself a shocking proposition – so familiar to the general public that it had become the butt of music-hall jokes – but it still embodied a strictly Left Bank culture, which audiences did not expect to encounter within a ballet company or an opera house. Lydia certainly believed that *Parade* was 'the first time that Diaghilev

Picasso drawing, Diaghilev, Lydia and Massine, Rome, 1917

Lydia, Mariuccia, *Les Femmes de bonne humeur*, Rome, 1917

set himself to really upset the public',[7] and even though Paris was clearly a city at war – its streets unnaturally quiet, its shops half-empty – a very pre-war buzz of controversy awaited the ballet's première on 18 May, with most of the seats sold out two weeks in advance, and supportive claques of students and artists drafted into the theatre to combat anticipated protests.

At first the performance appeared almost conventional. During Satie's overture the stage was screened by a front curtain, which Picasso had playfully designed in the style of a nineteenth-century circus poster, its figures possibly representing Ballets Russes celebrities in exotic disguise: Cocteau a harlequin, Diaghilev a sailor, Stravinsky with a turban and blacked-up skin, and Lydia balanced gaily on the back of a winged Pegasus. But when the curtain rose, it was on a harsh urban street scene in which the buildings had been painted in flat slabs of orange and grey, and the perspectives were fiercely awry. More sensationally still, in place of the *commedia dell'arte* or folkloric characters who had typically inhabited Diaghilev's repertory, the scene was fronted by two inhumanly stomping gesticulating figures, their bodies encased in towering eight-foot Cubist 'sculptures' of papier mâché and wood.

Nothing like this couple had ever been seen on the ballet stage. The characters they represented were a pair of rival fairground managers, one French, the other American, and to differentiate between them Picasso had constructed a collage of iconographic national images that bristled unwieldily, and seemingly at random, from their 'costumes'. The French manager sprouted a top hat, a pipe and a wing in the shape of a Parisian chestnut tree; the American was identified by a hat shaped like a ship's funnel, a scarlet pleated shirt, cowboy chaps and a tilting skyscraper.

Hardly less odd were the various acts who were introduced to the audience by the competing managers, among them a pantomime horse sporting a doleful African mask and a precocious young 'American Girl' (Cocteau's idea of a twentieth-century princess) who showed a brazen amount of white knicker as she danced a medley of ragtime steps and mimed scenes of modern 'daring' in imitation of the silent-screen serial *The Perils of Pauline*. (These included swimming across an imaginary river, snapping photos and cranking up a car.) Massine himself portrayed a devilish Chinese conjurer, painted in malevolently garish colours, while Lydia, to her slight regret, danced the 'much more usual'[8] role of a female acrobat, dressed in a close-fitting unitard, as she pretended to walk a tightrope and romped through a virtuoso ballet duet with her partner, Zverev.

If Picasso's designs were the most blatantly Cubist feature of the ballet, the other collaborators had also stylised their contributions to subversive extremes. Satie's score was a subtle, satirical collage of popular music, which had been punctuated, at Cocteau's insistence, with the noises of a typewriter, pistol shots and sirens; Massine's choreography was an equally irreverent clash of ballet, circus tricks and cartoon mime. Even Cocteau's libretto could be interpreted as a kind of Cubist 'still life', its narrative a series of disconnected fragments which were arbitrarily curtailed when the ballet juddered to a sudden, and inexplicable, halt.

The reaction of the audience at the Châtelet did not match the partisan frenzy of the première of *The Rite of Spring*, but Left Bank artists yelled support from the gallery, while Right Bank conservatives in the stalls shouted out, 'Shirkers! Draft dodgers! Foreign scum!' and called for the ballet's creators to be sent to the trenches. A group of society women were alleged to have turned on Cocteau with their hatpins. Over the next few days the press attempted to minimise the scandal, dismissing the ballet as a lame joke or a squib of poor taste, but the artists of Paris gave Diaghilev the endorsement that he craved. Proust assured Cocteau that *Parade* had been a 'foretaste' of the future,[9] while the poet Guillaume Apollinaire hailed its celebration of the 'sophisticated commonplace' as the start of a radical new aesthetic. Historically, he dubbed it 'sur-réalisme'.[10]

Having started out as an organiser of genius, focussing a generation's scattered revolt against the traditions of the past, Diaghilev had succeeded in transforming ballet into a modernist battlefield – the most talked-about art form of its era. His dancers thrived on the controversy of *Parade*. 'You can always tell when the company approves of a ballet,' recalled Sokolova, 'because you will find a number of them watching it from the wings.'[11] Lydia, too, remembered the atmosphere backstage being unusually affectionate. Picasso had flirtatiously undertaken the painting of her costume: 'Believe me, it was ticklish to be painted by Picasso who amused himself doing circles [and] coils on my body,' while the reclusive Satie had sent her flowers, with a card affectionately addressed 'to the most graceful acrobat'.[12]

Morale had in fact been high during the whole of the Paris season, lifted by good houses and mostly adulatory reviews; and it remained buoyant when the company moved south to perform in Madrid and Barcelona. The Catalan city was new to the dancers and they were enchanted by its lively population, who seemed to promenade outside the theatre night and day, along pavements crowded with flower stalls, canary cages and chicken sellers. Yet outside of the haven of Spain, the realities of performing in wartime Europe were becoming increasingly harsh. Paris was being encroached on by the Western Front; Rome was under threat from German and Austrian forces; and most of the company's other pre-war destinations were either behind battle lines, located in enemy territory or simply too problematic to reach. Even North America had become difficult to access after the United States too finally entered the war in April 1917.

Diaghilev had thus been forced to scout ever more inventively for audiences, and after Spain he planned to send his dancers on a two-month tour of South America. This would dispatch the Ballets Russes on their fourth Atlantic crossing in just over a year, exposing them yet again to the threat of German U-boats. But almost as unwelcome to the dancers was the fact that they would once again be exposed to Nijinsky's conflicted leadership. The latter had willingly rejoined the Ballets Russes in Spain, but was refusing to go on the long South American tour unless Diaghilev stayed behind in Europe. To most of the dancers, the chances of revisiting the disasters of North America seemed all too likely, and they were in a pessimistic, even mutinous mood when they travelled down to Cadiz to board ship in early July.

The journey was dreadful, with gale-force winds and violent seas, and when the company arrived in Montevideo to give their first performances they were feeling limp and battered. 'We had been a month on the boat and too seasick to practise,' remembered Lydia. 'My toes got out of order – I had no breath and no toes.'[13] The local audience seemed to notice nothing – Lydia wondered sardonically if it was because the women were veiled – but she was made sharply aware of her own inadequacies when Pavlova, who was coincidentally also touring South America, came to one of their performances. Lydia embraced the ballerina, and even more joyfully embraced Volinine, who had joined her troupe after leaving the All-Stars, but she was not so thrilled by the bouquet that Pavlova sent her after the show: 'She always sent me flowers when I danced badly! It seemed that she did not like you nearly so well when you were at the top of your form.'[14]

It was easy for Lydia to joke about the tour in retrospect, but the two months that she spent in South America were among the most horrible of her career, inducing such feelings of frustration and claustrophobia that she came very close to running away. Conditions for everybody were gruelling: the company were exposed to submarine attack during their 1,000-mile voyage up the coast from Montevideo to Rio; a spark set fire to one of the baggage trucks during their 200-mile rail journey from Rio to São Paulo; a failure in the ship's engine en route back to Buenos Aires left them marooned at sea for an entire day in thick fog. The heat, of course, was enervating. Yet for Lydia these discomforts and alarms were only background misery to the extreme personal distress that she was experiencing.

Nijinsky was the most immediate source of her problems. His difficult behaviour had resumed soon after he had rejoined the company in Spain, when he had begun making violent accusations that Diaghilev was excluding him from the repertory. In Barcelona he had become so disturbed that he had packed his bags and headed for the train station, and had only been coerced into dancing his final performances by threats from the Spanish police.* It was hoped that in South America, with his star privileges guaranteed, Nijinsky would settle, yet to many of the dancers he continued to behave erratically, ordering last-minute changes to the repertory and making inexplicable changes to the casting. For Lydia, as his stage partner, this was obviously irksome but it was Nijinsky's growing hostility towards her

*Under Spanish law he was required to perform all his contracted appearances, or face prosecution.

that was most upsetting. Her privileged position in the company had always rankled with him – she was Randolfo's wife and Diaghilev's favourite – but during this tour he became actively antagonistic, believing that she had entered into a conspiracy with his enemies to injure him and force him off the stage.*

Randolfo meanwhile was exerting all his charm and good humour to coax Nijinsky out of his tortured caprices, although he typically made a self-important drama of his efforts, wringing his hands over every crisis and muttering darkly to anyone who would listen, 'Poor Nijinsky, he's finished for good.' Randolfo was right; it would only be two more years before the dancer would be diagnosed as profoundly schizophrenic. But to Lydia, who could feel the bad blood of suspicion and resentment leaching into her work, Randolfo's diplomatic efforts did little good – in fact, they only exacerbated her irritation with her husband. It seems that Lydia rarely allowed Randolfo to glimpse her growing dissatisfaction with their marriage; his later description of her as 'sweet, decent and generous' suggests she was committed to maintaining the appearance of a loving wife.[15] But conditions on this tour, confining them to unusually harassing close quarters, had made the act harder for Lydia to keep up, and one particular incident seems to have exasperated her beyond endurance. When the Ballets Russes's boat had been stopped en route to Buenos Aires for a routine search for contraband goods, Randolfo had got it into his head that the raid was directed at him and had raced in a panic to hide his wedding certificate, which he was then unable to find again.

Lydia later described this incident to Maynard, long after she knew the full extent of Randolfo's bigamy and understood the reasons for his paranoia. At the time her husband's actions must have seemed at best inexplicably silly, at worst suspicious. If she had ever entertained any doubts about the propriety of her two American 'weddings', they surely came back to haunt her now, and by the time the company arrived at Buenos Aires on 10 September, she was close to breaking point. Pavlova was dancing in the same city and,

*He thought that Grigoriev and others were trying to force him off the stage so that he could then be fined $20,000 for non-performance.

according to her biographer, Keith Money, Lydia went to see her and in tears begged to be taken into her company. The conversation that took place between the two women is not recorded, but we can guess how desperate Lydia felt from the extremity of what she was suggesting. Lydia was beginning to make a habit of bolting from situations that did not work for her, but the consequences of this exit were far-reaching. On a personal level the move would spell an effective end to her marriage, as well as to all the friendships and loyalties that she had established within the Ballets Russes. Professionally it would mean a significant demotion, for Pavlova would certainly not allow Lydia many opportunities to outshine her own ballerina lustre.

It is impossible to know whether Lydia would have gone through with the move, for Pavlova apparently had no job to offer. After this tearful encounter, Lydia thus had no choice but to carry on with the miserable tour, drawing down protective shutters over her depression. The worst of her problems were soon to be resolved, for Nijinksy's own hostility towards the Ballets Russes had so intensified that two weeks later, when they danced their last performance in Buenos Aires, Nijinsky swore that it would be his own last appearance with the company. Lydia would never dance with her damaged partner again, and the next time she saw him, in 1924, he would be too ill to recognise her. All her resentment would be forgotten in the pity and waste of his life. As for her issues with Randolfo, once Lydia and the company had rejoined Diaghilev in Cadiz, marital disillusionment rapidly shrank to a minor concern in comparison with the problems that the Ballets Russes now faced. In the middle of Europe, in the middle of the war, so much was now stacked against them that all members of the company were locked together in a collective struggle for survival.

Diaghilev had been able to secure only a few scattered bookings for their return, the first of which were in Barcelona and Madrid. The dancers had looked forward to returning to these familiar, friendly cities, but when they arrived in Barcelona they found most of the population closeted indoors, traumatised by an influenza epidemic that would shortly be identified as the lethally virulent Spanish flu. A small core of fans ventured out to the Teatro Liceo to watch them perform, but when the company travelled on to Madrid they found a ghost city, with half of the population already sick and the other half having fled to the surrounding countryside. Several of the dancers also became ill, and whilst none of the cases proved fatal, the Ballets Russes felt themselves to be under siege, checking anxiously for the paralysing aches and chills that signalled the onset of infection.

Anxiety stalked them from Russia, too, as news emerged of the Bolshevik coup which on 6 November (26 October OS) had forced Kerensky's provisional government from power and installed Lenin and Trotsky in its place. Even though this second revolution had been virtually bloodless, it represented a violent acceleration of change, as the infant democracy was thrust towards a communist state and all vestiges of the tsarist order were ripped away. (There would, for the dancers, be a particularly piercing symbolism in the fact that Lenin installed his new headquarters in the St Petersburg mansion belonging to Kschessinska, a property that she had bought under Imperial patronage.)

As Lydia and her fellow Russians pored over what tatters of news they could lay hands on, they had no idea what would be left of their theatre or their profession, let alone their families, if they ever managed to find their way back home. Diaghilev, who had kept himself buoyant by assuming that his former patrons in St Petersburg would one day be lavishing support on his company again, feared that he was now cut off from his financial sources for good. There would, he suspected, be no return of the Grand Dukes, and he was correct. During the following months, as estates and palaces were ransacked and Russia cannibalised itself in a bloody civil war, the system that had created the Russian ballet was all but destroyed.

Wearily the dancers packed their trunks to journey on to Lisbon, where Diaghilev had managed to arrange a short season, but they had been only one day in the city when Portugal embarked on its own brief but convulsive revolution. It was a struggle about which the dancers knew nothing – the country's workers and troops had in fact joined forces under the demagogic leader Sidónio Pais to demand the overthrow of the government – but they were trapped in the middle of it. With shells and gunfire ripping through the city, the company were forced to shelter inside their lodgings, with the mattresses torn off their beds for protection. The first day of the fighting was the most dangerous. When Sokolova returned to her bedroom she found that half of her balcony had been shot away and the headboard of her bed was pitted with bullet holes. But even when the two sides had realised that they were shooting at foreign dancers and transferred their fire to more deserving targets, the company remained stranded for another two days. Occasional pot-shots continued to rattle against the windows and Lydia, huddled up with the others, snatching fitful sleep and trying to ignore her empty stomach, may not only have cursed her bad luck in failing to get a job with Pavlova, but also have wondered why she had ever sailed with Diaghilev away from the luxuries and freedoms of New York.

Then, almost as abruptly as the fighting had erupted, Pais declared himself victorious and the dazed company were permitted to start preparing for their performances. By this time, however, neither they nor Lisbon were in a mood for ballet, and when they opened at the echoing, unheated Coliseu dos Recreios, fewer than half the tickets had been sold and the jumpy, dispirited dancers were barely able to perform. Nor was it just cold and exhaustion that afflicted them, for once that season was over, Diaghilev had nothing to give his company. He had no more bookings organised; he did not even have sufficient money to transport the dancers somewhere more comfortable than the now-hateful Portuguese capital.

All he could offer was the vague possibility of a tour around Spain's smaller towns and cities, and in order to arrange this he had to abandon them and travel up to Madrid. This, for Lydia, was the one moment during the war when she was unequivocally grateful to be Randolfo's wife, since as business manager he too was required on the trip, and she was permitted to accompany him. Once in Madrid and under the patronage of King Alfonso, the small Russian party were installed in the luxury of the Palace Hotel, where, close to the Prado, isolated from the worst effects of the Spanish flu, Lydia was able to cram herself, guiltily, with every pleasure that Madrid could offer. For her fellow dancers there were no such privileges. As the days of Diaghilev's absence turned into weeks, all of their remaining cash ran out and they were forced to squash together into cheaper and cheaper *pension* rooms, living on whatever credit they could finagle. It was a chilly, interminable wait, and as the dancers whiled away the time playing poker, it seemed less and less likely that Diaghilev would ever come back to save them. But Alfonso, who now fondly regarded himself as the company's godfather, was able to smooth the planning of this tour, and towards the end of March 1918, money and instructions suddenly arrived in Lisbon for the dancers to travel up to Valladolid, in northern Spain, for their first performance.

In any other circumstances the Ballets Russes might have rebelled against the itinerary that had been arranged for them, an arduous 4,000-kilometre circuit of twenty-seven towns, during which they were required to perform forty-seven shows in two months. They might also have rebelled against the pittance that they were paid: 'Small towns in Spain did not flock to see us,' Lydia drily recalled, 'and we had just enough to pay our hotel bills. The soles of Diaghilev's shoes were worn out.'[16] But the dancers were high on the pleasure of being rescued from Lisbon, and a desperate sense of adventure, even of comedy, crept back into their spirit. Probably their most ridiculous performance took place in the Riojan hill town of Logroño, where they had been unable to transport all their scenery and costumes and had been forced to give a wildly ad hoc performance of *Schéhérazade*. Since only one sword could be found for the slaughter of the harem, Grigoriev, taking on the role of the Shah and wearing Lydia's *Firebird* cap back to front, had had to improvise the ballet's climax, stamping around the stage, waving his sword and muttering to the dancers, 'Die, you fools. Die any where,'[17] while they could barely stand for laughing.

Lydia, restored by her break in Madrid and perhaps shamed into a more stoical acceptance of her situation with Randolfo, seems to have been determinedly bright during this tour. It was with genuine nostalgia that she later described how she and her fellow dancers had 'sipped in the flavours of Spain. In Seville where the choir boys dance a ballet before the high altar the organist priest fell in love with us, allowed us in by ourselves to the dim cathedral and played Bach on the organ.' Even more magical was the memory of a Sevillian café cantante, set among orange groves, where gypsy singers and dancers performed for the Ballets Russes at sunset, with 'undulating grace and indescribable abandon'.[18]

But Spain had only a finite welcome to offer the dancers and by the time the tour reached Barcelona, in May, the Ballets Russes had played in almost every possible venue and squeezed every possible peseta out of the public. Even the sorcerer Diaghilev could not conjure any more bookings, and he knew neither where to go next, nor how to keep his dancers together. When he telegraphed to his friend Misia Edwards in Paris to ask for advice, he had nothing to set against her bleak reply: 'Give it up Serge.'[19]

For the first time in the Ballets Russes's history, Diaghilev was forced to release his dancers from their contracts. Yet even now he would not let them go without a final tug at their loyalties. During the previous October, while the company had been travelling back from South America, Diaghilev had managed to talk his way on to a troop ship that was crossing to England, and had entered discussions with Oswald Stoll, owner of the Coliseum, for a possible season in London. Before the war, Diaghilev would have winced at the humiliation of prostituting his company in a music hall. Now, if he could somehow get his dancers through France and over the Channel, the Coliseum held out his last hope for the Ballets Russes's survival.

That 'if', however, encapsulated a diplomatic and organisational nightmare, for in the summer of 1918, with a new Allied military push in preparation, it was difficult to find a boat or train that had not been commandeered for military use. Even more difficult was securing permission for all the dancers to travel. Lenin and Trotsky's recent signing of the Peace of Brest-Litovsk with Germany meant that the Russians in the company had lost their status as Allied citizens, whilst those from the Ukraine and the Baltic States, now under the control of Germany, were officially enemies. The French Prime Minister, Georges Clemenceau, was so incensed by Russia's betrayal that he refused to let any of its nationals or former dependants set foot in France. Within this stalemate, Diaghilev's only ally was King Alfonso, but while the latter was happy to initiate negotiations through his ambassadors in London and Paris, progress was excruciatingly slow, and Lydia remembered the weeks of stifling heat and uncertainty as among the worst moments of the war. She and Randolfo were in Madrid for part of the time, where they were witness to Big Serge's distress: 'With no money, no contracts and no passports Diaghilev's rich friends were urging him to leave the dancers and come quietly to Paris, he would sit with us for hours in the Park at Madrid, and then say "No I can't do it." '[20] Sokolova was also in Madrid, trying to find medical treatment for her baby daughter (who had been born during the South American tour). Diaghilev, unusually passive, unusually powerless, was peculiarly gentle with Sokolova, entertaining her baby with his monocle in the park and, when she was unable to pay her doctor's fees, taking her to his hotel room, emptying a bag of foreign coins on to the bed and picking out for her a handful of silver. It seemed to be all the money he had left in the world.

The other dancers who were still stranded in Barcelona were also down to their last coins, and theatrical agents began circling around the wounded company to pick off its talent. Fortunately for Diaghilev, the transit visas came through on 29 July and he had lost only a few dancers from the company that Grigoriev was finally able to herd on to the trains for Paris. The Ballets Russes had been permitted just three days to cross France (4–7 August) and even at this stage the itinerary nearly foundered. Diaghilev and Massine, who were travelling separately, were held up for hours at the French border by police, interrogating them about their acquaintance with Mata Hari (who had been accused of spying for the Germans and shot the previous October). When the two men eventually met up with the rest of the company in Paris, it was then discovered that the Ballets Russes's baggage trucks had become detached from the train. More bureaucratic panic ensued as the company sought permission to extend their time in France for an extra week while they waited for their scenery, their costumes and some of their trunks to reach them.

No one welcomed this prolonged stay in Paris, for the city that had so gamely applauded the Ballets Russes on their last visit was now grimy and tense, its shops boarded up, its population cowed by bombing raids and shelling from the Picardy front. It was the closest that the dancers had come to the fighting, apart from the revolutionary spat in Lisbon, and Massine was among several to experience the shock of a bomb blast at close quarters: 'Just as we turned into the rue des Capucines we saw a house receive a direct hit. Its walls and widows burst and splintered in the air and fragments of glass and stone pattered on the roof of our taxi.'[21] During this extra week the dancers struggled to find ration coupons to feed themselves, while Lydia strove too to tend a bedraggled pair of canaries that she had acquired during the Spanish tour and managed to keep with her during the journey through France. She had hoped to meet up with Picasso and Olga in Paris, but the couple were in Biarritz. She found only Stravinsky, who was, coincidentally, staying in the city during the summer.

Finally the baggage caught up with the company and, on 15 August, the dancers took the train from the Gare St-Lazare up to the port of Le Havre. The Channel crossing was the shortest leg of the journey but it was also the most tortuous, for the Germans had booby-trapped stretches of the water with mines. The following day, Lydia was photographed disembarking at Southampton docks. She had attempted to put on a show of jaunty insouciance for the camera: dressed in a striped, tailored suit, her eyes pencilled in kohl, her body sharpened by months of privation, she looked untypically glamorous, even foxy. However, her subsequent comment to reporters would betray how traumatic the last few days had been: 'I did not like the terrible journey,' she said simply. 'I thought we were never going to get here.'[22]

Chapter Eight

LONDON

> It was the grace, pathos, entrancing cleverness, the true comic genius and liveliness of a dancer new to this country, Lydia Lopokova, which made the chief impression. Her face was ... inquisitive, bird-like, that of a mask of comedy; while being an artist in everything she comprehended exactly the strengths and limits of her capacities; the personification of gaiety and spontaneity and of that particular pathos which is its complement ... Her wit entered into every gesture, into everything she did.
>
> OSBERT SITWELL[1]

When Lydia arrived in Britain, she was too scared and exhausted to see beyond the fact that this hazardous Channel crossing had delivered her and her colleagues to safety, as well as to a few precious weeks of paid work. She also had few expectations of London, which after four years of war was rumoured to be a dirty, defeated shadow of itself – wasted by Zeppelin raids, casualty figures and rationing. Yet everything about the city pleased and surprised her. Its Northern light raised nostalgic echoes of St Petersburg, whilst a gallant spirit of defiance seemed tangible on its streets, prompting Lydia to inform reporters, somewhat extravagantly, that London was the 'most cheerful city' that she had visited during the entire war, and that she could not believe the abundance of goods in the shops, singling out, for some reason, the cheapness of the coal and the stoutness of the boots.[2] Even more delightful to Lydia was the discovery that she was to be accommodated in almost pre-war levels of luxury, for in a rapid restoration of company hierarchy, the junior dancers were all dispatched to cheap lodging houses in Soho, whilst she and the rest of Diaghilev's inner circle were booked into the Savoy Hotel. Here, with all the pre-war luxuries of fine linen and attentive staff, it was not surprising that Lydia felt optimistic. And in these pampered surroundings she also seems to have softened even more towards her husband. During that autumn, Randolfo was to be seen in Lydia's dressing room after every performance, impressing visitors like Maynard Keynes and the painter Duncan Grant as an engagingly attentive husband and genial host. And according to the critic Cyril Beaumont – who struck up an early friendship with Randolfo – Lydia and her husband appeared to be a perfectly contented and domestic couple.

Most crucial to Lydia's happiness, however, was the prospect of work. She had been offstage for nearly three months and, whilst she and the other dancers had managed to improvise classes in hotel rooms and train corridors, they were feeling an acute sense of physical frustration, craving the adrenalin of performance. Diaghilev, in private, was worried that his dancers might not have recovered their form in time for the season's opening. The only rehearsal space that Grigoriev had been able to find was a grubby, abandoned club room in Shaftesbury Avenue, with barely room to drill the dancers back into a disciplined ensemble. At the same time, Diaghilev was brooding over the humiliation of presenting the Ballets Russes in a music-hall programme, sandwiched, as he lamented, between performing dogs and acrobats. Despite the Italianate grandeur of Frank Matcham's auditorium at the Coliseum, Diaghilev remained convinced that some taint of working-class culture would attach itself to his dancers, and he insisted that the thousands of sequins decorating the theatre's drop curtain be removed (it took a crowd of women most of a weekend) as well as demanding that a new lighting rig* be installed.

But the timing of the season ensured that Diaghilev's fears were groundless. Over the summer there had been a massive Allied assault

*Diaghilev was ahead of his time in understanding the poetics of lighting. He understood how crucial it was to have the dancers lit from the right angle, and to use colour filters to create flattering definition and tone.

against the Germans, and the British public were finally permitting themselves to believe that victory was in view. The arrival of the Ballets Russes, with their bright, stinging, theatrical colours, was a premonition of the end; the advent of 'pure beauty', wrote Aldous Huxley, 'like a glimpse into another world'.[3] Although the company were dancing only two ballets a day, sharing the matinée and evening programmes with a changing cast of music-hall acts, their Coliseum debut was nothing like the mortification that Diaghilev had feared. On 5 September, when the company opened with *Cléopâtre* and *Les Femmes de bonne humeur* (Anglicised for British audiences to *The Good-Humoured Ladies*), the Ballet Russes's pre-war patrons, including Lady Ottoline Morrell, Lady Cunard and the Sitwell brothers, were all in the audience. So too were the national and regional press, and their response gave Lydia her first glimpse of the intensity with which London would take her to its collective heart. If her dancing in the solo Bacchanale in *Cléopâtre* was praised for its 'electrifying' vitality, her performance of Mariuccia set her on track to becoming a cult.

For the British public, this role distilled all that was most singular in Lydia's talent, just as *Spectre de la Rose* had defined the genius of Nijinsky before the war; and Osbert Sitwell was not alone in hailing her as the revelation of this 1918 season. Cyril Beaumont, too, judged Lydia to have brought something new, but essential, to the Ballets Russes. Initially he had found her a 'complete surprise' after Karsavina's classical gravity: 'as lively as a London sparrow … she danced with her head, her eyes, her shoulders and even her lips'. But it had taken him only a couple of performances to appreciate the layers of intelligence and tradition that underpinned her animation: 'if she played the part of a soubrette it was not a modern conception clothed in historical costume: her soubrette had a mellow quality, the glaze of a past epoch, a suggestion of period graces which gave a final touch to her performance'.[4]

Beaumont's fascination found its voice in numerous published reviews, and in an early, lavishly illustrated monograph on Lydia's career.* But he was also able to study her offstage, as Randolfo,

***The Art of Lydia Lopokova* was published in 1920 and illustrated by ten album plates, plus reproductions of portraits by Picasso and Glyn Philpot. Lydia also demonstrated various steps and poses for a book that Beaumont planned to write about Cecchetti's teaching method.

having met Beaumont at his bookshop in Charing Cross Road, had affably offered him an open invitation to visit Lydia after performances. The Coliseum's 'number 1' dressing room had, within days of her occupation, become a vivid, untidy space, its chairs strewn with discarded shoes, its walls hung with sketches by Laura Knight, who was one of several British artists to hang around the Russian ballet this season.* Beaumont, a scholarly little man with thick spectacles and an abrupt brush of auburn hair, was more than content to simply absorb the dressing room's atmosphere, standing quietly as other fans were ushered in from the tiled corridor, admiring Randolfo's polyglot charm as he offered greetings in English, Russian or French, observing Lydia's smiles as she acknowledged her compliments.

The reward for Beaumont's patience came later, when he was invited by Randolfo back to the Savoy and in the intimacy of their suite was allowed to watch Lydia relax, brewing up cups of hot chocolate, scattering breadcrumbs for her two canaries. He studied her with the same dedicated attention he brought to the theatre, memorising every scrap of information about her life and career and noting for his later memoirs the capricious, occasionally indecipherable volatility of her mood. 'She had a vivacious manner, alternating with moods of sadness ... and a habit of making a profound remark as though it were the merest badinage.'[5] Respectfully, and silently, Kyril, as Lydia began affectionately to call Beaumont, seems to have fallen in love.

The British press expressed their own fascination with Lydia in a barrage of profiles and portraits. London had been starved of foreign visitors during the war, and Lydia could not have scrubbed up more obligingly for the part, chattering fluently to journalists about her extraordinary, itinerant life and responding to their compliments about her English with the boast that she had practised with the best – Shakespeare and the Romantic poets. What the British prized most about Lydia, however, was her easy normality. Spotting her in an old frock and a tam-o'-shanter as she walked back to the hotel from the theatre, or discovering that she had slipped among them at

*Early in 1919, Knight began to use Lydia's dressing room as a studio, and over the next four years produced many sketches and oil paintings of her, several of which were published in a 1920 portfolio, *Twenty-One Drawings of the Russian Ballet*.

the Coliseum and was laughing riotously at one of Stoll's latest comic acts, made Lydia very endearing to her new public.

They liked it even better when her ballerina image slipped on stage, for despite her meticulous training at the Theatre School, Lydia was impatiently, inherently sloppy about her stage wardrobe and frequently ended up dancing with a shoe ribbon trailing, or her clothes half buttoned. She knew, guiltily, that it exposed her dresser to Diaghilev's abuse, but she discovered in London that her untidiness might also add to her charm. Before one performance of *Sylphides* she had failed to secure her underwear properly and, according to Sokolova, when she began to perform a series of *relevés* in arabesque, 'her raised leg fell lower and lower; then to everyone's surprise she stopped, tucked her hand under her costume and stepped out of a pair of tarlatan drawers'.[6] In such a purely ethereal ballet this should have been a disaster. But Lydia not only carried off the incident with a grin, throwing her drawers into the wings and continuing as if nothing had happened, but also knew how to make theatrical capital from it. The performance became legendary, and the fact that similar 'accidents' recurred made some of Lydia's colleagues suspect that she occasionally engineered them deliberately.

It was incidents like these that made London in 1918 adopt Lydia as one of their own and christen her with the peculiarly British nickname Loppie. The public she was dancing for had changed from Diaghilev's pre-war audience; for while the 'kid glove and tiara' set still sat in the expensive seats at the Coliseum, low-priced tickets in the upper galleries allowed a younger and more demonstrative crowd to lay claim to the Russian ballet. These new devotees were often raucously loyal to their favourite dancers, some so rowdy that they had to be removed from the theatre by force. Others worshipped the ballet with a more religious fervour – 'gaunt angular women', as Cecil Beaton would later caricature this breed of enthusiasts, 'with lank, untidy, bobbed hair and shapeless clothes and red-bearded ballet maniacs who would think nothing of waiting ten to fifteen hours in the rain for a seat'.[7] Lydia received many earnest tokens from such admirers: poems, pictures, and dozens of letters were regularly delivered to her dressing room. But if their adoration could be tortuous –

a fan letter, written from Chelsea in July 1922, informed her, 'as yours is the greatest of all dancing so you are a benefactress of humanity and you belong to humanity' – it was the fervour of these 'galerites', as Lydia called them, that contributed to the Coliseum season becoming a pivotal moment for her.[8] During the following decade Lydia would dance in London more than in any other city. Becoming Britain's favourite ballerina, she would come to think of herself as almost British.

Diaghilev in 1918 wasted no opportunity to exploit Lydia's popularity and there was barely a performance in which she did not dance during the autumn, reprising much of her old repertory, and on 21 November premièring a short solo that Massine had choreographed for her in his 1915 ballet *Soleil de nuit*. Such was her draw at the box office that Stoll threatened to cancel the Ballets Russes's entire season when some financial spat between her and Diaghilev (its details unspecified in the press reports) put Lydia's casting temporarily in jeopardy. But she was also working hard to deserve her exposure. After Christmas, Stoll extended the Coliseum season for a further three months and she took advantage of this settled interlude by beginning serious remedial work with Cecchetti, honing her technique on the analytic rigour of teaching – and in the process earning herself a rare instance of his praise. (A photograph he gave to Lydia at this time was inscribed with congratulations on her 'véritables grandes progrès'.)

The Maestro had set up his own teaching studio in Soho, and every morning at nine Lydia braved the rats and the shabby membership of the British Bolshevik Society, who also shared the building, to take her morning class. By this stage in her career she had formed a deep, private preference for studying alone, although she did not apparently object when a young Irish dancer, Ninette de Valois, slipped in before her own class with Cecchetti to watch. The 21-year-old de Valois – who would later become a close friend of Lydia's and still later would found the Royal Ballet – was then an impressed and impressionable acolyte, studying with enormous interest the technique of this internationally famous ballerina who 'jumped like a gazelle, giggled like a school girl, and dramatised and projected every movement'.[9] Like Beaumont, de Valois was also fascinated by Lydia's temperament and would later struggle in her memoirs to analyse its volatile shifts:

> Her face had a grave sincerity, but when she laughed it was transformed; she suddenly resembled a hilarious cherub ... when Lopokova laughed she willed that the world laughed with her. Cecchetti would shout and scold at this diminutive dynamo and she would regard him, her small oval face fairly drooping with the gravity of the situation ... then suddenly the air would be rent asunder by a peal of merriment that reduced the old Maestro to the growls of a distant ineffectual thunderstorm.[10]

A less captivated observer of Lydia's power was Massine, who since Nijinsky's departure had been cast much more regularly as her partner. Nothing delighted the gallery fans better than seeing the two on stage together, Massine's supple brilliance heightening Lydia's effervescence. However, it was during this London season that the dancers' own pleasure in each other began to waver. The more acclaim Massine enjoyed, the more resentful he became of Lydia's seniority, and she was made uncomfortably aware of this when the two of them were invited to perform in a charity gala together. Lydia, as Diaghilev's premier ballerina, had had her name printed not only above Massine's on the poster, but in larger type, and when Massine had seen this he had taken mortal offence. In an unsettling echo of Nijinsky's tantrums, he had locked himself in his dressing room and only after the combined pleadings of Diaghilev and Grigoriev had he emerged in time to go on stage. Lydia might revere Massine's gifts as a choreographer – indeed, her career had come to depend on them – but she would not tolerate his vanity as a dancer, and she was sufficiently malicious to needle him a little. She knew, for instance, that Massine was mortified by the less-than-perfect classical line of his legs, a slight curvature that he made assiduous attempts to disguise with specially sewn trousers and tights. It used to infuriate Diaghilev, who complained, 'He has a pair of handsome eyes and bandy legs,'[11] and during the winter of 1918–19, Lydia would not have been above reminding her partner of that fact.

Yet balletomania was so much in vogue during this season that

Signed pictures of Enrico Cecchetti and Cyril Beaumont, London, 1919 and 1926

there was little reason for Lydia, Massine or any of Diaghilev's other principals to squabble for their share of applause. Nor did they have to squabble over the social invitations that had begun to snow down on them after the end of the war was finally declared. When London had celebrated victory on 11 November, it had been a revelation to the Russian dancers as they watched chanting, drunken crowds spilling out of every pub and down every street. Lydia, after dining with the fashionable Sitwell siblings, had ended up at the Adelphi Hotel at a party given by the wealthy art collector Montague Shearman. Most of artistic and intellectual London was present – Augustus John, D. H. Lawrence, Lytton Strachey, Roger Fry, Virginia Woolf, and Vanessa and Clive Bell – and as the dancing grew hot and riotous the millionaire Henry Mond had played the pianola stripped to his vest and with champagne being poured over his head.

These Armistice celebrations, releasing four years of nerves and frustration, set the tone for a winter of partying, during which Diaghilev and his dancers were predictably courted as guest attractions. Russia had suddenly become very fashionable in London, as the stream of refugees escaping from the civil war had generated a craze for Russian cigarettes, Russian clothes, Russian artists and Russian art. The Ballets Russes had never been more chic, and among their most eager hostesses was Ottoline Morrell, who, having been one of Diaghilev's most loyal patrons before the war, was once again determined to stake her claim.

This tall, effusive woman was, after her own fashion, more audaciously original in pursuit of her social career than anyone Lydia had encountered in Paris or America. With her beaky features recklessly dramatised by cosmetics, Morrell at forty-five still made it her duty to turn life into a daily fantasy, dressing for breakfast as a Russian Cossack, in red boots, silk tunic and astrakhan hat; setting out for a walk resplendent in crinoline, pearls and high heels; staging magnificent parties in which the aristocracy of Belgravia mingled with the artists of bohemia. The better to pursue the Ballets Russes, Morrell had taken rooms at the Garlands Hotel, a short walk from the Coliseum, where she invited the company to take refreshments between their matinée and evening shows. For many of the dancers the lure was simply Morrell's inexhaustible supply of treats, especially the blackcurrant jam she served with excellent Russian tea. But Lydia, with her fluent English, was also drawn by the conversation, as London's novelists, painters, musicians and intellectuals drifted through Morrell's tea parties that winter, curious to catch a glimpse of her ballet guests.

Some of these Lydia learned to identify as core members of the Bloomsbury Group, known to their intimates simply as Bloomsbury, a tight-knit, influential circle of artists and writers who had become unofficial arbiters of cultural London. Before the war Bloomsbury had kept their distance from the Ballets Russes – inclined to dismiss the repertory as a glamorous novelty even while acknowledging the dancers to be spectacularly gifted; but the new Massine ballets interested them very much, as did the company's links to leaders of the European avant-garde like Picasso and Cocteau. Enthusiastically the group recast Diaghilev's post-war company as a forum for modernist art, admiring the Futurist-inspired designs of Larionov and Gontcharova, and hailing Massine's innovations in animating the human figure and its relation to the stage. The serious magazines

English Review, *Burlington*, *Dial* and *Athenaeum* reflected this interest, so that by the spring of 1919 it had become commonplace to read the bylines of writers like Rebecca West and Ezra Pound attached to ballet reviews, and to see T. S. Eliot or the art critic Roger Fry in regular attendance at Diaghilev's performances.

It was also increasingly common to see such writers out and about in the company of dancers and, for Lydia, one consequence of her association with artistic London was that her social life acquired a new literary profile. Many of her acquaintances were busy diarists and correspondents, and if her movements before the war were often hard to track, in post-war London they came into lively focus. We can read of Mark Gertler, the painter, giving imitations of Lydia in her dressing room as she was visited by a succession of distinguished guests. We can read of her at a party given by the Sitwell brothers, where she fell in love with their collection of stuffed lovebirds and begged to be given the gaudiest, which she had nicknamed Pimp. It was also where the novelist Virginia Woolf painted pen portraits of her fellow guests: Ottoline Morrell 'brilliantly painted and garish as a ship wreck'; and Edith Sitwell 'a very tall young woman wearing a permanently startled expression, & curiously finished off with a high green silk headdress concealing her hair'.[12]

Also frequenting the Sitwells was Maynard Keynes, a conventional-looking man within this bohemian circle, who despite the mercurial brilliance of his intellect preferred the social camouflage of dark business suits and formal evening dress. His first reaction to Lydia and her dancing had been disobligingly negative. Watching an early performance of *The Good-Humoured Ladies*, he had complained to Duncan Grant that Lydia seemed a 'poor' substitute for Karsavina;[13] to his friend the stockbroker Foxy Falk he had grumbled: 'She's a rotten dancer – she has such a stiff bottom.'[14] This was the first and only time that Lydia received this particular criticism, but Maynard never claimed to have an expert eye. By 20 September he had cheerfully reversed his view and was hurrying backstage with Grant to join the line of admirers paying court. Speaking for both men, Grant described to Vanessa Bell how delightful 'Madame Lapohkova' had been. Dressed in a kimono, with most of her stage make-up still on, including the blue eyebrows that she had painted on for *La Princesse enchantée*, she had been 'absolutely charming without any sort of sham feelings and perfect manners and very pretty and intelligent looking'.[15]

A month later Maynard was again visiting Lydia's dressing room. He and the painter Edward Wolfe had been hoping for an introduction to the tiny virtuoso Stanislas Idzikowski, who had been her partner, but it was Lydia, in an entertainingly malicious mood, who dominated the encounter. She confided to her visitors, 'I don't like dancing with [Idzikowski]. It is not nice to dance with something only up to your breasts and I am always afraid he will drop me.'[16] And if Maynard and Wolfe were disconcerted by this rudeness about a man who they had been led to understand was 'the new Nijinsky', they were even more thrown by Lydia's mischievous invitation to 'pinch' her legs to see how strong they were, which, Maynard reported to Grant, 'we did very shyly'.[17]

When the mood took Lydia she could be a shameless flirt. Whilst she stuck to her own idiosyncratic code of sexual conduct (within her few love affairs she had always been discreet and, by her own lights, kind), she enjoyed testing her now considerable powers of attraction. To these British men she presented an exotic combination of childlike candour and ballerina grace, of implied sexual experience and wit. Quentin Bell, Clive's son, who grew up in Bloomsbury, would later judge Lydia to be 'really impressive ... her natural sincerity, her gaiety, her complete lack of side, could make an evening ... not merely delightful but instructive'.[18] Maynard, in Lydia's dressing room, may have worried that his friend Clive Bell, an enthusiastic connoisseur of women's bodies, could have done the offer of a pinch better justice, but he had been quick to claim Lydia's acquaintance when he saw her again at the Sitwells' house and at Shearman's Armistice party. When he sent Lydia a book for Christmas in token of his admiration, he was also careful to preserve the note of thanks that she sent in return, penned in a huge, scrawling, spidery hand, quaintly misspelled and quaintly formal in its efforts to master English etiquette: 'The book was most welcommed and I appreciated indeed your charming thought.'[19]

Lydia's note was the starting point of a correspondence that would eventually amount to hundreds, even thousands, of letters; however, at this point neither she nor Maynard had any premonition of the love affair that would unite them in three years' time. After the New Year, Lydia was probably working too hard to register Maynard's departure as he was sent to Paris as chief Treasury representative at the post-war Peace Conference. In the early spring of 1919 she and the company were distracted by the tragedy of Nijinsky, who had been diagnosed in Switzerland as clinically insane and had had to be admitted to an asylum. Lydia's own schedule became still more demanding at the end of April when Stoll transferred the Ballets Russes from the music-hall stage of the Coliseum to the Alhambra, where they could finally perform full programmes of ballet.

For Lydia this move added *Firebird** and *Petrushka* to her London repertory; it also meant that she could perform her much-publicised debut in Massine's new ballet *La Boutique fantasque*. This was another of Massine's works in which the naivety of the plot was in inverse proportion to the sophistication of its means. Set in a toyshop, it told the story of a pair of can-can dolls who, deeply in love with one another, prefer to run away from the store rather than face being sold off to separate customers. What sounded as innocent as *Coppélia* or *Nutcracker*, however, was a satirical, fantastical romance. Massine's visual models for his new ballet had been the dispassionately observed dolls in Seurat's painting *Le Cirque* and the grubby theatre world of Toulouse-Lautrec. Choreographically he had been inspired by the folk and flamenco dancing that he had seen in Spain, with its choppy, staccato footwork; and the style of his characterisation had been an extension of the caricaturing wit of *The Good-Humoured Ladies*. The dancing toys were never cute but deviantly quirky, whilst the human customers were reduced to almost forensic cartoons, divided by national stereotype into a fat Russian merchant couple, a fastidious Englishman and a crude American family.

Massine had worked closely with each dancer on the creation of their roles, but with Lydia and himself dancing the two can-can dolls, their collaboration had been especially intimate. 'Lopokova

*In *The Firebird*, Lydia received her first mildly negative reviews. Even Beaumont felt that she was less convincing than Karsavina, though when he made the mistake of expressing his views, Lydia made him suffer: 'If she happened to see me,' he recalled, 'she would often ask with a wickedly assumed anxiety, *was I better tonight*.'

knew instinctively the effect I was aiming at,' he later wrote, 'and without a word from me would speed up her kicks or tilt her head coquettishly in response to my sinuous movements.'[20] For Lydia herself this creative involvement was heady, far more so than when she had premièred the role of Mariuccia. Forgetting all the recent niggles that she had had with Massine over publicity and applause, she loved the choreographer for giving her a role that she could own from scratch, a character that had been made directly out of her body, her personality and her imagination.

The public were clearly expecting something extraordinary, for when Beaumont arrived on the night of 5 June he watched with wonderment as crowds streamed in to fill every seat and every inch of standing room. From the moment the curtain rose, the ballet's success was not an issue. Each new number elicited rowdy applause, and when Lydia and Massine danced their climactic can-can the audience began screaming and chanting their names. According to Beaumont, Lydia, in a pale blue dress, trimmed with bows and garlanded with flowers, bore an unnerving resemblance to a doll. '[With] her rounded limbs, plump features, curved lips and ingenuous expression, you could easily imagine her speaking *Ma-ma! Pa-Pa!*'[21] By her side, Massine cut an even more extraordinary figure, part Chaplinesque clown, part sinister rake, with a dead-white face and a greasy sheen to his curly hair and moustache. Out of this incongruous couple Massine had created an oddly touching pair of lovers. Beaumont felt that the true heart of the ballet was revealed when the couple heard of their impending separation and Lydia's doll gazed at Massine's 'with a look of ineffable love, which seemed to light up her whole face'.[22] The transfixing showpiece, however, was their can-can duet, which came, as Beaumont wrote, out of nowhere. Lydia herself stood quietly, 'stiff, inanimate as a china doll', until the bang of a drum transformed her 'into a Bacchanalian fury'. 'Her body bends and sways as though fashioned of India rubber, her foot leaps above her head, wrists twist, turns revolve amidst a sea of foaming lace and ribbon.' He concluded, 'It is a thing of delirious joy leaving not a trace of the vulgarity that it might obtain were it performed by a lesser artist'[23] – although Lydia later complained that the exuberant splits on which she ended her solo 'nearly cut me in two pieces'.[24]

Left: Picasso drawing of Lydia and Massine as can-can dancers. *Right:* Lydia and Massine, can-can dancers, *La Boutique fantasque*, London, 1919

This energy does not, disappointingly, come across in the posed publicity photos of *Boutique*. But Picasso, newly arrived in London with Olga, had been drawing Lydia and Massine in the studio, and from the swooping, sensuous lines of these sketches it is evident how devilishly the two dancers sparked off each other. Although Diaghilev had at first made cruel demurrals about Massine dancing the lead role (carping as always about the defective line of his legs), the choreographer had known exactly how to showcase his own and Lydia's gifts. The can-can became their mutual signature piece, and no one, according to Sokolova, ever danced it with 'quite the same accent and flavour'. As with most of Massine's work, Sokolova believed that *Boutique* became 'in a way *lost*' once it was separated from its original cast.[25]

On its debut in June 1919 the ballet was so successful that *Vogue* considered it to have become a 'popular cult',[26] whilst the British critics judged it to be the most intriguingly modernist work that they had yet seen from Diaghilev. Roger Fry claimed that André Derain's post-impressionist re-creation of the ballet's Victorian setting had refracted 'the artistic expressions of the past' into a brilliantly contemporary aesthetic.[27] Clive Bell argued that Massine's choreography had, at a stroke, revolutionised the art of ballet.

Bell devoted an entire essay to this claim, and the terms in which he framed it were a measure of how seriously Russian ballet was now regarded in London. Like the rest of Bloomsbury, Bell took it as axiomatic that art could no longer limit itself to surface representation; rather it should aim to reveal the underlying form and dynamism of its subject matter. This, he argued, Massine had uniquely achieved in ballet. Just as painters in 1918 were focussing on texture, colour and the rhythm of line, and writers were experimenting with language and narrative, so, he claimed, Massine had arrived at a new structural essence in choreography. In contrast to Fokine's naturalistic methods in *Petrushka*, Massine had 'emptied' the characters in *Boutique* of their 'superfluous humanity' and in so doing had created a ballet that was 'more of a work of art and infinitely more dramatic' than any of its predecessors, putting it on the 'level of literature music and the graphic arts ... detached from circumstances and significant in itself'.[28]

At its core, however, Bell's essay had been less a comparison of choreographic styles than a love letter to Lydia, for he asserted that it had been her performance that secured this essential quality of detachment in *Boutique*. Unlike Pavlova and Karsavina's generation, Lydia exemplified a new breed of stage artists, who did not communicate their personalities directly to the public but 'transmuted' them into the work as a whole. For Bell the essential illustration of the modern dancer was 'little Lopokova bouncing in her box, making vivid contacts with every line and colour on the stage, impressing her personality on each gesture of her own and so helping build up an organised whole'.[29]

Bell was not alone in elevating his favourite ballet dancer on the pedestal of critical theory. T. S. Eliot would later do the same in arguing that Massine embodied all that was 'most completely unhuman, impersonal, abstract' on the stage.* However, it is hard not to feel that Bell overstated his case. Lydia herself would have agreed

---

*Massine's dancing paralleled Eliot's concept of the pure 'objective correlative' in literature. In contrast to the 'conventional [stage] gesture which is supposed to *express* emotion', Eliot praised 'the abstract gesture of Massine, which *symbolises* emotion'. ('Dramatis Personae', *Criterion*, April 1923.)

that in *Boutique* she occupied the stage in a manner very different from a classical ballerina, who can, as she put it, 'shine and twinkle and radiate without limitations'.[30] Yet Bell's description contradicts all those anecdotal reports of Lydia kicking off her knickers mid-*Sylphides*, or seducing audiences with her luminous grin. Out of all her generation, Lydia enjoyed an extraordinarily complicit relationship with her public – it was the premise on which her celebrity was erected, the factor that allowed her to shine even in second-rate material.

On the other hand, Bell had stumbled part-way towards a paradox that lay at the heart of Lydia's style. While she might be the most consummate entertainer in Diaghilev's company, there was a lack of apparent self-consciousness or self-regard in her performances, which made them seem mysteriously instinctive. Lydia at her most sparkling could also be unfathomable. Beaumont too had been fascinated by this contradiction, but unlike Bell he had seen enough of Lydia to be fascinated still more by the enigma that she presented offstage. Initially he had noticed only the layer of seriousness that underpinned her gaiety, or the occasional shadow of melancholy, which he attributed to her long exile from home, or to the exigencies of a ballerina's temperament. But by the New Year he also realised that Lydia's marriage to Randolfo was not as happy as he had first believed, and in the months that followed, he felt that she was exhibiting signs of a deepening depression. Alone, in her dressing room, he observed that she 'would sometimes lean back in her chair, a wave of weariness would pass over her features and she would murmur half-plaintively *Kak yah oustala* (How tired I am)'.[31] Even after the première of *Boutique*, when Lydia was being plied with ovations and flowers and should have been exultant, she appeared to be 'half crying ... divided between sadness and delight'.[32]

Beaumont, innocent of the full history between Lydia and Randolfo, may have assumed that she was partly reacting to the stress of work. During the previous ten months Lydia had been dancing an unnaturally heavy schedule, and the strain had been intensified by a series of petty squabbles over money and casting. One innocent catalyst of these disputes had been Tamara Karsavina, who had recently sent word of her arrival in England and her desire to rejoin the

Ballets Russes. Karsavina had been trapped, with her English diplomat husband and small child, through the violent uncertainties of the Russian Revolution and the civil war, and of course her fellow dancers, including Lydia, applauded her safe arrival, but the fondness of their welcome was also muddied by professional pique, for a delighted Diaghilev immediately began offering his 'Tata' her pick of the principal roles. According to Ansermet,[33] Lydia and Tchernicheva had both been badly affected, and were quarrelling crossly over the reallocation of their repertory.

The watchful Beaumont had not presumed to press Lydia for confidences; and he had simply noted the disintegration of her mood with concern. He certainly had no idea that Lydia, under stress, was drifting back to her old patterns of withdrawal, and denial. She had begun seeking consolation for her unsatisfactory marriage with another new lover, and at the same time she was building up to yet another dramatic exit from her career. On Thursday 10 July, just five weeks after her triumphant première in *Boutique*, it was noticed that Lydia had failed to sign in at the theatre for her evening show. A search party was rapidly dispatched to the Savoy, and the discovery that most of her belongings were still in the room, coupled with a message left by Randolfo for the Alhambra's manager that he had 'gone to the Continent'[34] to attend to urgent affairs, led everyone to assume that she had decided to accompany her husband on some kind of brief business trip.

But Grigoriev then found a terse note from Lydia, which informed him that 'For reasons of health I shall be unable, from today, to appear with the ballet.'[35] Having noticed no signs of ill health in Lydia, the regisseur had no idea how seriously he should take her message, but the arrival of a panicked telegram from Diaghilev, who was in Paris on business, confirmed its gravity. He himself had just received a letter from Lydia, miserable and defensively formal, in which she had declared categorically that she was unfit to dance for the rest of the season, or perhaps ever again:

> Recently, for reasons of a personal nature, I have had a nervous breakdown so serious that only with difficulty was I able to get through the performances at the end of last week and of the current

> week, and, in particular, of yesterday. Under the circumstances, in order not to overstrain myself irreparably I shall literally be unable henceforward to take part in performances not only today, but on subsequent days generally. I very much regret that on the basis of the final clauses of our contract, my agreement with you will be terminated by this but I am consoled by the thought that my departure from the troupe now only a few days before the end of the season will pass wholly unnoticed.[36]

This last sentiment was of course absurd, for as soon as Lydia failed to appear on stage, the press were baying for news. Banner headlines 'Famous Ballerina Vanishes' were splashed over newspaper hoardings, and rumours began to fly around that Lydia had not just run away from the stage, but was in the middle of a marital scandal, having eloped with a Russian officer and caused her cuckolded husband to flee the country in despair. By the Saturday, rumour had tracked Randolfo to Rome, and Lydia and her officer to St John's Wood, where it was said the couple were hiding out with Russian friends. Virginia Woolf wrote with gossipy avidity to her sister Vanessa Bell on 17 July, demanding the latest news: 'I wish you'd explain to me the truth about Lopokova. Did she run away – and with whom – and why – and where is she? Mrs Hamilton pretended to know for certain she was ill in a villa in St Johns Wood. But dear old Molly Hamilton has a temperamental lust for the commonplace.'[37]

For over a week the company refused to respond to any of the rumours or gratify any requests for information, beyond maintaining the official line that Lydia was simply too exhausted to finish the season. When interviewed for the *Observer*, Diaghilev claimed it was 'not to be wondered at that she is suffering from fatigue after nearly a year of continuous dancing' – although he was sufficiently angry to add sarcastically, 'Many of the other dancers might also discover that they had the same reason for being ill if it were not for their intense anxiety to continue to give pleasure to the public.'[38]

Yet Diaghilev was obviously expecting that Lydia could be brought around for a few days later, on 26 July, he wrote a short but friendly note to her:

Going away for some days and would like to see you. Please name time & place where I could meet you today, tomorrow or the day after.

I hope that you are feeling better now after your emotional upheavals.

Affectionate greetings

Sergei Pavlovich[39]

Her reply, that same day, brought him no comfort:

Kind Sergei Pavlovich!

Thank you for your concern. I do feel a little better, but of course my decision to leave the stage is unchanged. You probably know that I have applied for a divorce and as soon as I receive it, I will be getting married to general Martynov. We will be leaving soon for Russia. I hope that somehow if you are passing by in Russia, you will not forget to look in on us.[40]

Chapter Nine

VANISHING SECRETS

Dancer May Cost Ballet Million.

HEADLINE IN *VARIETY*, 16 JULY 1919

Lydia's breezily censored note may have been more aggravating to Diaghilev than anything else she had inflicted on him. Just a few days earlier she had been claiming that extreme ill health had forced her to disappoint her public and throw the Ballets Russes box office into turmoil. Now, apparently having made a full recovery, Lydia was talking of running off to Russia with a new lover, about whom neither he nor Grigoriev knew a single thing.

Diaghilev had had long experience of the strength and secretiveness of Lydia's impulses. He had made her a star in Paris, only to have her suddenly sail away to America; he had watched her abandon Heywood and marry Randolfo without a flicker of disclosure to the outside world. But she had concealed this affair with General Martynov so effectively that, even after she had eloped with him, most of her colleagues were still ignorant of his character, his history or even his full name. When Ernest Ansermet wrote to tell Stravinsky about Lydia's flight, all the information that he could offer was that a 'young officer' had apparently 'taken possession' of her heart.[1]

The very few who might have guessed more about the affair did not choose to reveal it, for secrets were respected within the tight factions of the Ballets Russes. Sokolova, for instance, had known that a pair of Russian officers had been hanging around Lydia and her ballerina rival Tchernicheva; she had also witnessed a drunken argument when her own husband, Kremnev, had accused Randolfo and

Grigoriev of acting as pimps between the officers and their wives. But since Sokolova claimed to know of no connection between this 'appalling scene' and Lydia's subsequent disappearance, we have no idea whether either one of these Russian officers was her general.[2]

So reticent were those few people in whom Lydia may have confided, and so stubborn her own refusal to go public, that even today Martynov remains an enigma. The man for whom Lydia was willing to throw up her career, her security and all her friends has remained a virtual blank. Years afterwards, two or three scattered references to 'the general' would appear in Lydia's correspondence with Maynard, which cast him as a solitary figure, poor and a little bit mad, with ambitions to write and a vague ambition to emigrate to America.* An even more tantalising reference cropped up in 1935 when Lydia wrote of discovering a pair of the general's tortoiseshell spectacles in one of her old trunks.

None of these details, however, gives us a clue to a personality, let alone a life.

If Martynov was indeed a Russian general, then the most likely explanation for his being in London was that he was among the thousands of formerly loyal tsarists fleeing the civil war. Police records were kept of all such émigrés, and at some time all of his details would have been listed. Frustratingly, though, most of the files have long since been destroyed, and there are no Martynovs listed in any that survive. Nor does Lydia's general appear in other British documents from this period; among the various Martyns and Martinoffs who are registered as having given birth, married or emigrated, none fits Martynov's profile. Even the Russian files do not help, since without knowledge of his full name or confirmed proof of his military rank, this Martynov cannot be definitively identified. He was certainly not the more famous Martynov who served in the Russian army during the First World War and during the 1920s became one of Stalin's leading political theorists. Even if this general could be placed in England in 1919, at the age of fifty-four he would hardly have fitted Ansermet's description of a 'young officer'.

But the general's identity is not the only mystery in this episode,

*A few Martynovs were also listed as American immigrants at this time, but it is impossible to know whether any one of them was Lydia's general.

for the circumstances leading up to Lydia's final break from Randolfo remain equally hard to interpret. The latter's own version of events, which he recounted in a rambling letter to Diaghilev soon after he had fled to Rome, was predictably self-serving. There had, he blustered, been nothing wrong with his marriage until Lydia had suddenly fallen under Martynov's 'dire influence'. At that moment she had become unrecognisable, not only demanding an immediate divorce but flouting all of his requests that she maintain a veneer of normality until the Alhambra season was over. Lydia had put him through 'Hell', Randolfo claimed, abandoning the Ballets Russes, eloping with Martynov and, still worse, threatening him with some sort of 'shameful and provocative' act.[3]

From the short, clenched note that Lydia left for her husband, however, a very different picture emerges, of a woman who felt herself to be wronged and in pain:

> It is very hard for me to continue the life I led lately and I decided to go away from it. If you really want to help me you will send me the necessary papers. It is suffering for me to continue to dance also, so I informed Grigorieff and Diaghileff that I am no more in the troupe. Excuse me if I trouble you, but I can't do otherwise.[4]

There is other evidence, too, that undermines Randolfo's portrait of Lydia as a demonically transformed virago. While we do not know what story she eventually confessed to Maynard, he would refer to her flight as an act of 'courage and frankness',[5] and he clearly understood it to have been motivated less by passion for Martynov than by Lydia's desperate, even moral, need to get away from her husband. This is corroborated by press reports of Lydia's eventual divorce from Randolfo, in 1925 which claimed that she had walked out of the marriage in disgust after having finally found out the full scale of his bigamy.[6] Even more distressing to her had been the discovery in 1919 that Randolfo had been siphoning money out of her savings. Ansermet's gossip to Stravinsky that 'serious conflicts of a financial nature'[7] had erupted between the Borocchis were backed up by rumours that when Randolfo ran off to Rome, he had Lydia's wage packet in his pocket.

Randolfo's stealing might plausibly have been the breaking point for Lydia. In other circumstances she might have tried to accommodate the affair with Martynov into her relationship with Barocchi, just as she had been able to accommodate her long-unresolved feelings for Stravinsky. She might even have forgiven Randolfo's bigamy and tried to find a way of legalising their marriage. Lydia did not enjoy confrontation; as she later described herself, she was a natural 'appeaser', who found it difficult to 'fight'.[8] But like any freelance dancer at the time, she was haunted by fears of retiring into poverty. One reason that Lydia had appreciated this long London season was that it had allowed her to rebuild her savings, and for Randolfo to threaten her portion of financial security may have been a betrayal too far. Her discovery of his thieving could also explain the ranting, defensive tone of Randolfo's letter to Diaghilev. The dreadful act that Lydia had committed, 'so much beyond description that I might indeed have reacted in God knows what way', may simply have been to threaten Randolfo with the police. The truth behind his claim that he had had to flee London to 'avoid a probably irreparable disaster' may have been that he was trying to avoid prosecution as a thief.[9]

Randolfo, it seems, had given Lydia more than one good cause for running away, but even he could not be held responsible for the fact that she planned to run all the way back to Russia. This is another puzzle in the story that has yet to be solved. Russia in July 1919 was tearing itself apart, with towns, villages, even families turning against each other in the civil war, and with packs of murderous White and Red militia roaming the countryside. It was an astonishingly dangerous choice of destination for Lydia and Martynov, and even if they believed that they could make it safely back to Petrograd, they must have been aware that disease, hunger and violence also awaited them there. A letter from Diaghilev's old friend the music critic Walter Nouvel had arrived in London in late June, and it contained harrowing accounts of what it was like to live in the city. Benois had been forced to sell all of his precious paintings for food; Bakst's wife had been reduced to abject penury; the dancers at the Mariinsky had just performed through a bitter winter on starvation rations and in an unheated, freezing theatre.

Since Lydia left no explanation of why she was willing to forfeit the comforts of London and expose herself to these dangers, the best guess must be that she was motivated by family. It was now nine years since she had left home, and she may have feared that Karlusha, nearing sixty, might die before she saw her again. She may have formed a heroic idea of being at her family's side during these dire times. And perhaps to her this plan did not seem as suicidally rash as it now appears. In late July there had been signs that the civil war was on the turn. Western governments had begun threatening military intervention against Lenin's regime, and reports of White Russian forces advancing successfully towards Moscow and Petrograd were stirring rumours of the Bolsheviks' possible collapse. Martynov, almost certainly a White Russian, would have been fully alert to such information and may well have been encouraging Lydia with reassurances that the old Russia might soon be restored.

Certainly Lydia was impatient to begin her new life with Martynov, for by the middle of August she had secured her travel permit for the complicated journey that would take them via the Italian port of Taranto and across the Black Sea to Batumi on the west coast of Georgia. Batumi was, of course, about 2,000 miles south-east of Petrograd, but Lydia and Martynov may have been advised that it was a far safer point of entry than slipping in over the Baltic borders. Georgia was temporarily an independent republic,* and with a British naval force stationed off its coast it offered the couple a reasonable degree of security and comfort while they waited until it was possible for them to cross the border into Russia and head up north towards home.

If Lydia had successfully embarked on this long and risky journey, it would have been the most extreme vanishing act of her career. Quite possibly she would never have danced again. Quite possibly she would have disappeared into obscurity. But whilst she and Martynov had laid their plans with extreme care, something prevented Lydia from going through with them. Not only did she fail to get home to Petrograd, most evidence points to her never, in the end, having left London. Four and a half years later she would swear to

*Georgia had exploited the post-revolutionary chaos to seize independence in 1918, but by 1921 it was back under Russian control.

her divorce lawyers that she had remained resident in the UK during this entire period, apart from one short trip to France in the summer of 1920; and her statement was supported by her passport, which showed no further evidence of travel in 1919, beyond the initial permit that she had obtained for Batumi. We can be almost certain, too, that Lydia was in or around London by the autumn, because Beaumont reported that she 'still declined' all of Diaghilev's efforts to persuade her to rejoin the Ballets Russes.[10] And it is revealing that an anxious letter that she received from her sister Evgenia in 1922 displayed no knowledge of Lydia ever having been close to Russia, nor even any knowledge of her affair with Martynov. 'Tell me how you are getting on now?' urged Evgenia. 'Have you recovered financially and emotionally after Barocchi, [who] has cheered you up?'[11]

But if Lydia failed to get to Russia, it has not been discovered what she did instead, for during the next eighteen months neither the gossips nor the journalists of London had anything to report of her. It is possible to imagine that she and Martynov retreated to an anonymous suburb together, living frugally on the money Lydia had left after Randolfo's pilfering. But it is very hard to explain why, during all this time, Lydia failed to return to the stage. Diaghilev obviously wanted her, and since Randolfo had remained in Rome, licking his wounds, Lydia could have gone back to the Ballets Russes without any serious embarrassment or retribution. Even if, as she later suggested, she had grown 'tired of dancing',[12] there was another major stage project that she could have pursued. Lydia's extraordinary popularity with the London public had encouraged her to contemplate some sort of return to acting, and she had asked J. M. Barrie (whose *Peter Pan* she had much admired in America) to write a play for her. Barrie, both flattered and intrigued, had begun work during the spring of 1919 on *The Truth about the Russian Dancers*, a full-length comedy about the imaginary, fantastical life of a ballerina called Mademoiselle Uvula.

The play would have allowed Lydia to make a delicious switch to London's dramatic stage. And the fact that she did not resume the project after she had walked out of the Ballets Russes, and that she simultaneously dropped all contact with Barrie, with whom she had become friendly, raises exactly the same question as that prompted by her period of exile in the Catskills, six years earlier.* Had Lydia become pregnant? This would certainly explain the extreme tiredness that she had been suffering just before she ran away, and would resonate with Beaumont's alarmed sight of her on the night of her debut in *Boutique*, racing from the stage to her dressing room and vomiting into the sink. It could also explain Randolfo's anguished statement to Diaghilev: 'The situation is much worse today and since Mr M[artynov] is the one and only person responsible for it why would he not do anything about it.'[13] Perhaps Randolfo was trying to get Lydia to abort the baby and was being obstructed by Martynov; perhaps he was genuinely and selflessly alarmed by the idea of a pregnant Lydia trying to get back home to war-torn Russia.

But while it is easy to build a case for Lydia having become pregnant by Martynov, there is no evidence at all of a baby having been born. Years later a rumour would float around the ballet world of Lydia having had an illegitimate child, yet if this were true she had covered her tracks with remarkable efficiency. No baby Martynov, baby Lopokova or even baby Barocchi was registered in the UK between late 1919 and early 1920, and since Lydia did not travel abroad during that period she cannot have slipped away to France or Spain to give birth. What is more plausible is that the pregnancy, if it had ever existed, had ended in a miscarriage. This would be consistent with Lydia's later gynaecological history, since she failed to sustain a full-term pregnancy with Maynard; and it could also be consistent with the length of time she remained offstage. If Lydia had lost her baby late, if she had suffered some sort of infection or trauma, in that pre-antibiotic era it might have taken several months before she was well enough to consider resuming her career. The failure of her pregnancy could also explain why the relationship with Martynov, having flared up with such extreme and disruptive consequences, did not last. We do not know whether Lydia was with the

*A one-act version of Barrie's play was eventually premièred on 15 March 1920 at the Coliseum with Karsavina as its star. The role no longer had any dialogue, however, and significantly the plot had become the story of a Russian ballerina who is courted by an English lord and 'dies' a preofessional death in order to give birth to the latter's child. Barrie perhaps guessed more about the truth of Lydia's situation than she would have liked.

general when she travelled to Paris on 2 August 1920 – although the fact that Stravinsky was also in the city, celebrating the marriage of Diaghilev's old friends Misia Edwards and José Maria Sert, suggests not. But she had certainly parted from him by the end of the year, when some combination of restlessness, loneliness, boredom or brute necessity forced her out of her long exile. By 20 January 1920, Lydia had secured a visa to take her to America, and over in New York a flurry of press reports was announcing the return of Little Pet to Broadway.

Chapter Ten

A PRODIGAL RETURN

> I was in New York out of training, for I had run away from the stage. So, I thought it would not be a bad plan to appear in a musical comedy, where it is so easy to cover up your faults.
>
> LYDIA LOPOKOVA[1]

The new show for which Lydia had been engaged was *The Rose Girl*, a sentimental fantasy about a flower girl who falls in love with an aristocratic perfumier. Ten years had passed since she first travelled to the city of 'enormous fees', and this time, when she saw the steep shimmer of the New York skyline, her heart probably did not lift. She now knew what tedium could await her on the Broadway stage if she was lucky and *The Rose Girl* turned out to be a long-running hit. She knew, too, how instant the punishment would be if it flopped. But in her current financial situation, the chance of an American wage must have looked irresistible to Lydia. And she may also have hoped that the project would transcend the usual Broadway trivia, given that the choreographer with whom she would be working was her former teacher and mentor, Mikhail Fokine.

Fokine himself had only recently arrived in New York, having left Russia in 1918 with his wife, Vera, and slowly worked his way across Scandinavia and Europe. When he and Lydia first met up, their reunion must have been extraordinary. Between them they had over a decade of news to exchange – about their former colleagues in the Ballets Russes, about the drastic changes to their homeland, and about the complicated journeys that both had made. There was, however, no such animation or urgency in the work they did together on the 'Ballet of the Perfumes', the short number that was to form the decorative centrepiece of *The Rose Girl.*

Perhaps it was the grating silliness of the musical itself (judged by *Theater Magazine* to come 'pretty near the limits of stupid mediocrity')[2] that induced the once-conscientious Fokine to skimp on the seriousness of his own ballet. Or perhaps the choreographer thought that by providing a chorus of dancing roses, which made its entrance through a trap in the stage floor (putting one critic in mind of a 'group of unlucky pedestrians ... caught on top of a freight elevator',[3] and by giving Lydia a solo in which she wafted around the roses, pretending to unfold their petals, he was 'doing' Broadway.

But all the reviews of the show's première on 11 February 1920 suggest that Fokine had allowed the sensuous charge of his imagination to operate at the level of coarse, gimmicky kitsch. Worse for Lydia, the loud and loyal ovations that had greeted her first entrance on the Ambassador's stage had faltered as, according to *The Globe*, 'her old charm failed to shine and much of her dancing seemed unsure'.[4] Certainly in the one surviving publicity photograph from the musical she is barely recognisable as her former animated self, reclining plumply in front of a semi-circle of swaying women, like an odalisque from a burlesque show. Later even she would admit that her performance had been terrible – a 'female spectre de la rose without seed or flower'.[5]

One journalist, however, took a stand in Lydia's defence. Heywood Broun was covering the show for *The Tribune*, and while he deplored the 'crude theatrical devices' that had cheapened Fokine's ballet, he insisted that the stage had been distinguished by 'the return of ... one of the great dancers of our day', her 'graceful and feathery presence' as fresh as it had always been.[6] It was a review as gallantly protective as if Lydia had been his fiancée still, as if she had never run off with Barocchi. Yet if Broun's generosity warmed Lydia's heart, it could not save her. The 'Ballet of the Perfumes' was allowed to run for only a few performances before it was cut out of the show, and she was sacked with it.*

Lydia would be grateful that *The Rose Girl* was her last ever brush with Broadway, but at that moment, having travelled so far and

***The Rose Girl* was allowed to limp on for another three months.

staked so much on this engagement, she was facing a financial impasse and would have taken almost any work offered her. She was staying in the drably genteel Hargrave Hotel, on the Upper West Side, and soon even the price of a room would be beyond her pocket. Her later insouciant comment that 'It is good to be a flop sometimes but not at the time' could only hint at the fear she must have felt as she faced the New York winter, ill at ease in her body and with her formerly infallible charm in doubt.[7] Four and half years was a long time for Lydia to have been absent from the city, and she subsequently confided to the press that she had not found New York 'warm hearted'. There was a hint of desolation in her description of how she had spent her evenings: 'I watched people jazz and glide and once or twice when the company was jolly I jazzed too',[8] and it may have been loneliness that had made her hang on to a fan letter, which had followed her from England, filled with reassuring promises that if she ever returned to the British stage she would find 'heaps and heaps of people ready to go mad with joy. I do not think we ever loved anyone more than you.'[9]

It was this uncritical adoration that Lydia had thrown away eighteen months before, and it must now have seemed tormentingly inaccessible. But professional schooling had armed her with tough survival skills, for by early March she was writing to two Russian friends in London, assuring them that she had rallied from her disaster: 'My mental state is good and I have my head on my shoulders, I am pondering on things, thinking and read a bit when I can.' She implied that she was determined to stay on in America, even taking her chances in cinema ('I am not timid, something successful must come out of it, and I will probably find myself in something better than "Rose Girl". It was rubbish, but it helped me to get my legs in practice and unwind').[10] However, other, more daring plans were also forming in her mind. A few days later, two telegrams crossed the Atlantic. One, addressed to Diaghilev at an address in Paris, asked, 'Will you have Lopokova back?' The other replied, just as succinctly, 'If it is the same Lopokova I knew.'[11]

If Lydia studied herself dispassionately in New York, she must have quailed at the implications of Diaghilev's response. The body that she saw reflected in her mirror, still softened and weakened by her long period offstage, was far from the Lopokova that he had known, and it was a gamble for her to face him before she had recovered her form. The days were long past when Lydia could dip casually into her savings for the cost of an Atlantic crossing (she would in fact have to borrow the money from friends), and it is possible that if she had successfully found employment in New York, she would have stayed there. But shortly after Diaghilev's first telegram, detailed instructions arrived for her to meet up with the company in Madrid. It was a gesture of confidence and it was sufficient for Lydia to take the risk.

She would have felt more confident still if she had known that Diaghilev, at this point, needed her almost as much as she needed him. The Ballets Russes had currently lost its two main attractions – Karsavina, who, despite her fanfared return, was refusing to leave her young son for extended tours of Europe; and, far more ruinously, Massine. In an uncanny replay of the Nijinsky debacle in 1913, Diaghilev's cherished protégé had fallen in love with a woman – the English dancer Vera Savina – and as a result of his sexual treachery had been immediately sacked. The crisis had blown up in January, and it was lucky for Lydia that Diaghilev had still been thin-skinned and smarting when she arrived in Madrid, in early April. With her own bad behaviour dramatically eclipsed by Massine's, she was quietly put back to work by Big Serge and quietly re-embraced as his petted favourite. Some of her colleagues were surprised by Diaghilev's forbearance, for although he had always been fond of Lydia he formed famously bitter grudges. But during her absence he had tried out several substitutes in her roles, and whilst he had confidently declared, 'I shall make a Lopokova of that one',[12] he had always been disappointed. Lydia's apparently inimitable style ensured her privileged place within the company even more than her personal friendship with its director. 'You have never shouted at me like that,' she once remarked to Diaghilev after hearing him abuse a fellow dancer. 'No and I never shall,' he had replied.[13]

It may have been Diaghilev who also arranged matters so that Lydia would not immediately be confronted by her estranged 'husband'. Randolfo had eventually been coaxed back from Rome to resume his duties as the Ballets Russes's business manager, but when Lydia arrived in Madrid he was down in Seville, recruiting dancers and musicians for the flamenco project that Diaghilev was planning for his summer season. When the couple eventually met, it was mid-May, and from the lack of any anecdotal stories of rows or recriminations we can assume that Randolfo's facile good nature, aided by Lydia's own fear of confrontation, had smoothed the moment over.

Once again Lydia had taken a leap of faith, and once again she had landed more smoothly than she had dared hope. Whilst she returned to the company a little more cautious and a little more subdued, ballet was once again to be the centre of her life, and when the Ballets Russes prepared to open at Paris's Gaîeté Lyrique for a week in mid May, it was Lydia, strong and supple once more, who was its featured ballerina. A splashy feature in *Comoedia* headlined her return as the 'event' of the season, and the notoriously demanding Parisians, who had not seen her for over five years, apparently agreed. On 17 May she danced *Firebird* to accolades and she continued to hold the public's favour, even against Diaghilev's flamboyant Spanish import, *Cuadro flamenco*, with its Picasso designs and its freak attraction, Maté 'el sin pies', a gypsy who danced like a devil on the stumps of his amputated legs.

Paris should have given Lydia all the proof she needed that she had recovered her powers, yet she remained irrationally terrified of how she would be greeted when the Ballets Russes moved on to London. She feared that she had done irreparable damage to her reputation with her sudden disappearance in 1919, and, as she confessed to a reporter shortly after her arrival, 'I was so frightened after two years not to dance my best that I take off my telephone and I hide in my room all the first two days I was here.'[14] The London public, however, were waiting to give Lydia one of the most doting receptions of her career. Tickets for her opening performance at the Prince's Theatre on 26 May sold so fast that C. B. Cochran, who was managing the season, claimed that he could have filled the seats three times over; and from the moment she made her first entrance in *Boutique*, with Leon Woizikovsky as her partner, the evening was hers. The initial burst of applause was so loud that the orchestra were forced to stop playing, and to Cyril Beaumont, who was watching

Lydia from the stalls, it appeared as if the public were competing with each other to express their excitement at her return. Groups of fans chanted her name at moments throughout the ballet and continued to do so even after the safety curtain had been lowered, forcing Diaghilev to fetch Lydia back from her dressing room and lead her into a box where she stood, in her old kimono, to receive London's homage.

It was an exceptional demonstration of love, yet all that was written in the press suggested that Lydia had deserved it. The American columnist H. Willson D. Sher described with almost mystical delight the new maturity that he had seen irradiating her dancing, arguing that Lydia had 'broken the shackles that bind the soul of every young artist ... her eyes had a new eagerness ... her limbs had a quickness of movement unlike that of any dancer I have ever seen'.[15] And if Sher's metaphors had become somewhat mangled in his enthusiasm (Lydia, he claimed, was no longer just 'a Dresden shepherdess come to life' but 'a still pool whose depth cannot be seen because the light on the surface is too strong'), his judgement was endorsed by the more matter-of-fact *Sunday Pictorial*, whose critic wrote, 'We have not seen Lopokova for two years and two years can play havoc with a dancer. But Lopokova has improved. It is not merely that the exquisite plebeian beauty of that gay, tragic soubrette is unimpaired; her joints and muscles are in finer fettle. Long life to the joints and muscles of Lopokova.'[16]

The *Pictorial*'s pledge was underlined the following year when an attempt was made to immortalise Lydia's joints and muscles on celluloid. The Pathé newsreel company were commissioning a series of short documentaries on theatre and fashion at this time, and in *Dancing Grace* Lydia was invited to showcase the art of the ballerina.* It was the first time that she had danced on film, and the resulting few minutes of footage (stored in the archives of the British Film Institute) are a precious glimpse of how she appeared back in 1922, dressed in her *Boutique* costume and dancing a variation that exhibited her fleet, springing footwork and high jump.

To a modern eye, however, the film can make for disconcerting

*The series was collectively titled *Eve's Film Review*.

viewing. Eight or nine decades is a long time in ballet, and, even allowing for the limitations of 1920s film technology, Lydia's technique displays little of the athletically burnished finish that we expect from ballerinas today. Just as in early film footage of sportsmen, singers or actors, her captured performance looks smaller and more muted than her legend.

Her impact is also distorted by the experimental film effects that were assayed in *Dancing Grace*, as her sequence is repeated once in slow motion and again in double exposure.* Revealed in meticulously deconstructed detail, it is impossible for Lydia's celluloid dancing to match the stage performances so glowingly recorded by admiring critics, as her jumps move slackly across the screen, her arms and her feet dangle mid-stretch.

What is remarkable, however, is that the film, in all its old-fashioned cumbersomeness, still captures some live essence of Lydia's personality. On screen, her solid little torso twists and curves with a very individual mobility, the delicacy of her hands makes a subtle poetic appeal, a flicker of wit slants the gravity of her expression. The cumulative effect, an intriguing modern bounce tethered to a chaste classical restraint, is one that no dancer today could reproduce. And the fact that none of Lydia's colleagues could replicate it back in 1922 ensured that the hysteria of her first night at the Prince's Theatre settled into a steady triumph. During the Ballets Russes's ten-week season, Diaghilev cast Lydia in all of her old repertory as well as giving her Pimpinella, the ballerina lead in Massine's *Pulcinella*, which she would regard as 'second only to *Petrushka*'.[17] After the initial excitement had died down, Lydia picked up one or two gently corrective reviews but she closed the season in a programme that had been organised expressly around her talents. Dancing *La Boutique fantasque*, *Les Femmes de bonne humeur* and *La Princesse enchantée*, Lydia clinched her triumphal return to London with a personal apotheosis.

The fervour surrounding Lydia's reappearance had also been whipped up by Cochran, a more brazen publicist even than

*Pathé were particularly keen to showcase their advances in slow-motion filming, made possible by the new Ultra Rapid camera.

Diaghilev, and all through June and July a pack of journalists had followed her closely. A group were sent to watch her morning class with Cecchetti, prompting an admiring report in the *Daily Telegraph* of Lydia's diligence at the barre and her remarkable eschewal of 'haughty airs'.[18] On 22 July the *Daily Express* took her round the Women's Exhibition at Olympia, slavishly reporting her disingenuous comments that all the new household appliances on show were in danger of making women redundant – she who had never dusted or washed dishes in her life.

As Lydia re-established her command of the stage, she was also able to claw back some stability in her personal life, with a weekly salary of £100* restoring her finances and a steady stream of invitations welcoming her back into London society. By now her English was fully fluent, if idiosyncratic, and it was during this season that she seems to have honed her skill in playing her two languages off against each other. Improvising vocabulary, deliberately twisting pronunciation, became Lydia's party trick. 'I had tea with Lady Grey [a famous bird lover],' she would slyly inform a room, her head tilted slightly to one side, her eyebrows arched. 'She has an ovary that she likes to show everyone.'[19]

Yet if Lydia knew how to work her assets, she loved equally to be entertained, and her own infectious laughter became almost as much of a calling card as her humour. According to one of her later admirers, the historian Noël Annan, the sound of Lydia laughing was pure 'champagne', bubbles of quick, silvery brightness. Even complete strangers in hotels, trains or restaurants were said to be seduced by it. The choreographer Frederick Ashton once swore that when he had taken a taxi with Lydia, the driver had refused to accept her fare, claiming that 'to hear that lady laugh has done me more good than anything'.[20]

Lydia's laughter was heard that summer in the drawing rooms of Bloomsbury, as to celebrate her return, Maynard Keynes organised a lunch party with her and Karsavina as guests of honour. Quentin Bell, Clive's ten-year-old son, observed Lydia in the middle of an

---

*£3,000 by modern values. While Lydia's London wage was less than her old Broadway earnings, it was double what Sokolova, for instance, earned.

admiring group, all of whom were trying to speak to her in French (considered, then, to be the most stylish language for conversing with ballerinas). As Quentin watched the competition for Lydia's attention, he noticed that his own father was leading the field, talking to her in expert French and flirting with her very 'enthusiastically'. He noticed, too, that Maynard appeared furious at being sidelined. The economist was not a natural linguist and in his frustration he demanded irritably of Quentin, 'Why do they all jabber away in French like that? I don't believe they really understand what they are saying themselves.'[21] To the socially precocious boy it had seemed that Maynard was jealous of more than Clive's linguistic fluency.

Another admirer who hovered around Lydia in the summer of 1921 was the textiles millionaire Samuel Courtauld. He was a reserved, rather literal-minded man, tethered to his business interests and to his snobbish wife Elizabeth, or Lil; yet he was also deeply romantic, willing to spend immense sums of money on art as well as fast cars, and with a passionate susceptibility to women. Until he died in 1947, Sam would linger loyally and adoringly on the fringes of Lydia's life, and it was during this London season that he first began to communicate his devotion, sending carefully worded tributes to her artistry: 'in comedy you are of course supreme, but it is the poetic almost unearthly feeling that specially appeals to me'.[22]

When the season was over, Sam went a small step further, asking Lydia to join himself and Lil for a holiday in Scotland. He had issued the invitation discreetly and without great expectation but it was one that Lydia was unable to accept. She was genuinely taken with her new, very English admirer, admiring his decency even if she was amused by his limitations: 'Honesty, sincerity, competence, intelligence, modesty are Sam's feathers,' she would later write, 'but he can't soar, his little feet follow him.'[23] However, that summer she was – discreetly and without great expectation – involved in a reunion with her former lover Stravinsky.

Whether or not Lydia had met up with the composer the previous August when she had travelled to Paris, she had definitely encountered him in Madrid the following April when he had rejoined the Ballets Russes to conduct performances of *Petrushka*. The two of them had both been vulnerable, lonely and suggestible: Lydia still recovering from her failed relationship with Martynov and her New York flop; Stravinsky in the aftermath of an affair with the fashion designer Coco Chanel. Even if the couple had not turned to each other immediately for comfort, circumstances indicate that they were doing so in Paris, a couple of weeks later.

After Madrid, Lydia had travelled to London, possibly to sort out her travel papers, but rather than resting there and resuming contact with her Russian friends she had gone straight on to Paris, a full two weeks ahead of the rest of the Ballets Russes. Stravinsky was already in the city, working in his little attic studio in rue de Rochechouart, and the situation could hardly have been more ideal for the pair to recharge their affair. Paris was at its most seductive in the blossoming heat of early May; they were both temporarily free and unencumbered; and they had much of the summer ahead of them, given that Stravinsky was to spend June with the Ballets Russes in London.

Most indicative of the lovers having resumed their affair was the fact that when Stravinsky left London to join his wife and children in Anglet, in south-west France, Lydia followed him as soon as she was free. She had booked herself into a hotel in nearby Biarritz, which meant that she and the composer could continue to meet in private. And it may be significant that while she paid at least one 'social' visit to the Stravinsky household, a photograph taken of her with the conductor suggests that there was an awkwardness in her presence. In the garden of the Cottage l'Argenté, Lydia's gaze at the camera is both unfathomable and unrelaxed.

If the relationship had revived, however, it was never going to become permanent. Lydia needed more security than Stravinsky could give, whilst he himself was apparently searching for other qualities, perhaps more glamorous, more intensely feminine than Lydia possessed. In fact that summer he may already have found them, having made the opening moves in a new affair with the Parisian actress Vera Sudeykina. Vera was a dark, glossy beauty, far more seductively finessed than either scatty Lydia or the exhausted Katya, and having caught Stravinsky's imagination when they had first met, in February, she actually seems to have moved into his bed in July, while he was in Paris en route from Lydia in London to his family in Anglet.

All the time that Lydia hovered close to Stravinsky in Biarritz, a new rival was thus sending the conductor coded love letters. And if Lydia had been kept ignorant of this new situation, in September when she and Stravinsky were back in London with the Ballets Russes, it became impossible to ignore. Vera had managed to get herself hired as a mime artist for the company's autumn season and was now hanging around rehearsals, possessively watching over her lover and making every possible display of her own striking glamour. A small group photograph taken at the time shows Lydia with her arm possessively tucked in Stravinsky's, while Vera stands watchfully behind; and the tension between the three of them was evident to at least one member of the company, Boris Kochno, the clever, subtle young man whom Diaghilev had appointed as his secretary earlier that year. Kochno already knew Vera and her husband, Sergei, quite well, and he took it upon himself to send Vera a smirking little ditty about her relationship with Lydia and Stravinsky, informing her that he was watching their unresolved triangle very carefully:

> ... What is new in the company?
> What about Lyda, Lyda Lopokova
> And Igor – the old friends?
> But I find things out by chance
> I was blessed with a gift of omniscience ...[24]

The only surviving clue to what Stravinsky was feeling this autumn is his 'traitresse' dedication to Lydia, for it was at this point that he wrote the curious phrase on her music score, and from its reproachful charge we have to assume that he still felt involved with her in some intimate way. This could mesh with the theory later advanced by Richard Buckle (who became friendly with Lydia during the 1950s) that she had temporarily taken Randolfo back into her bed. It could also mesh with Buckle's further belief that Lydia's brief and unexplained marital rapprochement had resulted in yet another pregnancy scare.*

*Buckle points to a receipt, signed by Randolfo, for a room in a Bloomsbury nursing home, which could have been used for an abortion. There is, however, no other evidence for this theory.

Outside the Alhambra Theatre, London, 1921; from left to right: Vera Trefilova, Florrie Grenfell, Vera Sudeykina, Lydia, Igor Stravinsky, Bronislava Nijinska

If so, even more conflicting implications would have circled around Stravinsky's choice of the epithet 'traîtresse'. And issues of sexual loyalty, let alone paternity, would surely have started smoking, scandalously, if the situation had persisted. But by Christmas it would all be over. Stravinsky would return to France and remain loyal to Vera, eventually marrying her when Katya died in 1939.* Randolfo, finding it no longer worth his while to be employed by Diaghilev, would creep out of London, and out of Lydia's life for good.

By this time, too, Lydia herself would have little leisure to regret either of their departures. Even if she was inclined to feel bitter or self-pitying about the state of her private life, she could not afford to indulge her emotions. Her energies were now all being directed towards the challenge of Diaghilev's latest production, a staging of Marius Petipa's *Sleeping Beauty*.

*In a letter to Maynard in November 1928, Lydia would caustically note Stravinsky's monogamous devotion to Vera: 'he does not want to sin as much [as] with the other Madam'.

Reviving this treasure of the Imperial repertory was to be the most extravagant project in the Ballets Russes's history, and given the company's post-war embrace of the avant-garde it appeared to many observers to be the most aberrant. Diaghilev was perceived to be about the future, not the past. However, in 1921 the impresario's finely tuned cultural antennae had caught the stirrings of a neoclassical revival in France, and he believed that this was a timely moment to unveil *Beauty* to the West. It was a ballet he had always revered, both for Tchaikovsky's symphonically arching score and for the detailed magnificence of Petipa's choreography. More pragmatically, he also believed that there were strong commercial possibilities in presenting such a ballet in London. Diaghilev had been observing, with jealous admiration, the record-breaking success of *Chu Chin Chow*, a musical based on the story of Ali Baba (and, ironically, inspired by his own *Schéhérazade*), and he had wondered whether a full-length classic, sumptuously staged, might have a similar box-office draw. It might relieve him of the constant pressure to find new choreography (a pressure especially fraught after the loss of Massine), and if, as he calculated, the ballet could run for a six-month season, it might even make him rich.

Mounting a full-length classic in little over three months would, however, be an arduous, expensive enterprise for a company that was largely geared to staging one-act ballets. Diaghilev would have to borrow heavily to pay for it, and he would be demanding an exhausting commitment from his dancers to get it ready on time. Inevitably much of the work fell to Lydia, for whilst she could not be Diaghilev's first choice to dance the chastely classical role of Aurora, it was a box-office necessity that she remain central to the production. She was thus given the two secondary ballerina roles, Lilac Fairy and Princess Florine (the original incarnation of *La Princesse enchantée*), as well as limited performances of Aurora in which she would be partnered, and steered, by a new arrival from Russia, Anatole Vilzak.

Together these roles added up to a daunting volume of new choreography for Lydia to master. Aurora alone ranked as one of the most densely written roles in the repertory, while the choreography for the Lilac Fairy was also being expanded especially for her, with a new variation* introduced into Act II and an enlarged slot in the Prologue, which she was to fill with the fast, delicately ornamented Sugar Plum Fairy solo – interpolated with its music from *The Nutcracker*. It also added to the pressure on Lydia that Olga Spessivtzeva and Lubov Egorova, the two guest Russian ballerinas hired by Diaghilev to dance first- and second-cast Aurora, had brought with them intimidating reminders of the Imperial schooling she had left behind. In public Lydia might appear chirpily untroubled by her rivals (when Diaghilev announced that he would be changing the ballet's title to *The Sleeping Princess*,† she joked loudly that it must be on her account since a ballerina with a nose like hers could not be billed as a Sleeping Beauty). In private, however, she set herself to study long hours alone with Cecchetti.

Around her *The Sleeping Princess* was slowly being assembled. Teaching Petipa's choreography was Nicholas Sergeyev, a former regisseur at the Mariinsky who had managed to escape the revolution with a collection of notebooks in which he had notated the Imperial repertory. Choreographing the additional material was Bronislava Nijinska, Vaslav Nijinsky's sister, who had recently returned from Petrograd. Orchestrating and editing the changes in the score, as well as managing Vera and Lydia, was Stravinsky. Meanwhile, in the workshops of the Alhambra Theatre, Bakst and his army of carpenters, scene painters, wig makers, tailors and seamstresses were working sixteen hours a day to amass the costumes and stage effects that would take *The Sleeping Princess* through its five magnificent changes of scene.

So many conflicting demands crowded the company's schedule that when they moved into the Alhambra for the ballet's final rehearsals, the ballet still appeared to be a jumble of ill-fitting pieces. If there was enchantment among the half-finished costumes, the grumpy fairies and the swearing stagehands, few of the dancers could

---

*It was on Lydia's piano score for this variation that Stravinsky inscribed his dedication to the 'traitress'. Other dance material was added to the role in subsequent Russian productions and coincidentally it was Lydia's brother, Fedor, who choreographed the steps most frequently danced by the Lilac Fairy today.

†In fact the new title was to distinguish it from a competing pantomime production of *Sleeping Beauty*.

discern it. Yet on 2 November, when the curtains parted to reveal the baroque magnificence of the ballet's Prologue, the company did believe some spell had been cast. Some of the dancers, like Sokolova, had never been part of such an elaborate production, and stepping on to the stage was to her like being 'transported to fairy land'.[25] For the Russian exiles in the company like Lydia, the experience was acutely nostalgic, a direct return to their Mariinsky past and to the awe that they had felt as children when they had taken their first tiny steps in a Petipa ballet.

At first much of the audience had seemed as entranced as the dancers, but the moment did not last, for there were gremlins in the Alhambra's stage machinery that night that would undo much of the production's sorcery. First, the screen of creepers, which was meant to grow around the sleep-enchanted court, became jammed halfway, leaving Lydia, as the Lilac Fairy, stranded on stage and trying to make frantic sense of the hiatus. 'I waved my wand', she later recorded, 'and cast my spell and nothing happened, nothing. The machinery had failed, the whole illusion destroyed and the beautiful climax lost.'[26] Then the gauze curtains, descending in sequence to create the transformation scene in Act II, became caught on a piece of scenery, piling up until, as Beaumont observed, 'they resembled a monster bale of muslin on the shelf of a draper's shop'.[27] As the public began to break into derisive hoots of laughter, it was mortifying enough for the dancers; for Diaghilev, the evening was an artistic crucifixion. As soon as it was over, he fled to his hotel room, where Stravinsky found him sobbing like a child.

Diaghilev was convinced that this humiliating première must be a bad omen for the season – and he was right. Even though the faults in the machinery were quickly eradicated, the British public could not be persuaded to love *The Sleeping Princess*. While the first few weeks did brisk business, with a loyal core of balletomanes returning night after night to compare notes on different casts, they failed to build into the numbers that Diaghilev required. London had already enjoyed an unusually busy dance season, with Isadora Duncan at the Prince of Wales, and with the Royal Danish Ballet, Karsavina, Loie Fuller and Maud Allan all performing at the Coliseum. The public's appetite for the Ballets Russes had been slightly blunted. But even more damaging to the box office was the response of those who found *The Sleeping Princess* embarrassingly old-fashioned, a betrayal of the post-war modernism that Diaghilev had previously championed. Lytton Strachey's peevish complaint that the ballet had made him feel sick because 'the whole thing was so degraded,'[28] may have been extreme, but it set the tone for all of those who dismissed Tchaikovsky's score as saccharine tune-making, Bakst's designs as crowd-pleasing fancy dress (Raymond Mortimer scoffed sarcastically, 'What do the English like ... Clothes! Clothes! Clothes!')[29] and Petipa's choreography as blandly conventional.* Even the artistry of the visiting Russian dancers did not impress, and *The Times* was typical in judging that they had been effortlessly 'outshone' by the familiar brio of Lydia and her partner Idzikowski.[30]

Lydia was, in fact, one of the very few members of the Ballets Russes who did well out of this production. Her performances of the Lilac Fairy and Princess Florine were greeted with excessive enthusiasm and, with the help of some dextrous partnering by Vilzak, she received more cheers than she deserved for her performances of Aurora. Cyril Beaumont – who continued to watch all of her performances even if, in the wake of the Martynov affair, he felt less confident in claiming her friendship – believed that Lydia had been key to the ballet's limited success, her performances confirming her popularity among London balletomanes.

But even Lydia's most hysterical admirers would not keep returning to watch her in the same three roles, and by Christmas alarming numbers of seats were left vacant. It was at that point that Diaghilev understood he was facing financial disaster. He had not begun to repay the money he had borrowed, and if the box office failed to rally he would soon be unable to pay his dancers. On one occasion, Randolfo and Beaumont were lunching together and chatting animatedly about how the production might be rescued. There had been

*One dissenter was a seventeen-year-old schoolboy called Frederick Ashton. Smitten by ballet since he had watched Pavlova dance in South America, Ashton was fascinated to see in *The Sleeping Princess* what a full-scale classical production looked like. He admired, as many others failed to, the eloquent riches housed within Petipa's disciplined vocabulary and the masterful organisation of his stage pictures. When Ashton became a choreographer in his own right, *Sleeping Beauty* would become one of his most abiding inspirations – a work he always returned to as a reminder of ballet's essential principles.

several ideas mooted, each one wilder than the last, from Lydia and Idzikowski speaking a comic *entr'acte* dialogue by George Bernard Shaw (a sop to the intellectuals), to embellishing Aurora's awakening scene with some live animals (a sop to the children). Suddenly the two men's conversation was interrupted by a vicious snarl of 'Merde' from a hunched figure near by.[31] Diaghilev, sunk into a dumb debilitating depression, could not even bear to hear his disaster spoken of. It was at this point that Randolfo, recognising a sinking ship and anxious to save his own skin, returned to Italy.

No one seems to have cared that he had gone, certainly not Lydia, whose own loyalties were now focussed on her beleaguered colleagues. Oswald Stoll, as the Alhambra's owner and Diaghilev's main creditor, was eager that the company try to salvage the season by performing some of their other repertory, but Diaghilev refused to consider the option. He already feared that Stoll would impound the sets and costumes from *Sleeping Princess* until his £10,000 advance was repaid and he was determined that Stoll should not also get his hands on the decors for the other ballets. It was probably the right decision, but it forced the latter's hand, and at the end of January Stoll announced that the ballet's run would end on 4 February – a full three months earlier than Diaghilev had planned.* While the Ballets Russes had engagements scheduled for the end of April, the intervening months gaped shockingly, and in a black impulse of denial and despair Diaghilev abandoned his company to their fate. He borrowed £500 and disappeared to Paris, leaving the dancers to struggle through the remaining few performances on their own.

When the last curtain fell on *The Sleeping Princess*, it was Lydia who was co-opted to deliver a farewell speech to the public. She joked bravely that she and the company would all be returning very soon as 'good-humoured ladies', but the mood among the dancers was wretched. Most of them were owed weeks of back pay, and there was no word, and certainly no money, coming from Diaghilev. Grigoriev attempted to deflect their bitterness, assuring them that their director was even now organising a future for them and

*These days any ballet company would consider a three-month run of a single production – 105 consecutive performances – to be a remarkable achievement.

reminding them of the loyalty they owed. But to those dancers who were already threatened with eviction from their lodgings, his pleas sounded absurd. Two of them, Sokolova and her new lover Léon Woizikovsky, took it upon themselves to hunt Diaghilev down in Paris and demand cash from him personally. It was a futile journey. Diaghilev fobbed them off with a tiny sum and instructions to address all their further demands to Walter Nouvel, who had replaced Barocchi as business manager – but who of course had nothing to give them.

Back in London, several of the other dancers were beginning to disperse, responding to offers of work in revues or music hall. Lydia at first took it on herself to staunch the flow, sending Diaghilev a letter in which she begged him to return and hold his company together:

> Dear Serge
>
> By leaving us all here so long with no news of you, [you] make a terrible situation. The artists have no money. Everything is uncertain and there is no one here to encourage us or tell us what are the plans. Other Directors who talk of ballet in London make us offers and we do not know what to say.
>
> For myself I believe the great ballet will only be with you and what others may do will be inferior. Therefore I accept no other engagement ...[32]

However, although rumours drifted back that Diaghilev was trying to expedite plans for a tour of Europe, he sent Lydia no reply, and both her patience and her loyalty began to waver. Pious as her intentions had been in assuring him that she would dance for no one else, she could not wait for long, especially as an extremely attractive engagement was now being offered her. The next message that she sent to Diaghilev was still earnest with expressions of 'personal respect and regard' but these were undercut by a new insistence that if Lydia were to remain free for him, Diaghilev must pay a £200 guarantee into an account set up for her at Lloyd's Bank in Paris.[33] It was a disingenuous request, for Lydia must have known that such a sum was beyond his pocket, yet she may have been using it to clear her conscience. The engagement that she had been offered was not only attractive, but it was also one that Diaghilev would regard as a rank betrayal. With almost malign timing, Massine had just arrived in London to search out dancers for a short season of divertissements that he had been commissioned to stage at Covent Garden. The misfortunes of his old company offered him the ideal recruiting opportunity and, free to cherry-pick his favourite artists, he had made moves on Sokolova, Thadée Slavinsky and Woizikovsky. On 30 March, Lydia, too, signed a contract for 'four weeks certain'.[34] She may have felt a remorseful qualm for Diaghilev as she did so. But she had one very potent reason for ignoring it – and one that would deliver her into an entirely new phase of her life.

Chapter Eleven

MAYNARD

> Loppy [sic] came to lunch last Sunday, and I again fell very much in love with her. She seems to me perfect in every way. One of her new charms is the most knowing and judicious use of English words. I am going to the ballet tomorrow.
>
> MAYNARD KEYNES[1]

As *The Sleeping Princess* had played out its final weeks at the Alhambra, one loyal admirer had returned to the theatre night after night. Solitarily entranced by the spectacle on stage, Maynard Keynes had been untroubled by the fact that the stalls around him were almost deserted. Unlike the rest of his London circle, he had genuinely admired the ballet, which reminded him of the pantomimes and melodramas to which his father had taken him as a child. But it was not Petipa or Bakst who had kept him coming back. As Maynard had watched Lydia dancing Aurora and the Lilac Fairy, illuminated in the production's period grandeur, he had been paying rapt attention to the woman with whom he had fallen in love.

It was a devotion that would astonish his friends, and it would do so not only because Maynard was Britain's most famous economist and considered far too clever to be 'dished' by a pretty pair of legs. In circles where it was possible to confess such truths, the far more significant issue was that Maynard had been actively homosexual since he was sixteen and had never yet fallen in love with a woman.

People knew, of course, that he admired Lydia for her dancing, since after his initial disparaging reaction to her London season in 1918, Maynard had loudly added his voice to the general adulation.

He also liked to associate with fame, and even before knowing Lydia well he had made proprietorial use of her nickname, 'Loppie'. Yet despite his enthusiasm, Maynard had never expressed anything like a fan's ardour, and when Lydia had run off with Martynov in 1919, he had reacted with little more than friendly curiosity, coupled with the self-interested regret of a thwarted host. 'Isn't it shocking about Loppie?' he had written to Duncan Grant. 'Has she been discovered yet? Clive and I are giving a grand party on the 29th to which we hoped she would come.'[2]

During Lydia's absence from the stage, Maynard had had no reason to give her any further thought. Sexually he had been involved with several men, including a Cambridge graduate, Sebastian Sprott, whose quick brain and appealing manners suited him, even if they did not engage his deepest emotions: 'shallow waters are the attraction,' he had admitted to his friend Lytton Strachey. 'Up to the middle, not head over ears at my age.'[3] Even when Lydia had returned to London in May 1921, Maynard had not raced to the theatre to watch her (the only ballet that he recorded in his meticulous diary was *Le Sacre du printemps*, in which she did not dance). Yet it was during that summer, as Lydia socialised with Bloomsbury, that Maynard seems to have felt a quickening of possessive interest towards her. The extreme irritation that he had experienced as Clive flirted with Lydia over lunch in Gordon Square intimated that even if she did not yet provoke in him the predatory ardour that he felt towards his own sex, she was starting to fascinate.

Like many men, Maynard found Lydia exotic. Her idiosyncratic command of English pleased him, as did the graceful physical imprint of her Imperial background. But it may have been the easiness of her company that drew him deeper into intimacy. Not only did Lydia deliver her opinions with engaging frankness, not only was she beguilingly ready with her jokes and her chatter, but she came refreshingly unencumbered by English social baggage or class. This mattered to Maynard, who was more defensive about his own relatively modest background than he cared to admit. Despite the confidence with which he had learned to move in high political and social circles, several of his Bloomsbury friends – innately snobbish beneath their acquired bohemianism – were inclined to look askance on his manners. Maynard had a tendency to be bossy in conversation and greedy at table, evidence, it was felt, of his Victorian ancestry in trade and chapel. During one detailed Bloomsbury anatomisation of his character, from which Maynard himself was absent, it was judged that he 'had a lot of low blood in him'.[4]

The fastidiousness that Maynard sometimes sensed from his friends was vaguely oppressive to him, and Lydia – who disliked dressing formally, preferred to eat with her fingers, was casual about time and disinclined to conceal her impatience when bored – was interesting and even reassuring to him. He sensed a fellow maverick, and as he paid closer attention to her he was flattered to see her respond. Even though she herself was possibly still entangled with Stravinsky during the summer of 1921 and was tactfully fending off Sam Courtauld, Lydia evidently enjoyed the flirtatious static that began to develop between them.

Love had still not been on Maynard's mind, however, when he had attended the opening night of *Sleeping Princess*, nor when he had taken his brother Geoffrey backstage after the performance. Even on 18 December, when he arranged to have lunch with Lydia, he seems to have anticipated no more than a casual date. Yet desire evidently sparked at that meeting and it flared so fast that within two weeks Maynard had become Lydia's lover, and within seven weeks had established her in rooms that were just four doors away from his own house in Gordon Square.

If Maynard had felt confused by the speed with which his feelings had intensified, they had also confounded everyone close to him, who assumed that the patterns of his life had settled into a predictable, middle-aged self-sufficiency. Maynard might, in the past, have attempted one or two experiments with women but they had not induced any profound doubts about his homosexuality, nor, by the age of thirty-eight, had they brought him close to proposing marriage. He might have hovered on the fringes of bohemia but little had stalled the steady upward curve of his career, both as an academic at Cambridge University and as an international expert on economics. Aspiration, in fact, had been as deeply wired into his genes as restlessness had into Lydia's.

John Maynard Keynes, who was known to his friends as Maynard, was born on 5 June 1883 to parents who would set a high standard of duty and application for their first-born son. Neville, his father, lectured in Moral Sciences at Cambridge University and was head of the university administration. His mother, Florence, the vigorous, sweet-faced daughter of the eminent Nonconformist minister John Brown, had been one of the first women students at Cambridge and would, in 1932, become the town's first female mayor.* As soon as they had discovered Maynard's prodigious intellectual gifts, they had poured all their ambitions into nurturing his progress,† and Maynard, in turn, had rewarded his parents willingly, securing a scholarship to Eton College and winning a total of sixty-three prizes at school. Yet despite Maynard's inclination towards a schoolboyish, list-making pedantry he was no ordinary swot. He developed an appreciative curiosity about poetry and ideas, and among certain boys his popularity was also fuelled by his curiosity about their bodies. Homosexuality flourished in the dormitories and study rooms of Eton, and although for many boys it remained at the level of sentimental confidences and crushes, Maynard, by the age of sixteen, had dared to lose his virginity, or at least come very close.

By October 1902, when he was accepted to King's College, Cambridge, to read Mathematics, Maynard had grown into a tall, thin youth, confident of his intellectual and sexual maturity, if still convinced of his own ugliness. Late adolescence sat awkwardly in his lanky limbs, in the sharp jut of his brows, in the rubbery thickness of his lips, and in the long nose that had earned him the brutal nickname 'Snout'. Yet despite his obsession with his poor appearance, Maynard's inquisitiveness and prepossessing cleverness made him more attractive than he realised. An expressive gleam lit his grey-blue eyes, described by one subsequent admirer as a 'window' on to his 'leaping' mind,[5] and despite the formal camouflage of a military moustache his full mouth promised sensuality.

---

*Florence was only the second woman in Britain to be elected mayor; the first was Elizabeth Garrett Anderson, who became mayor of Aldeburgh in 1908.

†Maynard's siblings were less academically pressured, but clever. Margaret married the Nobel Prize-winning physiologist Archibald Vivian Hill and became a borough councillor in London. Geoffrey became an eminent surgeon and distinguished Blake scholar with a polymath's enthusiasm for rare books, art and the theatre.

In Cambridge, as at Eton, Maynard shone, but it was his extra-curricular activities that most profoundly shaped his undergraduate years. During his first year he was elected to membership of the Apostles, an elite discussion society that held semi-secret meetings over tea and anchovy toast, and it was here that Maynard had his first encounters with the moral philosopher G. E. Moore. Moore's rejection of solid Victorian pieties in favour of an ethics defined by art, intellect and love came as a revelation to Maynard, whose own childhood had been crowded with the heavy moral furniture of Church and school. The liberating proposition at the heart of Moore's *Principia Ethica*, that 'personal affections and aesthetic enjoyments include *all* the greatest, and *by far* the greatest, goods we can imagine',[6] brought light and air into Maynard's thinking and would continue to influence him for the rest of his life. Even though money and politics would be the worlds where his practical genius flourished, his spiritual compass would be set by a reverence for art and a contempt for rigid Establishment mores. He would become the kind of economist who could startle the world by falling in love with a ballerina.

If Maynard discovered his life's creed in Cambridge, he also made lifelong friends there, including Lytton Strachey, a pale, spidery-limbed aesthete with a lethally original intelligence and a devastatingly direct approach to matters of sex. Maynard, who had considered himself emancipated at Eton, was both unnerved and enraptured by Lytton's confident embrace of his own homosexuality. Only a decade had passed since the public ruin of Oscar Wilde, and the two young men were far from outing themselves. Yet in private they pledged themselves to a brotherhood of 'Higher Sodomy', regarding their sexuality as evidence of unimpeachable intelligence and superior caste.

For Maynard, these undergraduate years passed as an intellectual 'heaven on earth',[7] but in 1906 Lytton left to attempt a literary career in London, and Cambridge lost some of its lustre. Maynard's plan of working towards a Fellowship also lost its appeal, and instead he opted to follow Lytton to London where, after sitting the Civil Service entrance exam (and typically scoring the second highest mark of his year), he secured a post in the India Office. Here, however, he had his first experience of a world that did not yield to his ambitions. However fast Maynard's own mind might process lists and juggle numbers, the creaking bureaucracy of Whitehall maintained its own agonisingly slow pace. Once he claimed that all he had succeeded in doing, during his two years in the service, was arrange the delivery of a special breed of bull to India. Feeling bored and disappointed Maynard thus escaped back to Cambridge whenever he could which was one reason why he failed to become involved with a new London circle that Lytton was forming on the other side of town.

A former Cambridge friend, Thoby Stephen, had recently been liberated by the death of his father (the eminent man of letters Leslie Stephen) to relocate himself and his siblings, Adrian, Vanessa and Virginia, to a house in one of the shabbier Georgian squares of Bloomsbury. To the Stephens, having grown up in genteel Kensington, hemmed in by the rituals of four o'clock tea parties and calling cards, this move had felt like a pioneering step towards freedom, and they had embarked on it, as Virginia would later write, 'filled with experiments and reforms. We were going to do without table napkins ... we were going to paint; to write; to have coffee after dinner instead of tea at nine o clock. Everything was going to be new; everything was going to be different. Everything was on trial.'[8]

Reports of these domestic experiments, as relayed to the Stephens' elderly friends and relatives in Kensington, suggested that they were shocking, with young people of both sexes mixing at 46 Gordon Square without the constraints of either visiting hours or chaperones. In reality, the Stephens' embrace of bohemia was little more than a timid London version of the Apostles club. Small groups of Thoby's friends called round to converse gruffly with each other, finding the two Stephen sisters far too intimidatingly beautiful to address, let alone flirt with. Vanessa, aged twenty-six, was a promising painter, tall and dignified, her face moulded in strong Pre-Raphaelite curves; Virginia, three years younger, appeared skittish and sharp, with a suggestion of ungovernable emotion hovering in the angles of her face. She was rumoured to have a brilliant tongue and a vocation to write, but during these stilted 'at homes' she and Vanessa mostly sat apart, maintaining a shy, ironic silence.

Over time, however, these gauche young men and women learned to unbend in each other's company, and it was partly Thoby's sudden death, in 1906, that triggered the change, as grief prompted Vanessa into accepting a proposal of marriage from her brother's friend Clive Bell. The son of a coal tycoon, Clive was the plump and garrulous hedonist of this little circle, and he introduced a slight but perceptible razzle of luxury into Gordon Square. As Virginia and Adrian set up their own household near by, the small knot of friends expanded into a larger, more confident social network. Even though it was not yet the influential and notoriously cliquish 'Bloomsbury Group' that Lydia encountered in 1918, it was rapidly becoming a distinctive circle, known for the cleverness of its conversation and for its disdain of social taboos.

Lytton was the other catalyst in liberating Bloomsbury sensibilities. Still the most intellectually daring of his peers, he egged on Virginia and Vanessa to talk openly about sexual issues and encouraged them to read his smuttiest poetry. His casual enquiry one day as to whether a stain on Vanessa's dress was semen became, in Bloomsbury legend, the moment when Victorian prudery was definitively banished from their drawing rooms. Maynard, however, continued to remain a minor player in these bohemian dramas. Although he occasionally tagged along to Gordon Square with Lytton, his formal, civil servant suits, coupled with his modest disavowal of any artistic pretensions, muted the impression that he made on the Stephens and their friends.

By the summer of 1908, Maynard was also anxious to put some distance between himself and Lytton, for he had become physically and poetically besotted with his friend's cousin, the young painter Duncan Grant. Awkwardly for Maynard, Duncan was himself the object of Lytton's territorial, and very uncousinly, lust and only recently the latter had written to his friend Leonard Woolf of how smitten he was by Duncan's astonishing, unruly beauty: 'outspoken bold and just not rough, with frank grey-blue eyes and incomparably lascivious lips'.[9] As Maynard had feared, when news of this affair became public, Lytton turned against him and began circulating jealous, defamatory comments about his miserable qualifications as a lover – a 'safety bicycle with genitals'[10] – too cerebral and emotionally cautious to deserve Duncan.

But Lytton, in his desire for vengeance, had completely underestimated the depth of Maynard's feelings for Duncan, which went far beyond the predatory, sentimental rhetoric of the Higher Sodomy. Even though the affair would last for only a couple of years, Maynard would cherish Duncan for the rest of his life. Only Lydia would come closer to him, and she embodied many of the qualities that he had loved in Duncan – intuition, humour, the transforming gift of the artist, the ease of physical beauty. In later years it would become one of Maynard's greatest pleasures to watch his wife and former lover dancing together at Bloomsbury parties.

Yet while Lydia would return Maynard's love with unswerving fidelity, Duncan was too restlessly promiscuous to commit himself, and around the end of 1909 the affair had scaled down to a precious, but platonic, friendship. Maynard suffered in the process, but work as always was his panacea. Having finally lost patience with the Civil Service, he had retreated back to Cambridge, where he gained a Fellowship at King's and an appointment as College Lecturer in Economics. He spent much of his free time in London, however, and by 1911 the double helix of his private and public life was established as he moved into the heart of Bloomsbury, taking on the lease of a house in Brunswick Square, which he shared with Duncan, Virginia, Adrian, and Leonard Woolf, who had recently returned from the Colonial Civil Service in Ceylon.

This large, mixed household felt like a thrillingly unconventional arrangement to Maynard, giving him, he told his mother, his own 'London family'.[11] The city seemed brilliant to him at this time. Roger Fry had just challenged the art establishment with his first exhibition of post-impressionist painting; the Ballets Russes had just performed their first season; and at Ottoline Morrell's salon in Bedford Square, discussions about Freud, Einstein and Shaw were followed by dancing till dawn.

By 1914 the dance of the Bloomsbury households had reconfigured. Virginia and Leonard had tentatively, but happily, become Mr and Mrs Woolf, while Vanessa's marriage to Clive had settled into an arrangement of semi-prickly convenience, held together by their two small sons, Julian and Quentin, as well as by their willingness to tolerate each other's love affairs. It had become a fixed tenet of

Bloomsbury that domestic and sexual ties should remain open to reason and reinvention; in affairs of the heart – as in art, morality and table manners – the circle prided themselves on having broken free from their Victorian past. The result, however, was that sexual partners were swapped between them with confusing incestuousness. Duncan had moved on from Maynard to have an affair with Adrian; then, most unexpectedly, Vanessa had fallen in love with Duncan.

This, to some of her friends and family, appeared a hopeless cause, for while Duncan cared deeply for Vanessa and would father her daughter Angelica, he could never deny that his sharpest desires were for men. Early in 1915, when they were more or less living with each other, he began an affair with David, or Bunny, Garnett, an aspiring writer whose athletic beauty and uncomplicated high spirits reduced Duncan to the kind of jealous infatuation that he usually aroused in others. The two men were lovers for four years, and the strain on Vanessa hardened elements in her character. She formed a dread of outsiders invading her close circle, and it would be this same defensive hostility that Lydia encountered a decade later, when she herself was introduced into Bloomsbury as Maynard's mistress.

The 1914–18 war, however, threatened far more division than sexual rivalries, especially for Maynard. Whilst most of Bloomsbury took the leftish, libertarian line that Britain should negotiate peace with Germany, and many of the men declared themselves conscientious objectors, Maynard was conscripted into the centre of the government's war machine, with a post in the Treasury. Professionally his career had been rising steadily towards this elevation, with a string of new appointments, including editorship of the prestigious *Economic Journal* and growing influence in government circles (the Prime Minister, Herbert Asquith, and his wife both counted Maynard as a friend). Yet this move to the wartime Treasury exposed what was an already implicit moral divide between Maynard and his London circle. Bloomsbury's values remained ranked under the banner of G. E. Moore – proposing art, friendship and contemplation as the unsullied goals of the civilised mind. When Maynard's work took him into the compromised world of politics, money and especially war, his intellect was judged to have been misdirected, even debased.

Nor did the gap between him and his friends lessen when in 1916 Maynard was offered the lease on 46 Gordon Square. Clive had got himself work as a 'gardener' on Ottoline Morrell's country estate in order to avoid prosecution as a conscientious objector and could no longer afford to run the house alone. But by the time Maynard moved in, virtually everyone else in Bloomsbury had retreated elsewhere, Lytton was living and writing in Buckinghamshire, while Vanessa had moved herself and her boys to Sussex, where she could look after Duncan and Bunny as they laboured on government-approved farm work. Their new home was a flint-and-brick farmhouse called Charleston, which was tucked under the ridge of Firle Beacon. Dominated by the South Downs, five miles from the closest station, in Lewes, it was geographically a world away from Gordon Square. Yet Vanessa had taken the latter's spirit with her, finding time between pumping water and feeding chickens to paint decorative murals on the farmhouse doors, and to hang the walls with her own and Duncan's work.

Bloomsbury had moved to Sussex and, missing his friends, Maynard began to follow them down for the weekends. The rustic domesticity of Charleston fascinated him (he spent hours weeding the garden path with his penknife), and the closeness of these new living arrangements brought a deeper intimacy with Vanessa. He and she were already bound by their love for Duncan, but it was at Charleston that Maynard learned to admire Vanessa's beauty and independence of mind. Also to enjoy the interest she took in what she called the 'sucking sodomy'[12] of his sex life. Vanessa in turn came to depend on Maynard's company as he entertained her with political gossip and with stories of the wartime party circuit that had sprung up around the Café Royal and the clubs of Soho. Even more crucially, she came to depend on him financially, as he started to subsidise Charleston's running expenses.

Moving between Sussex and London, Maynard was often happy and exhilarated. His involvement in the war had benefited him in certain ways, providing bracing intellectual and social challenge. Yet by the time it had dragged into its final year its logic had become dreadful to him. The government's determination, under Lloyd George, to win at any human cost seemed to him to breach essential moral values,* and by the end of 1917 he was despairing to Duncan, 'I work for a government I despise for ends I think criminal.'[13] He was also being kept at his desk for intolerably long hours, and the strain made him hectoring and boorish. Maynard himself could be overwhelmed by the energy of his brain, complaining that it never seemed to stop in its implacable, investigative tracks – 'an over activity of the cells, I suppose, like cancer';[14] yet in this period of exhaustion and disillusionment he went into such aggressive intellectual overdrive that even the Charleston household began to dread his visits.

The ending of the war brought some respite – parties in London, the Diaghilev season and meeting Lydia: all were signs of a world restored to sanity – but in early 1919 Maynard was sent as chief Treasury representative to the Peace Conference in Paris. Here the conduct of the victorious Allies was almost as brutish and senseless as the war itself; and Maynard looked on with grim disbelief as France, Britain and America conspired on a collective act of revenge, imposing crippling levels of reparation on Germany that seemed to him not only immoral but certain to impact perilously on Europe's political and economic future.

He left the conference feeling 'morally physically & spiritually ill';[15] but as he went on to exorcise his feelings in the now-classic polemic *The Economic Consequences of the Peace*, Maynard's disgust would make him famous. His scintillatingly rude attacks on the Allied leaders (Wilson a 'blind, deaf Don Quixote',[16] Clemenceau a xenophobe with 'one illusion – France'), coupled with his starkly prophetic analysis of where their blinkered policies would lead, were greeted with what he incredulously reported as a 'deluge of approval'.[17] After the book's publication in December 1919 it sold over 100,000 copies, and as *The Economic Consequences* brought Maynard international recognition, it also regained him the respect and intimacy of his friends. Lytton wrote admiringly that he had 'swallowed it at a gulp',[18] and by early 1920, Maynard felt himself almost restored to Bloomsbury – able once more to straddle the virtues of the 'examined life' with his own more pragmatic operations in the wider world.

---

*Maynard briefly considered resigning from the Treasury in protest.

Bertrand Russell, Maynard Keynes and Lytton Strachey, Garsington, 1915

Number 46 Gordon Square also remained Maynard's London home. There was still a communal feel to the house as Duncan and a somewhat resentful Clive (who had tried and failed to regain the tenancy) rented rooms on the top two floors whilst sharing the ground-floor dining room and first-floor sitting room with Maynard. Vanessa and her children, who were now living four doors away at number 50, also came into the house for meals (produced by the servants, who worked in the basement and lived up in the attic). The spacious second floor, however, was all for Maynard's use as bedroom and study, and it was here, with his high front windows looking out over the trees of the Gordon Square garden and flooding his rooms with afternoon sunshine, that Maynard settled comfortably into his new eminence.

Half the week he was still teaching at King's, which remained his intellectual centre of gravity, but the rest of the time he was in London, dealing with an expanding flow of invitations to lecture and write for the press, whilst also developing a talent for working the financial markets, which would ultimately gain him real wealth. Even though he was always engaged in too many projects, Maynard now seemed to juggle the life of academia and politics, money and ideas with panache. To others, and perhaps to himself, he appeared a man enviably in control of his destiny. In December 1921, however, he allowed Lydia into his life – and with her a challenge both to his autonomy and to his sense of identity.

When Maynard made the first crucial move towards Lydia, asking her to lunch on 18 December, he had been in an unusually solitary state. Sebastian Sprott was in Cambridge, while Vanessa and Duncan were wintering in St Tropez with the children. That he had only chaste expectations of Lydia was evident from the appointment he made for eight o'clock that evening with Gabriel Aitken, a painter and musician whom he occasionally took to bed. But it was only four days later that Maynard was confessing happily to Vanessa by post that he was 'very much in love' with Lydia and was planning to have supper with her at the Savoy. Vanessa at a distance would have dismissed Maynard's being 'in love' as Bloomsbury exaggeration, and so it may still have been. But the Savoy supper, which took place on 23 December, after Lydia's evening performance at the Alhambra, ratcheted Maynard's emotions to a higher intensity. He and Lydia talked together until 1 a.m. and arranged to meet as soon as Maynard had returned from spending Christmas in the country with Lytton, Lytton's domestic companion the painter Dora Carrington, and Sebastian.

It is possible, even at this stage, that Maynard believed he was in control of his feelings. Once he was reunited with Sebastian, the latter's obliging cleverness, long limbs and floppy brown hair would surely stifle any quixotic attraction that he might be developing for Lydia. However, Maynard's description of that weekend as quiet and very happy was highly censored, for he was falling seriously in love, plunging into a thicket of emotion, and by 27 December he was forced to admit to Lytton, 'I'm entangled – a dreadful business – and barely fit to speak to.' The following day he wrote to Vanessa, 'What's to be done about it. I'm getting terrified.' Even allowing for a degree of self-mockery, the note of panic was genuine.

From Lydia, however, Maynard was receiving very mixed signals. He had already written to arrange yet another meeting with her but the reply he received, while written by return of post, was the message of a sphinx.

Dear Mr Keynes
Do come then Friday about 5 o clock if it is possible.
Yours sincerely
L. Lopokova[19]

While Maynard had been scribbling to his friends a day-by-day account of his emotional turmoil, Lydia's communications to him could not have been more minimal. There were practical reasons for her reticence – from the looping scrawl of her handwriting it is clear that her written English was still less fluent than her speech. But she also seems to have been hiding behind the formality of her phrasing, flirting with Maynard perhaps but still deliberately withholding herself.

Months later, Lydia was able to write emotionally of the period when she and Maynard first became lovers: 'Fog. Truly it was so beautiful ... I believe all the fogs are made for Sundays, especially last season when we had our meetings ... Do you remember?'[20] But at the time she was guarding herself. She had only just emerged from messy relationships with Barocchi and Stravinsky, and she did not know Maynard, or his world, very well. All her instincts urged caution – a wariness that would be endorsed by her sister Evgenia in a letter that would eventually reach her the following spring: 'Take care in your choice of people and don't trust them Lidusha! ... You have lived through so much.'[21]

But if Lydia had counselled herself to move slowly, Maynard's disappearance to Tidmarsh over Christmas was timed with exquisite accuracy to force the situation. Whatever she had been feeling – curiosity, desire, frustration, nerves – had a long weekend to ripen, and by the time Lydia met Maynard again on 30 December she seems to have been primed for something decisive to happen.

Vanessa, in France, was now alerted to the aberrant force of Maynard's infatuation and wrote with hot, helpless prejudice to warn him against Lydia manipulating him into marriage: 'However charming she is, she'd be a very expensive wife and would give up dancing and is altogether to be preferred as a mistress.'[22] Yet while Maynard's reply reassured Vanessa that he was safe from marriage, he made no attempt to minimise his feelings: 'The affair is very serious and I don't know in the least what to do about it.'[23] He admitted in a second letter, 'I'm in a terribly bad plight, almost beyond rescue. Clive simply grins with delight at seeing me so humbled.'[24]

Once the lovers had moved into the bedroom, Lydia at least may have grown in confidence. If she had known about Maynard's taste for men, it would not necessarily have alarmed her – she was familiar enough with the histories of Nijinsky and Massine to understand that sexuality could be fluid. Maynard, however, had never been in love with a woman before and for most of his adult life had not even considered it an option. Back in 1912, when he had still been fully committed to the Higher Sodomy, he had been flirted with by the pretty, poetry-loving Brynhild Olivier and had reacted with something close to revulsion. 'I don't much care for the atmosphere these women breed,' he had complained to Duncan. 'Bryn is too stupid – and I begin to take an active dislike to her. Out of the window I see Rupert [Brooke] making love to her ... taking her hand, sitting at her feet, gazing at her eyes. Oh these womanisers. How on earth and what for can he do it?'[25]

By 1921, Maynard's feelings had admittedly undergone a benign modification. His affection for Vanessa had taught him to enjoy female company, and as London's young men had gone off to fight or farm, Maynard's social world had become increasingly populated by women. The war had, in fact, fostered a general drift towards heterosexuality. In 1915, when Bunny had been away on ambulance service in France, Duncan had turned to Vanessa for sexual consolation, although to his diary he had refused to admit that it was anything more than a crude form of relief: 'It is a convenient way the females have of letting off one's spunk.'[26] It had been in that year that Lytton had found himself 'profoundly moved'[27] by the boyish legs of Dora Carrington; two years later, his brother James had begun courting Alix Sargant, and Adrian had married an American psychoanalyst, Karin Costelloe. By 1921, Bunny too had settled for domesticity and married Ray Marshall.

If the war had helped transform bachelor buggers into husbands, age had also played a role. As Maynard's circle approached their forties, some felt the urge towards fatherhood (Duncan's daughter Angelica was born to Vanessa at the end of 1918), whilst others looked to marriage as social camouflage. Homosexuality could still bring scandal, possibly a prison sentence, to those who were exposed in public, especially in the reactionary backlash of the war years, and even Maynard had toyed with the idea of taking a wife.

The most likely candidate had been Barbara Hiles, an art student on the fringes of Bloomsbury. Though a delicately built woman, Hiles affected a rangy schoolboy swagger and Maynard was pleased by her rosy cheeks and blue eyes, a curly, doll-like prettiness that prefigured aspects of Lydia's own attraction. The relationship did not develop beyond an exploratory dalliance, however, and Maynard was shocked when, in the spring of 1921, he became the unwitting, unwilling object of female desire. His new secretary, Naomi Bentwich, had fallen in love with what she had rhapsodised in her diary as Maynard's 'long exquisite lines' and 'liquid lustrous eyes'.[28] She was convinced that her feelings were returned and was distraught to discover that, with his usual tendency to attribute 'unreal rationality'[29] to those around him, Maynard had simply interpreted her adoration as a rapt interest in his work.

Before Maynard fell in love with Lydia, the sum total of his heterosexual relationships had thus amounted to no more than a couple of self-consciously daring experiments with prostitutes,* a jolly flirtation and a grisly misunderstanding. He had never met a woman who aroused in him anything like the fascination he felt towards men, nor the sexual urgency. Rather, as he watched his friends' tormented ambivalence towards marriage, adultery and gender, he may have thought it far easier and less exhausting to stick to partners of his own sex.

He may also have found it more reassuring, for Maynard depended on sexual expertise to overcome the insecurities he still harboured about his physical appearance. Though Maynard loved beauty, was stimulated and delighted by it, the company of an attractive lover exacerbated his dislike of his own defects. With a man, at least he knew what he was doing, but with a woman he felt doubly vulnerable and, as he found himself 'entangled' by Lydia, part of Maynard's

---

*In Alexandria, in 1913, he confessed to Duncan hd had 'had a w-m-n'. JMK to DG, 17 April 1913.

terror was surely physical. Although she was not conventionally beautiful, she was a woman for whom physical finesse was a professional given. Nervously he may have wondered how this piquant little ballerina would view his lanky, unathletic frame; nervously he may have wondered how well he would succeed in making love to her, having once even shied away from Lydia's offer to pinch her leg.*

Yet whatever happened in her bedroom at the Waldorf Hotel, it fuelled their mutual desire. If Maynard was hypnotised by Lydia's energy and talent, then she was mesmerised by his astonishing mind. Lydia had been brought up to respect books and ideas. In an erratic fashion she had continued to educate herself, keeping copies of Tolstoy (in Russian) and Shakespeare (in English) among her belongings as she toured around America and Europe. It was immensely seductive now to have Maynard directing his brilliant conversation towards her, whilst at the same time paying her the compliment of concentrating tenderly on her own. When Maynard was attracted by anyone, he had an appealing habit of drawing out their thoughts and ideas, listening closely with his head on one side, his gaze unwavering. Basking in such attention, Lydia felt clever, elevated, cherished. And she felt equally cherished by Maynard's prompt desire to look after her practical interests. Love made him protective, and having first busied himself with setting Lydia up with a bank account (shocked by the discovery that she deposited her earnings with the hotel porter), when *The Sleeping Princess* closed and Lydia could no longer afford to live at the Waldorf, Maynard organised for her to move into 50 Gordon Square.

These actions weighed deeply with Lydia. She had suffered through enough uncertainty in the past four years to value a man who wanted to look after her – and with her professional future again in doubt she could not help but factor Maynard's generosity into his appeal. Yet if it had long been drilled into her that 'dancers have to look after their backs',[30] any reflex calculation that Lydia may have made did not cancel the truth of her feelings. She moved more cautiously than Maynard did, she fell in love less precipitously, but she

*Barbara Hiles would later claim that Maynard had begged her for advice and direction.

did want him very much, and the intimacy that grew between them during the early weeks of 1922 made her want him more.

The world, of course, did not stop for them. Throughout January, while Lydia was dancing her final performances of *The Sleeping Princess*, Maynard was busy with a hefty new commission, editing the first of twelve supplements for the *Manchester Guardian* on the problems facing post-war economic reconstruction. Yet it was a measure of his feelings for Lydia that he managed to squeeze private time for her out of his busy schedule, including driving her around the tourist sights of London in a hired Daimler. Quentin Bell, who was back in Gordon Square for the new school term, was invited on some of these trips, and it seemed to him that Maynard's detailed commentaries, as he led the trio around the Tower of London, or Hampton Court, were designed not just to entertain his new Russian mistress, but to draw her into his own world of British history and culture.

Lydia herself was humbly aware of the gaps in her education, writing to Maynard in an early letter, 'You are so brilliant I think sometimes I say things not as bright as you expect.'[31] Yet Maynard's tutoring became part of their lovemaking, and she would regularly offer up evidence of her progress as a gift to him: 'In one of Chekof's stories I met Malthus, I *was* pleased, if I would not have met you I would be ignorant about him - now I swell with pride.'[32]

Several of Maynard's friends and colleagues assumed that Lydia would be steamrollered by the force of his intellect. Maynard could be crushingly impatient with those he found stupid or slow, and even Bertrand Russell would claim that when he argued with Maynard, he felt that he 'took his life in his hands'.[33] Yet Maynard would never betray any sense that Lydia was his inferior. He considered artists to be privileged, even magical, beings, and he was captivated by the physical effects at his new mistress's command, not just on the stage but in the drawing room, on the street, and in the bedroom, where he was fascinated by her dancer's frank acceptance of her body, rare even in liberated Bloomsbury.

Still more fascinating as he got to know Lydia better were the odd, intuitive, occasionally startling insights of her conversation. For Maynard, who had been schooled in intellectual precision since he could first read, there was a constant novelty in the way Lydia's mind darted between ideas, and in the vividly reminted English with which she expressed them. Some of Lydia's more outrageous puns and neologisms were pure serendipity – accidental collisions between her Russian and English vocabularies – but many were fed by a genuine interest in words, and by a genuine idiosyncracy of vision. Maynard believed that she was a natural poet, and Lydia, quick to sense his admiration and to prove herself more than just a pretty ballerina, set herself assiduously to beguile him with her 'Lydian English'.

When she could not do this in person, she tutored herself to do it by post, cultivating for the first time in her life the discipline of regular letter writing. Whenever Maynard had to be away from Gordon Square she sent loving notes to him, writing two or three times a day and always with a dictionary by her side. Signing off one of her letters with 'ticking's and acheings in my heart for you', she added, 'In the dictionary is only ache but to me sounds not literary with tickings.'[34] Lydia's inventions were sometimes inspired, sometimes nonsensical, but they were always her own, as she wrote graphically of enjoying 'a promiscuous rattle of a day';[35] of possessing 'enormous gossips in my bosom';[36] or of Vanessa 'oxygenating' her daughter's Cockney accent.[37] Maynard reviewed her efforts with delight, both proud mentor and besotted lover, and it pained him if she ever relapsed into cliché: 'You mustn't write "I sat for 2 solid hours",' he chided. 'That's common English.'

Just as Maynard admired Lydia's language, so he admired the lyrical enthusiasm with which she responded to the writing of others, especially his own. Even though she suffered over her own analytic inadequacies – 'I am not like you talented in idea put into words, I express myself better in impulses'[38] – he set enormous store by her tributes. 'It is very nice to meet your articles,' she wrote, 'they *breathe* to me';[39] and in an earlier letter, 'When I read what you write somehow I feel bigger than I am.'[40]

If Lydia made fundamental emotional sense in Maynard's life, he also fitted the pattern of hers. She had always been drawn to the promise of security and power, and most of the men in her past had offered these things even if they had not delivered them – Mandelkern as her personal agent; Heywood as her fiancé and advocate; Randolfo as the Ballets Russes's business manager; and Stravinsky as its musical genius. If alcohol and absence had denied her a real father in Vasili, she had arguably looked for substitutes in her lovers. She had also looked to Diaghilev, and one other factor in Maynard's appeal to Lydia may have been the resemblance that he bore to Big Serge. Both men possessed protean intellects, with a rare talent for synthesising ideas; both men were autocrats – worldly, articulate and charismatic. It is surely significant that whilst Lydia never stopped revering Diaghilev, his mystique for her diminished after she had met Maynard and acquired a lover who was his equal.

During the early weeks of their relationship, binding threads of commitment were spun. Maynard had intended to go to India at the end of January, as Vice Chairman of a Royal Commission on fiscal policy, and right at the beginning the trip had promised a useful brake on his runaway emotions. 'Flight to India may save you', Vanessa had counselled,[41] and Maynard had agreed. Yet when the moment came he refused to leave, and not only withdrew from the Commission, but turned down Duncan's invitation to join him and Vanessa in Paris. On 8 April, Maynard was finally forced to part with Lydia, having accepted a commission to report on the Genoa Economic Conference for the *Manchester Guardian*. She promised to wait lovingly for his return, conjuring the scenes of domestic happiness that would greet him: 'I would come to your study,' she wrote on 16 April, 'sit on the couch and you speak simple words to me, peacefully joyful.'[42]

Chapter Twelve

CAMBRIDGE AND BLOOMSBURY INFLUENCES

Until I see him carrying on with L. I must give up imagining what happens – it beggars my fancy.

DUNCAN GRANT[1]

Over the years, Lydia and Maynard's relationship would acquire a near-mythical quality as friends and colleagues observed the tenderly self-contained world that they had created against the odds of their different backgrounds. Violet Bonham-Carter, for instance, would hold them up as an exemplary 'attraction of opposites' to the readers of her magazine column.[2] Yet it would be over two years before that attraction stabilised, and over two years before Lydia felt she had survived two very powerful threats to her security. One was Bloomsbury, and the subtle chill of condescension with which it collectively greeted her arrival in its daily life. The other was Maynard's homosexuality.

Despite Maynard's initial claims of being overwhelmed by his passion for Lydia, he had remained lucidly confident in his determination to hang on to his former sexual habits. If Duncan had been allowed to love both Bunny and Vanessa, Maynard assumed that he too could enjoy both his lover and his mistress, especially given Lydia's promising compliance early in February, when he had tried to explain the nature of his feelings for Sebastian Sprott. 'We had a good deal of *éclaircissement*,' he had reported to Vanessa, 'which was painful for a moment but seems to have made no real difference to us at all.'[3] But Maynard, as usual, was seeing largely what he wanted to see. While Lydia was too experienced to expect a sudden, radiant conversion to heterosexuality, she had no intention of settling for a 'civilised' relationship in which she took submissive second place to his clever young men. She might have appeared innocently full of gratitude, eager with love, but she was also quietly determined to oust Sebastian from Maynard's heart and from his bed.

To some of Maynard's friends this task had originally seemed one of almost farcical hopelessness. Yet the letters that began to pass between the two lovers reveal that Maynard, unlike Duncan, was finding sex with a woman surprisingly gratifying. The correspondence had been forced on them in April when Maynard had had to leave London for the conference in Genoa. But it was Lydia, with her dictionary close by, who began to coin for them both an unabashed and quirkily erotic language of love. The pages of her letters glowed, graphically, with remembered or anticipated references to sexual joy, as she wrote of 'gobbling and regobbling' Maynard; of 'blending [her] mouth and heart to his'; and of 'detaining infinitely our warm wet kisses'.[4] Maynard, by return of post, was not only smitten by Lydia's vocabulary but also freed by it to express his own desires, and by 24 April he was writing from Genoa of his yearning to 'be foxed and gobbled abundantly'.

Nor did these pleasures pall. In June, Lydia wrote of 'tasting [Maynard's] buttons', in August of being his 'dog', in September of 'warming him with [her] foxy lips', in October 'stand[ing] on [her] knees and kiss[ing him]'; and in November being his 'licking dog'. What Maynard did for her in return is hinted at in caressing salutes to his 'slender' and 'subtle fingers'. If Maynard had initially been unsure of himself as a lover of women, as a trained academic he knew the value of research; and as well as consulting Barbara Hiles he may have made a point of reading Marie Stopes's *Married Love*. This revolutionary text, published in 1918, not only stressed the emotional and physical significance of the female orgasm, but provided detailed anatomical information about how a man might 'rouse, charm and stimulate' his partner to 'local readiness'.[5] Maynard had already mastered the reading matter on homosexuality (he had all twelve volumes of Karl Heinrich Ulrich's *Research on the Riddle of Man-Manly Love* on his top bookshelf at King's) and it is hard not to imagine him extending his studies to Lydia.

However, the details of their correspondence suggest that the affair was consummated largely through an inventive play of fingers and mouths, and that Lydia may have been hoping for more. On 25 April 1923, writing to tell Maynard about a golfing ballet that Massine was planning to choreograph for her, she speculated teasingly, 'Can I seduce you in golf clothes ... as I have failed in masculine clothes perhaps I may win in masculine game?'* If this throwaway remark raises an image of Lydia coquettishly sporting trousers in the bedroom, it also suggests that Maynard may have been reluctant to embrace conventional heterosexuality. Was he unwilling or unable to attempt penetrative sex? Were there aspects of Lydia's own sexuality that unnerved him?

Certainly during the early years of their relationship Lydia was careful to play down her femininity. She habitually referred to herself in a masculine style, as a 'man' leading 'a simple working man's life'[6] or as a 'guilty man'[7] – and she scattered her letters with seductive references to cross-dressing. When she bought herself a pair of men's pyjamas, she made a point of letting the absent Maynard know; and it was with a touch of ribaldry that she described to him the famous male impersonator Hetty King, with whom she would share a stage later that year: 'If you should see her – at once you would acknowledge that she knows how to wear male trousers. She has acquired all man's habits to perfection.'[8]

But if Lydia's flirtation with androgyny started out as a sweet-natured offering to Maynard's sexual equivocation, her attitude began to turn less confident and more shrill. As the months passed, Maynard still showed no signs of weakening his commitment to Sebastian, while the latter obdurately continued to regard himself as Maynard's lover, with powerful rights and expectations. Sebastian was confident that Maynard was experimenting with Lydia and would soon return to the sodomite fold, a belief in which he was encouraged by Lytton. And as Lydia herself sensed how badly she had underestimated the 'Cambridge influence' in Maynard's life, and understood just how badly she wanted to hold on to him, her own

*Lydia had also been performing in 'man's clothes' in Massine's little ballet *Fanatics of Pleasure*, although Maynard would not have seen her, since at the time he was in Genoa.

feelings of insecurity became correspondingly fretful. During their first summer together, when Maynard had to travel to Hamburg for a lecturing engagement, she wrote to him miserably, 'Oh! Maynard do not have wild passions for other people.'[9]

But Maynard, fortified by his 'unreal expectations of rationality' in those around him, was either impervious to the tensions that he was creating, or else casually cruel in his determination to retain the best of both worlds. The awkward triangle between himself, Lydia and Sebastian persisted all through 1922, until he unwittingly forced it to breaking point by admitting to Lydia his plans for spending the following Easter holidays in North Africa with Sebastian. This choice of destination could not have been more wounding for her, notorious as it was for its relaxed attitudes to homosexuality and its reputation for available boys, and Lydia instantly sensed betrayal. She rounded on Maynard with uncharacteristic violence, demanding that he cancel the holiday and threatening to leave him if he refused.

Having delivered her ultimatum, however, Lydia either lost her nerve or reconsidered her strategy, for the following day she wrote a contrite, sorrowful note to Maynard, in which she berated herself for her overwrought state. She almost seemed to accept that she was asking more than he could offer: 'I can't put myself yet to that state of wisdom when all is over happiness and unhappiness. I am ashamed it all came out. Forgive me. I am your servus-regi.'[10] In late February 1923, Maynard did finally cancel the trip to North Africa, but he was not yet ready to cancel Sebastian, and a second exhausting fight on 1 March left Lydia once again weak, tearful and floundering for words. 'I know you are relieved to-day from yesterday's mentally stormy happenings. I struggle for sleep. I did not study this morning. I am a phisical invalid. Oh.'[11]

That final 'Oh' may have registered as a gasp of defeat, but Lydia had not given up fighting for Maynard. By 16 March she had controlled her emotions sufficiently to agree to a civilised tea with Sebastian and was sufficiently astute to describe their meeting to Maynard in terms that made her rival appear woefully dull: 'He has more intelect than others and told me about electricity.'[12] Maynard, either because he would not risk losing Lydia or because the affair with Sebastian had actually run its course, finally yielded. After that spring, Sebastian was eased from the role of lover to friend, and by 1925 had put himself at an extra distance by accepting a lectureship in Psychology at Nottingham University. Maynard never looked for a replacement. Although he flirted, and may even have continued to negotiate a little casual sex while he was in Cambridge, he never sought out another serious relationship with a man.

Lydia had won her sexual battle for Maynard, and it would not be long before the issue of male rivals could be turned into a joke between them. In October 1924, when Maynard invented a whimsical new formula for sending his love – 'I kiss the bacheloress as though she were something *quite the opposite*'[13] – Lydia pretended to misunderstand his reference to future matrimony, writing back with mock severity, 'I frown if you "kiss the bacheloress as though she were something quite the opposite" one of the meanings might be a bachelor (Cambridge influence) but I am *not serious*.'[14] She would even feel strong enough to taunt Maynard over the solitary sexual 'digressions' that he might indulge in Cambridge, ordering him not to 'write letters to me when you are enjoying yourself in an enlightened direction' and threatening to withdraw her own favours if he failed to obey: 'if you commit this adultery I will not serenade you with my fingers'.[15]

Most critically for Lydia, the removal of Sebastian cleared the air for Maynard to talk of marriage. Very soon after the North Africa holiday was cancelled, Quentin overheard Lydia 'suddenly and gaily' announce to his mother that 'Maynar' says I write to Barocchi and say to him: does he still considered himself married to me?'[16]

Vanessa's own response to this statement was not encouraging: 'matrimony is a very serious business,' she warned Lydia. 'I should be very careful about saying or doing anything.'[17] What Vanessa had meant, of course, was that marriage between Lydia and Maynard would be very serious for herself and for Bloomsbury.

The eighteen months during which Lydia had been installed as Maynard's mistress had only hardened his friends' incredulity concerning the affair. It was less that they disapproved of his seeking respectability with a woman – a clever Cambridge student or a Bloomsbury acolyte like Hiles would have been a respectable and understandable choice. What mystified them was Maynard straying so far outside his proper intellectual and social terrain, and expecting his friends to embrace this 'half witted canary', as Lytton was pleased to call her, as one of their own. Lydia might be adorable on stage or as an occasional party guest, but Bloomsbury had no desire to include her within their inner circle, nor to watch her annexing their most brilliant mind.

Years later, E. M. Forster would guiltily acknowledge their blindness to Lydia's intelligence: 'how we all used to underestimate her'.[18] Yet Bloomsbury's greater blindness lay in their failure to grasp how liberated Maynard felt by Lydia's difference from him. A bluestocking mistress, even a woman like Hiles, would have been a dull replication of what he already knew, and Maynard, to an extent not always grasped by his circle, derived much of his prodigious energy from moving between different worlds and inhabiting a subtly altered identity within each. Lydia, as a ballerina and as a Russian, was his fascinating opposite, and, as Maynard's niece, Polly Hill, would later observe, he delighted in her as a prize that he had snatched from another existence and as an expression of 'his own frustrated artistic humanity'.[19]

If Maynard had kept Lydia more separate from his social life, his friends might well have objected to her less forcibly. But back in February 1922, when he had opted for the convenience of moving her so close to him, at 50 Gordon Square, he had delivered her into the heart of Bloomsbury. Next door to Lydia at number 51 lived a shifting assortment of Strachey family (including Lytton, when he was in town) while nine doors along in the other direction, at number 41, lived more Stracheys, James and his wife Alix. Within number 50 itself Lydia was sandwiched between two sets of Stephens, with Adrian and his wife Karin in the bottom flat, and Vanessa and her children on the two top floors. Even at number 46, when Lydia visited Maynard she would encounter his friends, since Clive still occupied the top floor, as did Duncan when he was in London, while Vanessa and her children continued to eat most of their meals there.

These were, by any standards, exacting neighbours. Even Virginia Woolf claimed that visiting Gordon Square from her married home in Richmond had become as alarming to her as entering the 'lions house at the zoo ... the animals are dangerous, rather suspicious of each other and full of fascination and mystery'.[20] It did not help that during the first and most difficult two years in which Lydia was cast among them, she was experiencing unusual stretches of unemployment in which she was forced to hang around Gordon Square with time on her hands. It did not take long for the lions to turn on her, expressing their resentment at her intrusion in a subtle assault of snubs, impatience and small rudenesses.

This situation had been unforeseeable when, in early 1922, Lydia had first fallen in love with Maynard and when she had assumed that her new association with Massine would secure her a reasonable run of work. Massine had already proved his credentials as a potential successor to Diaghilev, having led a company of dancers on a highly profitable tour around South America. Now he was in London at the request of the movie producer Walter Wanger, with a commission to mount a substantial new season of ballet at Covent Garden and with generous funding at his disposal.

Wanger himself was not in the business of ballet, but was looking for ways to revolutionise the image of cinema in Britain. To that end he had hired the Opera House to host a season of 'classic' films from the past decade (including Wesley Ruggles's *Love* and Jacques Feyder's *Atlantide*); and to give extra cultural and fashionable gloss to the event he had decided to tack a programme of Russian ballet on to some of the screenings as a live 'second feature'. Massine had been offered sufficient money to choreograph four programmes of work* and to hire the best available dancers – and it was not remarkable that Lydia, if she had been surprised by the context of this engagement, had found it a hopeful one. It would put her back on an opera house stage; it would add several new roles to her repertory; and it would revive her partnership with Massine, which still remained lodged in the public's affections as the stellar pairing of the era.

Billed as 'The world's greatest dancers', Lydia and Massine gave their first reunion performance on 3 April 1922 in a programme headed by *Ragtime*, a short, deadpan pastiche of popular dances set to Stravinsky's titular score. All of their admirers were out in force to

*In fact Massine produced only three.

watch, from the Chelsea galerites to the Belgrave elite – Margot Asquith was spotted waving her handkerchief – and even though reactions from the critics were guarded, with the *Sphere* feeling that the Russians did not sparkle as brightly away from Diaghilev, their views had no effect on the public or the box office. To Maynard, now in Genoa, Lydia scrawled daily reports of the successful season, alternating between bursts of 'animalistic energy'[21] and delicious languor: 'All morning in bed pure delight!'[22]

For the second programme, which included a fiendishly bravura duet to Cimarosa's *Le Astuzie femminili*, Massine had choreographed Lydia a new solo, a Scottish reel set to music by Percy Grainger, for which Duncan Grant had been commissioned to design her costume. She was eager to show Maynard her approval of his friend's work, especially the series of sketches that Duncan had drawn of her in her kilt: 'like a Scotch whirlwind, so much activity and not only in the legs – everywhere'.[23] She was even more artful in the descriptions that she gave of the 'negress dance'[24] that she was learning for the final programme,* in which she had to cover her body with dark paint. Mischievously commiserating with Maynard's lonely 'intelectual' state in Genoa, Lydia offered him casually provocative reports of her naked, blacked-up body in the dressing room, and of the slippery consequences of the cold cream that she had to use for its eventual removal: 'Massine complaints that he cannot grasp me as I slide from him like a frog.'[25]

As Lydia was seducing Maynard with this enticing nonsense, she was also assuring him of her happiness in Gordon Square – and initially she was right to feel optimistic about her new living arrangements. When she had first moved in to number 50, taking over two empty rooms in Vanessa's part of the house, her landlady had been largely absent in France, leaving Quentin and Angelica in the charge of their pretty young maid, Grace Germany. This trio had formed an instantly cosy alliance with Lydia, and Quentin recalled her mesmerising them in the kitchen with her stories of 'Russia and the

*The 'negress dance' appeared in a mixed programme of divertissements titled *The Cockatoo's Holiday*. Individual numbers were listed as Valse, Papillon, Minuet (danced by Lydia and Massine), Les Gisettes, Tarantella (from *Boutique*), Pass Pied, Sylvia, Arabella (danced by Lydia and Massine), Clog Dance and a Finale led by Lydia and Massine.

L'Écossaise: sketch of Lydia in *Scotch Reel* by Duncan Grant, 1922

Nevsky Prospekt and droshkis and zakusis and wolves and samovars'.[26] Even when Vanessa had returned at the end of March, Lydia had been too busy for any friction to generate. Her dancing schedule had been hectic, since her morning class with Cecchetti was followed by rehearsals at Massine's studio in New Oxford Street, and by two daily performances. Her social diary, too, had been full, with parties hosted by the conductor Eugene Goossens, a photo session for *Vogue* and socialising with three of her most persistent admirers: Sam Courtauld, Basil Maine (an Irish songwriter and pianist whom Lydia referred to fondly as her 'platonic lover') and J. M. Barrie. Despite Lydia abandoning Barrie back in 1919, he continued to admire her talent, liked to chat with her sitting on his knee and promised that he would write a new play for her.

So crammed were Lydia's days that she had little time to intrude on Vanessa, beyond waylaying her for chats at bedtime. Vanessa herself might comment snidely to Roger Fry, 'there is some truth perhaps in Clive's complaint that [Lydia] has only one subject ... the ballet',[27] but she assumed that her presence in the house was only temporary, and was more than happy to exploit it by annexing Lydia in gossips about Mary Hutchinson – Clive's mistress – who had been the subject of unfailing irritated fascination to Vanessa for the last six years. Duncan too had seemed fond of Lydia, and the day that he, Vanessa, Clive and Mary attended the unveiling of her tartan ballet costume had felt like a genuine Bloomsbury celebration. (The only blot on the occasion was Elisabeth Bibesco, Margot Asquith's daughter, who tagged along with the group. Bibesco had nursed her own hopes of becoming Maynard's mistress and gave Lydia the uneasy sense that her only motive for coming backstage was to see 'how I look very near'.)[28]

Feeling herself popular with Maynard's friends, and 'full of speaking spirits'[29] with them, Lydia had not imagined that they would be anything but sympathetic when the Covent Garden season ended and Massine encountered unexpected difficulties in finding further engagements for his troupe. She may even have hoped that this period of unemployment would allow her to get to know Duncan, Vanessa and Clive more intimately. In Gordon Square, however, the prospect of Lydia being at home, without a job, raised more apprehension than sympathy. Vanessa and Clive in particular panicked each other into a state of mutual alarm, imagining Lydia's noisy, energetic presence shattering the peace at number 50 all day and her gossip about ballet, hats and Russian émigrés dominating every mealtime at number 46. Far from flitting into and out of Gordon Square as they had assumed, Maynard's ballerina mistress looked as though she might become a permanent fixture, expecting to be involved in everybody's doings, even to be included in the party that would be going down to Charleston for the summer holiday.

Vanessa's wartime retreat had remained a second home for the Bell and Grant households and, along with a few favoured guests like Maynard and Lytton, they routinely decamped there for at least two months, sharing visits with Leonard and Virginia, who had a holiday house close by. These summers were enshrined in very specific rituals of work and play, and the idea that Lydia might intrude on them, her 'goings on' with Maynard awkwardly apparent to everyone, drove Clive and Vanessa into a frenzy of anticipated irritation. If anyone had consulted Lydia herself, she might reasonably have pointed out that she had no intention of sitting idle in the Sussex countryside for an entire summer – she still had a career to pursue. But no one did, and by the time Maynard came back from Genoa on 5 May, Gordon Square was in a state of curdled hostilities.

At first he did not grasp how complicated the situation was and, typically looking for the practical solution, suggested that he and Lydia should rent a holiday cottage close to Charleston, which would give everybody an acceptable degree of privacy. No one else, however, was inclined to be rational. Lydia, when she was told of the plan, was hurt by Maynard's failure to appreciate the social difficulties that she might encounter from living even a short time with him alone and unchaperoned in a small rural community. But Vanessa, too, was hostile to the plan, pointing out that Maynard and Lydia were so domestically inept that they would be sure to end up spending all their time at Charleston, and the summer would still be spoiled. She and Clive were united in their conviction that their holiday community could not survive any outside intrusion: '*no one* can come into the sort of intimate society we have without altering it'.[30]

Then, with a rapidity that bewildered Maynard, the ban on Charleston was followed by a demand that Lydia leave Gordon Square altogether. It was Clive who forced the issue, threatening to quit number 46 if Lydia was going to spend so much time in the house. But it was Vanessa, squirming and desperate, who sent the ultimatum, writing to Maynard, 'I'm afraid you may be forced to choose between us.'[31] This was Maynard's first real view of the drastic clash of culture and personality that he had initiated by moving Lydia into Gordon Square, and he was utterly wrong-footed by it. He knew that Bloomsbury, as a group, had a bad history with newcomers – Mary Hutchinson, Karin Costelloe and Dora Carrington had all experienced degrees of animosity and suspicion – but he seems never to have penetrated the reasons for Vanessa and Clive's demonising of Lydia. As he himself admitted, he lacked the imagination to empathise with irrational emotion, and this particular situation was tangled with an unusually dark and historic confusion of issues.

For Vanessa, it was always difficult when a new woman hovered too close to Bloomsbury. Half willingly, half ironically, she had allowed herself to be positioned as the Madonna, the matriarch of the circle, the domestic genius who made Bloomsbury houses beautiful, the mother who produced Bloomsbury's second generation (the two girls born to Adrian and his wife Karin were cruelly tolerated as an inferior breed). The notion of Lydia becoming a rival homemaker to Vanessa was, of course, laughable, but in many ways she was still a dangerous interloper: as the principal object of Maynard's attention, as the possible mother of his children and, worst of all, as a rival for Maynard's protective instincts. Over the years Maynard had become a crucial figure in Vanessa's life. Even though he was younger than her by four years he acted as a buffer between her and the outside world, investing her money, subsidising Duncan's art as well as hers, even becoming godfather to Angelica. It was understandable that she would be apprehensive of losing him to Lydia.

Yet there were other, more practical reasons why Vanessa resented Lydia's increased presence in Gordon Square. As oblivious in her own way as Maynard, Lydia had fatally underestimated English sensitivities to privacy and noise. The thumps that came from her room when she was practising at home shook Vanessa's nerves as well as her walls, and even when Lydia had still been busy at Covent Garden, she had given her neighbours cause to fear her return at night. Vanessa's report to Maynard – that Lydia did not seem to have enough work to use up her energy – was a nervous understatement, for, as Lydia herself admitted, a successful show could leave her in an almost violent state of physical euphoria: 'sometimes after the performance I feel I could destroy this house and build a new instead'.[32]

And then there was the chatter. Once the Massine season was over, Lydia had time on her hands, and as well as prolonging bedtime gossips with Vanessa, she began cornering her during the daytime, in her kitchen or studio. This was the gravest of violations, for while Lydia, raised in the intensely social world of the theatre, found talking an ideal way to 'rest my body',[33] Vanessa was usually working alone and against the clock, trying to make time for both her painting and her family. She was profoundly serious about both, despairing once to Roger Fry: 'You don't know how desperate I sometimes get about everything, painting, bringing up the children properly etc.'[34] Unscheduled talks with Lydia were the last thing on her agenda. With a very English restraint, Vanessa let slip tactful hints and withdrew into repressive silences; but when these signals failed, she was too nervous of wounding Lydia to tell her directly to go away. She thus retreated into a mute, conflicted rage with which no one else in Gordon Square seemed able to deal. Duncan – who liked Lydia in spite of finding her a prattler, and, as a painter, delighted in studying her – was too chronically averse to rows to mediate. Maynard, meanwhile, was probably inclined to believe that Vanessa was exaggerating the inconvenience. His own working life had been serviced by such a doting succession of parents, tutors, servants and colleagues that he could not grasp the difficulties under which she had to paint.

As for Clive, he was far too embroiled in his own issues to broker any of Vanessa's quarrels. His prime complaint against Lydia was that her mealtime appearances at number 46 trivialised and disrupted the table talk. Bloomsbury conversations might not always have been the glittering performances that their acolytes claimed, but they did range freely, and sometimes brilliantly, relying on shorthand of reference and on a shared cultural register. Lydia was badly equipped to follow and, misunderstanding an opinion or missing a nuance as she frequently did, had a tendency to veer off on a stream of her own irrelevant ideas. She had no 'head-piece', complained Virginia after one visit; one could not 'argue solidly' in her presence.[35]

Nor was it just Lydia's opinions that sounded wrong. Among the measured English cadences of Bloomsbury conversation, Lydia's swooping Russian vowels and explosive consonants stuck out as emotional, extreme, and were mercilessly parodied – 'Maynar liked your article so much Leonar,' mimicked Virginia Woolf, meanly to Vanessa, by post in April 1923.[36] Even Lydia's jokes tended to miss the mark, for while humour at number 46 tended to come packaged in elaborately articulate witticisms or exquisite dissections of character, Lydia's own very Russian taste was for silly puns, outrageous innuendo or childish practical jokes – what the Russians call *shtoochki*.

As she herself would write six years later, Russians could be exasperating: 'very often we are unreasonable, we talk nonsense, we exaggerate and we lie'.[37] But she had no idea how often or how deeply she offended Bloomsbury decorum, especially as Maynard seemed to take proprietorial pride in her comic outbursts and even encouraged them. A year later when Lydia was out walking with the Woolfs she spotted a frog by the path and recklessly butted into a discussion on the future of Socialism by asking everybody to stop and watch as she put it up into a tree. Virginia acknowledged that Lydia's spontaneity could be 'enchanting', but complained to her friend Jacques Raverat that since Bloomsbury preferred 'reason to any amount of high spirits ... Lydia's pranks put us all on edge'.[38]

It was Clive's antipathy, however, that had the nastiest edge. He exaggerated Lydia's lack of education, sneering that her 'spiritual home' was Woolworths; and the pleasure that he seemed to take in stirring up conflict between her and the rest of Gordon Square appeared to certain observers, like the diarist Edward Dent, to be motivated by sexual revenge.* Clive was accustomed to success with women and when Lydia had first arrived in London he had set himself, very conspicuously, to court her. As well as flirting with her at every opportunity, he had erected his whole earnest theory of modern ballet around her and had written a poem, 'To Lydia Dancing', in which his homage had gushed through lines of such gruesome whimsy as:

> Is it true?
> Are Ariel's Whims
> Embodied in your artful limbs?[39]

When all this had failed to attract Lydia, Clive took the humiliation badly. His sexual pride had always compensated him for the suspicion that his friends considered him intellectually second-rate.

*According to Virginia, Clive's malice was also encouraged by his mistress, Mary Hutchinson. The elegant Hutchinson had never felt confident in Gordon Square, Vanessa and Virginia making it apparent that they thought her 'made for salons'. She may have resented Lydia's arrival, both as a potential recruit to Vanessa's 'gossip wars' and as an unresolved temptation for Clive.

(Which they did. Back in 1911, Lytton had bitched ruthlessly about Clive having 'fallen into fatness and a fermenting self assurance – burgeoning with inconceivable theories on art and life'.[40]) It was Maynard, eminent and influential, who had always made Clive feel his inadequacies most, and relations between the two men had become especially difficult after Maynard had refused to relinquish the lease of number 46 when Clive had returned from Garsington. Several territorial spats had blown up, including an ugly quarrel over the ownership of a bed, which had ended with Clive offering Maynard the use of an old train seat and raising a crude finger with it: 'as you appear to fuck less than I do it may serve well enough'.[41] The fact that Maynard not only ended up bedding Lydia, where he himself had failed, but did so at number 46 could not have rankled with Clive more deeply.

So the situation in Gordon Square muddled on through the rest of May and June, a snarl of sexual, social and domestic hostilities that none of the participants were willing, or able, to undo. Maynard suggested that new living quarters might plausibly be found for Lydia at James and Alix Strachey's house, number 41. But he stood firm on her rights to number 46. 'I must feel that there is no awkwardness at all in her coming to the house whenever and as often she wants,' he insisted, and he ruthlessly disclaimed any responsibility for Clive's or Vanessa's sensibilities on that matter: 'A great deal depends on whether you can face Clive's leaving the Square. We all want to have and not to have husbands and wives.'[42]

Lydia, in the middle of all this, must have been both wounded and bemused. Although the rows were conducted out of her hearing, and although she had enjoyed a brief escape from Gordon Square, dancing with Massine at Bournemouth's Winter Garden between 25 and 27 May, she could not fail to notice the change in atmosphere when she entered a room of Maynard's friends. She, too, feared an open confrontation of the situation, and she may have felt too vulnerable in her relationship with Maynard to risk either criticising his circle or courting his pity. Occasionally, however, her letters hinted obliquely at her real emotions. On 9 June she described a dream in which she had found herself distressingly and mysteriously abandoned: 'I dreamt that I have been on a Chinese ship, which had a form of a lantern. I had only a pair of turkish trousers on, and I searched for you everywhere.'[43] An uncharacteristic note of tetchiness and reserve began to inhibit her pen. On 12 June she reported dismissively, 'Clive gave a tea party … as usual great many boring persons including Ottoline, Mary, J. H. Smith and others,'[44] and on 23 June she coolly described a walk home from the theatre with Vanessa during which 'We spoke a little, almost no gossip.'[45]

Later in the summer, when Lydia was alone in Gordon Square, she came as close as she would ever dare to admitting how crushed she felt by the impregnability of Maynard's world. One night after wandering through his empty rooms, she wrote, 'I tremble – I sit at *your* table without your permission. I do not touch anything, occasionally I glance my eyes over it.'[46] And even in her own quarters at number 50 she felt diminished, an intruder: 'The house is big – I am all by myself. Even my hands shake. I am a thousand years old.'[47]

It is possible that the tensions in Gordon Square might have forced Maynard into making a public choice between Lydia and his London friends. But circumstances combined to create a temporary truce. Lydia, by the middle of June, had been rescued from unemployment, as Massine had managed to pull together a summer schedule of performances. Vanessa, Clive and Duncan were preparing to leave for Charleston, taking their issues and their irritations with them. And if Lydia now sensed that Gordon Square had fallen out of love with her, there were other people close to Maynard who appeared enthusiastic for her company. On 27 June an invitation came to spend three days at Lindisfarne Castle as a guest of Oswald (Foxy) Falk. He and Maynard had organised a working holiday there, and although Lydia had been apprehensive about the genuineness of her welcome – 'I do not know your friend,' she wrote humbly to Maynard, 'perhaps he does not desire me, it is only in relation with you'[48] – the financier Falk turned out to be a keen balletomane whose graceful hospitality was balm to her injured morale.

In early August, Lydia was again holidaying with Maynard, in Ostend. He was interested in the town's casinos, having a mild addiction to gambling; she had been drawn by the Ballets Russes, who were dancing a short season there after finally being regrouped by Diaghilev. Their companion – and token chaperone – was Jack

Sheppard, one of Maynard's favourite colleagues from Cambridge. Perhaps to her surprise, Lydia found this tiny Classics don, with his schoolboy face and prematurely white hair, to be delightful company. Not only was Sheppard infatuated with the theatre and flatteringly thrilled to be in her company, but he possessed a fantastical, very un-Cambridge streak of mischief. During their few days together at the Belgian seaside, Sheppard's high-pitched, snorting laughter encouraged Lydia's high spirits, and he became one of her most loving supporters, berating Bloomsbury for their perverse refusal to accept her and Maynard as a 'perfectly assorted couple'.[49]

Sheppard was also invited to chaperone Lydia in Wiltshire for the three-week holiday that Maynard arranged for them in September. The issue over Charleston had now been stiffly resolved. Maynard visited Sussex alone, with Lydia, unsurprisingly, resisting Vanessa's embarrassed permission to accompany him. We have to assume that Vanessa was aiming for humour in her tortuous letter of invitation: 'tell her I hope very much she'll come here and not put us off vaguely at the last moment – English households cant be treated like that'.[50] We can equally assume that Lydia failed to appreciate the joke.

Instead, Lydia spent eleven days in Bedfordshire with a new friend, Vera Bowen. It was a well-timed visit. Vera, a fellow Russian married to an Englishman, had become Lydia's closest confidante during the past difficult months, and the time that Lydia spent with the Bowens allowed her to vent some of the hurt she had been storing up. By the time she travelled to Parsonage House near Marlborough to join Maynard, Sheppard and the latter's jolly schoolteacher lover, Cecil Taylor, she was feeling confident, purged and forgiving. She was also more than ready to throw herself into her companions' peculiarly English holiday routines, walking, reading and, the greatest novelty for Lydia, learning to ride. So good a time was she having that she turned down an invitation for a London dinner being held in tribute to Adeline Genée: 'even gay dancers must have holiday sometime from being so gay,' she wrote in apology, 'and I am now in country with horse as dancing partner'. She did, though, pay careful respects to the great ballerina who had taught 'the English to love ballet … and so made a home for us emigrating Russians'.[51]

Within this sunny interlude, Maynard's love again seemed certain to Lydia – weighing powerfully against his loyalties to Gordon Square. Certainly Vanessa, who was being sent written reports of their happy holiday, began to doubt her chances of saving him. Gloomily she wrote to Roger Fry, 'Lydia & he seem to have settled down to married life & I'm not at all sure it won't end in real marriage ...'[52]

Chapter Thirteen

PRIVATE AND PROFESSIONAL SKIRMISHES

> Poor little wretch, trapped in Bloomsbury ... Nobody can take her seriously, every nice man kisses her. Then she flies into a rage and says she is ... a seerious wooman.
>
> VIRGINIA WOOLF[1]

Vanessa's predictions of 'real marriage' would prove correct, but not as speedily or as straightforwardly as she imagined, and during the difficult period ahead of Lydia there would be many more incidents in which she would feel emotionally blindsided by Maynard's circle. Also unresolved for much of this period would be the issue of Sebastian, whom Maynard, in an astonishing display of tactlessness, invited down to Wiltshire immediately after Lydia had returned to London. Given the strength of Lydia's instinct to bolt from any situation or relationship that failed her, it was a measure of how much she wanted Maynard that during the next year and a half she stayed and struggled. And it was not only Lydia's private life that was veering between confusing extremes of happiness and disillusionment; her professional situation too was often in an unreadable state of flux.

By the summer of 1922 it became evident to Lydia that she had only a limited future with Massine and his troupe. The work that he had found for them all, a tour of regional music halls coupled with two short seasons at the Coliseum, where they had performed in the same programmes as the Marx Brothers, was successful for her personally (the *Dancing Times* noted record 'ovations') but Lydia had found Massine increasingly intolerable as a director. The 'stingy' or the 'dirty insect', as she began indiscriminately to refer to him, was displaying a near-pathological streak of meanness when it came to paying out his dancers' wages and expenses. Worse, he harboured what Lydia regarded as an obsessive rivalry towards herself, excising her name from certain publicity posters and upstaging her so flagrantly during performances that she felt forced into retaliatory action in their curtain calls, standing back from Massine as ostentatiously as she dared, in order to signal her disdain for his vanity.

This was an old quarrel between them, of course, and Lydia might have found it in herself to behave more forgivingly towards Massine if he had managed to provide more satisfactory working conditions. But their week of performances at the Manchester Hippodrome (14–20 August) had been miserable – 'dreadful no athmospere',[2] while at Harrogate no accommodation had been booked for the troupe and Lydia had come close to spending the night in a cab, using 'the new ballet's skirts for pillows'.[3] It was here too that she had danced for an audience composed almost entirely of the lame and the elderly, and wonderingly asked Maynard whether 'the rhematic people of Harrogate' had been hoping for some miraculous cure by attending the ballet. 'I am almost convinced while they watched our legs their legs became active too.'[4]

This had been the last date of the tour – 22 August – and Lydia by now had taken the decision that she would remain with the troupe only if she herself took over its direction. It was, of course, an unknown challenge for her – Lydia had never assumed professional responsibility for anyone other than herself – and initially she had imagined that Massine would at least stay on as her choreographer. The 'insect', however, had made that impossible. Imagining that Lydia was to be bankrolled by Maynard, he had demanded outrageous fees for the staging of any of his existing ballets, plus an extra 'guarantee' of £1,400 if he were to create new ones. 'Massine's mouth is full of sugar for me,' Lydia had written in vivid irritation; 'Oh he is so foxy,'[5] and by September she had convinced herself of the necessity of parting from him. From now on the troupe would be known informally as the Lydia Lopokova Ballet Company, and she would be in sole charge.

In retrospect, Lydia's severance from Massine could be counted as one of the artistic losses of her career. She had discovered her own comic depths in Massine's roles, and if he had ever come to regard her as his muse, he might have brought out other possibilities in her. Yet Massine needed no muse other than himself, and whilst he and Lydia would be reunited in two further projects, their partnership would be driven largely by expediency, never returning to the inspired collaboration of the *Boutique* days. Sokolova went so far as to characterise the break as a tragedy, not only for Lydia but for all of Massine's core dancers, who, she believed, 'lost' something essential after they ceased working with the choreographer and 'never did anything so great again'.[6] But in the autumn of 1922, Lydia was wasting no time in mourning and, in need of a new artistic collaborator, turned optimistically to her friend Vera Bowen.

When Lydia had first encountered Vera, backstage during the *Sleeping Princess* run, she may have seen little in this fashionably dressed thirty-three year old to distinguish her from any of the other elegant Russian émigrés floating around London. Yet she had discovered in Vera a combative intelligence, as well as a restless temperament similar to her own. Although Vera had come from a much wealthier background than Lydia, she had been only a teenager when she had left her family's estate in the Ukraine to finish her education in Geneva, and while she had briefly paused in her adventures to marry a young Swiss doctor, Victor Donnet, impatience for new experiences had sent her travelling on to Paris, where she had met up with Marie Rambert, a former dancer with Diaghilev. The two had become each other's 'dearest companion'. While the already stylish Vera initiated Rambert into the mysteries of French couture and philosophy (they both went to hear Henri Bergson lecture), Rambert responded by teaching Vera about ballet.

After war broke out, the two women sought safety in Britain, and it was here that Vera discovered she possessed a very practical and very versatile talent for the theatre. Offering to help Rambert launch herself on the London stage, Vera not only wrote several ballet librettos for her friend, including, ambitiously, a Cubist-styled *Ballet philosophique*, but also designed most of her costumes, make-up and lighting. Rambert found her formidable: 'Her advice in art as well as in life was *law* to me and I never ignored it,'[7] and Vera herself grew increasingly ambitious as she widened her field from ballet to opera and plays.

Left: Vera Bowen and baby Nicholas, 1923. *Right:* Lydia with Leon Woizikovsky and Thadée Slavinsky, 1922–3

It was while staging a production of *Three Sisters* in 1920 that Vera met her second husband, Harold Bowen, who had translated the Chekhov text. Harold had seemed in many ways the ideal partner: a talented linguist, Middle Eastern scholar and writer, and, as the youngest son of property tycoon Sir Albert Bowen, rich enough to support Vera in her career. It was only after Vera had been fully installed as mistress of Harold's large London house, and of his family's massive country estate in Bedfordshire, that she had discovered how hard it would be to combine serious work with a position in English society. In fact, it may have been because her talents and energies had been left so frustratingly underused that Vera had responded as energetically as she had to Lydia request for help with her own new professional venture.

Lydia had actually made a preliminary approach to Vera back in June, when she had begun to suspect that Massine would not deliver all the new choreography that he had boasted of. The 'golfing' ballet had certainly not materialised, and Lydia was beginning to fear that she might be stuck dancing trivial divertissements for the rest of her post-Diaghilev career. Tentatively she had wondered about initiating a new ballet for the troupe herself and, knowing Vera's history with Marie Rambert, had asked for suggestions of a libretto on which they might work together later that summer. Vera, with an efficiency that Lydia would soon recognise as dauntingly characteristic, came back in less than a week with the outline of a romantic comedy, to be set in eighteenth-century Venice and titled *Masquerade*. She was, as Lydia reported to Maynard, 'filled with delight to do something for me',[8] and so persuasive was Vera's enthusiasm that Lydia was soon allowing her friend to take over other areas of her life, in particular her wardrobe.

At thirty-one, Lydia still needed assistance in styling herself. While she shopped for shoes and hats with what she admitted was a helpless avidity, drawn often to the gaudiest, most eccentric styles, she lacked the patience for sustained smartness – her hair was usually screwed into an untidy bun, her outfits chosen for comfort rather than image. Obviously Lydia could manage professional glamour when required. During the period with Barocchi her publicity photographs testified to the fact that with the right make-up and the right outfit she could transform herself convincingly into a veiled beauty, a cute coquette, even a vamp. Her features could be surprisingly sharpened and shadowed by make-up, her body given length and elegance by well-fitted clothes. But it was Vera's intention that Lydia should look 'strikingly' groomed[9] in her daily life too, and as Lydia became immersed in her new role as ballet director, Vera marched her round the London shops in order to dress her for the part. It was vital, she insisted, that Lydia did not attempt to impress theatre managers or impresarios in one of her old cotton frocks or peculiar items of headgear, and humbly Lydia concurred. 'Vera told me', she reported to Maynard, 'that when I go to the Savoy and have diplomatic lunches I must be dressed well, more than that. She sais from it depends the price of my salary. So I have a new hat and a new coat for the day wear. All is worth about 20 [pounds]. Extravagant?'[10]

In reality it needed more than a smart new hat and coat to launch the new ballet company. Lydia had imagined that after taking over Massine's dancers, it would be reasonably straightforward to get them all on to the stage. She would work with Vera on choreographing *Masquerade* and, with her eye on a long run at the Coliseum, she would charm Oswald Stoll into paying a fee large enough to not only cover her expenses but take her into profit (she was hoping for eight weeks, and a weekly fee of £250). Yet Stoll, a misleadingly mild-eyed, dapper-looking Englishman, had not proved to be the pushover she had hoped. Lydia was a complete novice, both as a choreographer and as a director, and Stoll had no intention of launching her new company without testing her abilities. While pencilling in a three-week run for *Masquerade* for late November, he insisted that Lydia must first prove herself by giving him three short programmes of divertissements, for which he would pay £175 apiece.

This compromise was finalised on 14 September. But since Stoll wanted her to open at the Coliseum on 9 October, Lydia was left with shockingly little preparation time. She was holidaying with Maynard in Wiltshire when the contract was sent to her, and she seems to have dithered there helplessly for a few days, wavering between denial and brief, piercing moments of panic. One of her most urgent problems was numbers, for with Massine gone, and Leon Woizikovsky having defected to the commercial theatre to earn regular money, Lydia now had only one man in her troupe, Slavinsky, to divide between herself, Sokolova and her small chorus – Ninette de Valois, Dorothy Coxon and Margot Astafieva. It would be very hard to find a repertory for such an imbalanced group, especially as Stoll on the one hand was demanding that Lydia herself must dance in most of the programme, while Vera on the other was writing daily to insist that her 'darling Lidulechka' must choreograph the material as well, to avoid 'dependency' on Massine.[11]

Lydia, who had no real experience of choreography beyond re-cycling a few dancehall steps or ballet solos for Broadway, was thrown into a paralysis of nerves and wrote pathetically to Vera, 'I am so pale with fear Maynard say I look more like tragedian than world's leading ballerina.'[12] Her appeal, however, drew only a brisk scolding from her friend: 'My angel I am coming to the conclusion that you are a terribly frivolous woman.'[13] Bullied but fatalistic, Lydia dragged herself back to London and, under Vera's tough, humorous supervision, she did manage to construct two new, if probably not very original, solos for herself, one Russian and one Scottish. She also created two works in collaboration with the other dancers: a Harlequin-styled duet titled *Arabesques* for Sokolova and Slavinsky, and a trio 'on Grecian lines' for de Valois, Coxon and Astafieva.[14] The first two programmes of her debut run were to be padded out with divertissements from *Sleeping Princess* (including the ever-popular *La Princesse enchantée*), while for the third and final programme Vera offered one of the ballets that she had originally created with Rambert, a slight, flirtatious comedy titled *Les Élégants*, which gave Lydia a pretty role as one of three flighty women competing for the attentions of one man.

Cobbled together as these programmes were (and fielding raucous competition from rival acts at the Coliseum like 'Hickey's Circus, with its Beautiful Performing Ponies and the Unrideable Mule "Obey"'), Lydia still managed to make a convincing directorial debut. Cyril Beaumont, reviewing for *Dancing World*, judged her new repertory to be a significant improvement on the Massine company, with the Russian solo, in which she wore a vivid costume designed by Gontcharova, boasting all 'the precision, the fire, the frenzy reminiscent of her best performances in *Prince Igor* and *The Midnight Sun*'.[15] He predicted a promising future for her as a director, and by the final week, when Lydia led the company première of *Les Élégants*, wearing a dress that she claimed 'hides my true age and makes me look naughty innocent',[16] she herself was ready to agree.

'I am mad mad with excitement,'[17] she scrawled to Maynard, and barely paused to steady herself before swinging into an intensive month of rehearsals for *Masquerade*. Stoll, impressed by the speed and economy with which Lydia had turned her first three programmes around, had by now advanced her money for the new ballet and initially it had almost seemed to create itself. The ballerina role that Vera had sketched for Lydia was a feckless young wife who is tempted by the charms of a lover but is then cajoled back into the embrace of her husband through a series of benign disguises and deceptions. Both the character and the storyline were an unabashed conflation of ballets that Lydia had danced before, and as she began sketching out the choreography for herself, it seemed that she had only to draw on her well-tried assets of comedy and romantic pathos to make it gell.

The rest of the ballet proved much less tractable, however. *Masquerade* had been conceived on an ambitious scale, with two scenes and a cast of twelve, including Woizikovsky, who had temporarily re-joined Lydia to dance the role of the magnanimous husband. Orchestrating this amount of stage action took far longer than Lydia had anticipated, and on Armistice Day she could not even spare time to go out into the street and join the nation's tribute of silence, but instead had to pay her respects alone, standing 'nude in the dressing room'.[18] Problems accumulated. Because Lydia was using up so many extra hours of rehearsal, the dancers began dunning her for more money, and outside the studio too she was harassed by unexpected crises. The first was a row over the designs, which had been commissioned from Duncan but which Vera, pregnant with her first child and hormonally ill-tempered, had rejected. The second was a dispute over her chosen score, Mozart's Serenade in G (*Eine kleine Nachtmusik*), which the Coliseum's musical director, Alfred Dove, claimed was too much of a miniature to be played in a 2,000-seat auditorium. So adamant was Dove about the music's unsuitability that he called for the entire ballet to be cancelled. Even after Lydia had persuaded him to yield, he created a separate fuss over how the score should be performed, conducting it at much faster speeds than those set by the dancers in the studio, and discounting Lydia's objections on the grounds that she 'did not know how Mozart should be played'.[19]

By the morning of the première, 20 November, Lydia had ground herself into an exhausted collapse, writing bleakly to Maynard, 'I do not know where I am. I do not exist fully.' Even though her next day's reviews could hardly have been more encouraging – 'a beautifully presented one-act *ballet-comique*', according to *The Era*, 'a very beautiful medium for some of the most delightful dancing to be seen in town,'[20] and 'miles above Massine', according to Beaumont she felt too wrung out to enjoy her triumph. She was also too worried about money. Before taking over direction of her troupe, she had rarely had to confront the price of anything beyond a new hat or a hotel room; yet from the £900 that Stoll had agreed to pay for *Masquerade*'s three-week run, she had had to cover all of the dancers' wages, as well as the expense of the ballet's creation. She had already made a £40 loss on her three divertissement programmes (for which she had been shocked to discover that she had to pay for the Coliseum's electrician and fireman). Now, as she totted up the figures for *Masquerade* in the little black book that Maynard had bought for her (complaining, 'I am such a calculatrice nowadays'),[21] Lydia discovered that after paying £300 to Vera and £260 on design, she was in debt by a further £177 3s 0d. Even as she repeated to herself Maynard's consoling mantra that 'noble failure was better than cheap success', she was dismayed by the brutal price she was having to pay for artistic independence.

Lydia also had no idea of where her next salary would come from. Stoll had vaguely promised '1 or 2 weeks rest and then another "extraordinary engagement"', and by this she had hoped that he meant a second extended run for *Masquerade*.[22] However, no contract had appeared, and while Maynard seemed delighted to subsidise her living expenses, Lydia was not yet sure enough of their relationship to feel comfortable with the situation. Even two and a half years later she would find her dependency on Maynard difficult; the loss of a £5 note that he had given her induced a frenzied overreaction of shame and fear, humiliating for a woman who had once earned $2,000 a week: '*Oah oah* I feel so unhappy my throat is in pains and my eyes are so tearful and sad, why am I such a careless fool.'[23]

The other dancers in the troupe were in a far more precarious state, with even Sokolova and Woizikovsky 'often at a loss for a square meal',[24] so when Stoll finally revealed the 'extraordinary' engagement that he had planned, Lydia was in no position to refuse. His offer was flattering, since he wanted her to stage a ballet for the spectacular new revue, *You'd Be Surprised*, which he was presenting at Covent Garden in January 1923. Yet while it represented a significant step forward for Lydia as director, she would have preferred the more manageable prospect of a repeat season for *Masquerade*. All her Broadway experience had taught her how tricky it could be to position ballet within a commercial production; and she felt even more reluctant when Stoll announced that he wanted Massine involved, as both her choreographer and her co-star.

Lydia was right to be wary. Although Massine proved surprisingly keen to accept this job, having found no consistent employment beyond giving dance classes to socialites and celebrities, the prospect of making a new ballet at other people's risk and expense apparently let loose his most subversive devils. Lydia's brief had been to produce a work appropriate to an Arizona location (each of the revue's fourteen scenes or 'surprises' was to be set in a different part of America), and out of her draft idea of a honeymoon comedy, set in an Arizona inn, Massine had elaborated a violent little farce for three couples titled *Togo: or the Noble Savage*. This told the story of Signor de la Cueva and his new wife, Elaria, whose meeting with the Indian chief Togo, along with his wife and negro prisoner (coincidentally the husband of Elaria's maid), was to spiral into an unlikely series of threats, revelations and reconciliations. If the story was complicated for a popular revue, Massine's choreography was far more so, styled in a combination of gratuitously difficult steps and wild ethnic pastiche that prompted the *Dancing Times* to speculate later whether Massine had simply been having 'a joke at our expense'.[25]

Lydia and the four other dancers had wondered it too. From the outset the general mood in the studio had been tired and sullen, and Lydia, racing to learn her own role as Elaria, on top of overseeing the designs and organising the music's orchestral parts, felt miserably unappreciated: 'I do all the good I can and yet everybody says I am such a disagreeable man and I cant think why.'[26] Perhaps in another, less commercially pressured context, *Togo* might have been given time to smooth out its issues. All the ingredients were in place for a vibrantly innovative little ballet, with designs by Duncan, a score by Milhaud, *Saudades do Brasil*, and dancers who, for all their grumpiness, were technically superb. But *Togo*'s muted first-night reception on 22 January (from an audience who were not even appreciative of the rest of the programme) convinced Stoll that the ballet's colourful clash of jazz and post-impressionism was too avant-garde for a revue. After first requesting a major edit, he dropped the work entirely. It was for Lydia a galling disappointment, and even though she and her dancers were allowed to dance some replacement material,* by the

*This was *Lezghinka*, based on traditional Georgian dancing, which Lydia loftily accepted as being 'more suitable' for a revue audience, despite having no conceivable Arizona connection. She and Massine were also performing material in one other section, the 'Greenwich Village' surprise, including a duet titled *Trish Trash*.

end of March, when *You'd Be Surprised* transferred to the Alhambra, only de Valois was required to go with it. The long, lucrative run that Lydia been counting on to sustain her troupe was over and she saw no way of holding it together. Massine went back to his teaching; Woizikovsky and Sokolova returned to Diaghilev in Monte Carlo.

Lydia might have considered going with them if it had not been for Maynard. As it was, she was left with a professional blank that she did not know how to fill. Vera, by now heavily pregnant with her first child, could offer no suggestions, nor did Lydia have any means of pursuing a tantalising possibility that she had discussed with Cecchetti involving them both in a new staging of *Coppélia*, with the painter Walter Sickert as designer. In fact, Lydia's beloved Maestro was shortly to abandon her for good, for at the beginning of June he was to return home to Milan to become director of the La Scala Ballet School. Lydia could not decide which she would miss most, Cecchetti's teaching or his friendship. '*Oh* emotions!' she wailed to Maynard. 'When I arrived at the studio of Maestro everybody's eyes were so red that mine felt purple.'[27] She would not see Cecchetti in London again. He would die in Italy, five years later.

Ten days afterwards, when she travelled to Paris with Florrie Grenfell and another London friend, Muriel Gore, to watch Sokolova and Woizikovsky perform with the Ballets Russes, Lydia was still feeling sore. This was only the second time that she had seen her old company since the *Sleeping Princess* debacle and it was not an enjoyable reunion. While Diaghilev gave her an 'outwardly affectionate embrace', he seemed distant, even grudging, and Lydia also had a shocking encounter with her former partner, Nijinsky, now profoundly and incurably insane. The doctors had allowed Nijinsky to watch a performance, hoping that it would rouse him from the introvert shell of his madness, but when Lydia went into his box to greet him, 'he did not know me nor anybody, he does not recognise anyone'.[28]

All of Lydia's past animosity was forgotten. 'Who', she railed to Maynard, 'is so cruel to him.'[29] But more selfishly she was troubled at what this visit signalled for her own future. The Ballets Russes had moved forward in her absence, and while the season's most important première, Nijinska's *Les Noces*, had intrigued her – 'a well balanced madness in black and white'[30] – its fiercely geometric lines were in a disconcertingly different style from the Massine and Fokine repertories that she herself had formerly danced. Lydia suspected that she was in danger of becoming artistically stranded, and when she learned that Sokolova and Woizikovsky were planning to spend the summer in London, she suffered because she was unable to 'boast with engagements'[31] – either for herself or for them.

At this point she must have felt the irony of a letter that had recently arrived from her sister Evgenia, containing proud news that back home 'people are talking a lot about your success'.[32] This letter had taken months to reach London from Russia, and the success to which it referred had been Lydia's initial season with Massine in *Ragtime*. It had taken only a year for the optimism and emotion of her new life with Maynard to become stalled in a frustrating impasse.

Evgenia's letter had been the first detailed communication that Lydia had received from her family in over two years. The Lopukhovs had received, intact, several of her own parcels containing clothes, music and books, but all the letters she had written had fallen foul of the Bolshevik censors, as had most of theirs. Evgenia urged Lydia to write again or, better still, to come back home:

> Karlusha and I are very worried that we have no [news] from you and it's only from these parcels we see that you are alive and well. We sent you a letter for your birthday and then another longer one, but not a single word. How much I would like you to come here. I would immediately organise your choreographic [debut] and you would be a huge success. You would see all of us and we would be so overjoyed. I always feel somehow ... sad that we are so far away from each other.[33]

Lydia needed no prompting to imagine the pleasures of such a scene and of being restored to the uncritical, uncomplicated embrace of her family. She was often lonely in London, despite Vera and her other friends, and she was frequently brought close to depression by the uncertainties of her affair with Maynard. A slight distance had again developed between them during the winter of 1922–3, in part because Maynard had been working such an impossible schedule. Not only had he been engaged on his usual commitments to Cambridge, the City and journalism, but he was also travelling regularly to Germany as an unofficial advisor to Wilhelm Cuno's government, and had embarked on two consuming projects of his own: planning the takeover of the ailing Liberal magazine *The Nation and Athenaeum*, and arguing his way towards a new economic theory in his latest book, *A Tract on Monetary Reform*.

Lydia understood, even revered, the demands of Maynard's working diary, but it was in January 1923 that she discovered the large space that had been miraculously cleared in it for Sebastian and the North African holiday. Even before she confronted Maynard on this betrayal and instigated the trauma of their first open argument, Lydia's unhappiness had begun leaking into her letters, her inventive doodlings of love petering into dutiful formulae, a flurry of ambiguous gender images hinting at her feelings of sexual demoralisation. On 18 January she was mourning that she had not yet managed to be a brother to Maynard, only his 'brotherly dog', and two days later she was telling him about a nightmare in which 'you and I were soldiers and when the bullett went through me I did not die'.

Lydia was having many such bad dreams, her nights tangled in fears of being lost, abandoned or disoriented, and, as if to confirm the uncertainty of her rivalry with Sebastian, she had to endure a hideously embarrassing first meeting with Maynard's mother, Florence. Maynard had not yet thought fit to introduce Lydia formally to his parents, and in February 1923, when they were visiting his brother Geoffrey, and Florence unexpectedly called by, the awkwardness of the encounter and the careful vagueness of Maynard's introductions could not have told Lydia more cruelly that she was still an outsider in his world.

In Gordon Square, too, Lydia felt stranded within a social battleground. The previous autumn Vanessa and Clive had returned from Charleston determined to force a change in the living arrangements, and compliantly Lydia had gone along with them – moving into the ground-floor flat in number 41 so that Clive could take her place in number 50 and allow Vanessa to occupy his rooms in number 46.

Initially this domestic reshuffle had pleased everybody, and on 27 October Lydia was reporting happily to Maynard that she, Vanessa and Duncan had all got 'crazy drunk' drinking beers at Gatti's café on the Strand. During the months that followed, Lydia was too busy with her new troupe to do much more than sleep in Gordon Square, and well into the New Year everything had continued to promise conviviality. At a Twelfth Night party hosted by Maynard, Lydia danced a much-applauded star turn, sharing the floor with Walter Sickert's solo rendition of *Hamlet* and Marjorie Strachey's obscenely comic recitals of children's nursery rhymes. Three weeks later, on 28 January, she spent a happy, domestic Sunday with the Bells, trying (and failing) to draw a picture for Angelica and talking to Quentin about Mount Everest.

But by February, under pressure from the fiasco of *Togo*, Lydia began to drift towards Vanessa for sympathy and distraction. All of the latter's frustrations came rushing back, as she fumed to Roger Fry that Lydia had 'spent 3 solid hours sitting in my room gossiping. This now happens every Sunday which is usually my own day at home for doing odd jobs.'[34] Guiltily, Vanessa acknowledged her own responsibility for the situation: 'I don't show when I want Lydia to go and she can't be expected to know.'[35] But she could not control her resentment, and a doughy, unflattering portrait* that she painted of Lydia expressed all that she was unable to say. Maynard, for whom it had probably been intended, refused to buy it, causing Vanessa to grumble touchily to Duncan that Maynard 'never or hardly ever really likes my painting'.[36]

March and April of 1923 were uniquely horrible months for Lydia. *Togo* and her troupe had fallen apart, the atmosphere in Gordon Square was as tense as it had ever been, and she was still having to deal with the fallout from her battle over Sebastian. Even though Maynard had cancelled the holiday, a pall of mistrust still lingered. But by the end of May there was a renewal of intimacy. It was at this point that Maynard finally committed himself to talking marriage to Lydia and she, sending him 'a chirp from under the left breast',[37] allowed herself to feel optimistic again about their future together.

*It was hung at a London Group exhibition in April 1923 and reproduced in *Vogue* but the whereabouts of the original is not now known.

She made herself busy, visiting Vera after the birth of her baby, Nicholas, and planning outings with Sam and Lil Courtauld, Basil Maine and Florrie Grenfell – a pretty, cultured woman who was one of Diaghilev's patrons and lived on a grand scale in Cavendish Square with the banker Teddie Grenfell.

In the absence of any dancing work Lydia toyed with the idea of acting again. As always when her ballet career was faltering, she fantasised about the alternative riches of the dramatic repertory, and it was possibly in order to gear herself up for a change of professional direction that she set herself to study the works of Ibsen and to learn Shakespeare's Sonnets by heart. Yet after Lydia had returned from seeing the Ballets Russes in Paris, her dancing prospects suddenly improved. Stoll came up with an offer for a summer season at the Coliseum, which was to start on 23 July, and while it was only for three weeks the prospect of employment made Lydia glow. She celebrated by hosting a supper party with Maynard on 26 June wearing an unusually exquisite eighteenth-century dress, in which both Duncan and Roger Fry painted her.

Rarely had Lydia needed the adulation of her fans more than she did when she started on this Coliseum run. Ruby Coles, a young woman whom she had recently engaged as her maid, went to watch her new mistress perform and was an incredulous witness to the 'thunderous clapping' that Lydia received: 'the top hats being thrown up into the air' and the 'red roses' being thrown on to the stage.[38] But Lydia had high hopes too that the season would recoup some of her financial losses from *Masquerade*, since although Stoll had asked for new divertissements* in the opening programme, he had also agreed to a fortnight's reprise of her little Venetian ballet.

Money, however, would be the blight on her return to the Coliseum, for Vera too had been looking to profit from this season. As the originator of *Masquerade*, she assumed that she had a permanent claim to its earnings and proposed a deal whereby she should either be paid the full fee for the ballet's revival, from which she

---

*These included the pas de deux from *Sylphides* for Lydia and Slavinsky, with Lydia apparently wearing a new costume designed by Maynard; a Chinese solo for Lydia; and a Mexican-flavoured duet titled *Passedoble* to music by Moskowski for Lydia and Woizikovksy.

Lydia Lopokova by Duncan Grant, 1923

would then pay Lydia a weekly wage of £75, or receive a straight 50 per cent cut. With all the Bowen wealth apparently at Vera's disposal, this request infuriated Lydia, who had long resented her friend's 'complex of meanness' (as well as her inclination to patronise Lydia for her fecklessness). On 4 August a 'thunder of words'[39] was exchanged backstage in Lydia's dressing room, after which the two women retreated into hurt, angry silence.

Left to themselves, Vera and Lydia would certainly have made up, as Russians do, over tears and cups of tea, but their English partners seemed intent on prolonging the row. Harold had certain reservations about Lydia, her unpredictable behaviour an irritant to his nerves, and after a party on 28 July he had complained Pooterishly to his diary about her unruliness: 'Lydia ... wearing a crimson sack of Vanessa's ... became rather drunk and skimmed what might have proved rather an engaging strawberry mess of its cream. We left first.'

Yet he had even greater reservations about Maynard, claiming that the 'self consciousness' of his manner made him feel uncomfortable. Maynard in return did not fully trust Harold, resenting the latter's privileged knowledge of his and Lydia's business, and the two men embarked on a stiff exchange of letters. One of Maynard's, brusquely demolishing Vera's claim to any financial rights, was considered by the Bowens to be not only unfair but 'amazingly rude',[40] and it is possible that Maynard was unconsciously seeking to undermine the women's friendship. He may perhaps have been blaming Vera, for the bloody fights over Sebastian; he certainly did nothing now to soothe Lydia's hurt and resentment over this financial squabble. Although she finally paid Vera £100, she was still feeling miserably divided from her friend when the short season was over and she left London to join Maynard for a holiday on the Dorset coast.

Here she would experience the division from Vera even more keenly, for this holiday would leave Lydia as alone as she had ever been. Far from sealing the closeness that she had only just managed to regain with Maynard, it would almost persuade her to leave him.

The first chill to her expectations was Knoll, the house Maynard had rented, which, in contrast to their cosy property in Wiltshire the previous year, was the stately seaside home of the Duke of Hamilton and was run by an intimidatingly starched army of servants. The second was the guest list that Maynard had assembled, which could almost have been designed to make Lydia feel ignorant and small, including as it did Hubert Henderson, editor of the *Nation*, Leonard Woolf, the magazine's literary editor, and two of its writers, pretty, blond George (Dadie) Rylands and the bitchily brilliant Raymond Mortimer. Not only would Lydia have little time alone with Maynard, she would also be running the gauntlet of a very competitive, very intellectual coterie. Apart from her old ally Jack Sheppard, who was also among the party, she would find scant appreciation for her own stock of jokes and theatrical anecdotes.

Lydia's worst miseries, however, were created by Virginia Woolf, who, while only staying at Knoll for three days, apparently found time to reduce Lydia to a state of wretched demoralisation. In clever, meticulous Leonard, Lydia had interestingly found only sweetness. His own Jewishness and his seven disorienting years working in the Colonial

Knoll House, 1923. Standing: Dadie Rylands and Raymond Mortimer; seated: Leonard Woolf, Lydia and Virginia Woolf

Civil Service in Ceylon had allowed him to empathise with her feelings of exclusion as few others in Bloomsbury could.* Virginia, in contrast, shared Vanessa's resistance to outsiders, and while she had been entertained by the idea of Lydia as a temporary mistress for Maynard, she was as appalled as her sister when it looked as though Lydia might become his wife. At the end of 1922 she had written to Vanessa a sparklingly venomous portrait of what such a marriage might entail:

> I can forsee only too well Lydia stout, charming, exacting; Maynard in the cabinet; 46 Gordon Square the resort of dukes and prime ministers. M. being a simple man, not analytic as we are would sink beyond recall

*Lydia and Leonard were bound together as 'foreigners', but he was genuinely fond of Lydia, bracketing her with Virginia as a 'silly' – a term coined by Tolstoy for individuals who have retained a 'wonderfully direct, simple, spiritually unveiled' integrity. (V. Glendinning, *Leonard Woolf*, p. 36)

> long before he realised his state. Then he would awake, to find three children and his life entirely and forever controlled. That is how it appears to me, without considering my own grievances. Lydia is far better as a Bohemian, unattached hungry and expectant, than as a matron with nothing to hope and all her rights secure.[41]

As with all of Lydia's relationships with Bloomsbury, there is no simple explanation of why she aroused such excessive, analytic hostility. Part of it, in Virginia's case, was driven by a pure political reaction to her marrying Maynard. Like most of Bloomsbury, Virginia despised marriage as a bourgeois institution, despite, like most of the group, being married herself; and she feared that Maynard's union to Lydia would be the most disastrously bourgeois of all. Friends of Lydia's such as Lil Courtauld, Vera and Florrie featured high on Virginia's hit list of women who had been 'dulled' by too much money, and it seemed to her all too likely that under their influence Lydia would lure Maynard inside the drawing room of a very Belgrave, and very un-Bloomsbury, form of wedlock.

This, of course, was a wilful misreading of Lydia's character. She was far too socially inept to run a salon for dukes and prime ministers, and far too protective of her freedom to enjoy the relentless round of obligations that would entail. (Several years later, an invitation from the doggedly social Lady Colefax would fill Lydia with fear at having to reciprocate: 'I do not want her in 46 … she is filled with a desperate courage that has no use to you or me or the world.'[42]) She was also far too proud of her own professional status to covet the world of the unemployed upper-class wife who, as she put it, is 'ever on the run in search of unumerable excitements, liking manicure sets with the same enthusiasm as Rembrands'.[43] In fact, when Lydia did eventually marry Maynard she would not only confound Virginia's predictions by continuing to work, but also retain her own name – an act of independence that was beyond both Virginia and Vanessa, who all their lives worked professionally under their husbands' names.

But double standards were rife in Bloomsbury. Virginia might deplore the idea of Lydia becoming a slightly stout member of the upper classes, but in 1926 she herself would be in thrall to something like that type when she fell in love with the aristocratic, and rather solidly built, Vita Sackville-West. Virginia might deplore the possibility of Lydia dragging Maynard into snobbish society, but if she examined her own antipathy to Lydia she would have to acknowledge that it was rooted in a deep, unexamined snobbery of her own. The terms in which Virginia discussed Lydia, to her friends and to her diary, were routinely shot through with a revealing social malice. She found it so much fun to raise her eyebrows over Lydia's 'parokeet' brain; to sneer over her lowly origins; to parody her accent. Nor could she resist mocking Lydia's deference towards social 'proprieties', which appeared to her merely vulgar and hypocritical. She had once caused Lydia to blush in confusion by making a pointed enquiry about her and Maynard's sleeping arrangements, and had judged this reaction to be a hilariously prudish contradiction of all the 'Russian generals and Polish princes or Soho waiters' that she had heard about from Lydia's past.[44]

It was this mix of snobbish, fascinated, parochial amusement that Virginia brought to her scrutiny of Lydia during the holiday in Dorset. As she herself shone, smoking her home-rolled cigarettes, launching flights of literary brilliance for Sheppard, Mortimer and Rylands to admire, she also took brittle, accurate note of the unusual fraying of Lydia's temper as she 'got cross, frowned, complained of the heat, seemed about to cry precisely like a child of six'.[45] Lydia's own attempts to distract herself with Shakespeare seemed to her absurd: 'Lydia has the soul of a squirrel … she sits by the hour polishing the sides of her nose with her front paws … I assure you its tragic to see her sitting down to King Lear.'[46]

Yet Virginia was not only watching Lydia's misery, but also exacerbating it by her own subtle snubs, and by forming an exclusive complicity with the other guests. She had a talent for needling emotional reactions out of people; it was a writer's reflex, a dispassionate method for gathering material, and one reason for her acceptance of Maynard's invitation was to study Lydia for her latest novel, *Mrs Dalloway*.* She

*As a writer, Virginia would make other uses of Lydia, and while working on the first draft of her play *Freshwater* in 1923, she had her in mind to play the young Ellen Terry. However, when it was finally performed in 1935, Lydia played neither Terry nor the non-speaking part of Queen Victoria for which Virginia had also earmarked her. All that remained of her was the line given to one of the characters, Mr Cameron, referring to an 'exquisite but not altogether ethereal nymph … a dancer from Muscovy who snatched me by the waist and whirled me through the currant bushes'.

had planned that the male protagonist of her book, the traumatised war veteran Septimus, was to be married to a little Italian milliner called Rezia, whom she imagined as a woman rather like Lydia. While there would be no biographical connection between the two, there would be such an unmistakable connection of type that Virginia would muddle Lydia's and Rezia's names in her diary.[47] In the finished novel when Septimus marvels, uncomfortably, at his wife playing with a child, it could have been Lydia that he was observing: 'Rezia went down on her knees; Rezia cooed and kissed; Rezia got a bag of sweets out of the table drawer. For so it always happened. First one thing, then another. So she built it up, first one thing and then another. Dancing, skipping, round and round the room they went.'[48] When Septimus goes out walking with Rezia, it could have been Lydia's idiosyncratic passion for hats that animated their conversation: '"It is the hat that matters most," [Rezia] would say, when they walked out together … "Beautiful!" she would murmur, nudging Septimus, that he might see.'[49]

But in Virginia's portrait of Rezia she also highlighted what she saw as Lydia's flaws: her limited intellect, her naivety and, above all, her inadequacies as a partner for Maynard. It was perhaps a measure of Virginia's critical animus that she would also mete out to Rezia the harshest judgement of all, making her so ill equipped to understand Septimus's mental state that she would contribute to his ultimate suicide.

However, if Virginia was anatomising Lydia with literary ruthlessness, her attitude was also rooted in a less analytic distaste. Virginia suffered from precarious mental health (today she would be diagnosed as manic depressive), and the magically heightened sensibility that fed her greatest writing also subjected her to periods of alienation during which she perceived people around her as physically oppressive or hostile. Even when she was well, any moral or social ambivalence that she felt towards individuals would register as a peculiar, visceral queasiness, and she was experiencing this in Dorset, not only towards Lydia but also towards Maynard.

Virginia's feelings for the latter had always veered between admiration and antipathy: his eminence, his information and his intellectual certainties could make her feel 'flittery and stupid'; his masculinity could repulse her as 'thick & opulent'.[50] On her return from Dorset she was jotting down in her diary that he had 'grown very gross and stout' with 'a queer swollen eel like look, not very pleasant',[51] and even in his presence she had not been able to fully disguise her aversion. A photograph taken of them together at Knoll shows Virginia looking tense and reluctant, her hand covering her mouth, while Maynard leans slightly away, as if sensing that his contact is unwelcome.

The combination of Lydia and Maynard together could at times distress Virginia even more. Alongside her vision of them as future hosts to dukes and prime ministers, she saw their current relationship as something physically grubby, almost gluttonous – even the sight of them toasting crumpets 'steeped in butter' would induce a wave of revulsion in her against their 'tallow grease grossness'.[52] In Dorset, Maynard had arranged for his guests to visit the sunken tomb at Bindon Abbey, where Thomas Hardy had described Tess of the D'Urbevilles being laid in the ground by the sleepwalking Angel Clare. It was traditional for literary tourists to re-enact the scene, and when Lydia had been the first to oblige, Virginia had observed her prone figure with squeamish fascination: 'her pink fur jacket with the white fur ... her muscular dancers legs in white silk stocking's lying with the soles of the feet touching.' 'What,' Virginia speculated grimly, 'did she think about? About Maynard, & her death, & and what would happen before.'[53]

The situation that aroused Virginia's most appalled interest, however, had arisen when Lydia had casually thrown one of her used sanitary towels on to an empty fire grate. This disregard of menstrual proprieties had both disgusted and mesmerised Virginia, prompting her to wonder, shrilly and inaccurately, just what kind of upbringing had made it possible. 'Lydia, whose father was porter in a Petersburg hotel and whose entire life has been spent hopping from foot to foot with the daughters of publicans, did not know this perhaps most binding of all laws of female life.'[54] It had also, Virginia reported, generated a hysterical crisis among the Duke of Hamilton's staff. 'The cook's husband and the Duke's valet did the room. Soon the Cook herself requested to speak with the lady. There was such a scene ... rages, tears, despair, outrage.'[55] In fairness to Virginia, her correspondent, Jacques Raverat, was seriously ill and the exaggerated account that she had written of the scene had been designed to entertain. However, its tone of class contempt was unfeigned, and the fact that Lydia had eventually negotiated an emotional reconciliation with the cook had simply confirmed Virginia's perception of her irredeemably un-English ways: 'if you knew Lydia, you'll see how naturally it follows, lifelong friendship upon a basis of – well, bloody rags'.[56]

Lydia would hear miserably of the speed with which this story had subsequently travelled down the telegraph wires of Bloomsbury: 'they all know about our lives in Swanage (Virginia's gossip of course)'.[57] And having endured three days of Virginia's snubs, having been patronised by the rest of the company and undefended by Maynard (who was perhaps too preoccupied as a host to register her discomfort), Lydia evidently began to feel that she would never find a place in this barbed, difficult society. She also began to feel that Maynard, bound as intimately as he was to Bloomsbury and its laws, might ultimately be beyond her reach.

In the past, Lydia would have simply given up the fight as hopeless and moved on, to another man, maybe even another country. But Maynard still held her. She loved him, whatever she felt about his friends, and, almost as critically, she had allowed herself to become dependent on him financially. Even after the Coliseum season, her savings were low (Maynard had recently put her assets at just £203 6s 4d), and there was no immediate employment for her beyond suing for a return to Diaghilev, with all the complications that would involve, or trying to break into acting, which would take time and more money. Unable to form any decisions about what her next move should be, Lydia drifted. Maynard had gone on to join a stag-hunting party on Exmoor, so she briefly went down to Kent to stay with the art collectors Mr and Mrs Johnston; then on her return to London she accompanied Sam Courtauld on a day trip to St Albans. Finally, her loneliness became too much for her and, ignoring the bad blood left by *Masquerade*, she fled to Vera, who was staying with Harold at the Bowen estate in Bedfordshire. Maynard, with characteristic obtuseness, assumed that Lydia had gone on a peace mission: 'Do your best to compose the quarrel with her, so far as I am concerned, I don't want to quarrel.'[58] But as Harold noted in his diary,

Lydia's desire was only to seek comfort from Vera's 'outspoken criticism of Bloomsbury and its ways'. It seemed to Harold that she had moved a significant step closer to breaking off the affair: 'Loppie looks on the end of her Maynard attachment as inevitable,' he wrote, 'and not even out of sight.'[59]

Maynard himself continued in a state of bluff denial. 'Why are you not well,' he chided Lydia on his return from Exmoor. 'I give you many warm cheerful kisses,' and throughout the rest of the autumn, his letters to 'Dearest Lydochka' were peppered with unperturbed endearments. He feigned jealousy about her jaunt to St Albans with Sam: 'I see Lil and I will have to get together to have a serious talk,'[60] and he was confiding serious plans for their future together. In October, busy on an article about birth rates, he quipped, only half jokingly: 'Shall you and I begin our work on population together?'[61] It was also around this time that he entrusted the family solicitor, his uncle Kenneth Brown, to expedite Lydia's divorce from Barocchi and track down the latter's wife, Mary Hargreaves. (Randolfo, typically, had stonewalled requests for help, claiming that as he had not married Hargreaves in the presence of 'any Italian consular authority', he still figured as single in the 'Registrar-Romar'. However, he had typically warmed to the drama, urging Lydia to 'Destroy this letter for if it falls into enemy hands you will be not be able to get your divorce.'[62]

Yet however affectionate Maynard's gestures were, Lydia stalled and struggled with her doubts. The letters that she wrote to him that autumn were indicative of her constraint, as her usual intimate confidences stiffened into conscientious expressions of gratitude for things that Maynard had done for her, or were channelled into detailed accounts of how she was passing her time. Lydia was trying to ward off pain with resolute busyness, reading plays, taking Spanish lessons and exploring the streets of London: 'I jumped from bus to bus experimenting new roads like a butterfly from flower to flower.'[63] She was throwing herself into a frenzy of socialising, going to parties where there were games of charades, foxtrotting, and fashionable discussions on 'psycho-analisis, Zionism and politics', as well as receiving her favoured 'galerites' for tea: 'I gave them muffins and a little bit of myself.'[64] There were also frequent visits from Basil Maine (now nicknamed Vasiline, or Vaz), who, despite Lydia's attempts to maintain him as 'a friend of the soul and mind', was inclined to turn mournfully ardent in her presence. She kept him tactfully busy at the piano, her pet entertainer, and one afternoon, on 4 November, he obliged with such a riotous medley of Broadway songs that 'Ruby the maid could not keep her feet together, their was an atmosphere of musical tipsiness.'[65]

Lydia was also distracting herself with shopping, and one of her new purchases included a pair of gloves to wear during her daily ballet practice 'so that I might prospire even there [her hands]'.[66] This fetish for sweat suggests that she was gaining weight again, for although she had installed a barre and mirror at number 41, no amount of solitary practice could compensate for the professional routines of class and performance that she had been used to.

And still there was no sign of work. At the age of thirty-two, Lydia was in her peak years as a dancer, but the scrapbook that she normally filled with reviews and cuttings was now occupied only by amusing news items that she had clipped from the papers (an article advocating 'feminist apartments' in which women could live separately from their husbands, a 'scientific' explanation for why cats have whiskers). Her two remaining dancers, de Valois and Slavinsky, had both left London for the Ballets Russes, and the only project that could give some structure to her days was sitting for the sculptor Frank Dobson, who began a bust of her in late October 1923. It had been Maynard, in another confusing gesture of love, who bad commissioned this, and Lydia became genuinely absorbed by its creation. 'Dobby's Lydia is charming,' she enthused, and reported to Maynard that Walter Sickert had told her that Dobson owed it to the world to do a good likeness, given the poor attempts made by Vanessa and others on canvas: 'already 3 English painters ruined their reputation,'[67] she quipped. 'I was artists doom and tomb.'[68] But while she admired the progress of Dobson's bust, its cost to Maynard, about £160, seemed to her extravagant and perhaps embarrassingly inappropriate. According to Harold, Lydia was reducing Vera to tears of exhaustion as she discussed 'interminably the problem of whether Maynard is to marry her or no'.[69]

Maynard chose to blame Vera for these long sessions, apparently oblivious to his own role in them: 'Oh what a Jew Vera is with her tirelessness. I see why you and she get on together.'[70] Yet there was some excuse for his blindness, for while Lydia might be steeling herself for an eventual break with Maynard, another part of her was still gambling on their future working out, and still maintaining a convincing performance as his prospective fiancée. On 16 November, Maynard finally arranged for a formal meeting between Lydia and his mother. As far as he was concerned, she was preparing for the occasion like any future bride, buying a new dress and admitting that she was experimenting with 'many different coiffures' so that she might find a style most likely to convey 'the scent of virginity' to her potential mother-in-law.[71]

It may have been either tact or cowardice that had prompted Maynard to arrange the tea on a day when he was in Cambridge, but it took place at his sister Margaret's house, in north London, and it evidently made up for the fumbled embarrassment of the two women's accidental encounter the previous February. Afterwards Lydia wrote emotionally to Maynard, 'You have her eyes and searching mind. I was excited so I spoke too quickly and forgot the words ... She kissed me before going away.'[72]

Yet it was only three days later that Lydia was working herself up to midnight agonies with Vera. A shuttle between desire and distrust, hope and despair, was her daily state throughout much of November, as she fretted about the wisdom of staying or running away. How close she came to running may be measured by the short message – 'Second thoughts are best' – she would later write to Vera on the back of a photograph of herself and Maynard. But there is no clue in any of Lydia's letters to suggest what finally prevented her from doing so. Perhaps she and Maynard shared another 'éclaircissement' that scotched some of her doubts, or perhaps she simply made a stoic decision to jam a lid over her uncertainties.

Whatever happened, by the beginning of 1924 Lydia's morale was transformed. The dreams that she described in her letters were now idylls: 'Last night my sister was introduced to you. She was very pretty with white ballet skirts. I wore a long stately Greek dress. We loved one another very much, she gave you a kiss on the forehead with my approval.'[73] There was a second emotional meeting with

Florence: 'We, your mother and I unloaded our feelings for you and for each other in relation of your being our entire idol.'[74] Lydia even set herself to read Maynard's newly published *Tract on Monetary Reform*, which she proudly admired for its 'fresh literary style' and for 'the zest of life in constructive sentences – although there was surely a glint of mockery in her comment that 'Purchasing Power Parity or Forward Market in Exchange are pure matters and more difficult to grasp for a usual person.'[75]

Her situation was even improving in Gordon Square. Four months earlier, Vanessa had ratcheted up the hostilities by insisting on separate mealtimes for herself, Clive and the children, leaving 'the chilly couple',[76] Maynard and Lydia, to dine on their own. Yet while the atmosphere in number 46 had been temporarily fraught, Vanessa's rejection had, in the end, simplified the situation. Lydia benefited from having more private time alone with Maynard, and as their relationship regained its strength at the turn of the year, she became steadily more confident in setting limits to her involvement with his friends. She would never be fully accepted by them, but she would learn not to mind. In May 1924, Lydia was able to respond with cheerful disinterestedness to Maynard's account of an evening spent with Lytton and Sebastian: 'Your party is the dear old Bloomsbury, I would not be suitable but I like to hear from you',[77] and when Virginia and Leonard moved from Richmond to a house close by in Tavistock Square, she refused to feel threatened. By November she was able to make blithely mocking reference to her own irreparably un-Bloomsbury ways: 'Why do I blab so much ... I ought to be like Lytton when he is in society, but then there is no beard attached to me.'[78]

Lydia did not, however, blab to anyone, even Maynard, about the wounds that she had suffered from Bloomsbury. While she might risk the occasional joking reference to Vanessa's aloofness – Quentin Bell recalls her declaring comically, 'Oh Wanessa you frighten me to death'[79] – she was careful to indulge her own anger rarely and always in private. Once, having spotted Vanessa walking on the opposite side of the street, Lydia dared to shake her fist, but only because she knew herself to be unseen. As for the disillusionment that she had felt over Maynard's division of loyalties, it was swept away by the

Lydia and Maynard, 1925

currents of desire that again began to flow between them. 'I had such fluctuations for you in bed last night,' he wrote to her from Cambridge in February 1924, 'and felt very fond of you,'[80] while she in return sent 'fountains of feeling'. By the following year, when Vera asked Lydia about their relationship, every doubt had been cast aside. Maynard was, she replied simply, 'the big walk of my life'.[81]

Chapter Fourteen

ANGLO-RUSSIAN TREATIES

> I am so active over the telephones and visitors that I prospire in the places where the hair grows.
>
> LYDIA LOPOKOVA[1]

It remained typical of Lydia's life during this period that the vacillations in her emotional state were shadowed by abrupt changes in her professional fortunes. Early in January 1924, just as she had thrown off the doubts hanging over her relationship with Maynard and had allowed herself to believe in the reality of their future together, she received a call from Massine that immediately lifted her career from its months of torpor.

Massine had been hired to create the choreography for a six-week season of ballet and theatre in Paris, which, he boasted, would be artistically equal, if not superior, to anything that had been produced by the Ballets Russes. *Soirées de Paris** was to be paid for by Count Étienne de Beaumont, an immensely rich aesthete whose staging of extravagantly theatrical costume balls had inspired him with visions of becoming a rival to Diaghilev. Beaumont had told Massine to hire his pick of dancers for the Paris season, and the choreographer, ignoring the bad blood of his recent associations with Lydia, had asked her to be his leading ballerina. Passing on the count's lordly invitation for her to 'name her price', he had told her that there would be several new roles for her in the season, plus a very good chance of an eventual transfer to London. It was a proposition tempting enough to cancel

*The title was taken from the arts review founded in 1912 by the poet Guillaume Apollinaire. Most of the season was to be ballet but there was experimental drama as well, such as *Mouchoi de nuages*, a 'dadaist tragedy' in fifteen acts by Tristan Tzara.

every one of the grudges that Lydia had nursed against Massine, and she did not hesitate in accepting, reporting to Maynard that she was making herself sick with excitement as she absorbed Massine's seductive promises 'of new channels in choreography ... All that is best in painting and music shall unite.'[2]

Then, to pitch Lydia's mood still higher, Stoll approached her with the proposal of a short season at the Coliseum, with sufficient fees to cover the cost of a new ballet. The timing could not have been better. Stoll had offered the first two weeks in April, just before Massine needed her to start rehearsals in Paris, and Lydia believed that it was a heaven-sent chance to resurrect her directorial project. Competitively fired by Massine's vision of new 'channels', she was determined to make a success of it and, rather than risk the choreography herself (Vera was unable to advise her, having just had an operation to remove '6 stones in her bladder'),[3] she hired Nicolas Legat, a former Mariinsky ballet master who was now living in London. Luck was with Lydia too in that her old partner Stanislas Idzikowski, 'the legs of my heart',[4] had recently walked out of Diaghilev's company. With his 'method of dancing a la maestro, his French a la nègre and his English a la cockney',[5] Stas was an entertainingly cosmopolitan colleague and a fine partner, and by dint of shameless flattery and tough financial negotiations Lydia managed to secure him for her new ballet.

Legat was a professional of the old school and, knowing exactly what would suit Lydia and Idzikowski, he choreographed a droll love story for them, set in nineteenth-century Paris and accompanied by extracts from Alexandre Lecocq's operetta *La Fille de Madame Angot*. At its opening performance on 31 March, *The Era* judged *Soldier and Grisette* to be 'a sublimely racy' showcase[6] for the two dancers, and Lydia, whirled along by Legat's speedy, airborne choreography, had felt transformed by the old kick of performance adrenalin. By the time she travelled to Paris to meet up with Massine she was physically as well as emotionally charged with a sense of new beginnings.

Already in the city were Florrie and Vera (now fully recovered from her operation), who had volunteered to be Lydia's companions for the next two months. More usefully still, they had volunteered to share the costs of her hotel apartment, for the count's initial offer for Lydia to name her price had been retracted once he had discovered the real costs of producing a ballet season. Beaumont could now pay only 15,000 francs (£200) per month, which not only required Lydia to live on a much-reduced budget but, to her embarrassed annoyance, kept her dependent on the subsidy of Maynard's weekly 'papers'.* The reduction in her fee, however, had not dampened Lydia's enthusiasm. On 25 April, Vera and Florrie were at the station to meet her, and whilst they mocked her preposterous superfluity of baggage (which Vera exclaimed must contain a 'cadaver', although Lydia insisted it was mostly dictionaries and shoes, 'both important elements in human nature'), the three women felt liberated and adventurous as they drove through a 'beautiful and unknown' Paris to their hotel.[7]

Perhaps, given the fullness of Lydia's expectations, it was inevitable that a reaction set in. Two days later the soft April sunshine was depressingly veiled by 'detached pourings of rain', while Vera's choice of accommodation, the Cayres Hotel, was proving a mistake. Outside Lydia's window, the boulevard Raspail was noisy with traffic and with the dawn clatter of 'milkman's pots'; the rooms were too small for her to do her daily practice; and the drinking water gave her an upset stomach. Lydia was a melodramatic invalid and wasted no time writing pathetically to Maynard, 'To be in room all alone with pains was indeed a suffering although I looked at you [his photograph] on my table and that was the mental improvement.' She wailed too at the effects of her self-medication, a soothing diet of 'cream cheeses with cream', which made her phobic about going near 'the weighing machine'.[8]

Initially at least, these physical discomforts did not diminish Lydia's hopes for *Soirées de Paris*. After the opening rehearsal, held in the count's vast *hôtel particulier* in the rue Daru, Lydia reported back to Maynard that 'Massine look well and seem pleasant to everybody. I have not yet the full impression but dancers look to be not in bad order.'[9] She was also very taken with the first role that Massine had created for her in *Beau Danube*, a two-act Viennese romance set to a

*Maynard not only sent Lydia weekly instalments of £5 or £20 but also took over her commitment to send £10 a month to her family in Russia.

selection of Johann Strauss music. Lydia had been cast as a flirtatious street dancer who meets up with a former beau while walking in the park; and her easy progress with the choreography – waltzing romantically with her officer and dancing a spirited solo of defiance after he has returned to his fiancée – generated reassuring flattery from the other dancers.

However, the more she saw of the rest of the repertory, the more suspicious and restive she grew. Paris in the 1920s was slavishly in thrall to the new, vibrating to the latest black jazz musicians, to the latest Surrealist outrage, and Massine and Beaumont were determined that their own collaborations should be as stridently provocative as possible. While *Beau Danube* might please their popular audience, they had much more ambition invested in ballets like *Salade*, with its Cubist staging by Braque and Milhaud score, or *Mercure*, a surreal, mythological pastiche with designs by Picasso.

Lydia, already developing a more conservative approach to ballet, was inclined to view the more self-consciously avant-garde works as childish bids for attention, desperate attempts by Massine and Beaumont to outflank Diaghilev in the race for the ultimate 'dernier cri'. *Salade* she learned to admire but *Vogue*, a ballet that the count himself had devised for the season, she rapidly came to detest. Lydia's character was a rich, society woman involved in a sexually ambivalent love triangle with the pretty young dance actor Rupert Doone (currently Cocteau's lover), and she loathed the whole concept:

> [Our] tableau last about three minutes, with a young man and young girl who is like a boy, and I the woman of smart set. We lie on the beach in Lido, the man and the boy are getting on so that I must produce a vexed face and standing in the middle, showing a costume made up of miroirs (dernier cri, naturally). I do all I am asked except that I cannot look jalous, not in my nature of such circumstances.[10]

Harold Bowen, who had come to visit Vera in Paris, thought jealousy was very much in Lydia's nature, and believed that the reason that she ultimately withdrew from *Vogue* was that it raised painful echoes of her own recent 'circumstances' with Maynard and Sebastian. But Lydia continued to rail against the ballet's meretricious modernity, as well as the cliquish mentality of Beaumont and Massine: 'They also should aim at the "grand public" and not for little groups,' she grumbled. 'Big Serge always knew that ... Older I am more critical I become.'[11]

As the opening night of 17 May drew closer, and the company moved into La Cigale, the fashionably louche music hall Beaumont had rented for the season, Lydia began to miss Big Serge's professionalism even more. Beaumont, while essentially an amateur, was attempting to mount a self-promotingly packed season of new work; he had also amassed a quarrelsomely egocentric group of collaborators and Lydia despaired that there was 'not one controling voice in the situation except the Count's polite but weak falsetto'. She was particularly appalled at the liberties taken by their lighting artist, the celebrated Loie Fuller, complaining to Maynard that all the dancers had been forced to hang around for a whole afternoon while the 'big fat toad' played around with her effects.[12]

Increasingly it was to the comfort of her London friends that Lydia retreated. Vera and Florrie did everything to amuse her: taking her to the shops and theatres during her free time, throwing a champagne party for her, lying down in bed with her and chatting when she was tired. Maynard was both startled and titillated when he eventually heard, tut-tutting from Cambridge, 'Three women in one bed! I felt a little shocked.'[13] At the beginning of May, Muriel Gore arrived, along with Sam and Lil Courtauld, who took Lydia racing at Longchamps and fed her vast, stubbornly English meals at the Meurice – 'lamb chops, green peas and filet of sole,' reported Lydia, 'as if we were Berkely square'.[14] Even Vanessa, Clive and Duncan turned up, and while Lydia resented Clive's aggressive, reflex flirting, she escorted the three of them to Picasso's studio and was happy to report to Maynard that during an evening of impromptu Russian dancing, in the company of the painter Segonzac, Vanessa had been 'tipsy and very nice'.[15]

Maynard was gratified by the devotion with which so many people had followed Lydia to Paris: 'If you had an engagement in Pekin they would all be in Pekin,' he assured her. 'You are their elixir and without you they are not fully alive.' But he longed to have 'some elixir' for himself.[16] Unused to being abandoned, he made himself miserable in the 'darkness and desolation' of Gordon Square.[17] Anxiously he reread Lydia's letters, 'to see how fond of me you are';[18] in his 'dozing imagination' he dreamed of her, mixing her up with thoughts of his new book; and sexually he missed her badly: 'I wish you were by me. I have been badly conducted and pinched myself where you forbid it.'[19]

Interestingly, too, Maynard was fearful that Vera might, even now, turn Lydia against him. Perhaps he finally understood how he had figured in the two women's late-night conversations the previous winter, for when he was overdue in sending Lydia's weekly subsidy, he sent his apologies with an uneasy humour: 'Vera will be able to say that at last I have "dropped" you.'[20] His anxieties were further activated when Vera took advantage of the Paris shops to make another overhaul of Lydia's wardrobe. The style in which Maynard preferred to see his Lydochka was very much bohemian Bloomsbury.* She had taken, in his company, to wearing gypsy-style skirts and smocks, wearing headscarves or scraping her hair back in a very severe bun. This hairstyle suited her, emphasising the buttery smooth oval of her face and the sharp accent of her eyebrows,† but in Paris, Lydia had not impressed. A fastidious marquis, seated behind her at the theatre one night, had refused, outright, to believe that she was a famous dancer: 'He was', Lydia had reported cheerfully, 'almost disgusted by my appearance.'[21] Even though Maynard had resignedly sent extra 'papers' to fund the repair to Lydia's reputation, the list of her Parisian booty – two hats, a suit and a 'saucy' coat – had upset him. 'You will be completely dressed up as Vera's Lydochka,' he had fretted, 'and I shall have to look through the wrappings for Maynard's L.'[22] Nervously he felt that he should make similar efforts with his own appearance, and when he was able to clear some time to visit Lydia, from 24 to 26 May, he had his hair cut 'so as to look young' for their reunion.[23] Even his writing style began unconsciously to mimic and ingratiate itself with Lydia's, as he signed off his letters with 'crossings' (her word for kisses)

---

*Clothes were a moral issue in Bloomsbury. Virginia and Vanessa disapproved sharply of Mary Hutchinson's fondness for couture, even though they suffered occasional shame and discomfort at their own unfashionable dress.

†When Lydia experimented with a shorter hairstyle in 1926, Maynard was very upset, grieving dramatically for the loss of her bun.

or used her Russian-inflected sigh, 'Oah', to express his misery at their prolonged separation.

Yet Maynard's anxieties had never been more groundless. Lydia, with her dictionaries at her side, was writing to him every day, her letters rosy with love: 'I am here alone with your face and your letter ... and my feelings for you grow immeasurably, passionately.' Angelically she promised to 'prepare my vices' and give Maynard a 'calm hand' when they met in the small, discreet hotel that she had booked for them.[24] And when they were finally together, the intensity of their pleasure seems to have taken both of them by surprise. Afterwards Lydia wrote, 'we did promote something – outstanding, vivid and conquering',[25] while Maynard grew whimsically poetic in trying to find new ways of communicating his devotion: 'in my bath today I considered your virtues – how great they were. As usual I wondered how you could be so wise. You must have spent much time eating apples and talking to the serpent! But I also thought that you combined all ages, – a very old woman, a matron, a debutant, a girl, a child, an infant so that you are universal.'[26]

Lydia blushed by post at Maynard's homage: 'I am not all what you say, but I shall improve with time and eat more apples'; professionally, however, she felt that she had become little more than a 'theatrical rat' stuck on a relentless treadmill of rehearsals, costume fittings and performances.[27] *Soirées de Paris* had opened in style during the week before Maynard's visit, with a gala attended by all the princesses and painters in Beaumont's address book. Lydia had made her debut in two ballets, *Beau Danube* and a courtly trio titled *Gigue*, and, according to Vera, who wrote a review of the season for *The Nation*, she had been 'utterly exquisite both in dancing and appearance'.[28] Yet with seventeen performances scheduled for *Beau Danube* alone, and three other, smaller ballets to rehearse,* the strain of the season was escalating, one of Lydia's knees was hurting and she complained to Maynard that she felt 'no better off than proletariat'.[29]

**Les Roses*, set to music by Henri Sauget and designed by Marie Laurencin, required Lydia to do little more than pose. In *Premier amour*, set to Satie's *Trois morceaux en forme de poire*, and judged by the Bowens to be 'inconceivably feeble', Lydia portrayed a doll with whom a little girl has fallen in love. She did not eventually appear in the third ballet, *Mercure*.

An additional stress had been the arrival of Diaghilev, whose own season was opening at the Théâtre des Champs-Elysées on 26 May. The impresario had been maddened by the challenge that Beaumont and Massine appeared to be mounting to his name, and for months in advance he had been doing everything possible to undermine it. Dancers, designers and composers had been bullied to stay away from the upstart project. Poulenc and Auric had been threatened with permanent exile from the Ballets Russes if they worked on it, and malign prophesies had been spread about its certain artistic disaster. Lydia had sympathised: 'Big Serge must look enormous to Massine';[30] and once in Paris, Diaghilev had indeed appeared to be everywhere. He made terrifying, unscheduled appearances at La Cigale, positioning himself next to a *Soirées de Paris* poster and commenting loudly to the crowd, 'Only my name is missing'; he paid for extra-large claques to applaud his own dancers and to heckle the Beaumont troupe.[31]

Beaumont, in retaliation, hired his own claques, and for several days fashionable Paris was entertained by the battle of the rival impresarios. Sides were taken even in London, where the indefatigable hostess Lady Colefax announced that she would spread the word that 'Beaumont's ballet is the art of today'.[32] But Lydia guessed that 'another Lady C would fight on Diaghilev's side to spite Lady Colebox', and, like the rest of her colleagues, she was pessimistic about their chances of winning this war.[33] Diaghilev had mounted a superb season, with four new ballets by Nijinska, new scores by Milhaud and Satie, designs by Chanel, and a gorgeous drop curtain supplied by Picasso – the now famous image of two giantesses striding along the seashore – which Lydia thought 'moving and alive' when she spent sixty francs on her own ticket to the Ballets Russes.[34]

By 10 June, La Cigale was half empty and Lydia's own morale was close to exhausted. Normally too proud to vent her dissatisfactions in public, she threw a tantrum over some ugly flowers that Beaumont had ordered her to wear on a costume, and was picking almost daily quarrels with Massine, whose arrogant attitudes she was once again finding intolerable.

Lydia was not alone in having problems with Massine. Professionally, the choreographer operated within a ruthlessly solipsistic world in which his own art counted for everything; the injuries, exhaustions and egos of his colleagues for very little. Even Picasso began to complain of his ego this season. And while Lydia could accept Massine's hubris as a necessary evil when he was creating flattering work for her, she could not forgive it when he was making her perform in a ballet like *Mercure*,* whose surreally staged tableaux struck her as no more than stupid posing.

The old poisonous antipathy began to seep back into their relationship, and by 31 May the two were openly at war. Massine had asked Lydia, as a favour, to perform in a special charity gala and she been incandescent with rage to discover that in the publicity she was featured only as an unnamed member of 'an amateur society', while on stage Massine expected her to dance half-screened behind a net. 'I register facts that do not encourage me with devotion to M,' she wrote grimly to Maynard.[35]

Massine, however, had his own complaints against Lydia, as bad temper made her bossy, disruptive and petty in rehearsals. Even her fellow dancers, who normally looked to her for entertainment and encouragement, began finding her difficult. Only a few days before the première of *Mercure*, she flounced out of the ballet, causing a scramble of recasting; and when the company were required to dance a late-night performance for the Queen of Romania she complained bitterly, especially when she was forced to stay in the theatre to watch a spectacular light display orchestrated by the hated Loie Fuller. '[It] looked like the insides of the stomach or oysters or kinds of easter eggs or simply eggs,' fumed Lydia, 'and we poor worn out dancers had to wait and admire it.'[36]

At moments, Lydia fantasised incoherently about giving up ballet altogether: 'Oh I had a desire yesterday and today to become a rich woman again independently by my legs or comedy power; I saw so many old dancers they are mostly poor or mad, "Life is difficult" I sigh all over ...'[37] However, she was also casting eyes at Big Serge's

*Lydia hated *Mercure*'s choreography: 'No ballet no parody but somehow a stupid fake', and believed that Picasso's designs had simply been intended to 'pull the noses of the public' (especially the three 'graces' who appeared in a bathtub with papier-mâché breasts fixed on to their chests). This was the only work in Beaumont's season that was admired by Diaghilev, however, and he eventually acquired it for his own repertory.

company and wondering how to coax him into giving her a guest engagement when the Ballets Russes moved on to London. Even though Lydia had been dismissive of Diaghilev's new repertory – 'nothing or no one stirred me. I long … for very old fashioned ballets without abstract ideas, I want simplicity and Poetry'[38] – she had genuinely enjoyed *Les Biches*, a satirical comedy of modern sexual manners by Nijinska, and she would have been wonderful in the role of the gay, sophisticated Hostess. The choreography's garrulous energy, its speed and elevation would have suited her technique and, more importantly, would have taken her beyond her usual soubrette range.

Lydia, at thirty-three, needed more complex characters to inhabit than sparkling ingénues, yet the obvious sources for new roles seemed once more beyond her reach. Diaghilev had reacted with discouraging coolness to her enquiries about guesting with his company, sending word via Walter Nouvel that she had grown too fat for him. Meanwhile she and Massine were not even talking to each other; and Beaumont's company had obviously run out of steam, with bad reviews and low box-office returns scuppering any chances of its transfer to London.

Lydia's professional expectations had slumped all over again. However, when Maynard returned to Paris to see her through the final days of *Soirées de Paris*, he brought wonderfully compensating news. The lawyers working on her divorce case had recently tracked down Barocchi's first wife, Mary Hargreaves (she had been discovered singing with an opera company in Philadelphia), and a date for the preliminary court hearing had been set in July. Without hesitation, Lydia and Maynard cancelled the holiday that they had planned in the Pyrenees and caught the boat train back to London. In the event, that hearing had to be cancelled after one of the judges became ill, but the delay could not dull the sheen on Lydia and Maynard's happiness. They remained in London just long enough to participate in a rackety Gordon Square party (Lydia dancing in a transvestite ballet of Duncan's devising), before heading off for a two-month holiday in Sussex.

Here they found a kind of paradise. Tilton, the house that they had rented for the summer, was a large, semi-gentrified farmhouse a few hundred yards up from Charleston, hidden from the world by a large garden, and by miles of encircling fields and woodland. Lydia's willingness to throw proprieties to the winds during this largely unchaperoned holiday was a measure of how confident she now was of becoming Maynard's wife. But her happiness was also fed by a deeper sense of homecoming. Even though Lydia had not spent her childhood summers in country dachas, she seems at Tilton to have felt the atavistic pull of a rural Eden, so rooted in the Russian psyche. It was with a beatific feeling of 'losing time' that she discovered the joys of the house, sunbathing on the terrace or ambling with Maynard through the surrounding countryside, trying to identify the bright scatter of wild birds and butterflies, gazing at the exhilarating views that opened up through Sussex hills. Hours passed, too, as Lydia discovered a new hobby in gardening. There were thickly planted fruit and vegetable beds at Tilton of which she appointed herself chief 'harvester': 'Beans in the garden are not fading away,' she assured Maynard, 'and each family begins with not less than a quadruple. I plucked a few turnips and forgot the sitiation of a Brussel sprout designed by you.'[39]

This impressionistic gardener's report was one of very few letters that Lydia had to write this summer, for although a couple of work trips forced Maynard up to London, he was always reluctant to leave and always quick to return. He relished the novelty of playing married life with Lydia – their two months in Sussex was the longest time that they had ever spent together – and he was discovering that happiness and Tilton had a remarkable effect on his writing, as over the summer he effortlessly penned a 20,000-word memoir of Alfred Marshall, his former economics teacher who had recently died.

Down the track at Charleston the mood was, predictably, less contented. In June 1924, Duncan had written nervously to Vanessa, 'It's I see rather serious the Keynes' taking Tilton. I daresay we shan't see too much of them – I trust not',[40] while poor Vanessa, hearing Maynard enthuse about his hopes of renting Tilton every year, began wildly to talk of relocating to Norfolk. Yet if Lydia knew that she was still being picked over by Maynard's friends, she was too contentedly absorbed to care, and even when she had to leave Tilton and return to her 'bachelors quarters' in Gordon Square, she felt armed by the

Lydia and Maynard, Sussex Downs, 1925

happiness of that two months. Very occasionally, the slow progress of her divorce case produced a wobble of nerves: 'Do you think judge will give me a divorce,' she wrote despairingly to Maynard on 22 October, 'after all he might not, and I am a pessimist at present in "decree nisi". Please be very fond of me, otherwise I'll pour oceans of tears in the night and instead of bed I'll have a flood.' But she was immediately ashamed of her outburst, adding as a postscript, 'I find the sense of this letter is just like a woman. *Oh* I suffer from my own mentality.'[41]

Even though she had no work to distract her, Lydia was determined to enjoy the novelties of the London season, which this year promised to be more than usually diverting. Arm in arm with Florrie and Vera, she did the rounds of cultural events, enthusing over the Mond collection at the National Gallery and over the rival collection that Sam had recently donated to the Tate. With her friends, too, she became a fascinated observer of the crazes sweeping the city, as bright young things experimented with new dance steps, new sexual partners, new drugs (the cocaine era was just beginning) and new hairstyles. Lydia had no intention of cutting off her bun and was defiantly, unfashionably coiffed when she sat for a portrait by Walter Sickert. Everyone around her, however, seemed to be getting shingled. Lydia was shocked by Florrie's acquiescence to the trend, although conceding that it showed off her 'nice little chicken neck'; and she was entertained by Margot Asquith's attempt to follow suit, which was stalled by a hairdresser who explained it would not suit her because 'already her nose was prominent'.[42] Even Virginia made a temporary concession to fashion, borrowing a wig that Lydia herself owned, so that she could go to a party at Mary Hutchinson's 'à la mode'.

As the new hairstyles were paraded at the usual round of parties, Lydia also watched as fashionably naughty girls competed for attention – Elizabeth Bibesco put a kitten down the front of her evening dress; Nancy Cunard sat herself, suggestively, on Leonard Woolf's knee. According to Lydia, Leonard had not found Cunard's attentions pleasing – 'it bores him [the] most sensible man in Bloomsbury' – and she herself had dismissed these younger women impatiently.[43] She could remember a far more scandalous era, when Flora Ravalles had posed for the Ballets Russes with a python round her neck, or had travelled across the States with a baby alligator in her basket.

But she was also, loftily, attempting to concern herself with more serious issues, as Britain, and Maynard, geared up for the general election of October 1924.

Maynard had been a critical but essentially loyal supporter of the Liberal Party throughout his adult life, and concern for its failing membership – as Ramsay MacDonald's Labour Party encroached on its political territory from the left, and Stanley Baldwin's Conservative Party from the right – had got him reluctantly involved in making speeches at party rallies. He had felt press-ganged and compromised, writing wretchedly to Lydia, 'I hate political meetings. They are always *exactly* the same – the same vamped up atmosphere, and the same underlying boredom. It makes me feel a fool and a liar.'[44] Lydia commiserated with Maynard, read the newspapers carefully and acquainted herself conscientiously with the debates. However, if she was left to herself, her political interests tended to be more emotional and hazy, and she could never commit herself to one party.

In some fundamental respects Lydia was still drawn to the progressive beliefs of her past. She felt an instinctive distaste for snobbery and pretension: 'the rich are not lovable,' she would write tersely from a five-star hotel in Cannes; 'my sympathies go to the waiters',[45] and she routinely berated Vera and Florrie for their Tory views, boasting of the 'socialist' discussions that she had enjoyed with the still fierily idealistic Marie Rambert. With regard to the scandal of the Zinoviev letter, which was dominating the election, she was also in adamant support of the Left, believing rightly that the inflammatory document that had allegedly been sent from Russia to incite Britain to revolution was a fake and was being used by the right-wing press to topple MacDonald's government.*

Yet whatever natural sympathies Lydia felt for socialism, they fought with her equally instinctive embrace of caste. She disliked the working classes when they appeared to her vulgar or overassertive of their rights and felt no embarrassment in referring to sections of the Labour membership as 'uncouthe mongrels'. She also had a fixed, unalterable belief in natural hierarchy. It was entirely right and proper to her that an individual's talents should accrue them wealth and privilege, just as her own talents as a dancer gave her the right to occupy centre stage. She felt no sentimental attraction to working-class culture; she scorned the concept of a socialist utopia; and she had never deviated from her hatred of what the Bolsheviks had done to Russia.

Russia was in fact at the forefront of Lydia's concerns that autumn. She and Vera were dutifully attending a series of cultural relations meetings designed to orient new Russian émigrés, who were still crowding into London. At the same time, an increasingly regular flow of letters from her family was allowing her to picture life in the new

---

*The letter was said to have been written by Grigori Zinoviev, chairman of the Communist International, inciting the British Communist Party to revolution. When it was published in the *Daily Mail* on 15 September, it did irreparable damage to the Labour government, despite protests that it had been faked by a force within the British Establishment to counter the spread of socialism. This proved to be true. In 1999 it was revealed that Britain's own Secret Intelligence Service had engineered the scandal.

Russia in more intimate, and in some ways more reassuring, detail. Professionally at least, the Lopukhovs were on the move. Evgenia had retired from classical ballet to become a 'complete musical comedy star', while Andrei (whom Lydia had briefly tried to get to Paris for the Beaumont season) had been promoted to solo character dancer at the Mariinsky. Most impressive of all was Fedor's elevation. In 1921 he had launched a showcase for new choreography, Evenings of Young Ballet, attempting even in the chaos of the post-revolutionary period to nurture a new generation of dancemakers and build bridges between the classical past and the experimental future. The success of his project, coupled with the emerging quality of Fedor's own choreography, had led to his appointment, a year later, as ballet director of the Mariinsky – now known briskly as the State Academic Theatre for Opera and Ballet, or GATOB in its Russian acronym.

Fedor in his new demanding role bore no resemblance to the 'mad Russian' depressive over whom Lydia had fretted thirteen years ago. One of his protégées, Alexandra Danilova, recalled that during the harsh deprivations of the early 1920s, when wages had been slashed and the future of Russian ballet was still in doubt, Fedor had been a heroically positive force: 'not handsome, but *vivaci*, with a long-nosed profile like Gogol's. He was very fond of the young dancers and would scold us when we got morose. "What's the matter? You are young and talented! Go to the theatre. Go to the museums. See everything ..." I followed his advice ... Without him I don't know what I – or any of us – would have done. Despite all the gloom that pervaded our lives then, Lopukhov never let us lose sight of the goals he had set for us.'[46]

But if ballet was being slowly restored to official grace and Lydia's family with it, living conditions in Lenin's Russia were punishing, and many dancers were opting to flee. During the autumn, Lydia met up with several of them: Danilova herself; her boyfriend Georgi Balanchivadze (his name shortly to be Anglicised as George Balanchine); and her former adversary, Mikhail Mordkin.* The

*Danilova and Balanchine were dancing at the Empire, but in a few weeks would be accepted into Diaghilev's company. Balanchine would eventually become director of the New York City Ballet as well as one of the seminal ballet choreographers of the twentieth century. Mordkin also went back to America, choreographing and directing there until his death in 1944.

stories that they brought with them made her flinch: 'in Russia,' she informed Maynard, 'one must burn oneself with work to please the masses and at any moment comrade Mordkin should be ready to dance at a political meeting and yet nothing in return'.[47] Even Fedor earned very little, and while Karlusha had been able to retain the Nevsky Prospekt apartment, keeping a maid on the money coming in from two new lodgers plus the cash and parcels sent by Lydia, the Lopukhovs' life was hard. Lydia, cosseted in Gordon Square, felt embarrassed and impotent: 'They praised my brother but he is so poor what can I do for him? I feel so shamed to have all these comforts.'[48]

It shamed Lydia, too, that these comforts still came to her without work – for as the weeks passed, she continued to be unemployed. Massine and Idzikowski performed short seasons at the Empire but did not request her participation; nor was she offered any performances when the Ballets Russes came to the Coliseum in mid-November. Lydia had hoped to use the unpaid salary that Diaghilev still owed her from *The Sleeping Princess* as leverage in her negotiations for guest roles. But while there were ripples of interest, and some talk of her dancing *Boutique*, no concrete invitation came either for that winter season or for the Ballets Russes's return in May. Lydia's frustration was acute: 'what a crooked mind of Serge's he is a born wicked prima donna with intrigues',[49] and by Christmas it seemed to Bloomsbury that she had become stuck in a rather pathetic rut. Virginia, dining with Lydia and Maynard on 24 December, reported to Vanessa that 'the poor sparrow [was] already turning into a discreet silent serious motherly respectable fowl with eggs feather cluck cluck clucking all complete. A melancholy sight indeed and I forsee the day when she dislikes any reference to dancing.'[50]

Virginia, however, had seen largely what she expected to see. The previous few weeks might have been dispiriting for Lydia's career, but they had also seen a rapid burst of progress on the divorce case, and now that a date had definitely been set for the hearing, Maynard had had to restrain her wild spirits: 'you must be very tactful in law courts,' he coached her, 'and must not call Barocchi a baboon, Mary Hargreaves a cat or yourself a horse, dog or bee; and *me* you must not mention at all'.[51] The case would of course be compromised if Lydia let slip that she had a lover for whom she wanted to leave Barocchi. But heroically she kept her tongue, and three weeks later, on 15 January 1926, her decree nisi was granted and she could abandon herself to a theatrical outburst of gratitude. 'How fortunate I am, after these swift dramatic developments, my mental state no more bedraggling, "Gods divine" have been benevolent to me ... I bow into your knees and sink to my feet.'[52]

Maynard's own reaction to the news had, on the surface, been typically pragmatic. While Lydia had felt so 'shakey in the legs' that she was obliged to 'ride in taxis without reserve', he had immediately marched out to buy the papers in order to check the accuracy of the court reports.[53] Yet during the last few months he too had been badly affected by all the setbacks in the divorce case. They had even disturbed his work, and while he had managed to get deep into the planning of his next book, *A Treatise on Money*, he had uncharacteristically seized on any excuse – indigestion attendant on a college feast, the need to tidy his room – to delay its writing.

As soon as the hearing date had been announced, however, Maynard's concentration returned. *A Treatise on Money* represented a fundamental advance in his attempts to think beyond the economics that he had been taught as a student and towards a modern theory of state-managed capitalism. In two dense volumes he was attempting to demonstrate how an unregulated market, the basic model of traditional economics, was no longer viable in a post-war world where boom and bust cycles, fluctuating exchange rates, rising inflation and high unemployment had become endemic. These were problems, Maynard argued, which required new forms of state intervention, including the control of price levels through raising and lowering of interest rates – and in making this claim he was establishing what was then a visionary link between the principles of economics and government policy.

He was also laying the theoretical ground for his great, revolutionary writings of the 1930s, since, contrary to Bloomsbury's glum verdict on Lydia's obstructive influence – 'they say you can only talk to Maynard now in words of one syllable'[54] – domestic happiness was unlocking the most fertile reserves of his intellect. It stimulated

Maynard's imagination to have Lydia's intuitive, fantastical take on the world – 'there is no one's tongue like that in Cambridge,'[55] she observed complacently – and, more importantly, it steadied his confidence to have her close by. When Maynard was with Lydia, he felt contented and focussed; when too long away from her, he felt his creativity wilt: 'I am leading a dry life and time passes. You must moisten me again with your springs.'[56]

The sexual as well as the intellectual implications were deliberate, for Maynard took pride in the frank physical intimacy with which he and Lydia now shared their lives. His father, Neville, had surely never enquired after the state of Florence's menstrual cycle, yet almost every month Maynard would encourage Lydia to report on her 'bleeding guests' and sympathise over her graphic accounts of feeling 'fluffy with pains and blood'.[57] Their sex life continued to flourish, as despite the drab, motherly fowl image that Virginia had projected, Lydia maintained a very unmatronly style of seduction. Her letter of 22 May was signed off with the wanton promise to 'kiss your own lively pink 2 sucks', and she continued to sport her 'man's' wardrobe for his private and public pleasure. The following year she made a lively entrance at a Gordon Square dinner dressed in an Eton blazer and flannels and 'accompanied by a girl friend' in Harrow School uniform.[58]

Contrary to Bloomsbury's predictions, too, Lydia was adopting a briskly modern line towards her wedding, which would take place in early August as soon as the decree nisi became absolute. Lydia might be conventional enough to want Maynard's ring on her finger, and she was virtuously checking out the times of the birth control clinic, which she would soon, legitimately, be able to attend; but she claimed to have no further interest in the trappings of marriage, insisting that 'what we plan in 46 is only a practical solution of a inteligent arrangement of life ... I am prosaic with the society and romantic with you tete a tete.'[59] When Maynard suggested that they might publish news of their engagement, Lydia rounded on him in a rare fury of contradiction: '*No*, for the dear Lord God, do not ever put announcements in the papers. It is well for "virtious, very young, and innocent" but we two with our more or less scandalous reputations (especially mine) were never engaged to one another.'[60]

Somewhat sheepishly, Maynard had shortly to confess that the news was 'all over' Cambridge and that he had even begun to receive wedding presents.'[61]

Ideally Lydia would have occupied the months leading up to the wedding with work, but she had only one short engagement offered her, a three-week season at the Coliseum, in April. This was a second collaboration with Nicolas Legat, a comic duet titled *The Postman* which was set to Beethoven's piano sonata number 18 (opus 31 no. 3) and gave Lydia the role of a maid who is forced to beg her local postman, Idzikowski, to return a letter in which she has hastily and wrong-headedly broken off with her lover.* Again Legat's choreography proved wittily apt for Lydia's purpose: 'we all labour like dogs,' she hummed. 'I am afraid to praize before time but it is so charmingly humourous.'[62] She worried, however, that Duncan, as her designer, would hijack the ballet by insisting that Idzikowski make his entrance on a bicycle and that she exit the stage on the same machine, with the retrieved letter snatched triumphantly between her teeth. Neither dancer knew how to cycle and since both of them had rather short legs they found it especially hard controlling a man's bike.† But by the time that ballet was premièred, the two dancers had evidently mastered the art of pedalling, for *The Dancing Times* noted approvingly that the ballet had confirmed Lydia's status as 'the popular idol she is with the London public today'. It also reported that after their final performance on 21 April, the audience refused to let her and Idzikowski leave the stage as the dancers were showered with bouquets and caricatured portraits of themselves.[63]

After the three-week run Lydia suffered her usual post-season slump of adrenalin, and it was during this time that she began to get nervous about the approaching wedding. Maynard's family were not a problem. Florence and Neville, whom Lydia now fondly dubbed

*The idea for its libretto had originally come from Tom Marshall, who had observed Lydia dancing along Gordon Square one day to post a letter. Maynard discovered that his grandmother had been in the same situation as Lydia's character and speculated nervously that if she had not retrieved the letter written to his own grandfather, he himself might never have been born.

†A woman's bike was the obvious alternative but Lydia was worried that it would be inappropriate for a postman and an 'atmosphere of burlesque might creep in'. LL to JMK 26 February 1925.

the *starychki*, or 'old ones', had seemed genuinely delighted to embrace her as their daughter-in-law, and most of the rest of the Keynes and Brown clans had appeared equally welcoming. Maynard's brother, Geoffrey, and his wife, Margaret, had been charmed when Lydia had taken their little boys to the Coliseum and then romped with them afterwards at number 41: 'They all danced on their toes, and as a hostess I put the ballet shoes and stood on mine, then we walked on heels and finished our excitements on the floor.'[64] In April, Lydia had also been approved by a large family tea party in Cambridge. Although she had retreated from the embrace of one of the aunts – 'She has moustaches. I thought I smelt whiskey near, otherwise she is bright, ugly and nervous dressed in artificial silk' – she had very much liked Maynard's 'oncle the doctor' (actually Sir Walter Langdon-Brown): 'What a nice wooly [sic] creature! ... he is sweet nature and warm.'[65]

There had also been the appearance of a warmer rapprochement with Bloomsbury. Duncan privately growled that the marriage was 'a grim fact to face'[66] and Vanessa proffered a great deal of unwelcome advice as to where the new Mr and Mrs Keynes might live – which was essentially anywhere other than Gordon Square – but otherwise they tried to be graceful in defeat. Vanessa volunteered herself for 'gossips' and assured Lydia that, despite her aversion to the legal business of making and unmaking marriages, she was very glad the divorce from Barocchi had succeeded: 'Smiling and very nice ... she said that she had special sympathy for me and you.'[67] Virginia too had softened. After she and Lydia had gone to the theatre together (a programme of Euripides, which both women had found a trial), she had mused in her diary, 'Little Lydia I liked: how does her mind work? Like a lark soaring, a sort of glorified instinct inspires her.'[68] And even though Lydia does not seem to have spotted herself in the character of Rezia, she had enthusiastically read *Mrs Dalloway* when it had been published in May, impressed by the novel's inventive prose, if sceptical of its experiments with character: 'It is very rapid, interesting and yet I feel in that book all the human beings only puppets, Virginia's brain is so quick that sometimes her pen cannot catch it or it is I who is slow.'[69] When she discussed this with Duncan and Adrian the latter agreed that the novel lacked psychological depth. Lydia added that she preferred Virginia's essays, and with surely wicked disingenuousness claimed to have admired what she saw as Lytton's influence on them. Duncan roared with laughter and made her promise never to pass on the observation.

But while Lydia could be reasonably confident of Maynard's family supporting her marriage, she was apprehensive about how it would be treated in the press. She had always patrolled her private life so carefully, and the last thing she wanted to attract was the kind of publicity that might send zealous journalists dredging up details from her past, or encouraging comment from those who might still regard her as a disreputable partner for Maynard.

There were no tawdry headlines in the end, but Lydia was right to fear a fuss, for no sooner had her decree nisi become absolute on 27 July 1925 than news of their wedding on 4 August hit the headlines across Britain. Much comment was made of the unlikeliness of their union: 'Anglo-Russian Treaty Signed,' blared the *Newcastle Evening Chronicle*; 'Lopokova engaged to an economist,' reported the *Daily Graphic*; and *Vogue* would later publish a full-page photo of the couple with the plodding observation that 'The marriage of the most brilliant of English economists with the most popular of Russian dancers makes a delightful symbol of the mutual dependence upon each other of art and science.'[70] With the story even appearing in the international press, there was no chance of Lydia having the discreet ceremony that she had planned, and on the morning of her wedding a jostling, noisy press of journalists and photographers were among the crowd of well-wishers waiting for them outside the St Pancras Registry Office.

This aggressive welcome party was in marked contrast to the modest and oddly assorted group gathered inside. Maynard and Lydia had invited just two friends, Vera and Duncan, who were both standing as witnesses, and there were only four family members present: Florence and her eighty-eight-year-old mother, Ada; Maynard's sister, Margaret; and his solicitor uncle, Kenneth Brown (Neville perhaps having been detained at home by illness). From the start, the fifteen-minute ceremony appears to have been painfully self-conscious. Duncan, although having remembered to polish his shoes (an exceptional event), had forgotten that it was his duty to

Lydia and Maynard outside the St Pancras Register Office, 1925

bring the ring and was thrown into a confusion of panic until Maynard wryly produced it himself. Lydia, already unnerved by the crowd outside, then became upset and tongue-tied when the registrar required details of her father's profession for the forms. Possibly she had been embarrassed to admit Vasili's modest status in front of her new relatives, but it took her a few haunted moments before she could settle on the innocuous description 'theatrical assistant'.

By the time the ceremony was over, the crowd outside had grown. Maynard, looking 'big, solid and very professorlike',[71] took charge, reassuring Lydia that they would stop and pose for just a few photographs. However, as both the public and the press surged forward, they were in danger of getting mobbed. A group of invalid women in bath chairs wheeled forward to get a better view, along with a seemingly deranged fan who hurled handfuls of confetti straight at Lydia's face and then tried to stuff the empty bag down the neck of her suit.[72] According to Florence, who wrote an account of the wedding to Neville that day, Lydia looked 'like a little ghost, as scared of the newspaper people and photographers as if she had never faced the public before',[73] and she was almost trembling by the time Maynard got her into a taxi and back to number 46.

Here a small party, with a 'lovely and delicious'[74] wedding cake contributed by Florrie, were waiting. But Lydia had to accept more compromises and delays to her 'tête-à-tête' life with Maynard. Tilton had been unavailable for their first married holiday together, and although an alternative house had been rented, just south of Lewes, Maynard had given in to a perverse instinct of collegiate hospitality and invited a stream of academics to stay. Few proved to be sympathetic company for a honeymoon, and particularly punishing was the philosopher Ludwig Wittgenstein, who arrived on 20 August and used the whole of his six-day visit to exhibit his most antisocial traits. He dominated the conversation during walks and mealtimes, and Lydia he treated with unconcealed contempt. When she ventured a mild remark about the beauty of a tree, he crushed her with the blistering epistemological challenge, 'What do you mean?'[75] Lydia, who was already unnerved by the philosopher's incomprehensible monologues, burst into tears, and even Maynard was appalled by his behaviour. He himself had found many of Wittgenstein's arguments impenetrable, and later in November when he tried to relay them to a meeting of the Apostles, he had to confess that he was unable to remember even half of them.

Over at Charleston there was little relief. Maynard's friends may have resolved to put a brave face on the marriage but their goodwill was already lapsing. Duncan was sulking that his 'future prospects' as Maynard's heir had been 'blighted';[76] Clive was bitching nastily that it would take years for Lydia to produce a child because 'Maynard is too fast on the trigger'.[77] Lytton, who came to stay with the Keyneses at the end of the summer, was also inclined to be truculent. He did not make himself directly offensive but could not fully disguise his disappointment in Lydia and his resentment of her effect on Maynard. 'The Keynes visit was rather lugubrious, somehow or other,' he confided to Carrington. 'For one thing the house was so hideous. Then Lydia is a pathetic creature to my mind – and so plain ... [with Maynard] there is a difficulty of some kind in one's intercourse with him – he seems rather far off.'[78]

It was the old Bloomsbury view writ large and clear, yet it revealed far more about Lytton's state of mind than it did about his newly married hosts. The circumstances of the wedding, the awkward summer guests and the entrenched prejudices of Maynard's friends were all disappointing to Lydia. But such setbacks could no longer make her doubt the truth of Maynard's love, as he assured her constantly of the 'enormous pleasure I have in being with you [which] has got greater every year'.[79] And even during Lytton's visit she could not have felt more happily impervious to any criticisms being cast at her. Barely a fortnight earlier, Maynard had given Lydia the best possible wedding present: taking her on a journey home to see her family.

Chapter Fifteen

MARRIAGE

> How lucky we never bore one another. Can one go on being in love with someone who bores you? Your old hopes-he-never-bores-you M.
>
> MAYNARD TO LYDIA, 1926[1]

It had been a point of pride to Maynard that he had so quickly been able to give Lydia her longed-for reunion with her family, as well as make his own first contact with his Russian in-laws. Travel between Britain and Russia was no longer dangerous, but it remained difficult to arrange for private individuals, so Maynard had seized the offer of an official invitation from Moscow (to attend the bicentenary celebrations of Russia's Academy of Sciences) in order to organise an extra week beforehand in Leningrad and gain permission for Lydia to accompany him.

For Lydia herself, returning home after her fifteen-year exile was a momentous prospect – both joyous and alarming. She knew that Karlusha was pleased by her marriage, having received loving congratulations from her mother that her life was finally 'acquiring better shape'.[2] But she did not know what else to expect from this return, and during the long train journey, as Maynard ensconced himself in his usual mass of papers and books, Lydia was left to her own turbulent thoughts, staring through the windows as her past came back to her – the towns, fields and forests of Europe giving way to the plains and birch trees of Russia, and finally the low, graceful skyline that she remembered as St Petersburg.

Petersburg had, of course, been Leningrad since 1924, and during the drive to the Nevsky Prospekt flat Lydia would have seen everywhere on the streets the violence and the rhetoric of the new order. The battle-scarred buildings and the revolutionary statues; the red-starred uniforms of the ubiquitous state police; the drab clothes of the pedestrians and the empty shop windows were all brutally strange to her and it may only have been when Lydia was inside her family's flat that she felt she had arrived home. Here at least the knick-knacks of her childhood were still crowded into glass cupboards and the familiar photographs and pictures were still covering the walls. Here too was Karlusha waiting to meet her.

Lydia left no written record of this reunion, nor do we know exactly who was present. Nikolai, the rebellious engineer brother, was never mentioned in any family correspondence. Yet it is easy to imagine the confusion of embraces and exclamations, the unloading of parcels, the conversations started and interrupted, the cataloguing of physical changes. Karlusha had been a middle-aged wife when Lydia had left; now she was a widow, honed to a stoical self-reliance by the upheavals of the past years. Photographs from this period show that at the age of sixty not only did Karlusha look thinner and tougher, but her glance was keen behind her spectacles, and she wore her clothes – a woollen waistcoat, shiny patterned blouse and a man's necktie – with a practical disregard of convention.

For her own part Karlusha must have been startled at seeing the capricious teenager that she had waved off to Paris returned to her as a slightly plumper and infinitely more experienced woman. Maynard, too, as he watched Lydia being re-embraced as Lidusinka by her family, must have felt his perceptions shift. For the first time he could see how his wife had been formed. He could see her face in her mother's broad, pale cheeks, and how the domestic habits and social instincts, which he had thought unique aspects of Lydia's personality, were rooted in a family dynamic. During that week in Leningrad, as Lydia exchanged fifteen years' worth of news with Fedor, Evgenia and Andrei, Maynard could also identify exactly where his 'Lady Talky' had got her chattering gene from.

He adored Lydia's relatives and they adored him equally. Even though he had only a few halting Russian phrases to offer, Fedor found Maynard a 'fine person, very friendly, courteous and intellectual',[3] and Karlusha clearly felt that he was a superb catch, instructing

Lydia 'to be a good woman' to him always.[4] It pleased Karlusha too that Lydia had found an affectionate mother-in-law in Florence, and after the visit was over she sent a moving note to Harvey Road, acknowledging how painful she had found it to 'live so far away from my child' and how consoling it was 'to know you have grown to love Lydia … and will take my place'.[5]

'It was wonderful to see her again,' confided Karlusha, mother to mother. 'But the time of her stay is so short.'[6] Between reminiscing and storytelling with her family, Lydia had only limited time to show Maynard around her birthplace. During their brief tours, however, she was reassured to discover that more remained of her former life than she had first thought. Interviewed later by a British journalist, she reported that there were still 'delicious cakes at Gourmet's Restaurant on the Nevsky if you have enough money', and that her old school and theatre were much as she remembered. While memories were still recent of the near-starvation conditions through which the dancers had had to perform, 'with the temperature of the theatre below zero and a cabbage and a herring's head to eat', ballet was now fully reinstated as a state art form so that, as Lydia put it, 'the proletariat may feel themselves as good as Romanovs'.[7] A year later it would become even more favoured, as General Kirov, a dedicated balletomane, was appointed chief officer in Leningrad. At the court of Stalin it would soon become commonplace for high-ranking officials to seek their mistresses among pretty dancers, just as the Grand Dukes had before them.

From Leningrad, Lydia and Maynard went straight to Moscow, transported in magnificent style in a train that had once been reserved for the Tsar's use. This second stage of the visit was to be elaborately formal, a heavy schedule of meetings for Maynard with GOSPLAN, the committee for economic planning, and the State Bank, plus a programme of hospitality that included trips to the theatre and art galleries, and also a banquet for 500 assorted dignitaries in the Hall of Nobility. Lydia, still trying to absorb the contradictions of this new Russia, sat between an English professor and a 'parsee scholar', drinking wine left over from the Imperial cellar and eating a nine-course meal that lasted till 2.30 in the morning.

Maynard was equally fascinated, and even if he did not approve of

Lydia and children in Russia, 1925

his hosts' politics (and typically tried to press on them the logic of a more liberalised form of communism), he fell in love with the idea of Russia as Lydia's homeland. When they arrived back in Sussex he was full of the trip, walking the Downs in a Tolstoy blouse and black astrakhan cap, and talking unstoppably of what he had seen. Virginia was intrigued and reluctantly charmed: '[A]n immense good will and vigour pervades him,' she noted in her diary. 'She hums in his wake the great mans wife. But though one could carp one can also find them very good company, & my heart ... slightly warms to him, whom I've known all these years so truculently pugnaciously & unintimately.'[8]

Lydia appears to have been less voluble in her account of the trip, but perhaps she felt that Virginia would not appreciate her own most cherished moments from the visit home – which must have included showing off her husband to Karlusha and boasting of her future life with him in Gordon Square. She and Maynard were to take sole possession of number 46 on their return to London, and this was hardly a subject that Lydia would want to raise with Virginia. Given the long, territorial squabbles that had already taken place over the house, Lydia could easily anticipate the trouble that this final domestic shuffle would generate.

The move did in fact turn into an unedifying farce. Vanessa and Duncan, the ousted tenants, were only having to transfer to number 37, nine doors along the Square, but their relocation was accompanied by a disproportionate amount of bickering over outstanding rent and rates, and by disputes over furnishings and decor. The ownership of one painting by Duncan came under particular dispute, and after Maynard had defensively screwed it into the wall to prevent it being taken, Vanessa had retaliated by sneaking in with a screwdriver and carrying it off.

To Bloomsbury's greater horror, once Lydia was installed in number 46 she called in the decorators. Murals that had been painted by Vanessa and Duncan just after the war were whitewashed over, while the drawing room was laid with a thick, sky-blue carpet and hung with fake antique candelabras and primrose satin curtains, sprinkled with violet wreaths. As Virginia reported to Vanessa in fascinated dismay, the effect was all 'tight and shiney'.[9] Nor was she any happier with Maynard's own plans, which included building a grand new library and extra bathrooms. Having once been a showcase for Bloomsbury art and Bloomsbury lifestyle, number 46 was being transformed into an anathema of stiff, bourgeois luxury.

It was true that interior decoration was not one of Lydia and Maynard's talents – both of them were haphazardly blind to the finer points of decor and they possessed none of Vanessa's instinctive grace and simplicity in dressing a room. But there was a certain festive rebellion in their rejection of Bloomsbury aesthetics. When Lydia expressed delight with 'the passages in their new outlook and that they have no frescoes', she was revelling in the fact that the house had become a blank canvas for her own future.[10] As far as she was concerned, the essential luxury of number 46 was that it had become

Lydia practising in Gordon Square, 1925

her home, the first she had ever truly inhabited, and that she and Maynard were finally living together alone and unscrutinised.

Maynard still spent half the week in his suite of rooms at King's but Lydia no longer felt insecure and restless when he was gone. While she had once prowled around the house, hardly daring to touch his things, now she sat contentedly 'on your big chair with the fire sniffing around my feet'.[11] Nor did she fret his absences away by worrying about the 'Cambridge influence'. She knew that Maynard would continue to find young men arousing but she had learned to joke at his flirtations. One evening in the early 1930s, Lydia brought two young dancers to the house, Frederick Ashton and William Chappell, whose camp, easy manners were misread by Maynard as sexual complicity. He led them on to the balcony and, under cover of pointing out famous Bloomsbury residencies, tried to give them both 'terrible, great, smacking kisses'. The two men were violently embarrassed, especially since they assumed that Lydia had witnessed the assault. Yet Chappell recalled admiringly that she had appeared utterly unfazed and on their return to the room had simply asked them, very archly, whether they would like 'some more *Bols*' – a drink whose name always struck her as irresistibly rude.[12]

Lydia also knew how to pique Maynard's jealousy. Her dream life was vivid, and she was careful to keep her husband closely informed of its raunchier details, writing in October 1926 of 'a disreputable dream' that she had about the then-playboy politician Oswald Mosley. 'I was kissing Mosley he offered marriage I said yes but in a minute changed my mind to a No, then you came in ... and gently led me away.'[13] 'Words fail me,'[14] was all an appalled Maynard could write in reply. Lydia also remained an instinctive, opportunistic flirt. She enjoyed the sight of a handsome man in uniform, and when Gordon Square was burgled in 1934 (by a thief posing as a chimney sweep), she charmed a path through the officers at Scotland Yard when she was required to make a statement, boasting to Maynard that the police said, 'next time they will steal me'.[15]

There were also admiring young men at number 46, when Lydia began her regular habit of hosting long, informal Sunday lunches. During term-time weekends Maynard was always up in Cambridge, and while he would be eating a stolid English roast with his family in their house in Harvey Road, Lydia would fill number 46 with her own gregarious mix of dancers, musicians, painters and Russian émigrés. Generously Maynard would leave out bottles of his claret for Lydia, along with careful instructions to warm them by the fire. Every time she left them too long. Two details always remembered by the guests at Lydia's 'Russian lunches' were, first, the lack of ceremony with which she served her food – tearing up chunks of cold chicken and passing them around with her bare hands, and second, the fact that the wine always had to be rescued from the fire and was poured out 'gently steaming'.[16]

What mattered to Lydia was the conversation. She disliked socialising as Maynard's wife and shrank especially from her newly acquired duty of replying to their shared invitations: 'All my lingo stops for those occasions, the pen droops out, I become illiterate and illegitimate.'[17] At home, on her own ground, however, she was unconstrained. Her lunches blurred into cocktails, her supper parties extended till dawn, and she prided herself on the intimacy that developed between her and her friends, boasting to Maynard that Sam Courtauld had confessed his delight in the 'unrestrained' quality of their 'relations', and Boris Anrep (the mosaicist) had claimed that even with his wives 'there never happened frank conversation as took place with me'.[18]

Yet however confident and happy Lydia felt as mistress of number 46, it was Tilton that became her and Maynard's emotional home. In the spring of 1926, after protracted negotiations with the owner, Lord Gage, Maynard acquired a twenty-one-year lease on the house, and from that point he and Lydia spent most of their holidays there. Holiday was a relative concept to Maynard; he wrote almost every day at Tilton and completed most of his books there. Yet the peace and the seclusion of the Sussex countryside became the element in which the Keynes marriage assumed its most natural and most fulfilling equilibrium. Maynard might joke that Lydia was a dangerous distraction to his work (he threatened to dedicate the *Treatise* 'to his wife without whose influence the book would be published a year earlier'),[19] but in reality she was perfectly content to let him be. During the mornings, as Maynard wrote, Lydia did her ballet exercises (Bunny Garnett prized the memory of being allowed to observe her 'wonderful elastic body ... doing high kicks over the barre in her room'),[20] after which she occupied herself with her gardening, her books and her music. There was always a piano down at Tilton; Lydia had graduated from Theatre School with both a love of the instrument and some genuine expertise. By 1928 there was also a gramophone, to which Lydia, with her growing collection of records, became addicted.

It was at Tilton that Lydia also became a connoisseur of nature. Wandering the grounds outside, she tutored herself rapturously in the changing seasons, noting details in the diary that she had begun intermittently to keep* and showing off her discoveries to Maynard when they took their afternoon walks: 'Eggs of a thrush found in a small bush. I never saw such eggs before.'[21] She was also usually accompanied by a changing succession of dogs. Prior to Tilton,

*The diary was a wall calendar from Heffers on which she scribbled appointments, observations, or a treasured phrase of Maynard's. Lydia used it for personal entries primarily between 1926 and 1929.

Lydia's experience of animals had not gone beyond her pet canaries but she now discovered herself to be a sentimental dog lover. Her first puppy, Bruno, was inherited from her maid Ruby in the summer of 1926; her second was a black Labrador, Pushkin, which she loved for his 'bright, tender and independent character'.[22] Patsy, her third, was a short-haired, yappy bitch that suffered from eczema and from the aggressive attentions of the local dogs when she was on heat. Her fourth was a greyhound, Ross, whose passion for streaking after hares and rabbits came to an end under the wheels of a lorry.

These walks with the dogs usually followed a route up Firle Beacon or through the woods. Like many Russians, and like many dancers, Lydia was not a rigorous walker; a two-hour ramble was her limit, but she loved to feel herself part of the countryside. 'What a melody of a morning,' she wrote ecstatically one early spring, 'music in the air smells of strength and softness; one squeaks, stretches and blinks in perfect bliss.'[23] In April 1927 she went on a brief, hectic trip to Paris, taking in Olga and Pablo Picasso ('charming'), the Folies Bergère ('thousands of breasts more than [one] asks for') and an exhibition of Surrealist painting. As soon as she returned she headed straight down to Tilton to recover, writing contentedly on her arrival, 'peace Perfect peace nature is lyrical.'[24]

In an extra bid for fresh air and exercise, Lydia was temporarily and faddishly enthused by tennis, practising with Maynard on the scruffy court that had been laid out by previous tenants at Tilton and occasionally holding tennis parties. She liked, perversely, to dress up for these events (her tennis whites accessorised impractically with a pixie hat and a bead necklace), but she was never a natural player. Whilst dutifully signing up to a course of lessons with a Mr Perry (who may have been the legendary Fred), 'playing balls', as she called it, never came easily. As she chortled to Maynard, 'the only progress I've made is that although I attack my balls recklessly they fly nearer the boarder'.[25]

Their Charleston neighbours were sometimes roped in to play, provoking predictably disdainful mutterings from Vanessa and hilarity from her sister. 'They are off to Tilton,' warned Virginia with gleeful spite, 'how you must be looking forward to your tennis parties.'[26] But visits between the two households were limited.

Left: Lydia and Maynard practising the Keynes-Keynes. *Right:* Lydia and Maynard dressed for tennis

Left: Lydia with Pushkin. *Right:* Lydia gardening at Tilton

Vanessa and Duncan were now dividing their summers between Sussex and the South of France, and even when they were at Charleston, the few hundred yards of track that separated them from Tilton continued to be disproportionately tricky to negotiate. Invitations were dutifully given and received, yet always with an edge of duty and self-consciousness, and Roger Fry leaves a picture of Lydia still over-anxious to please in Bloomsbury company, making 'too much effort to entertain to be gay and dispense herself'.[27] Duncan eventually resumed his former fondness for Lydia and, despite his fears of being disinherited by Maynard, retained deep, grateful feelings for the latter's continuing love and financial patronage.* Vanessa's rooted antipathy to the Keyneses' marriage, however, remained unalterable. According to Bunny Garnett, when he spoke to Duncan on the subject the latter 'wept and could not reply',[28] and even Virginia felt that there was an almost psychotic element to her sister's dislike. She herself, at the safer distance of her house in Rodmell, reacted in a whiplash alternation between pleasure in the Keyneses' 'urban and admirable'[29] company and comically exaggerated fury when they chose to call in on her, unannounced. 'What should we find at the gate,' she wrote to Vanessa in 1929, 'but a seedy grey Rolls with the detestable Edgar and the Keynes. I don't see that one's friends have any right to mutilate ones life in this way. There I was forced to rake the cinders of Bloomsbury gossip with Lydia – it was an insult – a murderous act and one has no remedy.'[30]

But Lydia and Maynard's domestic happiness was blithe and thick-skinned, and mostly they found it easy to ignore their neighbours' froideur – surprisingly easy, Vanessa realised, as she commented to Duncan in 1926: 'It dawns on me that they are no more anxious to see us than we to see them.'[31] The Tiltonians – as they were called – had all the company they needed away from the Charlestonians. Apart from Maynard's family, regular guests included Jack Sheppard and George Rylands, or Dadie, who had become a Fellow at King's and was now much loved by Lydia. There were colleagues like

*The two men would nevertheless still come to occasional blows, for instance over the London Artists Association, a painters' collective that Maynard set up with Sam Courtauld in 1925. Duncan profited from this, as did Vanessa, but they resented what they saw as Maynard's philistinism in selecting the participating artists.

Dennis Robertson and also Mary Paley Marshall, the widow of Maynard's old teacher, who contentedly dug weeds from the lawn during the day and declared herself to be one of Lydia's greatest admirers, commenting to anyone who would listen that Maynard's marriage was the 'best thing' he ever did.[32]

Another unexpected admirer was Beatrice Webb, who, with her husband, Sidney, came to Tilton quite regularly. Virginia was inclined to be caustic about the Keyneses' relationship with these veteran Fabians: 'Lydia and Maynard are both completely under the sway of the Webbs. Beatrice and Lydia exchange headdresses. How charming it is,'[33] while Duncan, in a rare burst of cattiness, thought that it had a purely expedient motive: 'Socialism is now going to become for them a moral excuse for meanness.'[34] Yet it was a genuine friendship, and along with other political acquaintances, like H. G. Wells and George Bernard Shaw, the Webbs offered Lydia a reassuring foothold in Maynard's world. Beatrice Webb was impressed by Lydia's intelligence, took an interest in her views and was quick to perceive how she had enlarged and stimulated Maynard's own mind. 'Hitherto he has not attracted me,' she wrote in her diary, 'brilliant, supercilious and not sufficiently patient for sociological discovery even if he had the heart for it. But then I had barely seen him, also I think his love marriage with the fascinating little Russian dancer has awakened his emotional sympathies with poverty and suffering.'[35]

Not all the visitors to Tilton came from Maynard's world. Lydia began to invite several of her own friends down to Sussex, including Ninette de Valois, who was developing a distinctive talent for creating and staging ballets; the gifted young choreographer and dancer Frederick Ashton; and the composer Constant Lambert. By the beginning of the 1930s these three were becoming key figures in the emerging British ballet scene, and Maynard, with his high regard for artists, admired and enjoyed their company. They in return were inclined to be overawed by his brilliance, although that did not prevent Ashton and Lambert (both outrageous mimics) from satirising their host and his circle in private. Lydia must surely have felt some delicious malice on the evening that the two young men treated her to an imitation of Maynard and Lytton sitting by the fire and 'repeating the dialogue of Tilton on free trade' – the latter's voice rising higher and higher until it disappeared in an attenuated squeak – or planning a skit on the notorious bisexual marriage of Vita Sackville-West and Harold Nicolson.[36]

Old friends from London came as well, though Sam and Lil Courtauld did so cautiously, for during the Keyneses' first years of occupation the comforts of Tilton were notoriously patchy, especially in winter, when the coal fires gave out more smoke than heat and the supply of hot water was disrupted by burst pipes. Lydia and Maynard became adept at layering themselves in woollen clothes, but their guests discovered that the best place to sit during cold weather was the wide hallway, where a grille in the floor issued gusts of hot air from the boiler in the cellar.

In the country, Maynard seemed to assume a very English upper-class ambivalence towards comfort, especially to catering. Whilst he would lay on hearty, munificent feasts for special occasions, regular meals at Tilton were often meagre. Maynard's unreliable digestion and his basic impatience with the niceties of cuisine inclined him to stint his guests at table, and it became a joke among the 'Bloomsberries' that it was best to eat a precautionary meal before dining at Tilton. (Virginia, gossiping to Lytton about a supper that she had attended in September 1927, dwelled with special relish on the smallness of the helping: 'We picked the bones of Maynard's grouse, of which there were three to eleven people. This stinginess is a constant source of delight to Nessa – her eyes gleamed as the bones went round.'[37])

If Tilton was not a particularly comfortable house, neither was it a specially beautiful one. After taking on the new lease, Maynard had commissioned the architect George Kennedy to design a new library and loggia from the sprawl of outhouses at the end of the south courtyard, as well as to open up the hall and the upstairs landing. Yet the dining room at the front of the house remained poky, as did the warren of bedrooms, and while Maynard was to fill Tilton with a superb collection of pictures and books over the years, much of the furniture, as well as the decoration of the house, was unattractive, even mean. Maynard was happy to spend hundreds of pounds on rebuilding, but it gave him unreasonable pleasure to buy a 'sound but ugly carpet, large enough to cover two servants' bedrooms, if cut, for £4', and he was wilfully drawn to pointless bargains – a stud box, for instance, when he possessed no studs. Most of these were bought in Cambridge, either at auction or from his favourite antiques dealer, and as they piled up at Tilton and Gordon Square even Lydia was driven to protest: 'I see that soon all of Cambridge will be bought by you.'[38]

Yet haphazard, even hideous, as Tilton might appear to its detractors, it was in its own way as organic a household as Charleston, thanks to the tending of Edgar and Ruby Weller, who lived in the cottage next door. Ruby was the same Ruby who had been hired by Lydia back in 1923, a shy country girl who on her first arrival at Gordon Square may have been tempted to turn tail and run back home to her mother. When she had knocked at the door of number 41, Lydia, either busy or awkward in her new role as employer, had simply said to her, 'You are Ruby who is working for me', shaken the dumbfounded girl by the hand and marched back upstairs.[39]

But Ruby had had the basic courage to stay and would end up working for Lydia for the next fifty years. The perks offered by her new job could be unexpectedly entertaining, as on any given day she might be taken to the theatre and see the King of Spain throwing armfuls of red roses during Lydia's curtain calls, or be opening the door to a fabulous personage like Anna Pavlova. (On the day that the latter had paid a visit to Lydia, Ruby had bent down to pick a letter from the mat as she opened the door, so that her first view of Pavlova had been of the ballerina's famously slender legs. Sheathed in black stockings, these had reminded Ruby irresistibly of the 'legs of a black Minorca chicken', an image that she later recalled had produced shrieks of laughter from Lydia and the reply, 'Yus but lays "noer" egg.'[40]

Ruby swiftly became established as family. When she met her future husband, Edgar, down at Tilton, it was Lydia who hosted Ruby's 'farewell party to maidenhood', providing 'balloons, gramaphone sandwiches ice cakes' in the kitchen of Gordon Square.[41] It was Lydia, too, who sympathised with Ruby when her marriage became troubled. Edgar had, for a while, been unrequitedly in love with Vanessa's cook, Grace Germany, and, now employed as the Keyneses' gardener and chauffeur, he turned out to be a heavy drinker, with a surly temper and, possibly, repressed homosexual leanings. Lydia disliked him and feared his bad driving, but she adored the blue-black pigs that he began breeding in partnership with Maynard and which she liked to brag had 'such gloss on them that any film star would envy'. It became one of Lydia and Maynard's favourite holiday rituals to drive with the pigs to Lewes market, where they were sold. She also adored Edgar's Aunt Penny (known as 'Auntie'), who joined the household as Lydia's seamstress and personal dresser, and was fond of the three children that he and Ruby had managed to produce. Andrew, named after Lydia's brother, was Lydia's godchild, and every birthday he received from her a new sweater and a pound note.

But while Lydia and Ruby were close, an unquestioned traditionalism defined the terms of their relationship, as it did all Lydia's dealings with her staff. However easily she gossiped in the kitchen, and however generously she participated in her servants' lives (arranging, for example, for their newly married cook, Beatty, to borrow 46 Gordon Square for her honeymoon), Lydia expected to be called madam at all times and have her needs unquestioningly serviced. In 1936 when she had to hire some younger help she was shocked to discover what a lively sense they had of their own rights: 'younger generation of servants are selfish to an astounding degree,' she complained to Florence, 'even if they are nice'.[42]

The 'servant problem' was in fact to dog Lydia all her married life. She had not been raised to handle staff and when her default combination of cosiness and bossiness failed her she was at a loss. On moving into number 46 she had inherited Maynard's live-in couple, Mr and Mrs Harland, who functioned as butler and cook both in London and down at Tilton. They were, she felt, a repellently depressing pair, addicted to peppermints and prone to 'complaining day and night that life has become weariness itself'.[43] However, she was frantic when the Harlands suddenly disappeared on an unexpected, and possibly fictional, winter holiday; and hiring new staff was always a problem for her. One new maid, Mary, whom she kindly took on because she was 'small, one crossed eye, glasses, no men would snatch her so ... feel we should give her a chance' turned out to be 'vacant in her mind', and Lydia suffered agonies having to sack her.[44]

Before her marriage to Maynard, Lydia had been sternly advised by Vera Bowen that she must acquire some domestic skills: 'no matter how interesting a woman is, when she has a house the man will like her still more if she is a good housekeeper.'[45] But the gestures that Lydia made towards self-improvement were fitful and largely impractical. She developed a sudden fetish for fine linen, forcing dinner guests to admire her new stock of 'snowy white' tablecloths and napkins, and dragging them upstairs to view her sheets and towels. Planning the week's menu was a mystery to her, and cooking remained obdurately beyond her. During the brief interregnum between Mrs Harland and her replacement, Lydia was helpless. 'What shall we do without a cook,' she wailed to Florence. 'Karsarvina can make scrambled eggs. But can I?'[46]

One role at which she naturally excelled, however, was nursing her husband. The two of them had always enjoyed detailed discussions of each other's symptoms, and Lydia had become very alert to Maynard's weak digestion, his susceptibility to colds and to the state of his 'cycles'. (He swore that his fluctuations between activity and sluggishness kept pace with the rhythms of her menstrual cycle.) After they were married, Lydia fussed even more assiduously, bullying him, as any good Russian peasant might do, to wear his vests as protection against the Cambridge wind and recommending a new cellular brand of underwear whose 'little holes' she considered an excellent means of airing the body. She also made it her duty to overhaul Maynard's wardrobe, complaining that he came to bed looking like 'Christ in the last stages' and berating him for the fact that most of his 'pantalets' were full of holes; that he had hardly any socks; and that he possessed more dress shirts than he could ever wear.[47]

Maynard loved to be fussed over, finding it both hilarious and comforting, and as they settled into married life the balance between them grew even more constant. Individually they retained professional lives and friends, yet independence deepened their mutual attraction. When Maynard left for his long Cambridge weekends, Lydia would send extravagant claims of frustration after him – 'the silver saddle gave me such stamina I long for you to come back ... I could fiddle tears out of me'[48] – and while he was away she would send seductive promises of what she might do on his return – 'I could warble any little place you choose.'[49]

Ringing steadily through their letters was trust. Lydia, for the first time in her life, had found a man she could rely on both practically and emotionally, and she put down deep roots in her new security. Maynard, as Webb and many others observed, also let down his guard. His work colleagues might still be browbeaten by his devastating cleverness, terrified by the moment when he would deliberately remove his glasses and place the tips of his long fingers together, in readiness to deliver some crushing point. His friends might still observe a core of obtuse, pushy self-absorption in his relationships. But he was much readier now to show simple tenderness and sentiment. Entering a contented middle age with Lydia, Maynard grew emotionally mellow and physically plump.

Above all, this was a marriage that both partners found engrossingly entertaining. Lydia frequently vowed to sit as quiet as 'a mouse' when the great and the good gathered at their meal tables; and when Bloomsbury assembled for meetings of their informal discussion society, the Memoir Club, she kept especially silent. But Maynard treasured her conversation, which was for him a fascinatingly transparent expression of herself, her judgements and observations uncorrupted by fashionable opinion. He was livid with Clive when the latter snubbed a remark that Lydia made about Proust, while his esteem for H. G. Wells rose still higher when the novelist observed that Lydia was not just 'clever for a ballerina, she was clever for anyone'.[50]

Of course Maynard was influenced by Lydia's reverence for his own intellect – it was delightful to him to be assured that 'the truth lies in your eyes'. But he believed that there was an untutored spark of genius in her unpredictable take on the world. Maynard despised conventional thinking, putting great faith in what he called intellectual 'crankiness'.[51] For him even Lydia's most childishly outrageous behaviour possessed a privileged authenticity, and observers of their relationship would comment on the benign smile that flitted over his face when, for instance, she silenced the conversation at an official dinner by brightly cross-examining her neighbour on the subject of lesbian sex: 'Two men – yes – I can see they've got something to take hold of. But two women – that's impossible. You can't have two insides having an affair.'[52]

Alone, Maynard and Lydia talked and gossiped, shared the newspapers, read poetry aloud. And whilst it may be dangerous to conspire with legend, their letters betrayed few signs of their marriage being tarnished by dullness or conflict, and in public they never appeared to tire of each other's company. On the contrary, guests at Tilton and Gordon Square regularly commented on how uxoriously Maynard's gaze lingered on Lydia and how romantic he continued to find her. Bunny Garnett, who was down in Tilton in the autumn of 1933 with Lydia, Maynard and Sam Courtauld, left a detailed, if slightly florid snapshot of the marriage's dynamic: 'We three men rejoiced in watching [Lydia], hearing her eager voice. And then, just as the sun recedes and all the colour changes – like that – a look of sadness, of doubt eclipsed her gay vitality. What was she thinking? Was she feeling lost in a strange country? She turned to Maynard and a look from him restored her.'[53]

If Lydia bloomed in her husband's uncritical devotion, she was also warmed by the affection of his parents, both of whom were unexpectedly seduced by their Russian daughter-in-law and more than ready to find her lovable. Lydia wrote regularly to Florence (now her 'Dearest m.i.l.'), finding her a warm confidante, as willing to respond to Lydia's dislike of certain colleagues of Maynard's as to intimate details of her health. 'My deposits of food are leaking out of me with speed and courage,'[54] she would inform her startled mother-in-law after successfully overcoming a bout of traveller's constipation; 'placing ice in my passage', she confided, had done wonders for an 'annoying itching pile'.[55]

Lydia even drew close to the more introverted Neville when, in the summer of 1927, they spent a fortnight together in Switzerland chasing butterflies. The two of them made eccentric travelling companions – both heavily cold-creamed against the sun; Lydia outfitted in a hat of Florence's, a bead necklace and Russian boots – but they admired each other greatly: 'F.i.l is very good and gentle,' Lydia wrote to Florence, 'and naturally we get along very well.'[56]

Had Maynard and his parents been less in love with Lydia, however, it might have troubled them that, in two crucial areas, she was unwilling or unable to be a conventional wife for him.

Lydia knew, when she married Maynard, that she was also

marrying into his public life. He was fast gaining in eminence (during their first years together he was invited to become consultant to the National Bank of Hungary and advisor to the French Minister of Finance, and he was even asked to consider becoming the Finance Minister of Romania – an offer that he naturally refused). Yet proud as she was of his status, Lydia could not adapt herself easily to its social consequences. She loathed attending functions as Maynard's consort and found many of his professional associates excruciating company, especially the economists: 'tiresome, no wide outlooks, no touch with life, inferiority complexes and no great ideas ... Sir John Symons on free trade I imagine too dull even for moths.'[57] She also found it hard to disguise her horror when, in the spring of 1926, Maynard told her that elections were being held for a new Provost (head of college) at King's and that the younger Fellows were campaigning for him.

Lydia had by now gained some confidence within Cambridge, visiting Maynard's family and socialising with some of his fellow academics, but she was not completely comfortable there, admitting that it made her feel 'like a guest in my own house'.[58] If Maynard were elected Provost, Lydia as his wife would be pressured into spending more time in Cambridge, presiding over parties at the Provost's Lodge and managing polite conversations with tight little groups of university wives. The prospect was unimaginable, and fortunately Maynard finally accepted that it was so. He himself had been uncertain about standing for Provost, given the burdens of responsibility and respectability that came with the post – and the even more distressing possibility that he might not even win the election – so it was perhaps not too hard for him to assure Lydia that 'The answer must come out of my own poupsik.'[59] Clearly it was a negative, for Maynard withdrew from the election and the issue was dropped.

A much more painful and protracted issue between the two of them was children. Maynard had desired and expected to become a father; even before they were married he had begun talking about 'starting their work on population' and imagining the 'poet' that they would produce together. According to Vanessa, Lydia too was 'beginning to want a baby very badly'.[60] By early 1926 they had apparently begun to try, with Maynard's letters displaying more than usual anxiety about Lydia's menstrual cycle. 'Nothing about the guests,' he wrote in May, 'which is the only thing that interests me.'[61]

However, a year later Lydia still showed no signs of becoming pregnant and Maynard was begging her to limit her dancing, perhaps believing that she was inhibiting her chances of conception by too much physical activity. In the spring of 1927 there seems to have been one brief moment of excitement, as Lydia's 'guests' failed to appear. Yet either an early miscarriage or the onset of a delayed period crushed their hopes; and while Maynard wrote sombrely and tenderly to reassure Lydia that 'we shall have in the end what we so much long for',[62] his confidence was unfounded. No further references to conception or pregnancy appeared in any of their letters, and by early 1928 all prospects of babies seem to have faded.

It is hard to know exactly what went wrong. The Keynes family were told that Lydia had eventually been advised against having children because her pelvis was too narrow for safe delivery. Yet there was no medical corroboration for such a claim and it may have been a fiction that Lydia herself invented to deflect awkward questions. In the past she had almost certainly suffered one or more miscarriages, possibly an abortion, possibly a secret birth, and any one of these events could have incurred an infection that left her clinically unable to conceive. Equally it could have been Maynard who was the source of the problem. At the time, he was in his mid-forties and a heavy smoker, so his fertility could have been impaired. Yet there is no record of either of them taking medical advice, beyond the routine tips that Lydia would have got from her birth control clinic, nor is there any suggestion that they made systematic attempts to overcome their difficulties. The issues of babies remained a private subject between them, one that they barely touched on in their letters, and one that they certainly did not choose to discuss with anyone else.

When they were eventually forced to abandon their hopes of parenthood, Maynard probably did not grieve for long. He was genuinely fond of children, in a donnish, bantering way (his nephew Milo remembered at the age of six asking why Lydia wore her hair in a bun and being delighted with Maynard's reply that it was so that he, Milo, could take out all the hairpins). But his life was already so tightly scheduled and he was already so fussy about his own health that it is hard to imagine him yielding readily to the demands of a tiny baby, whose state of digestion and warmth of vest would take priority over his. Lydia's grief on the other hand was surely more complicated. As well as mourning her failure to give Maynard a baby, she may have suffered an extra legacy of guilt and loss from those other, unwanted pregnancies. These were not emotions that she would confide either to her diary or to Vera, even though Vera herself was struggling with similar emotions, having suffered a miscarriage and experienced further difficulties conceiving her second child.*

Thus 1927 and 1928 were hard years for Lydia and she had to struggle against a recurrence of loneliness and depression. She confessed to a 'brooding feeling of sadness' to Maynard[63] and did not care to be around small children – contriving to be away when Geoffrey and Margaret brought their boys to stay at Tilton. She also lavished a great deal of compensatory affection on Bruno and it hit her very hard when the dog died. 'Bruno is dead,' she mourned in her diary, 'poor dear good fellow Ill never hear your groules any more. It is so sad.'[64]

To sharp-eyed Virginia, Lydia's misery, and her attempts to conceal it, were edged with desperation: 'Lydia has her little stories and jokes, talks of fresh fish at Selfridges and how by making eyes at a certain shop man he pulls the kidneys fresh and bleeding from the sheep (or is it cow) in her presence. I see in all this the tragedy of the childless which will no doubt corrode her entirely.'[65] But Virginia (who nursed the disappointment of her own childlessness) underestimated Lydia's ingenuity as a survivor. Despite her unhappiness, Lydia wrote to Maynard with a game and tender flirtatiousness, as if banning between them any further links between sex and procreation. She teasingly renewed old jokes about Sam Courtauld's hopeless passion for her, and graphically reported on the findings of some cod scientific research that connected the state of a woman's libido directly to her bust size: 'those whose breasts are amplified are desperately lustful,' she assured him. 'I believe it can be true I touch my own, there is a <u>bit</u> of lust in them I swear.'[66] When she and Maynard hosted their Christmas party, they danced together in a comic

*Vera's daughter Clarissa would be born in 1930.

Keynes Keynes by Vanessa Bell

double-act, the Keynes-Keynes, as if nothing had clouded their happiness. (This duet, choreographed by Lydia, was a burlesque on Massine's can-can and, according to Bunny Garnett, showed off their marriage to delightful effect, with Lydia tactfully making Maynard look a much more graceful partner than he really was. Vanessa, however, painted a less enchanted image. Her now famous cartoon of the Keynes-Keynes portrays a foolish, furtive-looking Maynard offering a bouquet of flowers to a rather plump Lydia.)

But Lydia knew better than to rely solely on Maynard for consolation. While she had been focussed on getting pregnant, she had obediently curtailed her attempts to pursue her dancing career, and still in a temporary professional vacuum she searched out other ways of filling her time. One was volunteering her services to Leonard and Virginia, who in 1917 had set up a small independent publishing house, the Hogarth Press. The Woolfs were always in need of an assistant to help their printer, Angus Davidson, assemble the type. Lydia began her apprenticeship with them in November 1927 with typical, inquisitive enthusiasm: 'it is a neat craft to put letters so near to each other that they cannot breath, only kiss'.[67] She was also flattered by Virginia's request for help in checking the accuracy of the Russian scenes in her new book, *Orlando*; and still more flattered when she saw herself acknowledged in the published work, which she rapturously judged to be a 'world of exquisite words'.[68]

However, the printing turned out to be a bewilderingly fiddly task. 'Angus laughs when he sees me creping out of the little rooms with a hundred letters in my hand,'[69] Lydia told Maynard, and after six months of stoic effort she guiltily declared herself defeated: 'V and L came to take the printing book away to instruct a new man. I felt unhappy in my discontinuity but that room is a sort of gorgone on my chest.'[70]*

More satisfying to Lydia were her own first published attempts at writing. She had begun, almost as a hobby, to review the occasional ballet performance, commissioned by *Vogue* and, more nepotistically, by *The Nation*, and in spring 1927 had even been invited by the *Evening News* to write a series of articles about her favourite recipes. This was, as she freely admitted, an absurd imposture since she knew nothing about cooking: 'last night I copied Ukranian Borsh ... it is simply stealing',[71] and few of her dishes were likely to appeal – cabbage soup served with sour milk and buckwheat cakes was not the diet of the average *News* reader. But Bunny Garnett, who helped edit her prose, thought the recipes were just an excuse to show off Lydia's 'enchanting'[72] English, and in March 1929 the *Daily Chronicle* offered her the chance to show it off effortlessly, her subject being social differences between the Russians and the English.

This commission would, in fact, elicit from Lydia the best prose she had ever written – hurtlingly ungrammatical, brilliantly biased and delivering an exuberant snub to anyone in Cambridge and Bloomsbury who had ever made her feel like a blabbing, badly behaved intruder.

*Lydia lasted longer than most of the Woolfs' assistants. Alix Strachey walked out after just one afternoon.

> The English are not exactly dumb – I do not say that. They even make after dinner speeches. But they do not talk as we do in the train, in the tram, in the café, eagerly, endlessly, uproariously just for its own sake ... When I ask an English lady to lunch she begins to put on her gloves – what a horrid, rude unsocial by-the-clock custom that its! How I hate to see it! almost as soon as we leave the table. But when I ask Russian friends they arrive it is true an hour late, but they stay on to tea and to dinner if there is any encouragement, and will think it natural to spend the night on the drawing-room sofa.[73]

This homage to Russian conviviality was also a journalistic love letter to Lydia's own family – whom she had been able to visit for a second time the previous Easter. Maynard may have organised the trip to console Lydia for their failed 'population' project, for he had no official motive for going and seems to have placed himself entirely at the disposal of her happiness, spending all of his time in Leningrad with the Lopukhovs or else being shown around the landmarks from Lydia's past. Spring had melted the packed winter snow, and Maynard and she strolled together along the great sweep of the Neva River, returning several times to the Mariinsky, where Lydia was impressed at seeing her little brother Andrei dance in Fedor's *The Ice Maiden* – even if she remained severely silent about the ballet's choreography, whose acrobatic innovations she did not admire.

Their welcome at the Nevsky Prospekt flat was, she reported back to Florence, as 'nice and loving' as ever.[74] But their room at a new 'communist hotel' was less so, and much of what Maynard saw on this trip dismayed him. Having initially admired the dynamism of the new Bolshevik state and seen political possibilities in it, he was now appalled by the inefficiency of its rulers and by the continuing mania of its ideologues. On his return, he wrote to Ottoline Morrell, 'Its impossible to remember until one gets in the country, how mad they are and that they care about their experiment more than about making things work.'[75] Maynard knew better than to broadcast his criticisms, however. Although Stalin had only just come to power and had yet to unleash his industrial-scale purges, political paranoia was rife and a network of spies was primed to report real or trumped-up offences, including contact with 'dangerous' Westerners. In private, Maynard would argue with Soviet Russia for the rest of his life, but for the sake of Lydia's family he would censor whatever he said or wrote in public.

The details of the Lopukhovs' life were not discussed even with friends at home. Perhaps Lydia did not care to attract pointless sympathy for what her family were going through, or perhaps she did not expect her secure and privileged British acquaintances to be able to comprehend. It was enough that Maynard loved Karlusha and the others and that he continued to do everything in his power to help them. After this trip to Leningrad, Russia was established as one of the private areas of their marriage, one of the exclusive bonds that they shared. Lydia and Maynard may have missed out on the emotional and domestic fulfilment of raising a family, but as they returned to Britain in 1928, neither Gordon Square nor Tilton were empty nests. There were family, friends and work to come back to, plus the absorbing future of their own marriage.

Chapter Sixteen

MRS KEYNES ON STAGE

Although she makes her living by the nimbleness of her toes and he by the keenness of his particularly mathematical brain, they find much in common.

GLASGOW BULLETIN, AUGUST 1925

The fact that Lydia would still have an interest in work after returning from Leningrad, as well as a happy marriage, was not an outcome that many had predicted for her. In Bloomsbury the mean-spirited assumption had always been that she would trade in the stage just as soon as she had Maynard's ring on her finger. Among her in-laws it was judged that the duties attached to becoming the new Mrs Keynes would simply take over her life. 'There will be no more dancing,' Margaret (Maynard's sister) announced to the press on Lydia's wedding day. 'That is all over now.'[1]

Yet while Lydia had never denied her luck in being rescued from financial insecurity by Maynard, she had never acquiesced to the idea of hanging up her shoes. Nor had he expected it. In the summer of her marriage, 1925, Lydia was still not quite thirty-four, and the only career issues that concerned her were whether she could find suitable material to dance and sympathetic colleagues with whom to work. The disappointing season with Count Beaumont had again underlined how large those issues could loom, and they would continue to shadow the final decade of her dancing career. Yet only ten weeks after her wedding, Lydia's professional future had suddenly and significantly brightened when an invitation arrived for her to guest with the Ballets Russes during their autumn season.

It is not clear what had made Diaghilev finally forgive Lydia's defection to Beaumont and decide that he again had a place for her. Perhaps he had seen the publicity surrounding her marriage and judged that hiring Mrs Keynes as a guest ballerina would be a useful fillip to his box office. He was serious, however, about what he wanted from her on stage, requesting that she take over six leading roles during the seven-week run at the Coliseum. As Lydia, 'with excitings all over me',[2] set herself to work at her recently installed barre and mirror at Gordon Square, she dared to hope that Big Serge's gesture of reconciliation might lead to a regular association. She dared to believe she might attain the ideal balance: the security of marriage, plus the stimulus of a guest career with the Ballets Russes. Maynard plus Diaghilev.

Inevitably the practicalities of regaining her position within the company were not quite that simple. Lydia's technique had been idling for an entire summer, her routine disrupted by the wedding and her first trip to Russia, so the work that she had to put in during this season felt dispiritingly hard. Her legs ached from dancing *Boutique* and she developed an excruciating blister while learning a fast, coquettish role in Massine's nautical ballet *Les Matelots*. Even more depressing was *Cimarosiana*, a duet that she had danced with Massine's troupe back in 1922. Even then she had found the choreography difficult; now she feared that it was simply beyond her, and for the first time in her career she entertained serious doubts about her physical ability to bounce back.

But she wrote stubbornly to Maynard, 'there is a devil residing in me and insisting on my performance', and when she first stepped on stage on 28 October 1925 the theatre rose to give her a standing ovation.[3] According to Frederick Ashton, who followed her closely during this season, Lydia still held sway over the London fans with her 'incredible charm', and one particular incident, when she lost a shoe midway through a performance, convinced Ashton that he was in the presence of a stage genius. Not only did Lydia blithely continue dancing, minus one shoe, but at the curtain call exploited the accident with outrageous élan, 'holding the shoe apologetically' up to the audience and eliciting adoring applause. Ashton, like Sokolova, suspected that these accidents were sometimes contrived, yet for him they only added to the illusion of spontaneity that Lydia created on stage: 'When she lifted up her skirt at the start of the Can Can she lifted it up with such a wild ecstasy of delight at the mere thought that she was going to do this dance: she started enjoying it before she had taken a step ... it was like champagne corks popping.'[4]

Diaghilev was equally gratified by Lydia's impact and affectionately embraced her back into the company, plying her for news of Russia and blowing extravagant kisses when she took her curtain calls. After the initial performances, Lydia began to relax, her pleasure in being reunited with her professional family overcoming the worst of her self-doubt and resigning herself more or less to the 'toothache'[5] in her blistered toe. She delighted in the communal gossip and silliness (during one performance of *Petrushka* she went on stage in her street clothes and galoshes to participate anonymously in a crowd scene, reporting to Maynard that 'those who saw me had hysterics').[6] And it pleased her to be earning serious money again. Diaghilev was paying her ten guineas per ballet, and from her new riches she was able to tempt Maynard with news of an evening dress that made her look 'divinely tall, you shall not tear away your eyes',[7] as well as a pledge to subsidise his furnishing campaign at Tilton. He was impressed. 'Think of that. Every time you lift your toe a complete article of furniture drops out and in one week you fill the bedroom.'[8]

When the season closed, on 19 December, Lydia boasted that she would able to furnish the entire house, for Diaghilev professed himself so pleased that he wanted her to continue as a regular guest. This was the confirmation that she had been angling for and, smugly, during the months of winter and early spring she settled into a contented leisure, her letters to Maynard gurgling with endearments, as she urged him to be 'contagious of me as I am of you'.[9] But her husband was requiring more solid support at the end of April as the General Strike brought British industry to a halt, dividing a traumatised nation and reducing Maynard to a state of agitation. The crisis, he believed, was an inevitable consequence of the government's bungled return to the gold standard – a 'barbarous relic' from the Victorian era – which had forced up prices and generated inflammatory reductions in the pay of coal miners. But sidelined as he was by Baldwin's Tory administration, Maynard was unable to interfere, and while he might sketch out a rescue package of compromise price and wage cuts, he had no powerful ear to propose it to. None of the parties seemed to him capable of sensible policy making: Labour intent on whipping up opportunistic class conflict; the Conservatives maintaining a patrician deafness to the workers' grievances; the Liberals under Asquith vacillating ineffectually.

Lydia sympathised with his frustration – 'I hate government and coal owners and newspapers. I am angry with the whole system'[10] – but she was frankly fascinated when Maynard found himself forced into common cause with the one leading politician who shared his position, his former bête noire David Lloyd George. The Welsh Wizard, as Maynard had castigated him in *The Economic Consequences*, was as interested in Maynard's vision of economic management as in his critique of the Liberal Party. He invited both Keyneses to stay for a weekend in early June, and Lydia was impressed: 'LG is a lion he is strong and has a good digestion and in full possession of charm – I had to flatter him.'[11] She would see more of him. After Lloyd George took over the party from Asquith, Maynard was moved closer to its policy-making core, his theories on reducing unemployment influencing the Liberals' economic programme until the party's effective collapse in 1931.*

In fact Lydia had become so closely bound up with Maynard's concerns that a month earlier, when Diaghilev had asked her to guest for a week in Paris, she had found herself unexpectedly reluctant, and only hours after her departure was writing plaintively that she wished her husband was in the train with her – 'it would be very much nicer'.[12] Lydia had not realised how insidiously snug her married life had become, and when she again danced with the Ballets Russes in London (at His Majesty's Theatre from 14 June to 23 July) she took an entire week off to accompany Maynard on a lecture trip to Berlin. Two years earlier she would have had to be dragged from the stage and studio, yet her letters to Florence gloated guiltlessly over the luxury of the hotel in which they stayed. When she returned to dance her final performances she admitted to being in a shockingly un-

*The Liberal Party split between Asquith and Lloyd George, causing an irreconcilable break in Maynard's friendship with Asquith.

ballerina-like condition, having eaten 'like a crocodile' and feeling as though she had 'a liver on both sides'.[13]

If Lydia had underestimated the siren charms of marriage, she had also underestimated the difficulties of reinserting herself into company politics. Once the novelty of her reunion with the Ballets Russes had worn off, she was uneasily aware of the rivalries that rankled beneath the dancers' camaraderie: 'though treated with respect and friendship the feeling is for some that I may take their places'.[14] And she herself felt insecure. There were some unnervingly precocious women rising up the ranks, including the tiny British teenager Alicia Marks, her name already Russianised to Markova. Karsavina too was guesting with the company. Some of the dancers bitched reassuringly that the latter was now showing all of her forty-one years. 'Everybody tells me how bad [she] dances'[15] – but Lydia winced at the heartless comments of Serge Lifar, Diaghilev's beautiful new male protégé, who advised her 'to retire soon as he thought Karsavina in spite of her charm was really old'.[16]

What undermined Lydia most cruelly was the realisation that each time she returned to the Ballets Russes, it became harder to claw back her technique. Without regular performances, she felt herself becoming 'mentally shakey' and feared that her control of her craft was wavering: 'yesterday I was full of proud spirits ... but today I cannot understand my dancing'. She was, as she confessed hollowly to Maynard, 'afraid of being second hand dancer'.[17]

Lydia was careful to keep her anxieties from her colleagues, but when she returned for the company's autumn season at the Lyceum, in 1926, both her body and her age became humiliatingly public issues. Diaghilev had particularly requested her to première his new staging of *The Firebird*, yet when she arrived for her first rehearsal he gave her a shockingly rude reception. Lydia was still, according to Ashton, 'so pretty, with pretty arms as in Frank Dobson's bust of her, and very delicate hands',[18] and she could still create exquisite effects. That autumn, Viola Tree would claim of Lydia's dancing that 'the turn of her head is Fragonard, the way she puts her foot on the ground is pure eighteenth century'.[19] But her crocodile greed over the summer was showing on her hips and bosom, and was ill suited to her new costume, a flame-red tutu cut short and tight in the modern style. As soon as Diaghilev set eyes on Lydia, he created a vicious fuss, telling her she was far too fat for a tutu and sending her reeling from the studio 'tipsy from all the ballet devils with big Serge on top'.[20]

She was all but ready to quit, apologising that night to Maynard for her 'weak stretch of character' as she debated whether to tear up her contract or not. Eventually her mortification subsided enough for her to admit that her bosom was indeed 'a little bigger' and to request a forgivingly loose tunic, with gauze trousers in place of the tutu. Her ego was also soothed by the solidarity of the other women in the company, who not only offered to loan their bras – 'every new and old female member offer me kindly their breast supporters' – but admitted to having suffered a similar ignominy.[21] Ballet costumes were being cut increasingly close to the body, following the new Chanel-inspired fashions offstage. Dancers, as well as image-conscious young women, were under pressure to acquire a narrow, flat-breasted silhouette, and Alexandra Danilova had already dosed herself with so many slimming pills that she had passed out.

Lydia, more judiciously, forced herself to diet, and by the end of the season was deliriously happy to find herself just under eight stone, the flesh lighter on her bones than it had been in years. Yet her newly slender figure did not guarantee her rave reviews, especially in *The Firebird*, where her performance was judged to lack sufficient ferocity. Lydia accepted that this had never been her best role – 'I was', she liked to scoff, 'more of a friedbird' – but she felt genuinely wounded by Diaghilev's failure to offer her other new challenges. As ballets by Bronislava Nijinska and George Balanchine injected a more austere aesthetic into the company, Lydia's curvy, extrovert style was less in demand. Other quarrels too simmered throughout the season, and by its close Lydia had convinced herself that Big Serge had no interest in her career, beyond exploiting her name to publicise his seasons or fill the gaps in his cast lists. She felt that she had been reduced to a pet celebrity, to be used or not as it suited him.*

This was not how Lydia had dreamed of passing her final ballerina

---

*Her importance to Diaghilev as a local celebrity was underlined by a press report in September that wooden 'Lydia' dolls were selling 'like hot cakes'.

Lydia and Serge Lifar, *The Firebird*, London, 1926

years, and the depth of her frustration was hinted at in a despairing, barely legible complaint that she scrawled in her diary: 'I am a born dancer made no progress since ...' (the final word may have been *Femmes*).[22] She swore that she would never submit to the affront of another engagement with Diaghilev and momentarily was even determined to give up dancing altogether. When asked to perform for a charity gala, in December, she reported defiantly to Maynard, 'my answer No was louder than motor truck'.[23]

Maynard was secretly pleased by Lydia's vehemence. He had done little to smooth over her quarrels with Diaghilev; on the contrary, his warning – that 'those devils just want to use and exploit you and will not in any way protect you if you need it' – suggests that he was actively keen to force the split.[24] It is possible that he resented his wife being so intimately in thrall to a rival influence, just as he had resented Vera Bowen, but he may also have genuinely believed that the Ballets Russes were no longer a good showcase for Lydia. Maynard's tastes in ballet were instinctively old-fashioned, and it had almost certainly been his editorial hand that had sharpened Lydia's criticisms the previous year when she had been commissioned by *Vogue* to write her first dance review. As she boldly took issue with the new artistic direction of the Ballets Russes – categorising the clashing geometries of Nijinska's *Les Noces* as 'an intellectual thrill ... the way to stir up a high brow', and predicting that Balanchine's modernist experiments would result in ballet losing 'some of its tenderness, some of its soul'[25] – Lydia was already putting an emotional distance between herself and Big Serge. In the past, even when she had abandoned him for other projects, she had retained her faith in his vision and trusted that her own best professional self lay within his keeping. By the autumn of 1926 that belief was tarnished, and whilst it is not clear how much more work Diaghilev actually offered, Lydia would accept only one more performance from him.

The final unravelling of their relationship cannot have come without some pangs, but it would be wrong to paint it as a traumatic split. Babies were much on Lydia's mind after 1926, and as she attempted to become pregnant she was happy to commit herself to small engagements, even if some, like the ballet interlude that she created for Coleridge Taylor's *Hiawatha*, felt like a waste of her talent.* In the summer of 1927 she was also occupied in a project far more engrossing than any Diaghilev could offer, creating the role of the Princess for a production of Stravinsky's *The Soldier's Tale*. This was the first British staging of this 1918 music drama, and Lydia's pleasure in being involved was coloured by personal as well as professional motives, Stravinsky having once assured her that she had been in his mind when he conceived the character of the Princess.†

The latter was certainly a very Lydia-like heroine – mischievous, appealing and not entirely reliable – yet it was with dedicated

*This was staged at the Royal Albert Hall during June 1928.

†Stravinsky had been hoping to cast Lydia in a projected UK première back in 1923 (see his correspondence with Ansermet). Also titled *The Tale of the Soldier*, this music drama tells the story of a Soldier who sells his soul to the Devil in return for wealth and the hand of a royal Princess.

seriousness that she applied herself to choreographing the three variations for her role: a tango, waltz and ragtime. The fact that the staging had been produced by BBC Radio, intended for sound broadcast as well as live performance, meant that the majority of her audience would remain unaware of Lydia's contribution. A few months later, when a journalist congratulated her on her performance, she laughed away his compliments: 'I suppose you heard my heels.'[26] But there was a full audience on 9 July at London's Arts Theatre Club to watch her and her fellow performers (led by Harcourt Williams as the Reader, Ivan Firth as the Soldier and Frank Cochran as the Devil); and while some of the music critics were unsure how to judge Stravinsky's idiomatic clash of jazz, vaudeville and folk traditions, there was unanimous praise for Lydia's dancing and for the 'witty, ingenious and imaginative drolleries' of her choreography.[27]

It was only a week later that Lydia gave her last performance for Diaghilev. After the disputes of the previous autumn, he had initially blanked her for this summer season, but the Ballets Russes were staging a gala performance for the King of Spain, in London on an official visit, and the latter had requested very particularly to see his former favourite. So, on 15 July 1927, dancing the Polovtsian maiden in *Prince Igor*, Lydia stepped back on to the Ballets Russes's stage. Affection for Alfonso, coupled with a proud determination to prove herself, kindled from her a performance that matched all her former 'barbaric abandon'[28] in the role. Even though this had not been advertised as her formal farewell, Lydia had suspected that it was to be her curtain call with the Ballets Russes and had been determined to make it superb.

Yet if she accepted this as the final severance from her old company, Lydia had no idea that she would shortly be losing Diaghilev too. Two summers later she was reviewing the Ballets Russes for *The Nation* and, meeting up with the impresario, she found him distressingly altered. He had developed diabetes and, although just fifty-seven years old, was leaning heavily on his cane, his ashen flesh hanging in folds around his jaw, the black gloss of his impeccable dyed hair now showing grey.

These signs of decrepitude in a man who had been the proudest of dandies overcame Lydia's remaining grievances; and when she paid tribute to him in *The Nation* a torrent of love and respect burst the always fragile grammatical constraints of her writing: 'What a wonderful man is M. Diaghilev. When I see the old Buddha (or is he Catherine the Great?) sitting in his box with his face as impassive as his shirt, I know that the springs of action are there. We leave him, return to him, abuse him, court him, grow old or pretend to be young, but he goes on forever.'[29]

But she could not have concluded her article on a more tragically ironic note, for a few weeks later the old Buddha was dead. During his adult life Diaghilev had been haunted by a gypsy fortune-teller, who had prophesied his death taking place by water, but he had never imagined his destiny overtaking him in his beloved Venice. He had travelled there in August for a convalescent holiday but his weakened body was beyond recuperation, and his three closest, if quarrelsome, friends, Serge Lifar, Boris Kochno and Misia Sert were shortly gathered to keep vigil through his final hours. They were in Diaghilev's favourite bedroom at the Grand Hotel, and directly below was the ballroom where seventeen years ago Stravinsky had played his epoch-changing score, *The Rite of Spring*. On 19 August 1929 the only sound in the room was the rasp of the impresario's dying breaths. The long journey by which Big Serge reinvented ballet for the twentieth century had come full circle.

For everyone who had worked with Diaghilev, the moment at which they heard of his death became fixed in their memories. Sokolova was on the beach when she saw the newspaper headlines; Danilova was having her hair done in a hotel room in the South of France; Grigoriev was in Monte Carlo when the telegram was delivered. Lydia, most unexpectedly, was on a film set.

She was working with Balanchine and Anton Dolin on a short ballet number for a new feature film titled *Dark Red Roses* and, as she later recalled, she had been sitting out a long, enervating break between takes when the news arrived:

> You know how long you have to wait for filming. The lights are never right, the organisation very queer. I waited for twelve hours dressed in my tights and ballet shoes, sitting out of doors in the cold

> garden before I was called on to do my bit. Whilst Dolin and I sat there waiting and shivering, the evening paper came with the death of Diaghilev. We were shaken to the bottom of our souls, for we knew that an age in our art of the ballet, so great an age, was over.[30]

Maynard, who had accompanied Lydia to the film studio in Wembley, in north-west London, described the scene to Florence: 'The dancers crouched on the floor in a little group talking memories of him hour after hour. It was an extraordinary scene – with masses of machinery all round, the crowds of supers in dress clothes with jaundiced make up faces (supposed to be watching the ballet) and they in their central Asian costumes.'[31] 'How we danced,' Dolin later wrote, 'I do not know.'[32] Ballet without Diaghilev seemed unthinkable, and when Lydia wrote his obituary for *The Nation* she tried to express the absolute void that his death had opened up: 'He leaves a big empty space which it is impossible to fill. For he was a Life Force something extraordinary which made the world more vital and moving than it can be when he is gone.'[33] The three dancers also had personal reasons to grieve. Diaghilev had transformed each of their lives, giving Balanchine his foothold in the West, Dolin his first international appearances and Lydia her long career of celebrity and travel. Without Diaghilev's conquest of the West she might well have remained in St Petersburg; without his eye for developing choreographic talent there might have been no Massine repertory to define her own career. Without Diaghilev's bold setting of itineraries, she might not have ended up in London to become Maynard's wife. And without him as a friend and mentor, Lydia would certainly have been denied a force that had inspired, galvanised and infuriated her for nearly two decades. Five years later she wrote of him again: 'I would say, first, that he was the most absolute and the most beloved of tyrants; second that his reign was the most splendid in the history of the ballet. As for the third sentence, Diaghilev would not have allowed me to add it.'[34]

So absolute had been Diaghilev's hold over the ballet world that Lydia may even have suspected that he was flexing his power from beyond the grave. Big Serge had been a devoted fan of the cinema, especially Chaplin, yet he felt that ballet had no place on the big screen and he would certainly have disapproved of the fact that, at the time of his death, Lydia had been producing and performing a dance for film.* Soon after *Dark Red Roses* had been completed, a fire broke out in the studio and nearly all of its copies were destroyed.†

Not that this was a cinematic tragedy. *Dark Red Roses* might now possess some historic interest as the first 'talkie' ever produced in Britain (just two years after Hollywood's *The Jazz Singer*), but it suffered from a woodenly stilted script and self-conscious acting; and Lydia's own contribution, a brief, lurid trio of adultery and revenge titled *Jealousy*, was hardly the finest moment of her career. Since the ballet's sole function was to provide a dramatic catalyst for the film's plot – inspiring a maniacally possessive husband to plot violence against the man he suspects of seducing his wife – its dance values were incidental and its opportunities very limited.

Nevertheless, Lydia had felt no artistic qualms when she had been approached in June by Oswald Stoll (his entertainment empire having now expanded to Stoll Picture Productions) to produce a short ballet with an 'oriental' style and an adulterous theme. The offer of a 'stupefying' £1,000 fee had been inducement enough, and she had immediately embarked on writing her libretto, researching her costumes and selecting her music: an extract from Mussorgsky's opera *Khovanshchina*. The story that she cooked up was set in the Central Asian steppes, where she cast a woodcutter as the jealous husband who discovers his wife in the arms of a wandering minstrel and exacts revenge by chopping off the latter's hands.‡ She planned, naturally, to dance the role of the wife, hoping for Balanchine as her husband and Dolin as the minstrel (selecting him more for his looks than his dramatic gravitas: 'He is one of the best,' she had informed

*During his lifetime, Diaghilev had resisted pressures to commit his own repertory to film although his desperation over the failure of *The Sleeping Princess* had caused him momentarily to waver.

†There is a surviving copy in the archives of the British Film Institute.

‡The film was directed by Sinclair Hill. Lydia's ballet was given as an entertainment at a party and it was while watching it that David, the jealous husband, is moved to imagine cutting off the hands of his wife's lover, Anton, a musician. Maynard, with typical literal-mindedness, wondered whether the lover's feet would not have been a more appropriate target in the context of ballet.

George Balanchine, Lydia, Anton Dolin: *Jealousy*, from the film *Dark Red Roses*, 1929

Maynard back in 1925, 'and yet there is a sort of silliness that you do not meet on the stage in great dancers').[35]

Lydia had also briefly considered choreographing *Jealousy* herself, but in the end entrusted it to Balanchine, offering him Tilton as an initial, makeshift studio. It seemed to be a promising alliance. Balanchine worked fast, Maynard was thrilled to have a choreographer creating a ballet under his roof, and Lydia was touched to see a rapport developing between the two men as they traded stories about economics and ballet. Yet the finished material on screen did not reflect the ease of its creation. When Vera Bowen saw it, she was horrified by the histrionic clichés that Balanchine had produced, and it is hard, today, to disagree with her verdict. Lydia's swoon in Dolin's embrace, her guilty start at Balanchine's sudden arrival, her breast-beating terror as the latter attacks her, are soggily overwrought, and the fact that the final edit of the film put the music out of synch with the choreography reduces certain moments to inadvertent comedy.

Yet stylistically, Balanchine's material was very much of its era in its mix of popular dance conventions and silent-screen melodrama;

and another early viewer, the dancer Frederic Franklin, recalls it being 'completely acceptable for those days'. The issue to him was the casting: 'It was so surprising to see these three big dancers together in a movie especially as Balanchine and Dolin had never seen eye to eye. But there they were together, with Lydia in the middle.'[36] Equally surprising to Franklin was the degree to which Lydia dominated the screen. She might have been thirty-seven, slightly overweight and suffering from an injured knee, yet the trajectory of her jump was still remarkable and, despite the excesses of her material, she worked it hard. Nearly a century on, her gaze still glitters through the ballet's melodrama, and the abandon with which she arches forward to kiss Dolin, the blank, destroyed expression on her face as she is subdued by the triumphal Balanchine, still work a potent effect.

What is most abundant in Lydia's performance is energy, for however trivial the film may have been, and however overshadowed by Diaghilev's death, *Dark Red Roses* marked a new phase in her dancing life. The previous three years had often been demoralising, blighted by the failure of her attempted pregnancies, as well as by the uneven progress of her career; and while she had managed to keep herself on stage, dancing a few novelty appearances at charity galas – including an ice-skating show – she had wondered whether the effort was worth it. 'My legs are getting middle aged', she had lamented to Florence,[37] and around her Lydia's peers appeared to be in even more distressing decline. She winced at photos of Isadora Duncan, 'her torso broadened very much by beer',[38] and worried about Sokolova, who was suffering severe health problems. She was very tempted to throw up dancing and focus on her acting career, which she had just tentatively restarted. Yet Stoll had then given her the flattering and profitable *Dark Red Roses* project, and six months later she believed that she had acquired a new choreographer, Frederick Ashton, to give one final creative push to her dancing life.

Lydia had met Ashton five years earlier, when she had been rehearsing *The Postman* at Idzikowski's studio and he had still been an eager student; but it was in early 1930 that she got to know him well, when both found themselves drafted into a new ballet organisation in London called the Camargo Society.

During the immediate, stunned aftermath of Diaghilev's death, the British ballet scene had found itself deprived of both its inspiration and its most intimidating competition. Not only had the Ballets Russes been dismantled, but much of its former talent had dispersed: Massine to New York to choreograph at the Roxy Theater; Balanchine to Europe to moonlight with various companies; Nijinska to Paris to work with Ida Rubinstein. Left behind in the schools and studios of London meanwhile was a pool of young choreographers and dancers, including the twenty-year-old prodigy Markova. All of them were looking for employment. It seemed to the profession an obvious moment for Britain to launch its own, native ballet company.

What was not so obvious was where the money would come from to finance such a venture – it would be fifteen years before the arts in Britain became fully eligible for state funding. Nor was it obvious who might lead it.* In fact, in the autumn of 1929 both the politics and the problems seemed so insuperable that, according to ballet writer Arnold Haskell, the London ballet scene was in danger of cannibalising itself before it even got established, as dancers began to 'split into small factions and were swallowed up by their own jealousies'.[39] It was to staunch this disintegration that Haskell himself, along with Philip Richardson, editor of the *Dancing Times*, formed the idea of organising a short-term performing society. It was named after the eighteenth-century French ballerina Marie Camargo and its agenda was simply to channel British talent into producing two or three short seasons per year. There would be no formal contracts and very little pay – member artists would have to earn their living by moonlighting in revues or working as film extras, whilst the budget would depend on the generosity of patrons and the sale of subscriptions. It would also have no overall director, for, given the absence of any figure remotely resembling Diaghilev, artistic policy was to be determined in a very English way by committee.

*Lydia prophesied correctly that de Valois would eventually play a crucial role: 'She is a pioneer and whoever in future is director of English ballet her effort must be recognised respected and pensioned for life' (13 October 1929).

Yet modest as Camargo was in its outline, the Society would at least offer British dancers the chance to perform on their own platform. Among the first to be voted into the heart of its organisation were Ashton and de Valois. Also, protesting all the while that it was 'like parting with one's virginity', was Lydia.[40] She had initially intended to be nothing more than a patron and sympathetic observer of this prosaic-sounding enterprise, and when she reluctantly attended her first committee meeting, it was even more tedious than she had feared: 'A great deal of time spent,' she wrote in pained amazement to Maynard, 'and very little done'.[41] Yet having been commandeered into official responsibility, Lydia took her new duties with Camargo seriously. By 16 February 1930, when the Society was formally launched at a lunch party in the Metropole Hotel, she not only had persuaded the great Adeline Genée to preside over the luncheon, but had signed up a spectacular list of subscribers, including H. G. Wells, Augustus John, Osbert Sitwell, Oswald Stoll, Margot Asquith, Ottoline Morrell, Lytton Strachey and the Woolfs. She had even yielded to Haskell's pleas that she deliver the main toast of the afternoon, and while the *Daily Chronicle* reported that Maynard had sat beside her in the dining room, looking 'solicitous and ready to prompt', the performance that Lydia gave was unexpectedly eloquent.[42]

Such was her eloquence that Lydia rapidly found herself positioned as the Society's principal advocate, and during the following months, as Carmargo geared up for its first autumn season, it was she who also emerged as its main broker of power. She began to host committee meetings at Gordon Square, where, lubricated by Maynard's claret, they often stretched into gregarious supper parties. She also gathered around her a cosy inner circle, her Camargo 'cronies', which included Ninette de Valois, now her dear 'Ninnie', the conductor Constant Lambert, and also Frederick Ashton, who at twenty-five was promising to become the Society's main choreographer.

Lydia adored Ashton's company, and between Camargo business began to take him out with her to parties, plays and films. He was a skinny, witty, sentimental boy, with hooded eyes, a long elegant nose and a veneer of camp sophistication that was undercut by his thin-skinned romanticism. As a schoolboy he had been blinded by the stardust of Anna Pavlova's performances and nursed dreams of becoming a great dancer. Lydia, roused to a maternal protectiveness, had to gently talk him out of his fantasies several times, as during the next few years he badgered for leading roles with the Camargo Society. 'Poor Fred,' she would report to Maynard, 'he does not want to see his defects.' It took 'a long silence & tea & polite conversation' to talk him out of his delusions.[43]

Ashton could not but be flattered to have the celebrated Lopokova take him under her wing, and he also came to love her. Like so many others he was seduced by her laughter – 'of a gaiety you'd never believe' – by her disarming leaps of logic, and by her sometimes shocking candour. Coming from a generation that considered itself to have a privileged monopoly on bad behaviour, Ashton was both delighted and appalled to hear Lydia, next to him at a performance, comment with excruciating distinctness on the appearance of the ballerina Nikitina: 'look at her mouth, its indecent! It looks as if it belongs somewhere else.'[44] It was less funny, Ashton found, when Lydia's frankness was directed at him: 'It wasn't affectation but in some kind of way she knew how to make an effect. She [made] you laugh by saying exactly what she thought even if it might be embarrassing or hurtful.' When, in 1932, he sought Lydia's opinion on his new and ambitiously long ballet, *The Lord of Burleigh*, she volunteered gleefully, 'Oh Freddie I *loved* the first three days.'[45]

Within the Camargo organisation it was Lydia's outspokenness that many remembered as her greatest contribution. According to de Valois, 'She did not like committees; but having found herself a member of one, she did not suffer from any sense of inertia or inhibition. Her outbursts of thinking aloud very often succeeded in removing hours of wasteful discussion.'[46] Haskell went even further and claimed that there were moments during the Society's three-year existence when it had only been Lydia's power to bully, charm, exasperate and entertain that had kept it going.

The artistic ambitions of Camargo had been pitched high, but its daily style of operations was often pedestrian, and Lydia began to appreciate how masterly Diaghilev's style of leadership had been, as she herself tried to manage the conflicting claims and egos of the

Society's contributing artists. The new Camargo repertory was to be a vehicle for British collaboration: its music solicited from Constant Lambert, Lord Berners and William Walton; its designs from Edward Burra, Gwen Raverat and Vanessa Bell; its choreography from de Valois and Ashton. All of these artists were ambitious, all of them had very different requirements, and not only were there frequent competitive spats between them but, as Lydia discovered, there was never enough money to pay for their creations.

Cash was a constant problem for Camargo. Its junior dancers performed for nothing (many were students at the small ballet studios run by de Valois and Marie Rambert and were happy to gain the experience) and most performances were given on Sunday evening and Monday afternoons, when theatres charged only small fees for hire. Nevertheless, principal dancers like Markova had to be paid and, factoring in the budget for sets and costumes, an average Camargo performance cost £500 to stage. The income from its patrons could not cover such sums, and it was wretchedly bad timing, too, that the Society was trying to establish itself in the middle of the global slump that was spiralling out from the Wall Street crash of 1929. Even Sam Courtauld's deep pocket had a limit. In February 1931, when a budget crisis sent Lydia running to her old friend for extra cash, she was shocked to the point of 'frigidaire' when he responded with just £25. Forbearingly, Sam avoided mention of the £54 million drop in his company's share value during the previous eighteen months and, even more forbearingly, did not remind Lydia of his private anxieties – Lil was suffering from cancer and would die at the end of the year. Lydia immediately regretted the insults that she had heaped on Sam's head – 'forgive me, I am extrovert and cannot keep in either my pleasures or my greviences'[47] – but the Camargo Society's finances remained so precarious that she had to beg Maynard to take on the role of Honorary Treasurer, relying on his practical expertise in balancing the books and on his unembarrassed brusqueness in curbing her colleagues' wilder flights of extravagance.

Chivvying, feeding and funding Camargo's operations during the early 1930s exercised organisational powers that Lydia never knew she possessed. But she had no intention of putting herself permanently behind the scenes, and in the spring of 1930 she decided to try out Ashton as her choreographer in an ambitious and original new project. During the preceding eighteen months Lydia had forged a relationship with the Amateur Dramatic Club in Cambridge, appearing as a guest in several of their productions, and she was now impatient to bring two of these to London: chamber dramatisations both of them, of Shakespeare's poem 'A Lover's Complaint' and of Milton's *Comus*. Her plan, hatched in collaboration with Dadie Rylands, was to programme these into a mixed evening of ballet and theatre to be staged at the small and friendly Arts Theatre, where at a stroke she could relaunch herself as an actress whilst at the same time showcasing her continuing powers as a ballerina.

Lydia was delighted that Ashton agreed to her request to choreograph two new ballets for her, but she knew that placing herself in the hands of an untried choreographer was not without physical risk. Her 'wobbly knee', diagnosed as a stress injury in the surrounding muscles, was causing her increasing pain, and at times she declared herself, melodramatically, to be getting too ancient to perform: 'my face is so old and winkled and my body needs starch'.[48] But in anticipation of this new phase in her career she had gone to de Valois for advice and, at the beginning of 1931, Madame Zanfretta had entered her life. This tiny 67 year old, who had once been a famous beauty, a celebrated mime artist and a ballerina at London's Empire Theatre, came recommended for her ferociously erect Italian posture and ferociously correct Italian classes – even 'more strict than Cecchetti'.[49] 'After one of their first sessions at Gordon Square, Lydia discovered that she also came with ferociously outspoken views: 'she couldn't bear my Scottish knitted stocking, my legs gave her a headache, she hardly could see if I had an instep.'[50] Yet the tyrannical and rapidly beloved 'Zannie' proved to be as effective as de Valois had promised, and when Lydia delivered herself over to Ashton's choreographic direction, the young man found her to be on very responsive form for a dancer approaching her fortieth birthday. 'She was forgetful,' he recalled, 'and one had to keep going back over points, but she did everything with such intensity. She was not temperamental and if she liked something she would exclaim "no it is glorious!" (She loved the word glorious. She knew how to project her personality as no other dancer knew, and it was a joy to work with her because she was so game and lively and funny.)'[51]

Initially Ashton had been more nervous than Lydia about embarking on this collaboration, apprehensive of choreographing steps for a ballerina who had grown up in the repertory of giants like Massine and Fokine. Yet once they began working together he had been bewitched by Lydia's enthusiasm. If he and his fellow dancer Harold Turner turned up hungry before a rehearsal at Gordon Square, then Lydia fed them in ebullient style, ordering up such quantities of liver and soufflé from Mrs Harland that they could hardly move: 'the food was so prominent in our insides that hysterical laughter accompanied every step. I couldn't be lifted.'[52] If ever Ashton doubted his own ability, Lydia was unstinting in her praise. 'Fred brings me out as a ballerina,' she crowed to Maynard, 'it looks most difficult for me but it is the two men that work hard.'[53] And on 10 December 1930, when the fulsomely titled *Masque of Poetry and Music: Beauty, Truth and Rarity* was premièred at the Arts Theatre, Lydia and Ashton's pleasure in each other was echoed by the acclaim of the public and the press.

The more lightweight of the two new ballets that they had created together, *Dances on a Scotch Theme*, had been a comic romp inspired by Duncan's earlier 'whirlwind' sketch of Lydia in her tartan kilt. Ashton's most substantial offering, however, was *Follow Your Saint: The Passionate Pavane*, which, set to the music of John Dowland, gave Lydia one of the most flattering roles of her career. She was cast as an Elizabethan gentlewoman gracefully juggling the attentions of her rival suitors, Ashton and Turner; and in her prettily flounced dress, her delicate hands catching the light, her face lifted dreamily towards her partners, she had rarely looked more lovely. The critic of the *Evening Standard* wrote, 'I sat last night trying to plumb the secret of Lopokova's fascination. I decided that the dominant element is dignity – the compelling dignity of a child. And against this stand out the vivid colours of her humour, her vivacity, and her complete mastery of technique.'[54]

This was a fabulous review for any thirty-nine-year-old ballerina, and for Lydia it confirmed her determination to continue dancing.

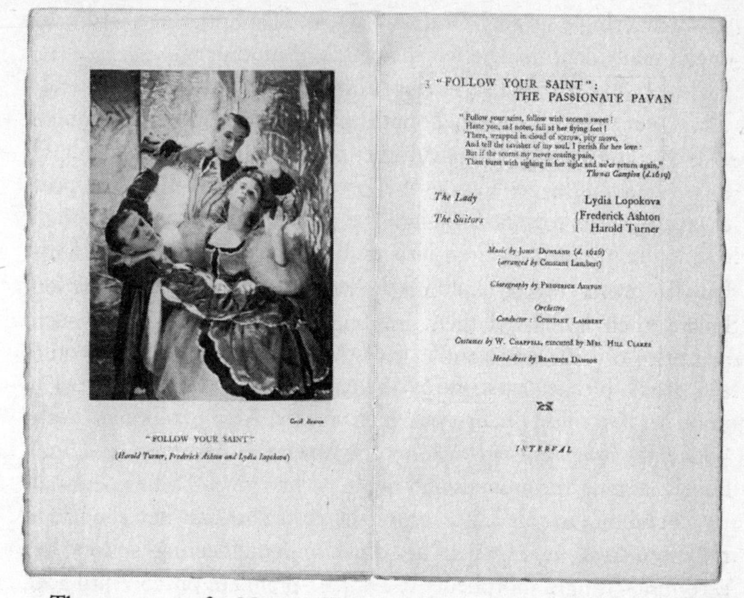

Cecil Beaton

"FOLLOW YOUR SAINT"

(Harold Turner, Frederick Ashton and Lydia Lopokova)

3 "FOLLOW YOUR SAINT":
THE PASSIONATE PAVAN

"Follow your saint, follow with accents sweet!
Haste you, sad notes, fall at her flying feet!
There, wrapped in cloud of sorrow, pity move,
And tell the ravisher of my soul, I perish for her love:
But if she scorns my never ceasing pain,
Then burst with sighing in her sight and ne'er return again."
Thomas Campion (d.1619)

The Lady	Lydia Lopokova
The Suitors	Frederick Ashton Harold Turner

Music by John Dowland (*d.* 1626)
(*arranged by* Constant Lambert)

Choreography by Frederick Ashton

Orchestra
Conductor: Constant Lambert

Costumes by W. Chappell, executed by Mrs. Hill Clarke

Head-dress by Beatrice Dawson

INTERVAL

The programme for *Masque of Poetry and Music*; Lydia with Ashton and Harold Turner in *Passionate Pavane*, London, 1930

She might now be looking forward to reviving her acting career full time, but she wanted to make this one, final push as a dancer, knowing suddenly that there were so few years left to her. Lydia felt a new sympathy and respect for Karsavina's bravely prolonged career and buried whatever rivalry she had once felt to seek out a friendship with the older dancer. They began to meet regularly, sharing confidences and bolstering up each other's egos: '[once] ballerinas at our age were getting round Victorian shoulders while today we are skimpy with exercises not only in dancing but taking the dogs out'.[55] Yet Lydia received a stark warning from Pavlova, whose sudden death was announced on 21 January 1931. The ballerina, aged just forty-nine, had contracted pneumonia on tour, dying in a hotel bedroom with only her maid, her doctor and her husband, Victor Dandré, at her side. Like Diaghilev before her, Pavlova had seemed indomitable, and when Camargo staged its farewell tribute, with the audience standing to hear the orchestra playing *The Dying Swan* and to watch a single spotlight tracking across the empty stage, Lydia was one of many dancers who felt the clutch of mortality.

Prolonging her own swansong, however, was not going to be easy. There were still only limited opportunities for ballet on the London stage, and only limited opportunities for Lydia to acquire new repertory. The younger generation of choreographers had their own peers to create ballets for, and although she would acquire two charming if essentially minor roles from Ninette de Valois, Fred, of whom Lydia had had such hopes, created only one more completely successful work for her.

This was in *Façade*, a pastiche of popular dances set by Ashton to the drolly vernacular score of William Walton. He had Lydia in mind for two roles, the first of which was the Alpine milkmaid in the 'Jodelling Song'. Perhaps inspired by images of her down at Tilton, bucolic among the animals and fields, he had given Lydia's personality gleeful rein in this dance, especially at its climax, when she had to milk the 'cow' into which her three mountaineering suitors had accommodatingly morphed. At *Façade's* première on 26 April 1931, Lydia had pulled so enthusiastically at the udders provided by one of the men's wiggling fingers that Ashton claimed, 'You could almost see the milk ... beginning to squirt.'[56]

But the other role that had created for her, in the 'Tango', was less effective. Ashton had conceived this duet as an oblique homage to *Boutique*, casting Lydia as a wide-eyed, innocent debutante and himself as an oily gigolo in the style of Massine. Yet while the *Manchester Guardian* claimed that 'No other dancer has ever been able to assume for comic ends an expression quite so vacant, like a doll in a dream, and to belie it so richly by the subtlety of her dancing',[57] the general verdict was that Lydia had been an embarrassment. The tone of Ashton's humour had been difficult for her to catch, and she had ended up exaggerating the jokes and overplaying her character's naivety. It was even whispered that Lydia had looked too old for the part.

Sensing the negative atmosphere around her, Lydia prickled miserably. 'I want none of <u>your</u> criticism for Façade,' she snapped by post to Maynard in a surge of pique.[58] She felt even worse when Rambert announced that her tiny troupe, Ballet Club, would be giving its own performances of *Façade* with Alicia Markova dancing Lydia's role in the 'Tango'. This was a double offence. Lydia may initially have been fond of Marie, or 'Mim' Rambert, admiring her energy and dubbing her 'my beetle' because 'beetles always run in all directions and very quickly',[59] but she now saw her and her studio as a potential rival to the Camargo Society. As for Markova, Lydia had never liked the younger ballerina. Whilst others might marvel at the rarefied beauty of her technique, Lydia simply thought her cold and, back in the Ballets Russes days, had sniggered enjoyably over the gossip that Diaghilev was trying to find her a lover 'to warm' her up. Now, however, she suspected that Markova might outclass her in the 'Tango', and she was right. Markova's precision-perfect style set up a comic tension with the debutante's naivety, and as Lydia registered the praise for her rival, she felt that she had been somehow made redundant. She might be happy to parade her age when there were loud voices to deny it; she might be happy to play the senior ballerina when that position gave her power. Direct, unflattering comparisons with a rising star like Markova were a different and humiliating issue.

Feeling her years more acutely than she had bargained for, as well as having sudden doubts about the wisdom of prolonging her ballerina years, Lydia had yielded with extreme reluctance to Ashton's insistence that she dance his next Camargo ballet, *Rio Grande*.* Maynard, mindful of her bad knee and still vulnerable ego, had frankly begged her to refuse. However, Lydia had boxed herself into a moral corner with this project. It had been she who had persuaded Fred to choreograph something to Constant Lambert's jazzy choral score. And when Fred had tried to wriggle out of it, pleading overwork, it had been Lydia who had urged him to continue. She had in fact been furious with Ashton when he had tried to withdraw from the ballet, scenting disloyalty both from him and from Rambert, who, she felt, was monopolising Fred with too many commissions for her own dancers. Relaying the incident to Maynard, her tone slipped into an unusually ugly bitterness. 'A Bomb-shell. Fred under influence of Mim is behaving disgracefully, he refuses to do Rio-Grande

*It was originally titled *A Day in a Southern Port*.

for the first programme ... I am disgusted yet I know he is a nice boy, & it is a matter of influence, the Jewess dominates him at present.'[60]

When Ashton's original ballerina, Anna Ludmilla, had then withdrawn from *Rio*, he believed that Lydia was under an obligation to take over her role as the Queen of the Whores. *Rio* was a knowing, sleazy ballet peopled with swaggering sailors and glossy tarts, and its tone was defined by a subversive humour that Lydia could not quite articulate. Even though her body in its provocative little skirt and skintight bodice looked taut and muscled from two years of Zannie's classes, even though her performance was showered with the usual critical confetti – 'divine dancing', 'delicious extravagance' – the more discriminating verdict was that, once again, she had been wrong-footed by Ashton's choreography. Responding uncertainly to its riotous lewdness, Lydia had forced her comic effects into pantomime; attempting to look sexy, she had looked brash.

It was, according to Haskell, a fundamental clash of generational styles: 'This mixture of an old tradition with new developments can never succeed,' he observed.[61] Even loyal de Valois suggested that Lydia's personality was too 'individual' for the new school of ballets. It had been little more than a decade since Clive Bell had extolled Lopokova as the essential modern ballerina, yet now it was being mooted that she was out of date. For Lydia it was gall and wormwood that shining on stage beside her was Markova, dancing the Creole Girl in *Rio* with a sure grasp of the role's witty perversities.

Yet Lydia was still not ready to hang up her shoes, nor did the world want her to. Boris Anrep, symbolically, was asking her to model for him as Terpsichore, the Muse of Dance, for a mosaic floor that he had been commissioned to create for the National Gallery (in which Lydia would be enshrined next to Virginia Woolf as Clio and Greta Garbo as Melpomene).* Then in March 1932, when she was rehearsing Ninette's latest ballet, *Origin of Design*, a piece appeared in the *New Statesman* that argued Lydia's claim to be ranked as one of the immortals of ballet:

**The Awakening of the Muses* was the third of Anrep's floors for the National Gallery and was funded by Sam Courtauld.

Rio Grande opening night; from left to right: Constant Lambert, Lydia, Frederick Ashton, Edward Burra, Walter Gore (kneeling)

> Directly she appears on stage [wrote R. Ellis Robert] you know … that you have wanted something without knowing that you wanted it: and she gives it you … you are part of a life she has summoned, a world she has created, the fantasy that she evokes has utter reality, her stillness has the effect of a poised bird, the way in which she holds her head can give a sudden arrest to the darting business of ballet … when she dances it is not just with her body; it is herself, her soul, what she seems to do is dance what she has always known.[62]

Lydia for her part felt both exalted and fraudulent at this panegyric: 'I read three times the glorification in print of my person. It is agreeable … but [I am] slightly ashamed that I can put over.'[63] She blushed at Ellis Roberts comparing her to the great Adeline Genée –

'she was a divinity, I am not but the public think I am' – and felt particularly spurious, given that she was currently rehearsing her role as Dibutade alongside the exasperatingly perfect Markova, who made her own 'puffing' body feel inadequate and ancient. Yet as Virginia Woolf wrote to the painter Ethel Sands, 'She is rather touching about her dancing, apt to say she must retire but sometimes is overcome like an old war horse by the sound of music and goes back.'[64] And in 1933 Lydia heard music that she was unable to resist.

Two years earlier, de Valois had moved her school and her small troupe of dancers to Sadler's Wells, a newly refurbished theatre in north-east London, where, funded by the philanthropist Lilian Baylis, she finally had the benefit of studios and a decent-sized stage. To celebrate the move, she was planning a production of *Coppélia*, and she wanted Lydia as her ballerina.* This could not have been a more tempting opportunity, given that mischievous, romantic Swanilda had been the role that Lydia had so badly wanted to dance with Cecchetti back in 1923 and, still further back, the role that had been denied her by Mordkin in 1911. Yet it could not have been a more poignant opportunity either. Lydia at forty-one was no longer an obvious soubrette – she was middle-aged, her knee was injured and her technique was in decline.

Certainly when she walked into her first company rehearsal, kitted out in her well-worn practice clothes, her fellow dancers had fallen silent with astonishment when they realised that Lydia was to be their guest Swanilda. As Frederic Franklin, a junior member of the cast, remembers it, she seemed to be entering the studio from another era: 'She looked very roly-poly, and very dear. She wore a pink crossover cardigan, a big shawl wrapped around her waist and legwarmers and she wore her hair in this very old-fashioned ballerina way, low down round the ears.'[65]

Divided between awe and criticism, the young British dancers had watched closely to see whether Lydia lived up to her legend. De Valois was not staging *Coppélia's* final act, with its most testing classical choreography, but the material that Lydia had to dance was still a challenge. Pirouettes, according to Franklin, appeared to be a slight

*According to Ashton, Maynard had financially subsidised *Coppélia*'s staging.

problem – 'you had to push her around a bit'; but during the brief section in which he himself had partnered Lydia, he had felt the jolt of 'dancing right next to a very great ballerina'. 'She was a little bit heavy,' he recalls, 'but her legs looked very good and you could see why Massine wanted her to do the cancan, she had such a vibrant personality. She was very fast and flew around on her points, she hadn't forgotten how to do it at all.'

An even younger fan, Leo Kersley, who watched Lydia dance from the audience, thought she appeared almost ageless in this ballet. 'Her brisés* were like merry hell,' he remembers, 'and her acting was glorious. When she entered, she came up to the front of the stage and told her story in mime. Everyone understood her completely. She had this way of addressing you personally as if she was whispering into your ear.'[66] For Kersley and his fellow fans, Lydia's celebrity was undiminished: 'she was', he insists, 'like a pop star to us', and on the morning of her debut, queues started forming at the box office long before breakfast. In the evening there were still 300 people lining up for returns – the biggest crowd that Sadler's Wells had yet seen.

Lydia's injured knee could take the strain of only two *Coppélia* performances in March, and during the rest of the run Swanilda was danced by de Valois. It wasn't clear whether Lydia would dance in public again, although after her second performance of *Coppélia* she had delivered a short, teasing speech to the audience, saying that she would 'not promise never to appear again'. Then on 28 and 29 June 1932 she did indeed return, dancing Swanilda for two gala performances at Covent Garden, which she was finally, and privately, determined to make her last.

It had been Maynard who had organised these extra performances. London was playing host to the World Economic Conference in June and he had had the idea of putting on *Coppélia* as an official entertainment for the delegates, soothing them after days spent grappling with outstanding war debts and the persisting global depression. With typical efficiency, Maynard had also seen the chance to raise some funds for the Camargo Society, which, after

*Kersley was referring to a fast diagonal of jumps during which the legs 'beat' or strike against each other, producing a fluttering energy.

three struggling years, was now being closed down and had its own debts to pay off.*

It was evident to everyone involved that the Camargo Society had outlived its moment. Marie Rambert was steadily expanding the scope of her Ballet Club; de Valois's own company, the Vic–Wells Ballet, had become fully established at Sadler's Wells; and for many months it had been hard for London's dancers to work Camargo into their busy timetable. Billy Chappell and Frederick Ashton had been complaining especially loudly to Lydia of overwork, and of suffering stress-induced, preposterously Freudian, nightmares: Billy dreaming that 'his teeth hanged out of his gums and turned into pencils'; Fred that he was being lain on by a cow and 'did not like the rubbing of the tits as they were rough'.[67]

Embroiled as they still were in the legacy of the Society's difficulties, it would be some time before Lydia and her colleagues appreciated how much they had achieved. From a modern perspective, however, it is clear that Camargo played a seminal role in the history of British ballet. Responsible for the creation of several lasting works, including de Valois's *Job* and Ashton's *Façade*, the Society helped to swell the repertories of both the Ballet Club and the Vic–Wells. Responsible, too, for pioneering productions of *Giselle* and *Swan Lake*, the Society allowed British dancers to lay claim to the traditions of the nineteenth century. Back in 1930, Lydia had fanfared the Camargo Society's first public performance as 'nothing less than the birth of British ballet'; in June 1933, as she presided over its closure, she had more reason than she knew to congratulate herself on her role as midwife.

But at the time she was preoccupied by her own farewell. These two performances of *Coppélia* had not officially been advertised as her last, and it is typical of Lydia that she opted to keep quiet about her plans to retire. Pragmatically she may have wanted to keep her options open, just in case some irresistible new role appeared for her. Emotionally, however, she may well have shrunk from the sentimental outpouring that would inevitably have greeted her had she

*As well as paying off the Society's debts, the performances raised £300 for the Vic–Wells ballet.

formally said goodbye on stage. We can only guess what mixture of regret and triumph she felt as she danced the 'exquisitely witty' Swanilda acclaimed by the *Sunday Times*.[68] We can only guess whether the critics watching in the stalls sensed a mood of finality, but there may have been a deliberate elegiac note in the review that appeared in the *Observer*, noting how, even after a career spanning three decades, 'the virtues of an Imperial training and the charm of her personality' had remained vivid in Lydia's every smile, gesture and step.[69] It was exactly the tribute that she would have asked for.

Chapter Seventeen

RETURN TO ACTING

> I should like to be a comedy actress. I wish I could find a manager to give me the small part of a soubrette. Could I do tragedy? How could one do tragedy with a nose like this! But I think I could do dramatic parts. I should like to do a dramatic ingenue if such a part exists. Ibsen particularly. What about that girl in *The Master Builder* I should like to do her.
>
> LYDIA LOPOKOVA[1]

Lydia may have danced her final performance with a sense of loss, but she despised pointless sentiment and she was already too deep in plans for her future to waste time mourning her past. Acting was finally to take precedence in her ambitions, and during her last major interview as a ballerina she had robustly demonstrated that fact, side-stepping all attempts by the journalist Hubert Griffiths to elicit dancing memories from her, and offering instead a blatant plug for her new career.

During the last few years Lydia had, of course, been laying the ground for this professional switch. Between her duties with Camargo and her ballet roles, she had made time to keep her voice exercised, reading poetry and plays aloud at home. She had also taken part in occasional amateur dramatics (including a dreadful play written by one of Clive's mistresses, Bobo Mayor) and, most usefully, she had developed her involvement with the Amateur Dramatic Club in Cambridge. The ADC had made their first tentative approach to her back in 1928 when they were planning to stage a production of Stravinsky's *The Soldier's Tale* for their autumn season and initially they had wondered only whether Lydia could be persuaded to reprise her dancing role as the Princess. However, Maynard, who had been consulted as an intermediary, instantly saw other, larger possibilities in the association. He was still worried about Lydia's state of mind after their failure to produce a child, and he was eager to find her new distractions. He thus suggested that she might not only be taken on as a guest ballerina but also given an acting role. Alongside *The Soldier's Tale*, the ADC were staging a dramatisation of Shakespeare's poem 'A Lover's Complaint', and Maynard put a new offer on the table. If Lydia were to be cast as the Afflicted Maid, the female speaking role, he would financially underwrite the entire programme.*

Lydia, when she was informed of the deal, was more excited than Maynard had hoped. The ADC aspired to unusually high standards, several of its student actors went on to professional careers, and its productions were regularly reviewed in the national press. With its high-minded, often innovative approach to theatre it possibly reminded Lydia of the Washington Players, where she had once spent her happiest months as an actress. Accepting the ADC's offer, she imagined she had found the stage that would prepare for her break into mainstream British theatre.

Her hopes, however, were running ahead of her. Although Lydia would go on to perform in other productions with the ADC, and although she would eventually be cast in professional roles – even performing Ibsen, as she had desired – she would not attain the acting triumph that had been predicted for her as a child. Success would be as bafflingly elusive for her in England as it had been in the States – and the main issue would still be her voice.

Despite the fact that it was now almost two decades since Lydia had left home, and despite the few clipped Bloomsbury mannerisms that had been grafted on to her accent, the music of her speech remained stubbornly Russian. The Os still slid into histrionic 'oahs',

*Maynard inevitably got involved in other ways. He was keen for Lydia to contact Stravinsky, in order to negotiate cheaper rates for the performing nights to the score (although apparently she did not know the address). He also persuaded Vanessa and Duncan to contribute the designs, although, according to Virginia, he did not pay 'a penny ... it is all for the glory of art of course'.

Ths still contracted into Zs, and when Lydia used her voice professionally, the rhythms of the English language were hard for her to catch. In Cambridge, in 1928, the ADC's young director Dennis Arundell had been awed to hear that the famous Lopokova was to join the cast of 'A Lover's Complaint', and when he had turned up to Maynard's rooms for their first read-through, had been enchanted to find Lydia sitting on the floor, appearing as eager as a child. But Arundell's excitement had turned to shifty embarrassment as he had listened to Lydia loop the poem's cadences around her Russian inflections and heard her clear, bright voice reduce Shakespeare's pentameters to the 'unvaried ticking of a clock'.[2]

Maynard seems to have been equally taken aback, and while he had loyally rebuffed Arundell's suggestion that Lydia attempt a more naturalistic approach – his wife's delivery had, he insisted coolly, been 'perfectly true to the poem's metre' – in private he set himself to coach her. During the weeks leading up to the Cambridge performance, he was nagging Lydia constantly about her accent, not only when they were at home together, but by post when they were apart. 'Sorrow, borrowed, owed,' he urged from his study at King's; 'can you hear me pronouncing them?'[3]

Over the next decade Lydia would work doggedly on her voice. Yet for every admirer who felt that her talent overrode her idiosyncratic diction – Robert Helpmann, for instance, who insisted that Lydia was 'an extremely good actress, and would have been wonderful [on screen] with a director like Bergman'[4] – there were detractors to judge it an insuperable handicap. John Gielgud, later a good friend of Lydia's, wrote regretfully, 'I don't think she could really be any good in straight theatre with such a strong accent and peculiar English.'[5]

Still, if her voice divided audiences and colleagues, the force of Lydia's charm was never in dispute and during her rehearsals with the ADC, Arundell's initial criticisms had been scattered by the gusts of her infectious enthusiasm. Equally seduced by Lydia had been her fellow actors, Hedley Briggs and a young, gifted undergraduate, Michael Redgrave. Soon Maynard was boasting that everyone in Cambridge had fallen in love with her: 'compliments flow round about you. I am threatened with divorce suits.'[6] Lydia must have brought some of this infectious energy to her lines, too, for the following year Frank Birch, an historian at King's and at that time the university's most respected director, offered her two further roles with the ADC. The most significant was Rosaura, the Russian heroine of Pedro Calderón de la Barca's seventeenth-century comedy *Life's a Dream*, and the role's subtle poetry brought out the best of Lydia's talents, earning her a euphoric review from *The Times* for her 'delicately humorous grace'.[7]

By the summer of 1930, Lydia's confidence was high enough for her to plan her London debut, in the 'Masque of Poetry and Music',* where alongside her ballerina roles in Ashton's *Pavane* and *Dances on a Scotch Theme*, she was of course taking the female leads in revivals of 'A Lover's Complaint' and Milton's *Comus* – in which she played the chastely puritanical Lady.† For this project she had surrounded herself with a team of her favourite young men: Dadie Rylands as her producer, Ashton as overall choreographer, Lambert as music director, and Cecil Beaton (then just twenty-six) as photographer. The latter's production shots, printed in the 'Masque's' programme, were among the most exquisite images of Lydia's career, showing her bathed in a silvery light that made her look, to her delight, almost ethereal.

In between incessantly demanding committee meetings for Camargo, Lydia worked hard on the 'Masque', and as she tracked between London and Cambridge – alternately rehearsing her steps and her lines; alternately holding court between her cronies from the Society and her actors from King's – she was as professionally optimistic as she had been in years. Yet in terms of the evening's dramatic content, disappointment followed hard on her flying expectations. Weakly, she had allowed Dadie to add new poetry items to the programme, including a staged reading from *Paradise Lost*, and whilst this dense, literary material might have been acceptable to a coterie

*In May 1930, just before Lydia began work on the Masque, she had acted in Velona Pilcher's anti-war play *The Searcher*. This did not qualify as a professional debut, however. When she temporarily forgot her lines on the second night, there was not even a prompt in the wings to rescue her. Maynard made Lydia promise never to appear in such 'a bad organisation' again.

†Lydia had already given two chamber performances of *Comus*, one in Dadie Rylands's college rooms, one at Maynard's annual party.

university audience, it did not please London.* When the 'Masque' opened at the Arts Theatre Club, on 10 December 1930, the critic of the *Evening Standard* was not alone in judging its cast of 'lisping' university men to have been insufferably Cambridge and insufferably camp. Nor did Lydia's own acting fare much better. Whilst *The Times* gently opined that her delivery had given the verse 'added pungency',[8] this verdict was undercut by the acid judgement of the *Standard*: that Lydia would please only those who liked 'their Shakespeare with a very broken accent'.[9]

The fact that her dancing had been greeted with hyperbolic approval left Lydia, at the end of 1930, professionally at odds with herself. Part of her wanted to devote more time to acting, yet with Ashton and the Camargo Society begging her to take on extra dancing roles, and critics still lauding her as a ballerina, she could not yet think of giving up her old career. Nor by this point did she have only herself to consider. As Lydia fretted over which direction to take her future professionally, she was also becoming anxious about Maynard.

Any modern doctor would have told Maynard that his lifestyle was a disaster in waiting – he smoked heavily, ignored his diet, and took so little exercise that by the summer of 1930, Vanessa observed him to have grown 'incredibly white and fat'.[10] To Lydia he also seemed to be crushing himself under an intolerable workload. The Wall Street crash of 1929 and the paralysing depression that came in its wake had left Maynard grimly preoccupied with future of the global economy. He was, in addition, burdened by complications nearer to home. The publication of his latest book, *A Treatise on Money*, had prompted a controversial response from the rest of the world, goading him into a frenzy of retaliatory correspondence and journalism. At the same time he was being forced into an urgent rescue plan to save his magazine, *The Nation*, whose dwindling circulation (accelerated by the decline of the Liberal Party) was forcing a merger with a rival publication, the *New Statesman*. By early 1931,

*The final order of the programme was: a verse prologue, 'The Preacher and the Young Man', which Dadie had drawn from The Song of Solomon and Ecclesiastes; 'A Lover's Complaint'; *Passionate Pavane*; *Comus*; a dramatised debate 'of the Infernal Peers' from *Paradise Lost*; and finally *Dances on a Scotch Theme*.

Maynard's system could no longer take the strain and a severe case of tonsillitis and flu left him feeling querulously convalescent, wishing only for the company of his 'dearest Countess of Talkie'.

He continued in this weakened state for several weeks, and Lydia was sufficiently worried to abandon all of her professional concerns and dedicate herself to his full recovery. In June 1931, when Maynard was scheduled to leave for New York and Chicago on an intensive round of lectures and meetings, she opted to go with him, even though it meant abandoning Camargo and her lessons with Zannie for over two months, while effectively putting her acting career even further down her list of priorities. Not that Lydia was being entirely self-sacrificial. They were booked to travel first class on the *Adriatic*, and during the first few days of the voyage out she and Maynard lazed like shameless sybarites in their modern suite, and glutted themselves in the dining room. 'The centre table is covered with huge meats, galantines, pork pies and ices,' Lydia reported to Florence; 'we swallowed all we could.'[11]

America, however, was no holiday. Maynard was on a fact-finding mission to analyse the causes and effects of the Depression, and his diary was filled with meetings with American economists. Lydia, left to herself, was distressingly aware of the human consequence of the crash. As she walked the streets of New York, she saw lines of women and children queuing for bread, and dull-eyed men with placards round their necks advertising for work. With no employment of her own, she passed her days in an aimless blur: some guilty shopping, a few trips to the theatre, some official parties with Maynard, all against the background anxiety over his health. And her concern sharpened when she and Maynard returned home, just as the British economy was itself poised to collapse. The knock-on effect of America's Depression had hit the City, and by August investors were withdrawing unsustainably large sums from the banks. Ramsay MacDonald's Labour government (back in power since 1929) was helpless to deal with the emergency, and the National Government, hastily formed to replace it, appeared to Maynard to be equally ineffectual. Its policy was simply to batten down the Treasury hatches, retrenching on public spending and refusing all loans, a feebly defensive response that in Maynard's view could only make the situation worse. Powerless to interfere directly, his nerves shredded by inaction, he began firing off savage articles to the press, advocating what had become his own basic principles of economic health: robust government spending to stimulate the sliding economy and an immediate retreat from the gold standard to prevent the collapse of sterling.

To Maynard's immense gratification, the government did eventually come off gold on 21 September, and a fortnight later Vanessa and Duncan found themselves in a London cinema watching him speak on the subject to the nation: 'Looking enormously big, in a well-appointed library blinking at the lights and speaking rather nervously [he told] the world that everything was now going to be all right. England had been rescued by fate from an almost hopeless situation, the pound would not collapse, prices would not rise very much, trade would recover, no one need fear anything.'[12]

But if the economy looked as though it was retreating from disaster, the crisis had an ominous effect on Maynard's own health. At the beginning of October he was forced into bed by stabbing chest pains, which Lydia rightly diagnosed as pleurisy; and as with his previous illness, he recovered alarmingly slowly, experiencing strange rheumatic pains 'flying about the body'. Lydia hated letting him stay in his bedroom in King's, where, with the onset of winter, icicles regularly formed on the inside walls. She fretted about his health, too, when Lytton died, of stomach cancer, early in 1932. Despite their rivalries and their quarrels the two men had remained essential to each other, always corresponding, always sending each other their books, and always requiring each other's philosophical ballast. When Lytton died, part of Maynard's past went with him and he was deeply shaken – although not too shaken subsequently to warn James Strachey to keep their correspondence – much of it libellous, much of it obscene – safe from prying eyes. 'The letters? – for God's sake lock them up for years yet.'[13]

As Lydia worried about Maynard she was also haunted by fears about her family. Like most of the Russian population, the Lopukhovs were again subsisting on a harshly reduced diet as Stalin's plans to collectivise the production and distribution of food had resulted in soaring prices, empty shops and famine conditions in the countryside. In addition, the family had also been disastrously affected by Stalin's new diktats on Soviet culture – under which the bold artistic visions that had elevated Fedor to ballet director of GATOB were now judged to be a subversive threat. His 1929 production of *The Nutcracker*, which had fragmented the ballet's action into a Futurist-styled collage of scenes, had resulted in his being removed from his post, and although he had been allowed to direct another, smaller ballet company at the Maly Theatre, his demotion had resulted in an immediate reversal of his own and his family's relatively privileged lifestyles.

The letters that Fedor now sent to Lydia appeared to be written on toilet paper, while Karlusha and Evgenia's once spacious quarters had been reduced to a tiny apartment, which they also had to share with Evgenia's husband – who for some reason was referred to as the Bourbon by the family. He and Evgenia had always been quarrelsome but the enforced intimacy of their living arrangements was creating impossible tensions. There were only two beds in the apartment, and since the Bourbon demanded to sleep in one of them, and Evgenia, who was still dancing, needed the other, Karlusha was obliged to nap through the nights uncomfortably in a chair. Mother and daughter were now barely speaking, and the rest of the family were also divided, with Fedor for some reason remaining friendly to the Bourbon, and Andrei taking Evgenia's side.

The damage inflicted on her family made Lydia feel even more savage towards Stalin's regime. The 'bolshies' among her émigré circle, like the Marxist writer Dimitri Mirsky, might talk of necessary sacrifices but Lydia saw only brutal attacks on those she loved and a wanton dismantling of the culture with which she had grown up: 'Before the war people kissed the feet of Jesus now they work for 24 hours and look miserable reading when they can 12 volumes of Lenin. How can one love a truck full of coal. Fred [Ashton] said in old times ballerinas were cheered, now it is a coal man.'[14] Lydia and Maynard briefly hoped to find a way out for Fedor and Andrei, faking a ballet engagement with Camargo, but even their friendship with the Russian ambassador in London, Ivan Maisky,* failed to

*Maisky himself became a victim of Stalin's regime when he was recalled to the Soviet Union after the war, arrested and tortured, perhaps for his closeness to Westerners like the Keyneses.

secure the brothers' exit visas. Instead Lydia had to content herself with sending back the usual envelopes of cash, and hijacking anyone she knew who was travelling to Russia, to smuggle in a few luxuries and clothes. (Sebastian Sprott, now a committed Socialist and calling himself Jack, was one of Lydia's mules, although he refused to accept the high-heeled shoes that she had given him, on the grounds that he would be unable to pass them off to the Russian customs officials as his own.)

By the autumn of 1932, Lydia was beginning to dread news from home, especially when it concerned her mother. Months of food shortages and lack of sleep had drained Karlusha of her once-dependable stoicism and she was now writing plaintively of her wish to see her youngest daughter 'one more time before she died'.[15] Lydia had never before heard this tone from her mother and was sufficiently alarmed to sign herself up as a companion to the philanthropic Lady Muriel Paget, who had put herself in charge of the welfare of several thousand British subjects still trapped in Soviet territories, and was planning to make visits to Riga and Leningrad in November. This trip inevitably turned out to be much more arduous than those Lydia had made with Maynard. Sailing over to Dunkirk in a bunk bed, she was kept awake by 'Lady M below grunting in her sleep';[16] on their arrival, French passport officials delayed the two women with wearisome queries about their travel papers, having never, apparently, heard of Riga; afterwards, during the two and a half day train journey to Latvia, 'Lady M's' ability to 'sleep 36 hours at a stretch' left Lydia to the mercies of a talkative American who insisted on called her 'honey'.[17]

It was even more frustrating that she then had to spend forty-eight hours in Riga following Paget on her humanitarian rounds. Lydia felt tantalisingly close to home in Riga, so close that she imagined she could 'taste ... the Russian frost again',[18] and as she helped Paget purchase supplies and accompanied her to a childcare centre, the delay was barely tolerable to her. By the time they caught the train for the final eighteen-hour journey to Leningrad, Lydia was physically shaking, caught between impatience to see her family and terror that she and her bulging cases of booty – 'millions of woollies with tooth brushes in between'[19] – might be held up at the Russian border.

On the afternoon of 21 November, however, Lydia was able 'to crush [Karlusha] in my bosom tenderly'[20] and wrote immediately to Maynard to reassure him that her mother was far from dying. But fear of the censor was evidently constraining her pen, for a disproportionate amount of this letter was taken up with a conscientious itemising of the virtues of modern Leningrad life, from the 'newly asphalted pavements near the Winter Palace' to the 'quite strong electric light'. Strikingly absent from Lydia's letter were any references to the chronic food shortages or the miserably confined conditions in Karlusha's flat. No mention at all was made of her suspicion that the Bourbon was now spying on her family, and only when she was safely back in London would Lydia tell Florence dramatically of how ominous the latter's presence had felt: 'We had to whisper our conversations so as not to be heard.'[21]

Nevertheless, Lydia was satisfied to see that, despite their shockingly reduced lifestyle, the Lopukhovs had kept a tenacious hold on their talents and careers. Evgenia had become something of a star in the musical comedy scene, with a cabaret repertory including several numbers by Fedor; Andrei was teaching as well as performing (Lydia went to see him give a 'superb' character dance class); and Fedor was making a success of his new company at the Maly (at that time known as MALEGOT). Some of his work had been retained at the Mariinsky, including his 1922 production of *Sleeping Beauty*, and when Lydia went to see the ballet performed she was entranced by its flavour of the Imperial past, disloyally confiding to Maynard, 'it is marvellous after the English ballet – such splendour, such dancers, such discipline'.[22]

Maynard himself felt miserably bereft during Lydia's absence. He had grown to depend on his 'dearest Loopoo' being as close as the next postal delivery, if not actually by his side, and he counted the days till she returned. When Lydia arrived back in London he was at Liverpool Street Station, impatient to meet her. A year later she could still recall the pleasure she had felt as she had recognised Maynard on the platform, the 'anxious expectant look' on his face a tender measure of how much he had missed her.[23]

It was only five months after this trip to Russia that Lydia was ready to send out her message to the theatre directors of Britain: that she was giving up ballet and hoping to move on to Ibsen. The moment seemed propitious. After the scares of the last two years, Maynard's health had stabilised and no longer required her careful concern. Karlusha was evidently not ready to die, and Lydia herself felt optimistic and energised enough to tackle a new professional future.

She was, however, forty-one, arguably rather old to be advertising herself for dramatic ingénue or soubrette roles, and it is hard to know how bothered she was by this. In some respects Lydia could be as touchily defensive about her age as any woman in her profession. She had never publicly reinstated the years that had been cut off by Diaghilev and Mandelkern (by the time she had married Barocchi, her passport showed her year of birth as 1895, rather than 1891). She had even tried to conceal her exact age from Maynard. After reading a profile of Lydia in a magazine, he teased her that the journalist had found out her 'birthday so that by cutting it out I shall know it too'.[24] On the other hand, Lydia made lackadaisically few attempts to disguise any depredations in her appearance. A trip to a beauty parlour, where she had her face deliciously 'patted sifted cool warmed eged and oiled', was a special event for her, making her catch her breath at its 'price enourmous'.[25] Equally unusual were the offstage occasions on which she could be bothered to apply cosmetics to her face, or dress herself up to look smart. Vanessa, when meeting Lydia out shopping in Lewes in 1935, would be shocked to see her looking 'very plain shabby and middle aged'[26] – and there are photographs from this period that justify Vanessa's surprise. Lydia in her forties was apparently quite happy to revert to her Lopukhov peasant inheritance – her body broadening and the planes of her face becoming coarser, more earthy.

If Lydia's beauty routines were perfunctory, so too was her attitude to bathing and hygiene. She had an especially criminal disregard for the state of her teeth, and a painful combination of decay and gum disease meant that in the spring of 1933 – just as she was advertising herself to play young heroines from Ibsen – she was also making trips to the dentist to have the worst of her teeth extracted and replaced with a denture. Many women would regard this as an indignity; Lydia, however, took inordinate pride in her new false teeth. She was fascinated by their design, fitted with 'little hooks so I cannot swallow them',[27] and she treated her most favoured friends to demonstrations of their ingenuity. Ashton, their first admirer, was winningly impressed. 'Fred was thrilled,' she jotted to Maynard, 'wants to have the same in his mouth';[28] and the following week, when she displayed her 'dentical jewel' to Sam Courtauld, he was not only admiring, but being 'an English sport ... drew his [own] out' in return.[29] This disgustingly reciprocal exchange was judged by Lydia to be a mark of 'intimate friendship', although Maynard was horrified. 'I was shocked at you and Sam clacking false teeth together. Intimate, I should think so.'[30]

Lydia's notions of intimacy had equally startled the painter William Roberts when, during a discussion of the double portrait that he was planning of her and Maynard, he had got something lodged in his eye, and she had nonchalantly offered to lick it out for him. Moments like these had long been grist to Lydia's reputation for inspired impulse. However, they were also one reason why many of her circle reacted with stunned disbelief to the first acting role that was offered her after she had advertised herself in the *Observer*.

Tyrone Guthrie was staging a production of *Twelfth Night* at the Old Vic, and in April 1933 he approached Lydia with the part of Olivia. That any director could envisage her as this most stately and solemn of Shakespeare's women seemed incomprehensible and a campaign was launched to dissuade her from accepting. Walter Sickert told Lydia that she would be putting her entire reputation in jeopardy, and Dadie Rylands begged her to ask instead for Maria, Olivia's quick-tongued lady-in-waiting. Lydia, however, was too excited and too much in love with Olivia's 'fine poetry' to consider refusing, already imagining to Maynard how she would play the role 'haughty and princess like [and] beautiful if possible in clothes, speech, ankles and wrists'.[31]

She was also very flattered by Guthrie's approach, for working with him at the Old Vic represented a significant advance in her career. Under the bullying care of Lilian Baylis (who ran the theatre alongside Sadler's Wells), the Old Vic had acquired the status of a national theatre, celebrated for its classic drama productions and for a stable of acting talent that included John Gielgud, Flora Robson and Charles Laughton. Lydia did, in private, worry that her accent might not be acceptable in such prestigious company and during the summer she again submitted herself diligently to Maynard's coaching. Yet if she was nervous when rehearsals started in September, none of her new colleagues seemed to register it. On the contrary, the actors working alongside Lydia seemed as quick to be disarmed by her as anyone else, with Athene Seyler (playing Maria) avowing that that they had all found her 'charming and intelligent and quick witted, a lovely intrinsic personality'.[32]

But perhaps Guthrie and his cast had been too charmed, for Lydia was allowed to interpret Olivia in a style delightfully true to her own nature, yet utterly contrary to the slow, fastidious and literal-minded heroine of Shakespeare's vision. As a startled, deeply divided audience witnessed on 18 September 1933, it was essentially Lydia, rather than Olivia, whom they saw on stage.

For her fans this was not a problem. Lydia physically dominated the production with her graceful handling of her Elizabethan costume and her deftly expressive gestures. According to Robert Helpmann, at the moment when Lydia 'drew down her veil and said *is't not well done* with adorable artless pleasure', she brought down the house; Flora Robson equally maintained that Lydia's interpretation of Olivia as a 'sentimental darling nit wit' had possessed a refreshing poetic truth.[33]

Anyone reading the hagiographic report in the *Daily Express* would in fact have assumed that Lydia had enjoyed an extraordinary tour de force: 'Great dancer turns actress,' trumpeted the *Express* headlines, 'Lopokova's superb Olivia. Audience of 2,500 held spellbound.'[34] Among the purists in the audience, and among the rest of the press, however, Lydia's performance was judged to be an impenetrable mistake. W. A. Darlington in the *Daily Telegraph* pondered, grimly, what could have 'possessed anybody'[35] to give her the role, and even the normally loyal *Nation* (now merged with the *New Statesman*) could offer only ambivalent balm.

Rather unwisely, Lydia had begged Virginia Woolf to review her for the magazine, not knowing that the latter, too, had already prejudged her casting to be an aberration. Loyalty and embarrassment had at least urged Virginia to fudge her dismay at what she had seen on stage, and Lydia may even have been flattered by the review's

Lydia with the cast for *Twelfth Night*, London, 1933

opening paragraphs, in which Virginia paid carefully poetic tribute to the grace of her stage presence:

> Madame Lopokova has by nature that rare quality which is neither to be had for the asking nor to be subdued by the will – the genius of personality. She has only to float onto the stage and everything round her suffers not a sea change but a change into light, into gaiety; the birds sing, the sheep are garlanded, the air rings with melody and human beings dance towards each other on the tips of their toes possessed of an exquisite friendliness, sympathy and light.[36]

Ironically, this description, fantastical and obligated as it was, ranks as one of the most vivid snapshots ever published of Lydia in performance. Yet the desperately reluctant Virginia had, finally, had to show her critical hand and admit how little dramatic relevance these enchanting physical effects bore to the role Lydia was playing:

> Olivia was a stately lady; of sombre complexion, slow moving and of few sympathies [but] Madame Lopokova loves everybody. She is always changing. Her hands, her face, her feet, the whole of her body are always quivering in sympathy with the moment. She could make the moment, as she proved when she walked down the stairs with Sebastian, one of intense and moving beauty: but she was not our Olivia.[37]*

For all its whimsical poetry, Virginia's review had, as she admitted to Ottoline Morrell, delivered a 'tough' verdict, and it was as damaging to Lydia's ego as were all the others. Not since the fiasco of *Just Herself*, back in New York in 1914, had she suffered such a critical bruising, and her agony was prolonged by the persistence with which her friends and acquaintances continued to go over it with her. Leonard Woolf, apparently siding with Lydia rather than his wife, suggested that the reviewers had been too small-minded to appreciate her virtues; others, including Christabel Aberconway, lectured Lydia on her folly in accepting the role in the first place. Gamely, Lydia tried to make a joke of the disaster, but Maynard had never seen her so obviously crushed by failure, nor her spirits so slow to revive. She clearly feared that her acting career had been aborted, and even his robust optimism was temporarily at a loss as he kept anxious check of her mood by post: 'How are you my dear dear duck whom I can't make happy.'[38]

Yet three months later Maynard's thwarted concern found an outlet as Lydia received an invitation to audition for the role of Nora in Ibsen's *A Doll's House*. The production was being planned by a small London repertory company, the Cosmopolitan Theatre, whose director, Mrs Grein,† was a woman of strict independence and integrity. The £125 that Maynard offered to underwrite the

---

*After writing her review, Virginia wrote to Ottoline Morrell on 7 October, 'Oh how I hated writing that tough little article! Poor dear little Lydia asked me to do it – she attached great value to her acting – she wants to be an actress – and the whole thing was a dismal farce.' (*Letters of Virginia Woolf*, Bell and McNeillie (eds), 5 vols, Hogarth Press, London 1977–84.)

†It may be a measure of how embattled female directors were in the theatre that Grein resisted the use of her first name even in private life (a practice to which Lydia, amazing Maynard, respectfully deferred), and that professionally she worked under the male pseudonym Michael Orme.

production cannot thus be interpreted as a bribe; however, the fact that Grein had very limited resources with which to stage the play did mean that his security was very welcome. If it did not directly win Lydia a part in *A Doll's House*, it did mean that the production could be guaranteed to go ahead as planned.

After Lydia auditioned for Mrs Grein on 18 January 1934, she was apparently accepted on the spot, writing in gasps of delight to Maynard, 'Well isn't it exciting! My god!' She was right to be thrilled – for, as Minnie Fiske had earlier suspected, she was a natural for the role. Physically she knew exactly how to convey Nora Helmer's ambivalent character – the doll-like compliancy of her demeanour and the frustrated will that seethed beneath it – and no actress in Britain was better qualified to dance the climactic tarantella, in which Nora, a frantic maenad, risked revealing her defiance to her husband, Torvald.

Nevertheless, the importance of this new role pressed on Lydia. Unable to face another failure, she was anxious to do well by the admirable Mrs Grein and her fellow actors, especially Walter Hudd, who she predicted would 'be a beautiful husband'. The persisting quirks of her pronunciation still worried her – 'nothing I say more like nathing ... I am learning to screw my face so that the o comes out.'[39] But as soon as the curtain had fallen on Lydia's debut on 4 March, Grein jotted her an ecstatic note: 'Once again Ibsen has raised a gifted actress to a place in the stars';[40] and most of the critics endorsed her admiration. *The Times* gave Lydia the longest and most respectful review of her acting career so far, analysing her interpretation in flattering detail: 'the emotional emphasis is brilliantly timed, every movement and frightened intonation contributing to an impression of a woman whose world is crumbling beneath her feet.'[41] Perhaps the most revealing praise came from Virginia, whose report to Quentin Bell of Lydia's success was clearly all the more genuine for its surprise. 'Dear Old Maynard was – this is exactly true – streaming tears; and I kissed him in the stalls between the acts; really she was a marvel, not only a light leaf in the wind but edged, profound and her English was exactly what Ibsen meant – it gives the right aroma. So she's in the 7th heaven and rushes about kissing and crying. Whether it means business I don't know.'[42]

It did not mean business straight away – disappointingly, the production had only been scheduled for two performances – but Lydia did not care. She 'read and read again' her review in *The Times*, ate 'like an animal' and cherished the fan mail that dropped through the letterbox of number 46. Christabel Aberconway rapturised, 'By the end of the play I felt quite broken'; Clive Bell judged her performance 'a masterpiece'; and Vanessa was a paragon of generosity: 'Now you must start on a new career of triumphs.'[43]

Feeling elated, with a 'load off my chest', Lydia floated through the Easter holidays at Tilton. The weather was beautiful, the pigs were fat, and the Keyneses each felt themselves to be serene and lucky. Their marriage had by now begun drifting into platonic middle age, and at times Lydia minded the lack of sex. Once or twice she suggested to Maynard that her bingeing onslaughts on the shops and restaurants of London were acts of thwarted displacement. Yet there was no souring of the air between them, no hardening into irritation. Tenderness for a man's underwear does not always survive a fourteen-year relationship, and the small fact that Lydia still wrote to Maynard with loving concern about his 'pantalets' was testimony of her continuing pleasure in him. Maynard's devotion remained equally strong. When he returned to Cambridge for the summer term he came across a couplet written by a Fellow of King's in the early seventeenth century, which he copied out for her. 'Only in love they happy prove / Who love what most deserve their love.' With simple certitude he added, 'I think it is true.'[44]

The happy equation by which Maynard summed up his marriage was also reflected in the smugness of his financial accounts. Clever investments in dollar shares had allowed him to recover, with almost indecent speed, from the Depression years, and the previous February Lydia had boasted to Florence that it had been a 'boom year', with her receiving 'the perks in frigidaire [refrigerator], fur coat, new bath and electric fires at Tilton'.[45] Then, at the beginning of 1934, she was promised another perk on a far more extraordinary scale.

It had long been a fantasy of Maynard's to see Cambridge equipped with 'a small, very smart modern theatre',[46] both to showcase the university's own plays and to present professional productions. Using King's College land, contributing his own money and expertise, he now planned to make this vision a reality; and if publicly it was to be a gift to Cambridge, privately it was his gift to Lydia. Operating as the power behind the new theatre, as its shadow impresario even, Maynard could do far more than subsidise the occasional play for his wife; he could directly initiate productions to suit her talent.

Lydia was overwhelmed by this generosity, writing shyly of the 'feeling of warmth and sweetness' it gave her, and fully aware of the magnitude of its cost.[47] Financially, Maynard would commit £20,000 (the equivalent of half a million today) towards the building, and the time and energy that he spent on it were even more draining. During the meeting in which he persuaded King's to let him build on college land, he made no fewer than eight speeches in the theatre's defence, one, he claimed, lasting three-quarters of an hour. Progress was very slow – by 27 May 1935 the theatre was still no more than a large hole from which the builders were digging out gold coins and the occasional skeleton – and for Lydia the delays felt especially long. Maynard had promised the first season to her, staging a cycle of four Ibsen plays that would allow her to reprise her triumph as Nora, as well as to make her debut as Hilda Wangel, the free-spirited heroine of *The Master Builder.* Now aged nearly forty-four, Lydia had only a limited time left for playing either role.

Nevertheless, the building project absorbed some of her frustrated energies as she and Maynard debated the details of the theatre's development, settling the size of its dressing rooms, the design of its 500 seats and the hiring of its restaurant staff (Lydia, supported by Vera, favoured using Russians in the kitchen, arguing that they were masters of the most eclectic cuisine in the world). There had been the distractions of a second trip to America, including the drama of a missed audience with President Roosevelt. Lydia had been in New York when the summons came and, as Maynard proudly put it, had to content herself 'with the glory of being the only girl in America who has refused a tea invitation to the White House'.[48] Most rewardingly, Lydia had also begun making a career for herself on radio. Back in November 1931 she had made a tentative broadcasting debut, narrating the story of Debussy's ballet score *La Boîte à joujoux* for a music programme on the BBC. It had been a challenging introduction to the medium, for Lydia had been required to speak her lines over the orchestra's playing and, given the primitive technology of recording studios, had been forced to control the balance of the sound herself by physically leaning into and away from her microphone. Not surprisingly, the effect had been peculiar, but it had won Lydia friends at the BBC and in the autumn of 1935 she was invited back for two more engagements: the first introducing a programme of ballet music with anecdotes from her own career;* the second narrating Hans Christian Andersen's story 'The Red Shoes'.

Lydia had selected this tale herself, and there may have been personal reasons for her choice. As a woman guiltily enslaved to her own shoe collection, she must have been amused by Andersen's gruesome fable about a young girl who jeopardises her soul for the sake of her new shoes. As a former ballerina, she must have felt a pleasurable shiver of horror at the ultimatum delivered to Andersen's heroine – either to dance for ever, 'till her skin shrinks up like a skeleton', or have her feet hacked off. But the reading was also an excellent vehicle for Lydia, her accent lending a lilt of magic to the narrative, and she 'swelled' to the excellent reviews that she received. Vita Sackville-West, herself a celebrated voice on radio, wrote to congratulate her: 'what an enchanting broadcaster you are', although Lydia was even more flattered by the shy 'girl at Raynes' (the Bond Street shoe shop), who told her that she had been 'enthralled'.[49]

Finally, on 3 February 1936, the Cambridge Arts Theatre was ready for its inaugural gala. The performing honours had been given to Ninette de Valois's company, which Lydia also took as a gift to herself, for Ashton, the company's resident choreographer, was still her beloved Fred, and de Valois was still her dear 'Ninnie'. The latter, despite her recent marriage and despite the demands of running her company, often drifted in to see Lydia at Gordon Square, to share lengthy chats in the kitchen on subjects ranging from period pains

*Lydia's script, heavily annotated by Maynard with directions for pauses and emphases, is the source for several anecdotes about her early career, including her theft of Pavlova's shoes.

(Russian girls cried: English girls took aspirins) to household management. (Lydia was shamed by de Valois's far superior powers of organisation: 'on Sundays she reads Mrs Beaton's book and makes a menu for a whole week'.[50])

Most frequently the two women discussed de Valois's trials in holding her company together. London was now on the touring circuit of the two new 'Ballets Russes' troupes that had been formed in the wake of Diaghilev, and British dancers were suffering from the competition. Lydia, although enthusiastically helping de Valois with several of her productions, including a staging of *The Nutcracker*, considered that the majority of her company were still 'puddings' by comparison with the Russians. She even had doubts about de Valois's new protégée, Margot Fonteyn, despite the beauty of her slanted dark eyes, elegant limbs and guileless smile. Whilst Lydia conceded rather viciously that 'Fontaine has more possibilities than Markova as nature endowed her without a hookey nose and with strict unwobbly knees', she was not yet convinced that the sixteen-year-old was ballerina material: 'I wonder if she has something of her own.'[51]

Nevertheless, she knew how remarkable it had been for de Valois to build her company almost entirely out of British talent, and she was proud of the role that she and the Camargo Society had played in its early formation.* As Lydia stood beside Maynard in their newly christened Keynes Box to applaud de Valois and her dancers, there was, throughout the new theatre, the atmosphere of an historic occasion. This gala might lack the social glitter that Diaghilev would have deemed necessary for a first night (the most famous person in the theatre after Lydia and Maynard was the university's vice-chancellor), but the vision that it embodied for British culture seemed impressively noble. Ten years later, when Maynard came to write the constitution for the newly formed Arts Council of Great Britain, the Arts Theatre would be part of his blueprint.

After the congratulations and the speeches were over, however,

*Lydia appreciated the achievements that Rambert had made with her Ballet Club but she felt that the smallness of its scale generated a 'destructive atmosphere' and lacked 'grandeur of view' (November 1934). The Vic–Wells, by contrast, seemed to her destined for great things, supported as it was by the vision of Lilian Baylis as well as by de Valois's ambition and determination.

Lydia had her Ibsen debuts to worry about. Maynard had been determined to make an ambitious statement with his first act of programming and was running *A Doll's House*, *The Master Builder*, *Hedda Gabler* and *Rosmersholm* back to back – a sequential logic, which, he claimed, would reveal Ibsen's own implied 'commentary on the emergence of the modern woman'.[52] He had also overseen a terrific pooling of talent, including Geoffrey Edwards (aged twenty-five), who was playing Torvald to Lydia's Nora; D. A. Clark Smith, who was playing opposite her as the master builder Solness: and also Jean Forbes-Robertson, an actress of renowned subtlety and depth who was taking the female leads in both *Hedda* and *Rosmersholm*. Directing the cycle were Mrs Grein, for *A Doll's House*, and Irene Hentschel for the remaining three plays, while the designs for the season had been commissioned from an experimental new team, three women who worked under the name 'Motley'.

Lydia should have felt reasonably confident about taking her place among this company. Despite the *Twelfth Night* humiliation, her fame, her connections and her personality had won her friends within the theatre community, John Gielgud, Flora Robson, Cecil Beaton and Robert Helpmann among them. More importantly, she had moved beyond Maynard's tutorials and now employed a voice coach, an actor she called Dicky. However, according to one of the Ibsen cast, John Laurie, the actors assembled for this season had been an usually 'tough lot', who were not entirely generous to a woman whom they regarded as a privileged outsider. Laurie's recollection that they had failed to 'extend' their 'most helpful encouragement to a very great little lady' suggests that Lydia's enthusiasm and sense of fun had won her less slack than usual, and that the idiosyncrasies of her acting style had been judged a little old-fashioned, even amateurish.[53] To read between the lines of the reviews, some critics agreed. Whilst Lydia was again given wonderful notices for Nora – her interpretation judged to be still more profound than her previous attempt – her performance in *The Master Builder* elicited a more ambivalent response. Physically she had known exactly how to play the iconoclastic Hilda, and production photographs that show Lydia with a dazzled light in her eyes, quivering with a barely contained energy, justify the enthusiasm of at least one critic, who compared

Lydia as Nora Helmer, *A Doll's House*, and Hilda Wangel, *The Master Builder*, Cambridge, 1936

her to 'a demonic force of destiny'.[54] Psychologically, however, Lydia had not got the full measure of her role, and the fierce, amoral wilfulness that lay coiled in Hilda's soul was beyond her. Once again she had come across as lightweight.

Lydia's reaction to her mixed success is not revealed in letters – she had no reason to write to Maynard since she was in Cambridge every day, staying with Florence and Neville in Harvey Road. Nor did she write much about her disappointment when the Ibsen cycle transferred to London's Criterion Theatre on 4 March 1936 and struggled to fill the seats for its five-week season. Maynard, along with his commercial co-producer, Leon M. Lion, had known that this transfer was a gamble – serious drama regularly did poor business in the West End and it had not helped that a production of *The Master Builder* had been staged at the Embassy the previous year. But for Lydia it was a galling novelty to find herself faced with half-empty houses. Although her old fans and galerites came out in force, she had to accept the fact that her name had lost its automatic power to pull a crowd.

Yet if Maynard's new theatre failed to launch Lydia into the heart of the acting profession, it gave her a new hobby – and she would absorb herself in its business for another three decades. During the summer of 1936 she was living virtually full time in Cambridge as she helped Maynard with the inaugural season, and she could hardly obsess over her own disappointment as production crises and post-performance parties followed each other in busy succession. T. S. Eliot was up during May to see the Cambridge première of *Murder in the Cathedral*, and Lydia took pleasure in his company. She thought he had a 'kind nature' and was intrigued by his and Maynard's friendship (during the eight years in which Eliot had supported himself by working in a bank, his special duty had been tracking foreign currency, a subject close to Maynard's heart). In June the Vic–Wells Ballet returned to dance a full season, in which Lydia not only acted as co-producer, organising accommodation for the dancers and discussing casting issues with de Valois, but also socialised with them tirelessly. Years later the historian Noël Annan (then an undergraduate) would write to Ashton recalling this as a golden season and a golden summer: 'endless laughter & fun & drink & delicate romances of no duration. I think of them as some of the happiest times & Lydia's champagne laughter.'[55]

So much time was Lydia now spending in Cambridge that Maynard felt she needed her own base, rather than staying as she usually did with his parents. During the summer he found a small college flat available for rent, situated in a narrow lane directly opposite the theatre's stage door. Although months of renovation were required before Lydia could take possession, 17a St Edwards Passage promised her a temptingly private space within the masculine collegiate structures of Maynard's world – and a far more convenient base than Florence and Neville's house in Harvey Road. Much as Lydia loved the *starychki*, it did not suit her to play the docile daughter-in-law for more than a few days at a time.

By the autumn, Lydia had another reason to be in Cambridge, as plans were laid to mount an Arts Theatre production of Molière's *Le Misanthrope*. The capricious and mildly malicious heroine Célimène was another ideal period character for her to inhabit, and the formal music of Molière's verse would be an ideal fit with her voice and her accent. For a mad moment Lydia had wondered whether she could persuade Edith Evans to read through the part with her – 'Her inflexions are perfect'[56] – but otherwise she was working as usual with her coach, Dicky, and having discussions about casting and design with Vera. (Lydia still depended on her friend's opinion and was still intimate with her, despite the occasional barbed quarrel. The previous year there had been one brief and silly falling-out after Vera had circulated a rumour that Lydia, down at Tilton, had constructed a pair of trousers out of uncured rabbit skin and, as Lydia indignantly reported, had 'inflicted a sort of leprosy in my private parts'.[57])

Rehearsals for *Le Misanthrope* did not begin until late January 1937, by which time Lydia was word perfect and was hopeful all over again that she had found the role to clinch her career. The creative team at work on the production seemed to her especially charmed – Robert Atkins, the director, she judged a 'Petipa of drama', while designers André Derain and Barbara Karinska (who worked simply as Karinska) had given her a 'dream' costume: 'I look so pert and crisp ... I wasn't dressed like that since Boutique.'[58] Maynard, however, in a state of profound agitation that this production should be a complete and unqualified success, began making unannounced visits to the rehearsal room in London, where his judgemental presence affected the cast. 'You crushed us yesterday,' Lydia wrote, half approvingly, half reproachfully. 'Your appearance of an eminent man produced that strange effect, including me.'[59] His nerves infected Lydia – 'I shiver and become a fidget case' – and she began to worry that Norman Higgins, the Arts Theatre manager, would not know how to manage the London critics when they came up to review: 'if Agate or Bishop come ... (Agate probably wont, he is lazy and fat) Higgens must offer champagne to one and spirits to other ... Agate collects gloves, shoes, where he fancies someone on the stage, I can supply him with half a dozen of outworn corrugated musty shoes, but he probably wont fancy my feet.'[60]

But the critics needed no bribes. When *Le Misanthrope* opened on 7 February, the *Telegraph*'s W. A. Darlington, scourge of her Olivia, judged that as Célimène she had given 'the best performance I have seen from her since she turned articulate on the stage'.[61] From his colleagues, too, there were similar compliments for Lydia's 'grace of movement and intelligence of attack' and for the dramatic improvements in the 'power and variety' of her delivery.[62] Lydia was judged to have been as natural a Célimène as she had been a Mariucca – engagingly comic yet precise in every physical detail, from the eloquence of her glance to the witty poise of her elbows and the aristocratic carriage of her head.

It was as close as Lydia had yet come to an acting triumph, and when the play finished its Cambridge run, transferring to London's Ambassadors Theatre on 23 February, she was giddy with hope that a commercial success was within her grasp. The first-night reviews were as complimentary as they had been in Cambridge, and Lydia was flattered by a comment from one of the Ambassadors' ushers that 'in the last 25 years he has not seen such good acting'.[63] She may have been thinking of her father when she affirmed that ushers were among the best critics in the world as 'they get to see so much'.)[64] But encouraging as the press were, the public remained cool. Molière was not a general favourite among British theatregoers and the fact that the play was programmed alongside a new Ashton ballet, *Harlequin*, seemed to confuse rather than tempt them. During *The Misanthrope*'s two-week run, ticket sales had faltered so badly that Maynard had to pay £200 to cover the deficit, leaving Lydia with the gloomy reflection that her greatest achievement as an actor had still not secured her a West End hit.

This was a delicate moment for her, since she was now forty-five and running out of time to establish herself in her new career. She had won over most of her critics but she still needed a stronger record at the box office; she still needed to widen her theatrical range. Lydia's professional tragedy was that she had no further opportunities to do either. Although she would appear in one more play (a badly timed and badly received pacifist drama by W. H. Auden and Christopher Isherwood in 1938), a new role would take over her personal life to the virtual exclusion of her work. In the early summer of 1937 Maynard suffered a serious heart attack and Lydia, without hesitation, sidelined all her stage ambitions to become his nurse.

Chapter Eighteen

ILLNESS AND POLITICS

> Dearest Lank, Try to forget shares markets fortunes because it must crumple the muscles of your heart and you must not decrease your strength because I am so fond of you.
>
> LYDIA LOPOKOVA[1]

When Maynard's health began to deteriorate again at the beginning of 1936, it was Lydia's assumption that overwork, as usual, was to blame. During the past four and a half years he had been writing his follow-up to *A Treatise on Money* and it had turned out to be the most ambitious endeavour of his career, confirming for many his status as the world's most creative economist. Fuelled by the 'queer imaginative ardour'[2] that Virginia had always admired in him, *The General Theory of Employment, Interest and Money* drew on the most formative intellectual concerns of Maynard's adult life: his early utopian responses to Moore and Bloomsbury; his radicalising experience at Versailles; his critiques of Soviet zealotry; and his new interest in Roosevelt's Democrat America.

At the core of the book lay Maynard's analysis of why mature capitalist economies, if left to themselves, inevitably tended towards sustained unemployment and depression; and why government intervention was the most effective way of countering that trend. It presented a model that would mark a revolution in economic practice – *the* Keynesian Revolution – demonstrating how periods of recession could be managed by a government policy of reducing taxes and / or increasing public spending: a strategy designed to expand the population's spending power, create jobs and so restimulate economic growth.

But what was most far-reaching was the book's commitment, as economic theory, to issues of social welfare and global politics. State-managed capitalism, according to Maynard, was not only good economics – the most productive possible balance between market forces and government – but also the only viable centre ground available to the Western world in the mid-1930s, and the only model powerful enough to prevent the accelerating drift towards fascism and communism. According to one of its admirers, the economist D. M. Bensusan-Butt, *The General Theory* had done nothing less than outline

> a very new sort of capitalism, controlled not by the greedy votaries of Mammon but by the intellect and joie de vivre of an intelligent and robust democracy. It had no more place for the dull, mean and fearful parrots of Birmingham and the City team in charge of affairs at home than for the suicidal tyrannies of the Left and bestialities of the Right then boiling up abroad ... [it] was less a work of economic theory than a Manifesto for Reason and Cheerfulness.[3]

By the mid-1930s, many observers were feeling that reason and cheerfulness were in diminishing supply as Hitler, having seized the German chancellorship in 1933, was riding a tide of nationalist hysteria to rebuild the nation into a new militaristic power. This was what Maynard had feared back in Versailles, when he had watched the Allies competing to exact brutal reparations from a defeated Germany, but his most pessimistic predictions had not envisaged the extremes to which Hitler and his 'party' were planning to fight back, terrorising political opposition and embarking on a systematic Aryanisation of the Rhineland.

Maynard and Lydia had both registered with horror the first wave of Germany's legislation against its Jewish population. In October 1933, Lydia had noted the 'Nazis treatment of the Jews getting madder and madder', and the following year Maynard refused an official invitation to Hamburg in protest at the anti-Semitic policies that had proved fatal to his great friend Carl Melchior: 'After the death of my friend ... there is nothing left that could attract me,' he wrote in stiff contempt.[4] Maynard himself had been instrumental in bringing German Jews over to the safety of Cambridge. Yet at the same time his and Lydia's daily response to Jewishness stood up less well to scrutiny. They both took for granted a prevailing culture of language and attitude that would now be judged obnoxious, routinely using the term 'Jew' as generic shorthand to denote greed, pugnacity, a kind of vulgar cockiness. In April 1933, Lydia had felt no guilt in laughing when a bus conductor, intimidated by a group of rough Jewish youths, had shouted to the rest of the passengers, 'Three cheers for Hitler.' Just as guiltlessly, Maynard had found this a witty anecdote and had passed it round the common rooms of Cambridge. Linguistic carelessness and routine racial arrogance of this type were endemic in their world – Leonard Woolf was subject to it even in his own progressive circles, and even from his own wife. Although both Keyneses had tempered their language by the late 1930s, it was not to their credit how long it took. In Lydia it exposed the lingering anti-Semitic prejudices that she had brought with her from Russia.* In Maynard it exposed a deficiency in translating large political issues into the detail of individual lives.

His eye for those large political issues had never been so keen, however, as when he was writing *The General Theory*. With growing concern he had watched the Depression-fuelled spirit of fanaticism spread to Britain during the mid-1930s, with Mosley's Union of Fascists tightening its grip on the Right, and communism gaining a charismatic hold on the Left. Marxism had become the ideology of choice among a new generation of Cambridge students, Vanessa's adored eldest son Julian among them, and it pained Maynard to hear this clever, pugnacious boy ruthlessly dismiss his own vision of state-managed capitalism as optimistic muddle, or to deny all the evidence that Marxism under Stalin was not just bad economics but a 'sickness of the soul'.[5]

This fashionable embrace of communism was especially galling for Maynard, given the misery that Lydia's family were now suffering. The monomaniac extremes of Stalin's first Five-Year Plan had inflicted famine across much of the Soviet Union, and routine purges

*On the other hand, in 1921 when Lydia had been in New York she had been shocked to encounter anti-Semitic prejudice against Albert Einstein.

of dissidents – real or imagined – had generated a noxious climate of paranoia and fear. In their cramped flat, Karlusha and Evgenia had finally managed to get shot of the hateful, spying Bourbon, but Maynard's monthly payments from England, the Lopukhovs' main defence against food shortages, had been stalled by a 'glitch' in Soviet bureaucracy. By May 1935, Lydia was agonising that her family's finances were 'on the brink', after hearing reports that their health was even worse: Genia had 'five carbuncles under her arm', Karlusha's blood pressure was soaring and Fedor was suffering from gastric ulcers.[6]

Worse followed when Fedor's new ballet, *The Bright Stream*, fell foul of the authorities. This witty, graceful comedy, which had been pioneeringly set on a collective farm, had been enthusiastically premièred at the Maly Theatre in the spring of 1935, but when it was transferred to Moscow in January 1936, Shostakovich's accompanying score was condemned by critics as a 'pretence against music', and an editorial in *Pravda* charged Fedor with 'aesthetic formalism'.[7] The only artistic crime he had apparently committed was to put the ballet's cast of farmworkers in pointe shoes, and to show them performing classical steps rather than 'local folk dances and games'; yet as a result, the librettist, Adrian Piotrovsky, was sent to the gulag (from which he never returned). Fedor had his newly announced promotion to director of the Bolshoi stripped from him, and his creative career was effectively terminated.

Far from being a help to his family, Fedor was now a political liability. He spent the next eight years as an itinerant ballet master taking whatever work he could, some of it as far away as Tashkent. He may well have been absent from Leningrad when Lydia made a brief visit there in November 1936, organised on the back of a lecture that Maynard was giving in Stockholm. It was a relief for her to be able to smuggle in presents for the family, which could, if necessary, be bartered or sold. There was some consolation too in seeing Karlusha's blood pressure reduced by leeches that had been sent over from Moscow and which, according to Lydia, had got 'lyrical and drunk' on her mother's back.[8]

But now she had Maynard to worry about. Writing *The General Theory* had been an exhausting labour for him, and even when the book was published (on 4 February 1936, just a day after the opening of the Arts Theatre), still more work was generated by the deluge of articles and letters that followed, all of them requiring close reading, all of them requiring a reply. There were the stunned admirers to acknowledge: 'In those years,' wrote Lorie Tarshis, 'many of us felt that by following Keynes, each one of us could become a doctor to the whole world';[9] but there were also the critics who condemned *The General Theory* as politically flawed. Antagonists on the Right dismissed its vision as arrogantly intellectual, denying the complex realities of the marketplace; antagonists on the Left denounced it as the expression of a defunct capitalism, perniciously antipathetic to the rights of the working class.

As Maynard dealt with his critics, goaded into a fever of argument, he seemed to Lydia to be putting himself under an intolerable strain. His health had been dreadful for the past few months, with a bout of flu followed by chronic rheumatic pain, and by 1 May 1936 she begged him to draw a line: 'Don't answer any more about your book, you have done it. You know why you have and it is not much use to correspond with anyone about it.' She dragged him down to Tilton for a few days, hoping that the early summer quiet might calm his racing mind. But while Maynard meekly submitted to Lydia's home remedies, including having his head rubbed with a pungent oil that made him smell like a 'sardine', on his return to Cambridge he was again corresponding furiously with his critics. 'I expect you are right – you always are,' he wrote to her apologetically. 'But I have such a dreadfully controversial temperament that it is difficult for me to keep away from it.'[10]

By the autumn the postbag had petered out, and Lydia imposed some kind of calm over the long journey to Sweden and Russia. Yet shortly before Christmas, Maynard was again in bed with flu, and was left with new pains, like 'wonky breathing muscles',[11] which made him fear that his heart was implicated. Lydia, busy preparing for her debut in *Le Misanthrope*, could only hope that the early Easter holiday they had planned in the South of France would speed his recovery.

Many others were also travelling to France in 1937. The civil war being fought across the border in Spain had escalated into an international stand-off between fascism and democracy as Hitler's

Germany, Mussolini's Italy and Stalin's Russia sent their respective forces in support of the Nationalists and Republicans. Also drawn into the struggle were the legions of unofficial sympathisers from both Left and Right who were converging on France, aiming to travel onwards to the battle lines of Spain. It was a situation that aroused Maynard's anxious professional interest, but Lydia was determined to keep him focussed only on his health. They travelled to France on the overnight boat train and reached Cannes the next day, where their hotel provided 'service with magic carpet touch, one need not leave the room just stretch one's eyes along the coast'.[12]

This luxury had been a necessity for the convalescent Maynard, who on his arrival was too weak to walk more than a few paces. But as Lydia restricted his diet and his drinking, he improved enough for her to let him out on brief forays to the casino: 'I hope he will come back with full hands as we have an agreement that what he gains I get half and what he loses I give half,' she wrote valiantly to Florence; 'of course it is all morale as I have no money only words.'[13] The combination of sea air, rest – and a few winnings – did seem to turn Maynard's health around. On their return, Lydia allowed him back to Cambridge, where he was examined by the family doctor, Uncle Walrus (Sir Walter Langdon-Brown), whose prognosis was reassuring. There was nothing fundamentally wrong, Langdon-Brown assured Maynard; his heart was fine.

That was on 31 March. Six weeks later, going as usual to Harvey Road for Sunday lunch, Maynard collapsed with violent pains in his chest. His heart was anything but healthy. Undiagnosed by his uncle, a severe streptococcal infection was raging both in his throat and in the valves of his heart. A furring of the coronary arteries, exacerbated by years of heavy smoking, was also producing what would be the first of many angina attacks. Lydia, called urgently to Maynard's bedside from London, had visions of finding him dead on her arrival. In fact he had rallied feebly by the time she reached him and, as she and Florence took anxious shifts in nursing, his strength slowly returned. The ever-optimistic Langdon-Brown still believed that the attack had not been serious – a case of 'pseudo angina' from which there was no danger of 'sudden death'.[14] But it was another month before Maynard could even be moved from his bed, and it was clear that his condition required a much more detailed diagnosis than his Uncle Walrus could offer.

On 18 June, Lydia and Maynard were driven by their new chauffeur, Fred Woollard, to a private sanatorium called Ruthin Castle, in North Wales. The clinic, housed in a gloomy Victorian folly of a building, had come recommended by Ottoline Morrell for its enormous beds and its up-to-date science; and as soon as Maynard arrived he was subjected to a barrage of tests. These were dramatically quick to identify the severity of his streptococcal infection – the swabs taken of his throat grew 'at once into an orchard', as Lydia put it[15] – however, without the benefit of antibiotics,* curing the infection was not a simple matter. All Ruthin's doctors could offer was the remedy of total, supervised bed rest.

Given Maynard's workaholic drive and 'controversial temperament', even this proved difficult to effect, and within days he was defying doctors' orders and scribbling secret letters and memos under his sheets. If Lydia had remained with him at Ruthin, she would have been able to alert the nurses to her husband's disobedience – but during the first week of Maynard's treatment she was required in London, where she was under contract to present a music broadcast for the BBC. Maynard himself had urged her to go, begging her to take a break from the long weeks of nursing, but Lydia had fretted at being away from him. The rehearsals were tedious to her; she disliked the script that she had written for herself; and although Fred Ashton visited her in Gordon Square, bringing gossip of the ballet war being waged between the two new Ballets Russes companies and their rival attempts to sign him up as a choreographer, even he could not seize her interest. On the evening of the broadcast, as Lydia waited to hear herself on the radio, she felt listless and morose: 'a piano grinder from the Square cheers me up, when that is over the time will be so long till 9 o'clock'.[16]

Maynard, up in Ruthin, was listening to Lydia's broadcast and even scribbling a commentary. 'Breathing and tempo were perfect,' he insisted by next day's post, 'and marred only by a couple of deviant

*Penicillin was not introduced until 1945.

vowels.'[17] Stoically he encouraged her to stay on in London, warning her that she would be dull and dreary in Ruthin. But Lydia could not stand to be apart from him any longer and, booking herself into a 'mousehole' of a room at Ruthin's local hotel, she braced herself for the prospect of spending her summer in the company of a dull 'hen party of Castle widows'.[18]

The widows themselves actually became very animated when they discovered that this new addition to their party was a celebrity dancer who had met, and performed for, the royal family. But otherwise the conversation was only of their husbands' symptoms, and Lydia admitted to Florence that the effect on her own spirits was 'very droopy'.[19] Seeking distraction, she set herself projects, translating articles in the Russian press to read to Maynard during visiting hours, and exploring the local countryside with Fred, his driving a 'great comfort', she claimed, in contrast to Edgar, whose drinking had frequently resulted in some 'ugly prank' and who was now mercifully restricted to gardening and pig duties at Tilton. She also penned detailed reports of Maynard's progress to the *starychki* and by mid-July was able to deliver positive news. On 19 July he had been allowed outside for an hour – 'it thrilled him to be able to touch the grass with his hands'; a week later he had had enough strength to walk 'like a human being instead of a poodle on its hind legs'; and by 8 August even the 'wounded bird's look in his eyes [was] disappearing'.

These improvements made life slightly more interesting for Lydia, as she was able to take Maynard out for drives or gentle walks. But as the weeks in Ruthin stretched into months, she came to hate the damp Welsh climate, the dismal ruins of the ancient castle that squatted next door to the sanatorium and the insidious vacillations of Maynard's recovery. The good days made her tense with hope; the bad days made her wretched. 'My nerves are getting very ragged,' she admitted to Florence, 'and sometimes I simply break up in torrents of tears.'[20]

However, at the end of September she was able to take Maynard back to Tilton, armed with a regime of diet and rest, which the doctors promised would complete the cure. Their joy in exchanging the bleak grandeur of Wales for a golden Sussex autumn made them willing to believe whatever encouragement was offered (even though they had by now reached the conclusion that Ruthin offered only a 'mixture of first-class medicine and first-class humbug').[21] And whilst Maynard would be a semi-invalid for many more months, and would terrify Lydia with sudden inexplicable reversals in his recovery, this period would be a time of peculiar domestic contentment. The two of them had never lived together, continuously, for more than a few weeks, and their enforced domestic intimacy altered the dynamic of their marriage, turning its focus inwards towards each other and towards Tilton.

It was now that the spirit of the house seemed especially benign. Maynard had recently extended their lease and commissioned his architect, George Kennedy, to oversee more renovations, including a new wing and staircase, new servants' quarters and extra bathrooms. Although Maynard was too weak to get up the stairs, sleeping in a hastily converted boot room off the hallway, he could still appreciate with Lydia the new spaciousness of Tilton and its improved comforts. During the mornings he wrote, in bed or on a couch, resting his papers on a large board, while Lydia did her exercises, read and played the piano. In the afternoons they 'sniffed' the fresh air, which Lydia stubbornly believed was essential to Maynard's recuperation. Arm in arm, they pottered on gentle walks around the grounds, drove with Fred along the lanes or took naps in the garden, wrapped up in bad weather 'like eskimos against the cold'.[22]

Evenings were spent by the radio or gramophone. Occasionally, if Maynard felt strong, they read aloud to each other from the newspapers or from a book of poetry or a play that Lydia was interested in. Yet whilst both of them thrived in the humdrum calm of Tilton's routines, Maynard could not be kept quiet all day. Under the terms of the new lease, the estate had expanded to include the adjoining farm, and Lydia could almost measure the state of her husband's health by the interfering interest that he took in the farm's running – checking with the newly employed manager, Logan Thomson, on the milking, the sheep shearing, the corn yield; discussing pheasant hatching with the new gamekeeper, Mr Churchill; or disputing with neighbouring farmers over issues like shared fencing.

Exasperatingly, it was often hard to believe Maynard was ill at all, as he applied the same dazzling feints of logic to farming affairs as he did to political or academic arguments. Quentin Bell, who came to work on the Tilton estate, said it was like 'a man armed with a rapier who meets rustics armed only with clubs';[23] and Maynard's abrupt brilliance did not ease relations with the local community, who were still inclined to view the Keyneses as alien outsiders. During one of their rambles round the estate, Maynard was being scolded by Lydia for walking too fast, and he verbally accosted a nearby worker for sympathy: 'What would you do if an old sheep looked at you as Lydia is looking at me now?' Quentin observed the shepherd staring nonplussed at his odd employers: the tall, stooped Maynard in his straw hat, and the stern Lydia fluttering at his side. It was, he commented, a question that 'anyone might have found ... difficult to answer'.[24]

But if Maynard liked to play lord of the manor, it was clear to all of the staff that Lydia was now the mistress of Tilton. Not only was she running the domestic staff (Ruby, two housemaids and the cook, Beatty), it was she who was now the ultimate arbiter of Maynard's days. Where once she had deferred to his timetable and his decisions, she now dictated his routines. She oversaw his diet and medication, and she ruled over his rest periods with an inflexible will. Although his secretary, Mrs Stephens, was permitted to come once a week to deal with correspondence, Lydia was vigilant about the volume of work that Maynard attempted, noticing that he became 'aggressive' and 'chippy' if his mind was strained. She even restricted social visits, imposing time limits and bluntly ushering guests out of the house the minute she saw that Maynard was tiring.

Unflaggingly, too, Lydia recorded in a daily journal every shift in Maynard's sleep patterns, his hours of exercise, his physical symptoms. To those who had previously dismissed her as a butterfly, this dedicated nursing may have been a revelation. Yet from childhood Lydia had been trained to respect the importance of physical regime. Maintaining this discipline over Maynard's care afforded her some illusion of controlling his sickness, and it helped to get her through the times when her confidence in his recovery faltered and the sight of his struggling system brought her close to despair. 'No one knows what I have to go through,' she wrote in a rare outburst to Florence, 'being on the string most of the time with hardly any strength left and then pretending to live normally with others.'[25]

During November, Maynard seemed to be making progress, and Lydia allowed him to host a Guy Fawkes party, commanding all the guests to wear masks, her own disconcertingly being that of a Tilton pig. She permitted a visit from the young writers W. H. Auden and Christopher Isherwood in order to discuss a play that Maynard had commissioned for the Arts Theatre's autumn 1938 season. And she dared to accept some work of her own. This was presenting another music programme for BBC radio, and also her first appearance on television.* Lydia had been invited to give a repeat reading of 'The Red Shoes' in front of the camera, and it may have been her confidence in her material, as well as her increasing lack of concern about her own appearance, that allowed her to view her debut as casually as she did. 'It will need a rehearsal or two,' she commented to Florence, 'but it will do me good.'[26]

By Christmas, Maynard was complaining of chest pains again, and just as Lydia was struggling to understand what might have caused the reversal, she and the rest of the household were caught up in a new medical emergency as Auntie Weller, Lydia's elderly dresser, contracted a near-fatal bout of pneumonia. However, when Maynard went back to Ruthin for a week of follow-up tests, in the middle of February 1938, the doctors' news was better than expected. Even though his blood pressure was still low and his heart enlarged, the streptococci were much less virulent, and the swabs, as Lydia reported to Florence, now 'refused to grow vegetable'.[27] The fine, blustery weather reflected their hopeful mood, and Lydia, taking Maynard on longer and longer walks, found the countryside around Ruthin exhilarating rather than oppressive: 'We ... walked with the winds behind, and the sun streaming, and the dead bracon to caress the eyes.'[28]

So well did Maynard appear that Lydia allowed him three weeks in Gordon Square. Here, as at Tilton, the scale of their living arrangements had expanded, with Maynard having recently taken a lease on the adjoining number 47 to house a new library. After their

---

*This was Lydia's only TV appearance, and it has not been preserved.

long exile in Tilton they both felt stimulated and urbane. There were walks in the parks, evenings with friends, and Lydia began working on a new radio project, *Studies of Childhood and Adolescence from the Russian Masters*, which was to feature extracts from the writings of Chekhov, Tolstoy and Dostoievsky, selected and introduced by her. Encouraged by her producer, a young Cambridge graduate called Guy Burgess, Lydia was writing and editing the scripts entirely by herself, causing Maynard to complain that she was showing alarming signs of intellectual independence.

This privately optimistic interlude was, however, set against a backdrop of intensifying international gloom. A terrible shadow had already fallen over Bloomsbury the previous summer when Julian Bell, driving an ambulance for the Republicans, had been killed in Spain. In the face of tragedy, all the animosity between the Keyneses and Vanessa had temporarily vanished, and Maynard, from his sickbed at Ruthin, had written an anguished letter on his and Lydia's behalf: 'Dear Nessa A line of sympathy and love from us both on the loss of your dear and beautiful boy with his pure and honourable feeling. It was fated that he should make his protest, as he was entitled to do, with his life and one can say nothing.'[29]*

Afterwards, during Maynard's long convalescence at Tilton, Lydia had tried to blank the worst of the political news from her mind. While appalled at the victories won by Franco's forces in Spain, horrified by Hitler and violently abusing the 'atrocious' Mussolini, she kept her sights resolutely on Maynard, looking 'not to the right, not to the left, just ahead organising my own life'.[30] Maynard too had encouraged Lydia's denial, for whilst many of his colleagues predicted that Europe was being pushed to the brink of war, he maintained a stubborn faith that the spread of fascism, even of Hitler's vaunting militarism, would eventually be curbed – either by muscular diplomacy from Europe and America or by some fatal blunder of fascism's

*Vanessa, half-dead with grief, could send only a brief acknowledgement, but three months later would correspond intimately with Maynard about Julian. Maynard also wrote a small memoir of Julian, which was much admired by Virginia. 'I wish you'd go on to do a whole portrait gallery, reluctant as I am to recognise your gift in that line, when it seems obvious that nature gave me none for mathematics. Is portrait writing hard work,' she anxiously enquired, 'compared to economics?' VW to JMK, 23 December 1937.

leaders. 'I ... believe that brigands are exceptionally liable to make mistakes,' he had written to his sister-in-law, Margaret, in 1937.[31]

Maynard's prophesies were not always sound. On 11 March 1938, Hitler ordered his troops into Austria and, with seeming impunity, claimed the country for the Reich. The news shook Maynard's equanimity, and when reports came through of a sudden slump on Wall Street, where many of his own assets were invested, his health also suffered another relapse. Lydia schooled herself to be phlegmatic, writing to Maynard's close colleague and former protégé Richard Kahn that a setback must be considered 'quite natural after so much work, change of weather, the world situation, Wall street and life in general'.[32] And this time her fortitude was rewarded. Just as Europe hung on to a compromised peace, opting to accommodate Hitler rather than confront him, so Maynard clung tenaciously to health. He was sufficiently recovered by the middle of May for Lydia to take him from London up to Cambridge, where the Arts Theatre was presenting a season of modern ballet by the German expressionist Kurt Jooss* – commended by Lydia in the *Cambridge Review* for his exceptional ability to bring 'the realism of life'[33] to the ballet stage. By June they were finally back in Tilton, settled with their 'pillows and bags'[34] after an unexpectedly long absence of two and a half months. Maynard's continuing improvement allowed Lydia to permit a second visit from Auden and Isherwood, who, along with the composer Benjamin Britten, needed to finalise details of the script and incidental music for the new play.

On the Frontier was the most experimental production that the Arts Theatre had yet presented, an anti-war drama that was part Marxist satire, part Greek tragedy, part love story. Maynard enjoyed having the three clever young men around him, especially Auden, whom he thought grubby (his fingernails especially) but a genius, and their presence was stimulating to Lydia too. She talked with them, unusually and vehemently, about Russia – trying to get them to see the iniquities taking place under Stalin – and she was also involved in discussion of the play, since she was taking on its lead

*Jooss had fled Hitler's Germany in 1933. He was one of several refugee artists and intellectuals who were supported by Maynard.

female role. Her character was Anna Vrodny, an idealistic young woman whose personal life becomes endangered when her native country, Westland, is threatened by the neighbouring state of Eastland, home to her lover Eric Thorvald. The unfolding *Romeo and Juliet* tragedy was intended by Auden and Isherwood to be a direct comment on the current situation in Central Europe, with Eastland's bellicose leader an unmistakable caricature of Hitler. Yet for the two left-wing authors the villain of the piece was less the strutting, gesticulating Führer than the cynical arms manufacturer, Valerian, manipulating him for profit. The play's message, communicated through Ann and Eric's ardently pacifist verse dialogue, was that wars could never be just or necessary, because they were essentially fought to fill the pockets of industrialists and oil barons.

Yet even as the play's production was under discussion in mid-September, Hitler prepared to invade Czechoslovakia, and Europe was teetering on the brink of actual war. Lydia, like most of Britain, felt sickened by her own ambivalence during the diplomatic stand-off that followed: 'it is dreadful one does not want it yet one must take a stand against Hitler'. And, like most of Britain, when Chamberlain sacrificed the Sudetenland for the sake of continuing peace she experienced a euphoric rush of relief. 'The state of nerves has been awful,' she wrote again to Florence. 'How wonderful Marg and Margaret must feel abut their beloved boys and millions of others. I say anything better than war.'[35]

The aftermath of the Munich peace was not, however, a good time to be premièring *On the Frontier*. The issues involved in Chamberlain's compromise were too complicated, too potentially shameful, to sit well with a pacifist satire, and Maynard confronted Isherwood over whether he really believed he could go ahead with it, in its current form, without feeling foolish. Yet the writers had already been required to make a number of edits (the national censor, with surprising deference to Nazi sensibilities, had ordered the most overt parallels with Hitler to be removed) and they refused to alter another word. With deep misgivings, Maynard allowed the play to go ahead, and by the middle of October Lydia was in rehearsal. She shared some of Maynard's doubts, whilst believing its satire to be 'good entertainment', and she relished being among an unusually talented team of collaborators, including Peters Pears, who sang and narrated, and the director, Rupert Doone. This was the same Doone whom she had encountered fourteen years ago as the pretty young man in Count Beaumont's hated ballet *Vogue* – another era, another infinitely more petty scale of upsets.

Inevitably, when *On the Frontier* was premièred on 14 November for a run of just six performances, it gained few admirers. T. S. Eliot wrote dismissively to Maynard, 'I'm afraid that Hitler is not the simpleton the audience make him out to be',[36] whilst the *Manchester Guardian* considered it 'too propagandist' to be credible.[37] The play received one further performance in London's Globe Theatre on 12 February 1939, yet while Lydia was loyally hopeful of success – 'there is something in that entertainment of ours ... I was thrilled again and again by that music'[38] – it had an even more savage mauling from the press. The *Observer*'s Ivor Brown judged the production to be irredeemably pretentious with its radical 'wise-crackery' and difficult music.[39]

It would be a small tragedy for Lydia that this clever, convoluted flop became the burial ground of her acting ambitions, the last professional stage production in which she would ever perform. But at the time events in the outside world were moving too fast and too dreadfully for her to focus on anything connected with her career. Only a month after Lydia, in the guise of Anna Vrodny, had argued passionately for peace, Hitler's forces seized the rest of Czechoslovakia and then trained their guns towards Danzig, with intentions that no one could ignore.

If all of Britain was focussed now on the likelihood of war, within Lydia's own lonely battle for Maynard's health there was a more immediate panic. After he had another serious attack of flu at the end of February, his condition had deteriorated with shocking speed, and on 1 March the sole entry in Lydia's journal had been a single terse line – 'Bad. Called Plesch.'[40]

Janos Plesch, the doctor whom she had called, was a new presence in their lives and one whom Lydia would several times regard as the sole bulwark between Maynard and death. A Hungarian Jew who had lived and worked in London since leaving Berlin in 1933, he possessed a ferocity of will against which Lydia's own dragon nursing paled, plus an unorthodox armoury of treatments that seemed to Maynard to fall somewhere between 'quack' and 'genius'. Some of these were in fact so brutal that Lydia (who referred to Plesch as the Ogre) feared her weakened husband could not survive them: three-hour 'freezing' sessions during which ice packs were placed on Maynard's chest, and a bizarre DIY form of shock treatment which involved Plesch bouncing vigorously on Maynard's bed while the patient himself lay supine, feeling, he claimed, 'like Desdemona'.

Most dramatically, Plesch also injected Maynard with a red dye called Prontosil, which had recently been discovered to possess anti-bacterial properties. He warned Lydia that there would be side effects: a temporary worsening of symptoms and also the bizarre possibility of Maynard turning bright pink. Yet this of all Plesch's maverick methods was the most effective. For a few days Maynard felt so ill that he was unable to stand (although he apparently did not change colour; Lydia's letters would surely have been full of a blushing Maynard if he had), then his strength suddenly rallied enough for him to return to teaching. By 15 August he was well enough to fly with Lydia to France for a therapeutic holiday in Vichy.

Given the rate at which tension was now escalating throughout Europe, with Hitler and Stalin positioning themselves against the democratic powers by their signing of the non-aggression pact on 23 August, it seems surreal that the two Keyneses should have spent a fortnight calmly cocooned in a health spa. Every morning Maynard underwent a regime of steam inhalations, massage and meditation in his 'cabin de luxe'; every evening he and Lydia sat in the restaurant of the Royal Palace Hotel, dining sedately as the resident orchestra played, as he told Florence, 'the sort of music father would like'.[41] Maynard remained supremely confident that Hitler was bluffing over his intentions to invade Poland, and even on 25 August he was sticking obstinately to his view that the situation was 'more like politics than war'.[42] It was denial on a quixotic scale. Around them the hotel staff were steadily melting away to join the French army. 'First our waiter went,' Maynard admitted to Richard Kahn, 'then the violinist, then the cellist, then both the pastry cooks, and the culmination was the departure of Monsieur Jacques, the nice and clever ... concierge around whom all the goings on in the hotel revolved.'[43] Lydia and

Maynard, left more or less unattended, had no choice but to leave as well, and it was in the sitting room at Tilton that they heard Chamberlain announce to the nation that Hitler's troops had crossed into Poland, and Britain was at war.

Chapter Nineteen

A TRANSATLANTIC WAR

My war work is looking after my husband and shopping.

LYDIA LOPOKOVA[1]

Lydia's assessment of her own war effort during the next six years was typically comic and typically evasive. With a shrug, a pout, a self-deprecating joke she liked to give the impression that she was immersed in the same anxious rituals as millions of other ordinary British wives. Yet in reality both her shopping and her nursing were done on a heroic scale. Between 1941 and 1946, Maynard was placed in charge of a Treasury task force jockeying with America for Britain's economic survival. The first stage of his mission was to extract more generous aid terms from Washington whilst Britain was actually fighting the war; the second was to carve out a British advantage in America's plans for the post-war reconstruction. Both were negotiations of extreme delicacy and urgency, requiring six protracted visits to the States. And as Maynard's fragile heart laboured under the strain, Lydia was with him at all times as nurse, companion and support. Travelling by his side, she would cover more miles during this war than she had during the last, sleeping in strange hotels, living among strangers, subsisting for months at a time with just a few traveller's possessions.

Most of Maynard's colleagues believed that without Lydia's terrier-like care, he could not have survived; that it was she who kept him alive for this most monumental task of his career. Yet it was also between the hours of tending to Maynard that Lydia waged a one-woman campaign against the rationing back home, raiding the American shops for basic goods that had become unobtainable in

London or Lewes, and identifying precious luxuries to raise the morale of her staff, family and friends. As Maynard reported to Florence with unfeigned awe, when Lydia shopped, she shopped for Britain: 'In the last week some two hundred objects purchased, including eighteen pairs of shoes, forty pairs of stockings, between twelve and twenty costumes, a new suit and a tie for me (the suit costing a thousand times as much as the tie), a new raincoat for me, a large trunkful of food, five safety razors, ten ferocious jewels, half a dozen head gear and in addition enough odds and ends to fix up a shop.'[2]

Obviously Lydia's duties were light, and her lifestyle privileged, in comparison to all that was endured by millions of others. Yet her experience of these years would still be one of disorienting and exhausting extremes as she was strung between the unreal plenty of life in America, and bombs and ration books back home; strung, too, between periods of draining anxiety about Maynard's health and dangerous hopes of his full recovery. However fortunate other people might think her, as she was swept off by boat or plane to the safety of New York and Washington, Lydia herself would feel little reprieve from a world overridden by the narrative of war.

Back in September 1939, when she and Maynard had listened to Chamberlain announce the failure of his 'long struggle to win peace', Lydia had felt almost calm. She allowed herself to shelter behind Maynard's conviction that Hitler could never successfully invade Britain, and she perhaps considered herself lucky that she had no sons of her own to worry about as the nation was mobilised to fight. Yet as the immediate crisis stretched into the blank weeks of the phoney war, Lydia became distracted and anxious. Once again she was to be divided from her family by a world war. And with Hitler and Stalin apparently determined to carve up Eastern Europe between them, and the atmosphere at home remaining one of pessimistic paralysis, her nerves became badly affected. Early in the New Year, when she attended the première of Ashton's ballet *Dante Sonata*, she wept at its apocalyptic vision of a world in chaos. She wept too at the knowledge that many of the men in the cast – including Fred Ashton – would soon be facing military call-up.

Lydia's morale wavered further in the face of Maynard's bullish determination to manoeuvre himself into a position of influence over the wartime economy. He had been typically outraged by the policies so far declared by the Treasury, a reflex package of defensive price controls and rationing, which seemed to him timid and unimaginative, and he had already come up with the alternative concept of a compulsory national saving scheme. To gain support for this he was writing a pamphlet, 'How to Pay for War', as well as networking with politicians and journalists in London, and Lydia found it increasingly hard to make Maynard accept that he was still a sick man. When the Woolfs visited at Christmas 1939, he was obediently lying on a sofa, with Lydia hovering watchfully by, 'a sort of fairy elf in her fur cap',[3] yet his conversation was as exasperatingly robust as it had ever been. 'A successful man,' Virginia noted, 'a farmer bursar a man of business he called himself applying for petrol, a heavy man with a thick moustache. A moralist. As interested in Patsy the black dog with the bald patch as in Europe.'[4] It was extraordinary to Virginia that while she agonised about the chances of her and Leonard being on Hitler's death list, Maynard was calmly lecturing her on matters like the effect of heat and cold on urine.

If the drawn-out uncertainties of the phoney war exaggerated these anxious cross-currents, their sudden termination in April 1940 detonated a bloody row. Lydia and Maynard were in Tilton when Hitler sent invading forces into Norway and Denmark, and as the British navy launched its counter-attack, news of the battle was the only topic of discussion when they drove over to visit Charleston. Maynard, professionally confident as always, was ready to assure the room that German defeat was inevitable, but Clive, always oversensitive to Maynard's hubris, irritably contradicted him. Clive's judgement was, in this matter, correct, yet his black prediction of German victory caused Lydia to become suddenly silly and overwrought. Quentin Bell, who was listening from the sidelines, recalled that she had violently derailed the discussion, shouting down Clive's arguments with a hysterical rant: 'You shall not say that you want the Germans to win. They shall not win and you MUST NOT say it.'[5] According to Quentin, this intervention had infuriated everyone, reducing the conversation to a 'shouting match', and he had been bewildered by Maynard's refusal to curb Lydia's disruption, like 'a fond parent whose spoilt child is smashing someone else's tea cups'.[6] What he could not appreciate, because Lydia so rarely spoke of it, was the strain she was suffering both from nursing Maynard and from worrying about her family in Russia. The scene Quentin had witnessed at Charleston was not so much an infantile tantrum as a cry for help.

The following weeks would be still more testing, as Hitler's forces swept on from Norway to attack Belgium, France and Holland; and Maynard, in Cambridge, suffered a minor but ominous heart attack. It happened early on 14 May, and Lydia, writing her medical diary from his bedside, noted with despair how the life seemed to have been leeched from him: 'very weak, bad under the eyes, blue lips, lies in pyjamas and rests with the lovely sun from the windows. It is very sad after 4 years illness.'[7] Three days later, just as Maynard seemed to be recovering, he was prostrated by a repeat episode, and Lydia mourned as much for herself as for him: 'I cried. I cannot stand the strain of illness and war.'[8]

Alone with her ice packs she struggled to stabilise Maynard, refusing to let him listen to the radio and its awful daily bulletins, even though he insisted on delivering his Cambridge lectures. But after Belgium and Holland fell and the defence of France began to cave in, Plesch arrived to deliver some more of his extreme aid. He prescribed a regime of icy baths, coupled with a ferociously restricted diet of coffee, tea, raw cabbage and sour oranges, and, once again, there seemed to be magic in his methods. On 14 June, the day that the Germans marched into Paris, Lydia noted a significant improvement in Maynard's condition. Almost perversely, as the war intensified, so his recovery seemed to keep pace with it.

When the Cambridge term was over, he and Lydia went down to Tilton and on 10 July 1940 were out in the fields to watch the first apocalyptic skirmishes in the battle for Britain. As German planes began their bombardment of the Channel ports, Tilton's familiar calm was shattered, the sky fractured by the glare of explosions and the raking arcs of anti-aircraft lights. Often it was possible to see the swastikas on the German planes, they flew so close above the house, yet Lydia seems to have stayed levelly philosophical. We hear all day bombs and anti aircraft guns,' she wrote to Florence, 'feel while it lasts a bit restless but English air men are wonderful and protect us. It is a strange war, we walk in the fields and yet we are right in the midst of it.'[9] She would only admit to being bothered when an air raid barred her from an urgent shopping trip to Lewes, or sent her down into one of the 'damp and smelly'[10] public shelters, which made her skin crawl. Lydia's main anxiety was still Maynard's heart, and what troubled her far more than the battles in the Sussex skies was the summons that came from Whitehall on 12 August, requesting her husband's services.

Chamberlain, a reluctant war leader, had been replaced by Winston Churchill, who, while having no sympathy for Maynard's peacetime theories, was impressed by his strategies for financing the war.* Determined to get him close to the Treasury, Churchill was now directing that Maynard be offered a special post, midway between consultant and policymaker, in which he would liaise with government on matters of trade, taxation, currency and foreign aid. This was an opportunity for Maynard to do serious work, and Lydia, faced with his 'abnormal will power',[11] had no way of preventing him from moving back up to London and accepting it.

Maynard had no thought of reconsidering even when the Germans began their systematic bombardment of the capital in September; and Lydia had felt never more helplessly sidelined as he insisted that she remain down at Tilton rather than joining him in Gordon Square. Scanning the skies anxiously for the Luftwaffe that flew with their deadly cargo towards her husband, Lydia found these weeks difficult to endure. Yet despite her terrors, Maynard seemed to walk with a charmed life through the Blitz that autumn. Rather than being weakened by his work at the Treasury, he derived a profound physical relief from having his pent-up intellectual energy put to use. Rather than being threatened by the devastation around him, he seemed almost braced by it. Whilst others would recall the horror of London's blazing skyline, the shock of seeing buildings pulverised to rubble, or the disgust of feeling ash sticking to their clothes and prickling their skin, Maynard breezily commented that the

*Churchill had admitted however that he should have listened to Maynard's arguments against going back on to the gold standard in 1925.

destruction was nothing that the building industry could not deal with in a few days, adding that the disruption to the transport system was very good for him, as he had not 'walked so much for years'.[12]

He attempted to reassure Lydia, too, with reports of the cheerful atmosphere prevailing at Gordon Square, which he shared during the week with Fred the chauffeur, the maid Mary, Mrs Stephens and Polly Hill, the daughter of his sister, Margaret, who, having followed Maynard into economics, was working with the Board of Trade. This little group ate hearty communal meals together and at night descended to the basement where, Maynard claimed, they all 'slept on bunks rather like life on board ship' and listened to the 'bombs whistling past'.[13]

Polly later recalled that she, personally, had not shared her uncle's insouciance – and on 18 September 1940 even his equanimity had wavered when a landmine burst opposite the house, shattering the windows and blasting the front door off its hinges. No one was injured, but a live bomb was discovered in the road the following morning, forcing them to evacuate the house until it was defused, and delaying essential repairs. Lydia tormented herself with images of the unattended house falling prey to thieves. But when she realised that the bomb damage would force Maynard home to sleep at Tilton, she recast the incident in a rosier light, foreseeing a temporary restoration of her own nursing regime: ice packs on the chest, early bedtimes and the chance to send him rested back to London with 'the beauty of the early country morning'.[14]

Maynard too accepted that Tilton was good for him, and from that point he took every chance to work in Sussex, receiving his papers from dispatch riders who roared impressively up the track on their motorbikes. In February 1941, when an army officer attempted to requisition Tilton for military use, Maynard reacted with pulverising anger, informing the authorities that the loss of his home would seriously interfere with his duties at the Treasury. No more attempts were made on Tilton. But if Lydia crowed over the fact that the 'possession of our bathrooms' had been repelled, the war inevitably encroached on her domestic life in a hundred other ways. Several of Tilton's staff had left, called up for military service or earning higher wages in munitions factories, and Lydia had to help Ruby, Auntie

Weller and Logan Thomson in the running of the house and estate. It was dreary work, for which she felt she had little talent. 'All seems so slow,'[15] she complained to Florence; and whilst she drew the line at washing up, the vegetable garden, care of the rabbits (raised for food) and the bedmaking all became part of her daily chores. Even shopping was no longer fun. Whilst Lydia scored a few gleefully unpatriotic successes in bribing the shopkeepers of Lewes to sell her extra rations, she mostly had to wait in line with everyone else. 'Charlestons to dinner,' she reported breathlessly to Florence, 'grabbed two chickens. No eggs anywhere in Lewes, vegetarian sausages instead.'[16]

But Lydia moaned only to Florence. She knew that others around her were having a very different war. Despite the campaign to get male ballet dancers exempted from military duty (to which Maynard had half-heartedly lent his support), Ashton and many of his colleagues had been called up for service, their careers, possibly their lives, under threat. Ninette de Valois and the remains of her troupe were now either dancing through London air raids, or touring around the country to cold, filthy, sometimes miserably unappreciative theatres. If the ballet was in tatters, so too was the property of many of the Keyneses' friends: Vanessa and Duncan lost their studios in German raids, and both of the Woolfs' two London houses (their new one in Mecklenburg Square and their old one in Tavistock Square) were badly bombed. The writer Peter Quennell, walking past the latter, was badly spooked by the sight of Duncan and Vanessa's exquisite paintwork flaking and exposed amidst the rubble.

Infinitely worse than the destruction of the Woolfs' property, however, was the impact of the war on Virginia's mental state. By the end of 1940 Britain's forces had become perilously overstretched, fighting at sea, in north-east Africa and in Greece, and Virginia became convinced that German invasion was close to inevitable. When Lydia and Maynard saw her on their annual Christmas visit to Rodmell, they found her badly depressed, reacting with bewildered resentment to Maynard's lofty prophecies of British victory and annoyed by Lydia's wifely endorsement of them. Unknown to them, she was also experiencing the terrifying early symptoms of mental breakdown.

Virginia had been flayed by madness before, and as she again heard sinister voices twittering in her head and sensed black horrors, she felt unable to endure the experience a second time. She made private, desperate attempts to starve herself to death, but when Leonard intervened, she waited for a morning when he was busy writing in his study and walked into the River Ouse with a heavy stone in her pocket, allowing the powerful currents to drag her down. The next day, 29 March 1941, Maynard telephoned unwittingly to invite the Woolfs over for tea and was stricken by news of her suicide. He and Virginia had argued, admired and watched each other for over three decades; however complicated their relationship might have been, it had revolved around a core of respect and love.

Lydia mourned, too. She had enjoyed Virginia for her wit and gaiety, and had recognised her rarefied intelligence. 'Virginia belongs to a very small chiselled top,'[17] she had concluded, and reading *The Years* had commented wonderingly, 'Extraordinary how she co-ordinates the words. When she has nothing to say she goes back to rain or blizzard next time she will mention sun spots or an owl's liquid voice.'[18] Even while she had winced at Virginia's erratic cruelties, she had understood something of the peculiar, exacting brilliance that had driven her to them – and reading through Virginia's posthumously published letters would exclaim, 'Oh! How intelligent she was. I see now how terribly stupid she must have thought me.'[19] Yet Lydia's real emotions were for 'wonderful patient'[20] Leonard. She knew from her own years of nursing what anxieties he must have endured as he had tried to keep his wife safe. And whilst Virginia's farewell note had assured Leonard, 'No one could have done more than you have done. Please believe that',[21] Lydia knew the anguish he would be experiencing, having failed.

In just over a month's time, however, Lydia and Maynard would be thousands of miles away from such tragedies, and thousands of miles away from blackouts, rationing and bombs. On 1 May, Maynard was sent on his first mission to Washington to negotiate aid, and he and Lydia were about to have their first dislocating experience of living in a city still innocent of war.

The political background to this trip was the continuing refusal by America to engage directly with the fight against Hitler. Despite

Maynard's sanguine forecast that Roosevelt would commit his country to the Allied cause, the US had not only stuck to its position of neutrality, but had been unexpectedly resistant to offering aid. By 1941 this policy had brought Britain close to its limits. Without a massively subsidised injection of American food and military equipment, the UK could not physically sustain the war, and it was this impasse that had forced Churchill to deliver his historic plea to Roosevelt: that if America would not go to war against Hitler, it should 'give us the tools so we can finish the job'.

Washington was not, in reality, as indifferent to Britain's plight as official policy indicated. Whilst hardline isolationists continued to insist that this was a European war, for which no American blood should be spilled nor American dollars squandered, the alarming advances made by Hitler's forces during 1940 had prompted a less belligerent position of neutrality in Washington, and in March 1941 a compromise aid package was agreed. Under the new Lend-Lease Act, America proposed to give Britain and its allies the tools that they so urgently required – $50 billion in total by the end of the war – but its terms dictated that these would be offered not as free aid, merely as a loan. Debts were to be repaid, with interest, after the war; and to further protect American interests there were to be strict conditions attached while the Lend-Lease Deal was in force, requiring the limitation of Britain's export trade, the running down of its gold and dollar reserves and the liquidation of its assets in America.

These were harsh terms, designed not only to depress the British economy, but also to seriously impede its recovery after the war. As Maynard's biographer Robert Skidelsky starkly summarises it, Britain had to mortgage its economic future in order to survive.[22] Yet the alternative was suing for peace with Hitler, and Churchill felt he had little recourse but to accept the Americans' deal, hoping all the while to ameliorate the worst of its terms. A team of officials was thus sent from Whitehall to Washington to argue Britain's case, and it was Maynard, with his juggernaut powers of argument, who was deputed to lead it.

Lydia felt wretchedly ambivalent about this appointment. She understood enough of what was at stake to anticipate the strain that it would impose on Maynard's system. On the other hand, a brief visit to Gordon Square in the middle of April made her see the advantage of getting him away to the safety of America. 'A night of terror,' she reported aghast to Florence; 'the raid lasted 7 hours we went into the cellars drank wine and crouched towards each other then looked on the square all ablaze as in the daylight. The next morning I never saw so much glass all over London. It took me 45 minutes to get to Victoria station in a taxi.'[23]

After over a year of domestic drudgery at Tilton, Lydia was also more ready than she cared to admit to find America attractive, and her growing anticipation of the adventure was sharpened by the fact that in order to avoid German U-boats, the Treasury party were to travel the whole journey by plane. Lydia had flown only once before – across the Channel to Vichy in the summer of 1939 – and the flying boat that was to take them on the first European leg of the journey, from Poole to Lisbon, intrigued her immensely. When the plane was parked on dry land, its swollen-bellied hold and boxy wings looked dangerously cumbersome. Yet as Lydia discovered on the morning of 1 May, it was a perfectly adapted flying machine, swiftly gathering speed across the water and, up in the air, offering its passengers 'perfect travelling better than the train so steady'.[24]

Unshaken and exhilarated, the party arrived at 7 p.m. to be met by 'dark Portuguese sailors in white British Airways uniforms' and driven into a city that was almost bewilderingly throbbing with light, colour and activity. Lisbon was far from the grim battlefield of revolution that Lydia had last encountered, a boom town, a cosmopolitan playground crowded with people attempting to escape Europe for the safety of America. The luxurious conditions enjoyed by the wealthiest of these refugees, as they waited for passages to become available, struck Lydia as a scandalous contrast to all that the British were enduring at home. But she was unable to resist the succulence of the huge unrationed meals that were served up to them at the Estoril Hotel, eating so greedily during her first day that she made herself sick and had to starve herself for twenty-four hours before she could 'face the world' again.[25]

On Sunday morning she and Maynard's team embarked on the next leg of their journey, aboard an American Clipper. Their accommodation was handsome, with sleeping berths, a separate dining room and even, Lydia boasted, 'a delicious cool drawing room'.[26] But the journey had to be broken twice, including a fractious change of planes in the Azores, and by the time the party arrived in New York, five days later, air travel had lost much of its appeal. Tired and claustrophobic, they were in no mood for the crush of journalists waiting to meet them. Maynard, however, had to go straight into meetings to be primed for the Washington mission ahead. Lydia, unable to persuade him to take proper rest, spent a day walking the Manhattan streets, so familiar to her, yet so disorienting after London in their busy unguarded normality and unrationed plenty.

Even greater opulence awaited when she and the team travelled to Washington and were installed among the sweeping lawns, lavishly appointed suites and marble-floored corridors of the Mayflower Hotel. Lydia had stayed here happily back in 1934, yet within days her palatial accommodation began to feel more like a prison. Maynard had told his mother that Lydia had agreed to the Washington trip only on condition that he would talk no more than was necessary, and that he remained fully obedient to her regime. But the punishing schedule at Washington was beyond her legislation, and Lydia could only watch helplessly as Maynard began his days with early-morning dictation, argued through twelve hours of meetings and attended long formal dinners in the evenings. He had not lost his schoolboy passion for lists and worked out that within the first five weeks of their Washington trip he had attended forty-seven official meals, including a sixteen-course Chinese dinner for his birthday. Lydia had 'trembled' for his digestion but had eaten voraciously herself, raving to Florence afterwards about the shark's fin soup and soya pastry, and her relief that there were 'no snake or cucoo nests that one reads about'.[27]

Nor was it just the schedule that imposed a strain on Maynard; a profound conflict of culture and philosophy also bedevilled these Anglo-American negotiations. Maynard had been warned that Henry Morgenthau, the US Treasury Secretary, was a tough, irritable man, instinctively suspicious of the British (who still had unpaid debts to America from the First World War). Even so, Maynard had gone into his first Washington meeting just as he would a Cambridge lecture or a Whitehall conference, in the full blaze of his intellectual arrogance. As he had delivered his opinions with a dazzle of esoteric reference and fine detail, the Americans had simply thought he was showing off, and one grumpy official advised him afterwards that in future he should keep his arguments short and to the point.

The discussions made slow progress, and, as the two sides stalled, froze and changed tack, Lydia struggled to keep Maynard on an even keel. While he was in meetings she had her own daily rituals to occupy her: a quick breakfast with the newspapers and her usual 'inhalation'[28] of scalding coffee, followed by letter writing, morning exercises, raids on the Washington shops and scavenging trips around the hotel. During the war years Lydia would purloin hundreds of complimentary toiletry items and thousands of packets of sugar. Yet every minute of the day she still had to be alert to Maynard's needs, and she wasted tedious hours waiting for him to come out of meetings, so that she could monitor his condition, decide whether he was due a rest and, with his diary in her hand, offer to rearrange meetings or deliver apologies for cancellations.

Even on the rare occasions that Lydia was able to squirrel Maynard away for a private meal, she was frequently hijacked by some importunate Washington official. One particularly tenacious man who had buttonholed Maynard at lunch had used his wife to distract Lydia with an interminable anecdote about some elephants she had encountered in Africa. When this tedious woman had moved on to the subject of zebras, Lydia's patience had snapped and, unable to control the 'signs of despair' on her face, she had simply marched Maynard away.[29]

Maynard himself was fully aware how zealously he was guarded, telling his mother, 'I shouldn't have survived without Lydia who provides constant rest, discipline and comfort.'[30] But he also benefited more than he realised from Lydia's charm when she accompanied him to official dinners and parties. Initially neither the British nor the Americans in Washington had known what to make of her. Lord Halifax, the coolly patrician British ambassador, wrote in his diary, 'An odder little person I never saw. I believe she used to be in the Russian ballet – very fresh and sprightly and after an initial shock I rather liked her.'[31] Most, however, came to rather love Lydia, finding her chatter, Russian graces and eccentricities a welcome emollient to Maynard's intimidating, and very English, cleverness. Even the irascible Morgenthau unbent in her company, and Lydia, having been seated next to him at dinner, concluded to Maynard afterwards that she thought him essentially 'a good man [who] will do you no harm on *purpose*'.[32] Maynard set so much store by Lydia's intuitions that he cabled her comments back to London.

The economist Roy Harrod, who would be part of Maynard's team during subsequent trips, claimed that Lydia became a minor legend in Washington:

> Her boundless gaiety, her manifest devotion, her resourcefulness in providing comfort on the most unpromising occasions with all sorts of queer contrivances, her shopping expeditions, her infinite sweetness with all his associates, her quips and sallies, unconventional and personal but always acceptable, suffused with some unique quality of simplicity and thereby of dignity, endeared her to American hearts. To be a friend of the great British economist – that was something to be proud of, but to be a friend of Lydia, – that was the supreme glory.[33]

Harrod's view was reiterated by others, yet the daily reality of Lydia's conquest of Washington must have been a great deal more lonely. Although she and Maynard had personal friends in America, including the political commentator Walter Lippmann and his wife, and although Margaret and Geoffrey's son Quentin Keynes was working in the embassy as a PA, Lydia had no daily companion with whom to confide her concerns over Maynard, nor to leaven the society of the driven, and mostly rather dull, Washington–Whitehall teams. The middle of June also brought fresh worries about her family as, the Soviet–German alliance having now dissolved, Hitler launched his first attacks on Russia. Lydia had been able to maintain sporadic correspondence with home and already the news had been disturbing: Evgenia was no longer performing; Fedor was not yet back in Leningrad; and while Andrei continued to dance at the Kirov, he was suffering from some debilitating medical condition, unspecified in the letters. Karlusha, aged eighty-one, was now extremely frail, and Lydia believed that she could not survive much more, writing in distress to Florence, 'my poor mother my heart aches for her'.[34] Six months later her fears would intensify, as German troops reached the outskirts of Leningrad and imposed a state of siege. With the city's food stocks destroyed by bombing raids, and a military blockade preventing all but a trickle of fresh produce coming through, the population of Lydia's former home would be starving to death in their thousands.

Lydia, closeted in a luxury that was becoming daily more oppressive to her, had little to distract her from the collective tedium and her own anxiety. Washington became 'just a negation of life', as the temperature and humidity soared, and whilst her morale improved with the move to an air-conditioned suite, the mere delivery of a letter from Florence, bringing with it a 'lovely sniff of England', made her pine for home.[35] Escape came finally at the end of July. The US Treasury was still trying to attach strict conditions to the Lend-Lease Deal (to Maynard's apoplectic fury, there had been a suggestion that the UK be limited to exporting only 'specialities' such as whisky and Harris tweed), but some significant concessions had been won, including the dropping of Washington's stipulation that London be barred from holding gold and dollar reserves while the Deal was in force.

During the slow ocean crossing back to England, Maynard seemed fairly satisfied with his results and less worn down than Lydia had feared. When he returned to the Treasury, ready to continue the skirmishes with Washington by letter, he also appeared to his colleagues to be functioning at surprising strength. As Wilfred Eady observed, in the autumn of 1941, illness seemed only to magnify his charisma: 'Tall and big-framed he walked through the Treasury in slow processional dignity. Above his dark clothes, the ivory pallor of his face and the fine dark blue eyes steady and reflective, or filling with amusement, had often the effect of a light moving.'[36]

Lydia did not, however, relax her guard and, now that there appeared to be a lull in German raids over London, she remained in Gordon Square, forcing on to Maynard as stern a regime of rest and diet as she could manage. After the expensive glossiness of Washington, a winter in London may have seemed a grey prospect but as Lydia queued in the shops for rations and attended to the laundry, she was busy, cheerful, even thriving. She now carried a shopping bag wherever she went, in readiness for bearing home some chance item of booty, and she had happily abandoned all pretence of fashion. Lydia did not belong to the breed of gallant wartime women who, in the absence of silk or nylon stockings, drew seams up the backs of their bare legs. The following year she would be spotted by John Gielgud 'trudging up Shaftsbury Avenue ... in a strange balaclava helmet, very thick stockings and oddly bundled up';[37] and by the writer Eddie Marsh, who could scarcely credit that this 'odd little figure in a fur-lined hood, carrying a basket full of empty wine bottles', had once been London's favourite ballerina.[38] On the other hand, the dancer Leo Kersley, who used to encounter Lydia in a Bloomsbury vegetarian store, claimed that her charm needed no accessories and that her effect on men could still be transforming: 'The shopkeeper of that store was the surliest sod on earth, except with Lydia. He adored her, and he was always smiling and chatting with her. Everyone was like that around her.'[39]

It was evidently a relief for Lydia to be back in her own territory and with her own friends. Florrie was regularly in town doing volunteer work: 'Her hands are cracked with wash up,' noted Lydia, 'but what a sport.'[40] Ninette, too, came to the kitchen of Gordon Square, sharing picnic meals and hair-raising gossip about her war-tattered company, now renamed Sadler's Wells Ballet. There were also regular weekends in Cambridge, where Maynard was keeping up a skeleton schedule of academic duties. The town had held on to its pre-war beauty despite a noisy influx of troops and military personnel, and Lydia revelled in having her days free of queues as she and Maynard took most of their meals at the Arts Theatre restaurant or at Harvey Road. Here the tradition of Sunday lunch was still faithfully observed, but the massed ranks of Keynes relatives and the ponderous family gossip belonged to the past. Neville, soon to turn ninety, had withdrawn serenely into his hobbies – his stamp collection, his bridge and his wine cellar – whilst eighty-year-old Florence seemed to become more vigorously adventurous every year; her contribution to the war effort was to take on the care of unmarried mothers.

Very occasionally there were also 'sublime' days in Tilton, where Maynard relaxed enough to read an Agatha Christie novel and Lydia refused to do any chores. Then came the climactic events of 7 December, when the Japanese bombed Pearl Harbor and the Americans were forced into the war. For a very brief moment Lydia dared to hope that relaxation periods in Sussex might become more frequent, for it had been supposed at the Treasury that if ever America became militarily allied to Britain, the more crippling terms and conditions attached to the Lend-Lease Deal would be rescinded – in which case the heaviest burdens attached to Maynard's own post would be lifted. However, Washington maintained a very different perspective and, far from ceding any economic ground after joining the war, Roosevelt's government was bent on enlarging the scope of its own advantages. Assuming (rightly) that it would eventually be leading the Allies to victory, Washington lost no time in formulating plans for how it would move on to dominate the peace.

At the centre of its plans was the creation of a World Bank and an International Monetary Fund, which would replace the discredited gold standard as a basis for fixing global exchange rates and also set up the conditions for post-war free trade. Britain in theory believed in the necessity of both institutions – Maynard had already been working on his own blueprint for similar plans. The issue was to prevent Washington having total control over their foundation, which if unchallenged would assure America's status as the post-war economic superpower and secure the effective demise of Britain and its empire. As Maynard and his Treasury team were driven into another hectic phase of planning, angling for a dialogue with Washington about its proposed 'pax Americana', there would be no time for Agatha Christie down at Tilton.

Still, there were positive repercussions for Lydia as they were forced back to London almost full time. German air raids had remained intermittent, allowing some semblance of daily normality to return, and Maynard's duties involved one new post that Lydia could directly share with him. In April 1942 he was invited to become chairman of the wartime arts organisation CEMA (Council for the Encouragement of Music and the Arts), and even though Lydia herself had no official role in the council, the association had for her something of a nostalgic return to the old Camargo days. Board meetings were held in Gordon Square, where, along with dispensing tea and carrots to Maynard's colleagues (the latter to sharpen their eyesight during blackouts), Lydia was deferentially consulted when any of the discussion related to ballet. She also acted as an unofficial mediator between Maynard and the younger committee members, who were inclined to be unnerved by his brilliance and bullying tactics. CEMA's secretary, Mary Glasgow, claimed that it took her three years to get over her 'paralysing awe'[41] of him.

Maynard's health continued to hold and by the autumn of 1942 Lydia dared to risk some work of her own. She had been invited to write and present a radio programme on the life of her former mentor, Mikhail Fokine. Then, in early 1943, in the most flattering opportunity of her radio career, she was cast alongside Leslie Banks and Celia Johnson in an eight-part dramatisation of Tolstoy's *War and Peace*. Lydia's role was the Female Narrator, and a rehearsal photo, which shows her intent at the microphone, conveys the enthusiasm with which she reconnected with her former acting life. It was a precious throwback to her pre-war self, to a time when her energies were not exhausted in the service of Maynard's care, to a time when she was regarded for her own talent, not for her professional abilities as a wife and nurse.

But another photograph of the entire cast emphasised how long it had been since Lydia had bothered with the image of a leading lady. Dressed in a shapeless coat, with two full shopping baskets stowed by her side, she appeared more like a favoured charlady who had been invited in for the shot. And if Lydia aged fifty-one could no longer be bothered to dress the part of an actor, there was even less about this photograph to suggest the other new role with which she had recently been invested.

When Maynard's name had appeared in the King's Birthday Honours List, in June 1942, Lydia's own concomitant elevation to the British peerage had left her fairly unmoved. She was proud for Maynard, of course, and glad for Florence and Neville, who saw this barony as the crowning achievement for their son. Yet while she diligently used her new title in formal correspondence, it made no positive difference to her life, and being Lady Keynes of Tilton sometimes felt like a liability. She did not fully understand the

Lydia rehearsing *War and Peace* for BBC radio, 1941

honours system, and in 1955, when Maynard's brother, Geoffrey, was knighted, she fretted over whether she should relinquish her title, in order to avoid confusion with her sister-in-law, Margaret. And back in 1942 among the 'Bloomsberries' Lydia knew that Maynard's barony could only become another source of friction. Gongs and decorations were despised among the circle's remaining membership, and when she and Maynard had first gone to Charleston with their new titles, Lydia had served herself up for a scolding, groaning comically to Clive, Vanessa and Duncan, 'O-ah we come to be mocked.'[42]

Nor was a title the best calling card for Maynard when, in September 1943, America finally invited Britain to submit its ideas for the future World Bank and International Monetary Fund. Harry Dexter White, the Washington economist with whom Maynard would be dealing, was a hardline Democrat with a strong political interest in the Soviet Union. If White already had little natural sympathy for the British, he would have even less for a delegation headed by a British lord. During the month in which the two men debated in Washington, the clash was frequently a titanic stand-off in styles and personalities. White found Maynard a classic English snob, ironically referring to him as 'your majesty', whilst Maynard in return found White to be a typically overbearing American, with a rasping voice, oppressive manner and what he judged a 'loony' disdain for 'the rules of civilised intercourse'.[43] The issues over which they joined battle were equally titanic as they debated rival proposals for the constitutions of the Bank and the Monetary Fund, and the rival advantages that would accrue to each of their governments within the hierarchy of participating nations.

Once more it was Lydia's job to force the temperature down, keeping Maynard calm in the privacy of their hotel suite and maintaining her now-reliable charm assault in public. One of the British team, James Meade, observed that in each other's company the two Keyneses appeared to be a 'perfect couple', combining the 'best qualities of a devoted Darby and Joan with the airs and graces of intellectualism and the arts'. During the train journey from New York to Washington he had watched fascinated as Lydia and Maynard had entertained themselves, and the rest of the carriage, with 'a tremendous discussion on modern painting', which Lydia had concluded by 'singing the *Casse-Noisette* music at the top of her voice and dancing it with her hands'.[44]

By the end of the month, Maynard had found some kind of shared language with White, and could report to Florence that 'London and Washington really are trying to make good economic bricks for the world however hopelessly difficult the political problems may be.'[45] Most importantly, he had won a crucial concession. The following June, when representatives from forty-four countries were assembled at Bretton Woods in New Hampshire to begin the historic work of launching the IMF and World Bank, Maynard had secured for himself, and Britain, the second most important seat at the conference table.

Lydia of course was accompanying him, and when they arrived at the Mount Washington Hotel, where the conference was to be held, she considered herself lucky to be there. The previous six months had been the bleakest of the war, especially for her. Although the siege of

Leningrad had been lifted in early 1944, neither her mother nor her sister had survived – Karlusha dying in the winter of 1942 and Evgenia the following year. Lydia, when she had finally heard, seems to have dealt with her grief with typical secrecy and stoicism. She did not express it in her correspondence with Florence, nor even commit it to her diary. If she felt bereft, exiled from home all over again, she may also have felt that death had become too commonplace a tragedy to make a fuss. The war was now in its fifth year and the fighting spirit of the nation as a whole was shrinking. Rationing was biting hard and Britain had shivered through the winter of 1943–4 with drastic shortages of hot water and fuel. When the summer finally came it had only brought more misery – the unleashing of Germany's latest terror tactic, the V1 bombs, which began dropping over London in early June.

Lydia had never been so relieved to escape the city, nor so receptive to the luxury that was awaiting her in America. The conference hotel at Bretton Woods was built in the style of a Spanish Renaissance palace with red-tiled turrets and classic white stucco. Yet it boasted every modern American amenity – an indoor swimming pool, a Tiffany glass conservatory, a palm court orchestra and a wooden cocktail veranda – and it was set in a landscape of tranquil, spacious beauty. Lydia's war-ragged nerves were stilled as she looked out of her window over vistas of woods and meadows, fringed by a distant range of mountains, and momentarily she even wondered whether this trip might not be good for Maynard. Although there had been signs over the winter that his strength was again failing, Maynard had assured her that this conference would not be especially gruelling. Harry White, realising that he needed British support to secure his control of the proceedings, had been lending an increasingly co-operative ear to the Treasury's proposals, so co-operative, Maynard was boasting, that the two of them had already settled most of the conference business between them, and there would be little for the 'monkeys' from the rest of the participating nations to argue about.

But Lydia's optimism was soon to buckle under the onslaught of 730 disputative delegates and their clerical staff. The Mount Washington had not been designed to accommodate such an enormous crowd. 'The taps run all day, the windows do not close or open, the pipes mend and unmend and no one can get anywhere,' she fussed to Florence.[46] Nor were the 'monkeys' anywhere near as compliant as Maynard had promised.* The workload turned out to be insane, with meetings and negotiations lasting till three in the morning, and Maynard, somewhere in the middle of it, was submerged. White had assigned him control of the commission for setting up the World Bank, and this position, coupled with the general assumption that he enjoyed uniquely privileged access to White, meant that he was hounded by delegates at every free moment, all angling to snatch a private conversation with him.

Lydia too felt herself hounded: 'I get out of temper waiting while everybody else asks me where [Maynard] is to be found,'[47] she grumbled by post to Florence. And while she found some distractions of her own, working as unofficial translator for some of the Russian delegates, she felt no temptation to seek consolation with the wives of the other British delegates, who, also invited to Bretton Woods, had united in a somewhat frosty disdain against her. An article that Florence had read back home in the *Daily Herald*, which gave 'an amazing account of how you and your shopping bag are known to all the nations and how great is your popularity',[48] reflected more the attitude of the male delegates towards Lydia than that of their wives. The British women regarded her uninhibited behaviour and slack dress codes as vaguely unpatriotic and vaguely unwomanly. Kathleen Lee, who was in Bretton Woods with her husband, the Treasury delegate Frank Lee, recalled that Lydia had invited a few of the wives into the Keyneses' suite, where they had been shocked by the chaos inside, with drying socks and underwear (washed by Lydia in the basin) hanging all over the radiators. These were hardly the standards expected from a Treasury wife, let alone a Lady. But the American

*All nations were required to pay into the IMF according to their capacity, but debates raged over the setting of those capacities and the currency in which payments would be made. Gold-rich America wanted a large proportion paid in gold – which put countries like Britain at a disadvantage. Compounding the dispute, all the highest-paying nations would be rewarded by membership of the Security Council of the new United Nations. Bretton Woods was determining the political as well as the financial hierarchy of the post-war world.

Lydia at Bretton Woods, 1944

wives did not care for Lydia much more. Mrs Morgenthau, who was staying in the suite next door, had plenty to say to her female compatriots about the thumps that came through the wall during Lady Keynes's late-night practice sessions.

Irritation and exhaustion seethed with increasing intensity until the conference finally wound up on 22 July. Maynard, at least, believed that the effort had been justified, for while Washington had secured greater control over the World Bank and IMF than he had desired, America was paying for that control with generous aid to other nations. He was also willing to predict that when the final deals were eventually hammered out, Bretton Woods could offer real chances for post-war economic recovery and peace. This enthusiasm was shared by the rest of the British delegation, who regarded Maynard himself as the visionary force driving the outcome. Wilfred Eady recalled that at their closing session 'the whole meeting spontaneously stood up and waited, silent, until Maynard had taken his place'. Afterwards they serenaded his exit with 'For he's a jolly good fellow'.[49]

Physically, however, Maynard was looking anything but jolly, for his health was now in a far worse state than even Lydia feared. Bacteria remained lodged in his heart valves, untreatable by the sulphur drugs prescribed by Plesch, and the blocked coronary artery was now a ticking time bomb in his struggling system. There had been a bad episode back in March when a return of the stabbing chest pains forced him to rest for a month, and in Bretton Woods, despite Lydia's application of ice packs and her enforcement of silent rest, he had suffered a minor collapse while running upstairs to catch a late meeting. His colleague Lionel Robbins had noted apprehensively in his diary that it now seemed to be 'a race between the exhaustion of his [Maynard's] powers and the termination of the conference',[50] and Lydia herself had been incoherent with relief at getting her pale, bowed husband out of Bretton Woods alive: 'What relief to be away,' she had gabbled to Florence. 'I do not scream or hysteria or lunatic asylum any more.'[51]

Maynard did in fact have another immediate mission to deal with: negotiating an increase in the Canadians' Mutual Aid agreement with Britain. But he had promised that this would be straightforward, and, as they were chauffeured north to Montreal to catch the flight to Ottawa, the serene, sunlit landscape seemed to irradiate Lydia's relief. By the time they eventually landed she was feeling not only light-hearted but irresponsible, and the novelty of the emotion inclined her suddenly towards exhibitionist mischief. An imposing welcome committee had been lined up to greet Lord and Lady Keynes – the High Commissioner, Malcolm MacDonald, flanked by two rows of senior officials – and as Lydia had descended from the plane, still wrapped in her fur coat against the cold of the flight, she may (apart from her sturdy shopping bag) have looked the part of a great statesman's consort. Yet as MacDonald later described the scene, the protocol of the reception had shattered in one outrageous instant when Lydia, despite never having met him before, threw her arms around him, exclaiming, 'Oh my dear High commissar, how are you. I dreamed zat I was lying in bed and zat you were lying in my arms.'[52]

The chorus of officials, solemnly uniformed in black jackets and pinstriped trousers, strove to keep their faces straight at this extraordinary revelation. If MacDonald had been a patrician snob like Lord Halifax, the moment could have been excruciating, but Lydia had chosen her victim well. The High Commissioner was a dedicated ballet fan and one of his most prized memories had been sitting in the gallery at the Alhambra Theatre to watch Lydia in Diaghilev's *The Sleeping Princess*. Far from being offended, MacDonald had barely been able to conceal his delight in her greeting, nor his fervent hope that 'in the hush of the early morning the whole population of Ottawa had overheard'.

Egged on by her success with MacDonald, Lydia seems to have been unable to stop herself showing off. The first meeting with Maynard had been delayed, because the key to the Treasury box, containing his papers, had been mislaid; but then, according to a goggle-eyed MacDonald, Lydia had appeared at the door wearing 'nothing but a short white chemise (presumably with a pair of brief drawers below) which hung flimsily round her otherwise bare body'. The memory of this moment had stayed vivid to him decades later:

> In that state of near nudity she stood in apologetic manner, casting a half-guilty, half-mischievous look at Keynes ... 'Oh Maynard darling I am so sorry. You did give me ze key and I forgot zat I hid it for safety between my little bosoms.' At that she clutched in her hands a ribbon hanging round her neck and as she lifted it over her head raised from between her breasts – which as far as we could detect were not quite so small as she suggested – the lost article. She blew him a kiss, turned in a ballerina's pirouette on her toes, glided through the door and closed it behind her.[53]

Lydia had spent so much of the last five years playing the worried nurse and careful spouse that it may have been an irresistible temptation to bring out the roles of her youth – childish ingénue, sexy bohemian, exotic foreigner. But she may also have been infected by the unexpectedly hedonistic style of this Ottawa interlude. Their hotel, the Chateau Laurier, was magnificent (the Keyneses' suite had nine rooms, decorated in superb Moorish detail); the food was unstinting; and, because Maynard was only working half-days, Lydia was able to arrange with MacDonald a timetable of excursions and picnics. The High Commissioner, 'wearing often his scotch kilt', earned Lydia's lifelong devotion by teaching her to swim properly. 'At first I was shy of the water but in the end I brought a bathing suit and swam like a dog in a smart pool of a country club.'[54] The only constraint on their holiday mood was the heat, which on most days blistered at over 100 degrees. It was in Ottawa that the legend arose of Lydia trying to find some relief inside the huge icebox in their hotel suite. Maynard swore to MacDonald that he saw her squeeze into it 'like Alice in Wonderland disappearing down the White Rabbit's tunnel'. Lydia apparently 'laughed at his tale but ... did not either confirm or deny it'.[55]

If Ottawa released Lydia's *shtoochki*-playing demons, they were reluctant to be confined again when, less than a month after returning to London, she and Maynard were back in Washington for more negotiations over the repayment of Britain's Lend-Lease debts. Whilst Lydia welcomed the 'luxe' of their penthouse suite at the Salter, America now spelled for her a predictable misery of tedium and worry, and as Isaiah Berlin, who was employed at the British Embassy, discovered to his cost, she was finding it increasingly difficult to control her frustration.

Their two-month visit coincided with the presidential election and a party was organised at the embassy to listen to the results. It was a long evening and, as Lydia grew restless, she began probing Berlin for his opinions on various Washington personalities. Maynard gently shushed her, but Lydia paid no attention and went on to quiz Berlin loudly about what he thought of Lord Halifax – who was sitting barely a yard away. Berlin recalled that in his strangled embarrassment he had only been able to 'produce a neighing sound'. But into the ensuing silence, during which 'nobody save the radio uttered a word', Lydia delivered her own airy verdict: that Halifax was 'quite popular' now but had not 'always' been so. Maynard, apparently unperturbed, had 'stared straight in front of him with a faint smile on his lips'. Halifax, while doing his best to conceal his mortification, had rapidly left the party.[56]

Childish, rude Lydia. Her only defence was the anxiety that she was now suffering as negotiations between Maynard and Morgenthau became mired in stalemate. So concerned was she about the effect on Maynard's heart that at one point she tried to intervene on her husband's behalf. The story flew around Washington that Lydia had bearded the Treasury Secretary in his office and pleaded in her most wheedling, ingenuous manner: 'Mr Morgenthau, *Maynar'* cannot sleep at night. He says he wants sixpence from you: only sixpence more. Why Mr Morgenthau why cannot you give *Maynar'* sixpence.'[57] It was also understood that Morgenthau had not only promised Lydia the sixpence but congratulated her on being one of the most skilled negotiators with whom he had ever had to deal.

Despite Lydia's diplomacy, the agreement with which Maynard came away was still below his expectations, with minimal concessions on the terms of Britain's debt repayments and insufficient compromise on the restrictions imposed on its export trade. Months of hard labour still faced him at the Treasury, as he attempted to limit the damage, and it was clear that his reserves were badly depleted. Ever since his collapse the previous March, his health had been veering between bouts of febrile nervous energy and bouts of total exhaustion. Lydia was not sure how much more stress his system could take.

The war at least was ending. No written comment survives from either Lydia or Maynard about the crowds in the streets, the streamers, the speeches and the boozy singing that followed German surrender, on 7 May 1945. But a few days later they held a party of their own down at Tilton, with beer, dancing and Bloomsbury theatricals: a staged trial of Hitler, who was represented by a grotesque straw guy. The Führer was examined by Maynard and Quentin as judge and prosecution witness respectively, then defended by Duncan in a hilarious monologue of mangled Germanic English. Finally he was taken by torchlight procession to be burned on a bonfire. 'It was', Vanessa reported to her daughter Angelica, 'a most lovely sight.'[58]

But Maynard still had in front of him the most dispiriting mission of his war career. Roosevelt had died of a stroke in April and his successor, Harry Truman, having taken the apocalyptic decision to end the war by dropping the atom bomb on Japan, had simultaneously decreed the termination of America's wartime alliances. Without warning, the Lend-Lease Deal came to an end on 19 August and with it all subsidised exports of food and machinery. For Britain, whose industry and agriculture were only just gearing up to peacetime operations, this was a disastrous blow. Just as bad were demands from America that Britain immediately begin repaying the money it owed. After five draining years of war this was impossible, and once again it devolved to Maynard and his team to negotiate with Washington for clemency – a gift of free money to tide them over these first difficult years or, at the very least, an extra, interest-free loan.

This time, however, the Treasury team went miserably armed. Now that the war was over, there was no longer any military justification for claiming American aid; now that a new administration was in place there were no friends or allies in Washington to help plead their cause. Maynard was being pitted against hostile strangers, and in the autumn of 1945 he did not remotely look the part of a warrior. Although it had been only five years since his first encounter with Washington, the strain of the intervening battles had left him an old man – his sixty-two-year-old body thin and frail, his hair white, his eyesight faltering behind thick glasses.

Lydia had felt serious alarm when she had packed their trunks, and although her letters to Florence kept up a cheerful commentary about the exhilaratingly crisp autumn weather, the delights of eating red meat and cream, and the hotel's generous provision of complimentary toiletries (all waiting to be smuggled back to London and Tilton), it was clear that Maynard was going to suffer. During the first three days in which he laid out Britain's cause, his rhetoric had never been more sparkling, nor his facts and figures more impressively marshalled. Yet his efforts to win over America by reminding them of all that Britain had sacrificed during its lone stand against Hitler proved self-defeating. The higher the moral ground he took, the deeper American resistance became: 'showing our medals', as he later acknowledged, was a bad idea. As the negotiations ground on into the middle of November, they also ground Maynard down. His heart flutters returned, and he was only able to get through each day by dosing himself with sodium amytal capsules and lying down for extended periods.

By mid-December, when they were due to board the *Queen Elizabeth* for the journey home, Maynard's observation that Lydia had

Lydia and Maynard arriving in America, 1946

become 'very cross'[59] with worry was an understatement. She was frantic. But Maynard refused to respond to all her efforts to keep him quiet during the voyage, for he was tormenting himself with the failure of his mission, having got from Washington concessions worth £1 billion less than what he had been sent to bargain for – and leaving Britain stuck with debts that it would in the end take over sixty years to repay. Maynard was also worried that certain members of the British Parliament, still sceptical over the alliance with America, would punish this latest instance of Washington intransigence by refusing to ratify the crucial agreements made at Bretton Woods. These were being debated in the Commons during their passage home, and Maynard, listening on the ship's radio to the criticisms voiced by MPs, felt that he and his Treasury team had been betrayed. Rather than going straight to Tilton for the rest that he desperately required, he was insistent on going to the House of Lords to defend his vision.

A photograph taken at Southampton Docks on 17 December 1945 shows a fragile Maynard clutching the stair rail for support as he disembarks. But there is a light of determination in his face against which Lydia, by his side, looks dazed and diminished. The following day he did indeed give his speech – a fierce, broad-ranging argument designed to persuade his colleagues that the World Bank and the IMF offered the world its first chance of a liberalised global economy from which Britain could only benefit. However, the effort prostrated him, and afterwards Lydia had Maynard driven down to Sussex immediately. During the following week she watched over him intently, and by the time they held the annual shoot party he managed briefly to take part, handling a gun and looking, according to his nephew Stephen, 'happy, if very frail'.[60] Lydia, however, struck everyone as utterly wasted from the effort of willing Maynard to remain alive.

Still her work was not finished. After the New Year, Maynard was back at the Treasury, where preparations were under way for a spring conference to inaugurate the IMF and the World Bank. And with that relentless appetite for duty, which Lydia both revered and feared, he was also overseeing plans for the reopening of Covent Garden as Britain's new national opera house.

Maynard's involvement with CEMA had made him a key player in plans for a radical post-war expansion of Britain's arts scene. It had been Maynard who had drafted the constitution for the new Arts Council of Great Britain, and Maynard who had spoken on the radio in July 1945, outlining the Council's future and offering an emotional testament to the creative talent it would serve: 'The artist walks where the breath of the spirit blows him. He cannot be told his direction; he does not know it himself. But he leads the rest of us into fresh pastures and teaches us to love to enjoy what we often begin by rejecting, enlarging our sensitivity and purifying our instincts.'[61] It was a tribute made all the more moving to those who fully understood Maynard's reverence for artists and who understood, above all, his love for Lydia and Duncan.

Although the Arts Council's remit was to stimulate the arts nationwide, Maynard had special plans for London, which he visualised as the new artistic capital of Europe. The symbolic launch of this vision was the opening of Covent Garden on 20 February 1946 with a gala performed by Ninette de Valois's company. To mark the occasion, the theatre was being restored to its former gilt and red-plush splendour after six years being scuffed and stained as a wartime dance hall. But with rationing still in force, this had involved an extraordinary effort of scrimping and improvising. One small but seemingly intractable problem had been finding sufficient fabric for the lampshades, and in the end the newly employed usherettes had had to volunteer their own clothing coupons. The sacrifice of these ordinary women moved Maynard, his nephew Stephen recalling that 'there were tears trickling down his face when he told us about it. Some people remember him as arrogant but his sympathies and his feelings for people were intense.'[62]

Maynard was also moved by de Valois's decision to stage a new production of *The Sleeping Beauty* for the inaugural gala. This had been his and Lydia's ballet – the gilded backdrop to the first weeks of their love affair – but it was also the most magisterial classic in the repertory, and its performance on the Opera House stage represented a gratifying coming of age for the troupe that he and Lydia had helped to nurture. With Margot Fonteyn and Robert Helpmann dancing the principal roles, palatial new designs by Oliver Messel, and Constant Lambert conducting, this production marked the moment that Sadler's Wells Ballet took its place among the historic companies of Europe. Maynard had insisted upon, and personally overseen, the transfer of de Valois's dancers from the Wells to become the resident ballet company at Covent Garden. Eleven years later its status as a national institution would be acknowledged by Royal Charter and forty-five years later, when de Valois looked back over the Royal Ballet's history, she would claim that without Lydia and Maynard's support she could never have succeeded in taking her company so far.

Lydia was proud of Ninette and her dancers, and proud that it was Maynard who had been deputed to escort the King and Queen to the royal box that night, but she would have a much more fraught experience of the gala than the innocent public, who greeted it as a fairytale ending to the adversities of war. Maynard had typically overfilled his diary that day and had hurried to Covent Garden after a three-hour meeting at the Treasury. As the audience had crowded through the doors, their pre-war evening dress still smelling of mothballs, he had been disabled by shooting chest pains and forced to let Lydia take his place greeting the royal party. While no record survives of how she fulfilled her duties, Fred Ashton recalled the relief she felt when they were over. By the second interval Maynard had recovered sufficiently to sit with the King and Queen; and Lydia, feeling delinquent in the aftermath of panic, had lain with Ashton on the floor of her own box, smoking cigarettes and sending a tremor of alarm through the heart of the theatre's fireman, who had to race up the stairs and order them to stop.

Ill as Maynard had been during the first half of *The Sleeping Beauty*, the poetry of the performance had remained with him, and the following month, when he was delivering the opening speech of the Savannah conference, he drew an emotional comparison between the official founding of the IMF and the World Bank, and the christening of Princess Aurora. The good fairies, he hoped, would bestow 'the virtues of Universalism, courage and wisdom'[63] on the two new institutions, and he prayed that there would be no malicious fairy to curse them with a future of political wrangling. Unfortunately, this glowing imagery was lost on the tough Washington team of delegates, especially on their leader, Frederick Vinson. 'I don't mind being called malicious,' he was heard to growl, 'but I do mind being called a fairy.'[64]

Maynard had gone to Savannah with hopes that a limit might still be imposed on America's dominance of the World Bank and IMF, but Britain had neither economic nor political clout to wield and, after an initial symbolic skirmish, he accepted defeat with grace. Others at the conference admired Maynard's diplomacy, but the truth was that he no longer had the stomach for a fight. After the conference was over, he and Lydia travelled back to Washington on the night train; in the morning, when he went alone to take breakfast, the effort of navigating the swaying corridors was too much for him and he collapsed. When Lydia reached Maynard's side he was lying on a table in the dining car, looking as bad as she had ever seen him, his breathing harsh and laboured. For two hours she sat helplessly by him while Harry White and a British colleague, Robert Brand, remained close by, offering help but having none to give.

Yet Maynard's dogged constitution was not quite ready to surrender. By the time the train arrived in Washington he was able to sit up and be driven by taxi to their hotel. He even insisted on attending one last meeting before Lydia was able to bundle him on board the *Queen Mary* for the voyage home. In London, Plesch came to deliver more remedies and some final reserves were kick-started in Maynard's exhausted body. Allowed, reluctantly, by Lydia to work restricted hours at the Treasury, he was still able to reduce James Meade to tears with some especially sarcastic argument; and back down at Tilton, for the Easter holiday, his recovery seemed to continue.

In the mornings he was able to cruise through two hours of paperwork, and in the afternoons he pottered with Lydia around the estate, she in her cardigan and headscarf, he in his straw hat and a favourite light blue jacket that he had bought in America. She watched his every move, but he showed no unusually worrying symptoms, nor did Florence see any when she arrived to stay over the long holiday weekend. The two women let Maynard go on his own to Charleston, on 18 April, where Clive found him 'extremely gay and full of projects'; and two days later, when he drove with them up to the top of Firle Beacon, he even felt strong enough to attempt the walk down. Florence, who had chosen to remain in the car, sat for a while watching Lydia and Maynard as they disappeared below the brow of the hill, he bending down to her in animated talk, she looking up in eager response. Lydia would later explain that Maynard had been telling her about a first edition of the seventeenth-century poet Thomas Parnell that he had recently bought, and about one poem that had struck him in particular. Parnell's message, he had joked, was: 'Don't worry there is always divine justice.'[65] The next morning, on Easter Sunday, Maynard was dead.

The exact circumstances of his death varied in the telling. It was reported to Roy Harrod that Florence, hearing strangled coughing from Maynard's room, had called to Lydia and the two women had hurried to his bedroom to discover him in the throes of a massive heart attack. According to Clive Bell it was Lydia, taking in to Maynard his morning cup of tea, who had found him, collapsed and with his face twisted in a grimace. The end certainly came fast, however, and if Maynard managed to utter any final words for Lydia or his mother, they were not recorded.

All the sunshine of the past few days, all the little hopeful improvements in Maynard's health were sucked into the horror that Lydia had anticipated for the last nine years. Yet perhaps because she had imagined Maynard's death so many times already, she seemed to those around her to remain strangely calm. All through the day, as the dreadful flurry of phone calls and visits gathered momentum, Lydia sat as if anaesthetised. When Vanessa and Duncan came over at suppertime they found her not weeping or wringing her hands, but quiet and composed.

Florence stayed on with Lydia in Sussex, and most of the burdens of the funeral were taken over by Geoffrey, who not only arranged for the cremation in Brighton on 24 April but, forgetting that Maynard had requested that his ashes be left in the chapel at King's, arranged for a small ceremony in which they were cast to the winds from the top of the Downs above Tilton. This was a merciful lapse of memory on Geoffrey's part, for in the years that followed it would be one of Lydia's main consolations that Maynard's body and spirit had somehow become merged with their shared beloved landscape.

In the days and weeks immediately afterwards, however, Lydia had few moments alone with her husband's memory. His death escalated into a full-scale public event as the first slew of obituaries were published. Judged by *The Times* to have been the greatest economist since Adam Smith, Maynard was revered as a war hero of the British Treasury, as a political visionary, as a national benefactor of the arts; and it would require three separate memorial services to cope with the official mourning. The first was held in Washington on 25 April; the other two in Westminster Abbey on 2 May and King's College on 4 May. At the Abbey alone were representatives from the British government, led by the Prime Minister, Clement Attlee; from Cambridge, led by the Provost; from embassies and foreign governments; from the worlds of ballet and Bloomsbury. Lydia, as she stood tiny and pale at the head of the congregation, must have felt all over again how crowded Maynard's world had been.

Yet when all the ceremony and all the rhetoric were over, the rest of the world would move on. Lydia wrote, 'And now I am so utterly alone without him. The light is gone. I grieve and weep.'[66]

She had another thirty-five years to live.

Chapter Twenty

AFTER MAYNARD

> You will go down in history as the most devoted wife a great man could have had. I always thought that it was through your will, devotion and care, that Maynard was spared to do the great work that he did, for your vigil was incessant both on his pleasure and his work.
>
> FREDERICK ASHTON[1]

For nine years Lydia's world had been organised around Maynard's care, and in losing him she had lost the structure of her life and its daily detail. She could not imagine work as a substitute, since she had all but abandoned her career, nor could she lose herself in family, however fondly she loved her in-laws. Her situation could not have been more poignantly emphasised by the fact that Richard Keynes and his wife, Anne, produced their first child on the morning of Maynard's death. While Florence was grieving for the loss of her beloved eldest son, she could at least look forward to seeing her new great-grandson. That solace would never be available to Lydia.

There was, however, one final duty left to her in relation to Maynard. As news of his death spread, the condolence letters began arriving in sackloads, sent by governments and banks, by pupils and former colleagues, by drivers, builders and others who had been employed by him, as well as by individuals who had barely met Maynard but still felt his loss. Lydia, having no idea who some of the writers were, relied tremulously and gratefully on the assistance of Richard Kahn, who had sent one stark, stricken note as soon as he had heard the news, unable to 'say' anything but offering to come to Lydia straightaway.[2]

Perhaps the most piercing letters were from friends, such as Dadie Rylands, who wrote tenderly, 'Your love for him and his for you was one of the most beautiful things I have known.'[3] With these, Lydia took heartbreaking care with her replies. She wrote several drafts, each one heavily pencilled with corrections and deletions as she experimented with the correct formulae for expressing her loss. It was painful, alien labour to her – nowhere is the old Lydia to be found in phrases like 'the universal admiration and esteem assuages my deep sorrow'[4] – but at least it was a pale simulacrum of keeping Maynard alive. When she was alone and unoccupied, she felt so deeply fogged in grief that she feared she would never see beyond it. 'The only feeling in my heart is a constant ache,' she mourned to her friend Muriel Gore, confessing that for long hours at a time all she could do was lie on Maynard's couch, thinking about the 'beauty' of their last week together at Tilton and agonising over the cruelty of his sudden death.

The Keynes family looked after Lydia for as long as she would let them, and in their company she maintained a façade of reasonable cheerfulness. But her old habits of privacy were too strong to feel comfortable in their continuing careful concern, and soon Lydia attempted to regather the threads of her former independent life, corresponding with Dadie about getting parcels through to Fedor, who was back in Leningrad with his new wife; writing solicitously to Sam Courtauld about his poor health; and by July attending a ballet performance at Covent Garden. She also returned to Tilton, having been coaxed down by Geoffrey in May, and, once she had faced up to the reality of being there without Maynard, the house became her refuge. Here she could surround herself with memories, taking herself to bed at night in Maynard's pyjamas and vests – many sizes too huge for her – and by day walking the familiar track to the top of Firle Beacon, feeling his presence in every twist and turn of the view.

But for many, many months, loneliness continued to ambush her. 'The house itself misses him,' she grieved to Florence. During the arctic freeze of 1946–7 she embarked on a 'nice affair' with a woodpecker that came to the garden every day to feed: 'I spread crumbs and rind from cheese to buck him up';[5] and when the bird stopped coming she missed it disproportionately. 'My woodpecker dropped me I must be patient and wait for his return if only he would have a bell to let me know.'[6]

Anniversaries were especially hard, and Lydia marked Maynard's birthday and Christmas with impassioned letters of mourning to Florence. 'He loved to be here at Christmas,' she wrote in 1948; 'the house and I sigh and sob for him';[7] and the following year she was still lamenting: 'except for the crushed leaves under my feet the noise [is only] of solitude and silence'.[8] The two women had always been close, but now their intimacy became more demonstrative as they kept Maynard's memory alive for each other. 'We give each other strength to bear the unbearable dear one,'[9] wrote Lydia in 1947. Florence in similar vein assured her 'dearest Lyddy', 'You know my darling that I understand your feelings more than anyone else.'[10]

Florence was not regarded by either her children or her grandchildren as a doting woman, yet Lydia was able to access an extravagant vein of emotion in her brisk, pragmatic mother-in-law. Towards the end of her life, when Florence wrote with gratitude, 'I always think of you and the happiness you gave [Maynard],' she was speaking of her own love for Lydia as well.[11] A year after Maynard's death Lydia had even more need of Florence, when news came from Russia that Andrei had died and with him his young son. The bitterness of losing her adored younger brother was compounded by a letter that she received from Adele Aleksandrova Laanson, a woman who had been Karlusha's neighbour during the Leningrad siege recounting the last months of her mother's life:

> In so far as I had the strength and opportunity, I tried to ease her terrible condition. I lived on the same stairs as her ... She came to us every morning to keep warm. Her poignant image remains in my memory: a thin uncomplaining solitary old lady, always recalling you and Andrei Vasil'evich as her best children ... poor thing, she did not manage to wait out the end of the war to embrace (as she always dreamed) her two loved ones Lidusink'a and Andriushinka.[12]

Laanson's well-meaning account of how Karlusha had been buried alongside Lydia's 'dear father' in the Okhtenskoe cemetery, and had been joined by Andrei and his son, had peopled Lydia's world with

Florence Keynes in 1956

yet more ghosts. Then, at the end of year, loyal, dependable Sam Courtauld also died. Lydia wept at his memorial service: 'It was all beautiful sad.'[13]

The claims of the dead made Lydia, for the first time in her life, cling to the past. Maynard had become a rich man (his estate was valued at over £12 million in today's terms) and, apart from bequests to his family and friends, the bulk went into a trust fund, which guaranteed Lydia an income of £1,500 per year until her death, when the whole of the remaining estate would revert to King's College. This was not an extravagant sum, and inflation, coupled with the rising expense of maintaining her three homes, would make it less so, but it still left Lydia a free and independent woman. Aged only fifty-four and in excellent health, she could have spent the decades to come travelling wherever she wanted and courting whatever society she chose. She could even have married again.

Yet Lydia did none of these things. If marriage to Maynard had settled her, his death had exhausted her, and she now had little curiosity for meeting new people and none at all for going to new places. It took her, she claimed, five years to get over her grief for Maynard, but even after that, she never left the UK again, nor did she seriously engage with the world outside her own small circle. The austerities of post-war Britain upset her, and her attitudes grew nostalgic and insular as she blamed Attlee's Labour government for the grey chill of the British mood and the 'barbarous' spirit of the modern age: 'I am not interested in politics, the whole situation is so difficult that words seem worn out.'[14]

In her retreat from the modern age, Lydia stuck closer to the private habits that she had formed with Maynard, dividing her affections between employees, family and old friends, and her time between London, Cambridge and Sussex. At Tilton her nearest woman confidante was still Ruby Weller, with whom she bickered constantly but still retained her old feudal intimacy. She also acquired a new male companion in the farm manager, Logan Thomson, who after Maynard's death slipped quietly into the role as the man of the Tilton household.

Logan was physically Maynard's total opposite, a short, red-faced Yorkshireman weathered by working outdoors. Yet his burly exterior hid a susceptible, romantic streak that endeared him very much to Lydia. He was a great reader of novels and affected a literary flourish in his letters – writing from Tilton in 1956, he assured her that the fire in the spare room was burning for her 'like the Olympic flame'.[15] During the war he had impressed Lydia with his tactful handling of some German POWs who had worked on the farm, and back in 1938 she had sympathised with his broken heart when his mother (who lived with Logan in the pink bailiff's cottage on the estate) had forced an end to his love affair with a young Norwegian maid who had briefly worked at Tilton.

It was natural now for Lydia to let herself be cared for by Logan. He became her regular escort, helping to fill her empty days with outings to restaurants and films, or the occasional trip to Brighton for fish and chips and a walk on the pier. Most evenings he dined at Tilton, chatting about the farm or the old days with Maynard, and helping Lydia with her money and her correspondence. Even when guests started to come again, from London or Cambridge, Logan would usually sit in with them, flushed from the wine and apparently unfazed as he listened and nodded to the conversation.

After the Norwegian maid there had apparently been no other

women in Logan's life and Lydia was delighted at his continuing single state. 'Logan is a rare nice fellow,' she wrote to Florence, apparently never speculating as to why she had never had to share him.[16] To anyone who saw Logan with Lydia, however, it was obvious that he was now deeply, if respectfully, devoted to her. He might be sixteen years Lydia's junior; he might call her madam; and he might never dream of transgressing the boundaries between them, yet he loved her with a selfless loyalty and delicacy. One Christmas, when Lydia went to bed feeling nauseous, Logan spent the night on the drawing room sofa, staying awake until he heard her 'snoring peacefully'.[17] There were also no household tasks that he disdained. In 1956, when Tilton was suffering one of its routine staff crises, Logan cheerfully took over the cooking, grilling steaks and chops, while Lydia under his direction boiled frozen vegetables and opened cans of tinned fruit. Ten years later, when Logan moved into Tilton full time, no one was surprised. He had virtually been living there for years.

For two years after Maynard's death Lydia buried herself as deeply as possible in Tilton, but by 1949 she began making regular trips to London and Cambridge. In Cambridge she kept faithfully to the habits that she and Maynard had formed together, eating Sunday lunch with Florence and Neville, and visiting what she now called the 'dear old characters' from King's, especially Dadie Rylands and Jack Sheppard, now College Provost. As a trustee of the Arts Theatre, she was also diligent, for Maynard's sake, in attending board meetings and performances, and was allocated a range of eager young students or Fellows to sit with her in the Keynes box. Several still remember their embarrassment on those occasions. Lydia treated the theatre as her personal territory and, while resenting other people talking through performances, delivered her own opinions frankly and very audibly. 'I *shall* applaud,' she typically insisted, during the hush of a performance of *Les Sylphides*, 'I know how difficult it is.'[18]

Lydia's London life, however, was all her own. Many invitations still arrived for Lady Keynes from Maynard's former world, but the only people she chose to see were old friends like Florrie and the Bowens; her favourite former 'galerites' Cecily and Peter; her neighbours in Gordon Square, Arthur Waley and Beryl de Zoete; the writers Sybille Bedford and Stevie Smith (the latter had written some monologues for Lydia back in 1937, in the hope that she might broadcast them on radio); and, most of all, her old colleagues in the ballet world. By July 1950, Lydia was impressing herself with her revived stamina, attending a post-performance party at the French embassy and insisting on taking her friends back to Gordon Square, where she gave them frankfurters, wine and bananas, retiring finally to bed at 4.30 a.m. According to Robert Helpmann, Lydia was returning to her old entertaining form and could once again be counted on to 'drive a ... party to absolute hysteria' with some 'absolutely extraordinary' pun or remark.[19]

A very few new friends were added to her theatrical circle, among them Laurence Olivier and his wife, Vivien Leigh, whom Lydia considered to be 'beautiful charmers'.[20] An invitation for her to stay at their country house in Buckinghamshire, in September 1951, however, created panic and consternation among her staff. Lydia had got it into her head that she was simply going for supper at the Oliviers' London home and, having accepted a lift from them dressed only in her evening clothes, had been surprised to find herself eventually arriving at a weekend house party. Typically, she had been unfazed, shrugging aside Leigh's offer of a spare toothbrush: 'Oh my dear do not worry. What is the point of cleaning your teeth? You have to lose them sometime.'[21] But as Lydia had cheerfully passed the weekend in her unsuitable finery, and with her unbrushed teeth, her concerned staff back home had no idea of her whereabouts. The Oliviers' butler had tried to phone the caretakers at Gordon Square, but the message had been misunderstood – and when Lydia failed to appear at Lewes Station on Sunday, Ruby and Logan had become frantic. The London police were alerted and, while searching Gordon Square, had discovered a chequebook from which a number of payments had been made to an unknown Mr Hawkins. Dark suspicions of kidnapping and blackmail began to form, until the next morning when Lydia was delivered back to Gordon Square and serenely informed the police that Hawkins was a local chemist who used to cash her cheques as a personal favour.

Another addition to Lydia's world was Richard Buckle, ballet critic of the *Observer*. He was only thirty-four when she first met him, in 1950, but his knowledge and his opinions impressed her and she began to ask him out to ballets and parties. 'It was handsome of you to escort me in such a grand manner,' she wrote coquettishly in May 1950. 'Thank you. I felt like a lady, quite. Did I behave?'[22] Buckle was conscious that some of Lydia's friends referred to him cynically as her 'London gigolo', especially once she began paying him a small allowance while he was attempting to launch himself, unsuccessfully, as a playwright. But he genuinely adored her company, and her 'invigorating' appetite for 'art, nature, people and life'.[23]

Above all, Lydia and Buckle bonded over ballet. While post-war Britain was struggling to regain its economic strength, dance at least was flourishing, with four full-size companies operating out of London: Ballet Rambert, Festival Ballet, Sadler's Wells Ballet, based at the Opera House in Covent Garden, and its smaller sister company, Sadler's Wells Opera Ballet, at the Wells. Lydia knew how much the success of these last two would have gratified Maynard, growing as they did out of his work with the Camargo Society and his commitment to establishing a national ballet. And she was delighted too by the progress of Fred Ashton, now resident choreographer at the Opera House and justifying her faith in his talent. 'At last you have come to your triumph,' she wrote lovingly after the 1948 première of *Cinderella*. 'My mind beams and my heart beats for you.'[24]

But Lydia was not an uncritical champion. At the Opera House she scolded the general administrator, David Webster, over a feeble staging of *Coppélia*: 'the costumes and décor ... should be drowned – it is a disgrace for Covent Garden not Surbiton';[25] and she once shocked Stephen Keynes by rubbishing one of de Valois's ballets directly to her face. 'It was on opening night and de Valois looked terribly, terribly upset. I don't think Lydia meant to be rude, or deliberately hurtful, but she always said, "You have to tell the truth otherwise they will never learn.'"[26] Robert Helpmann supported Lydia's tough approach, claiming that 'she was marvellous at spotting any falseness in performance' and could always identify what was 'first rate'.[27] Yet while Lydia did brief service on the Arts Council and the board of the Opera House, she refused to engage with her profession in any other formal capacity. Coaching younger dancers was of no interest to her. Even when de Valois mounted productions of *La Boutique fantasque* in 1947, and *The Good-Humoured Ladies* in 1962, Lydia was not tempted to help in the revival of her former roles. In 1954 she was happy to watch Karsavina coaching Fonteyn in *The Firebird* and even trekked up to Edinburgh to see the première, but on her return she commented briskly to Florence that she was now 'so glad not to be connected with the ballet'.[28] Beryl Grey, one of the Royal Ballet's new ballerinas, remembers that while Lydia frequently turned up to performances – 'a funny little lady, to us younger ones' – she never ventured backstage.[29]

Part of Lydia's wariness towards her old profession stemmed from the simple belief that the glory days of ballet were over. In private she grieved for the passing of Diaghilev's company, 'that it is no more nor I a part of it',[30] and admitted that some of the new choreography made her feel old-fashioned. Whilst she could enjoy Ashton's reinterpretation of the nineteenth-century classic *Sylvia* for its lack of 'squalor or social realism',[31] she had refused to see the newly formed Les Ballets Nègres (Europe's first black ballet company, founded in London by Richie Bailey and Berto Pasuka) on the shameless grounds that she was not 'much interested in negros nor in Hindus, I do not understand their religious taboos and plead ignorant'.[32] She was even shocked by the Bolshoi Ballet when it first visited London in 1956. In *Romeo and Juliet* she judged the great ballerina Galina Ulanova to be 'lovely', but the choreography to be indecently acrobatic.[33]

Yet in keeping her distance, Lydia was also protecting her privacy. Formal invitations from the ballet world frequently sent her into a tizzy of consternation, especially if they involved making a speech. Without Maynard's editorial assistance she was afraid of looking foolish, and when she was asked to deliver a public tribute to de Valois, in 1947, she went begging to Jack Sheppard for help. 'Please do scribble something to me in typewriting put yourself in my shoes and spread your general wits across my nervous system.'[34]

Even when Lydia was only required to put in an appearance, she was nervous of being fussed. In 1954, Buckle organised an exhibition of Ballets Russes designs and memorabilia, to commemorate the twenty-fifth anniversary of Diaghilev's death, and Lydia was happy to lend him precious items, including Frank Dobson's bust of her. Yet she refused to attend the exhibition's opening, or to turn up at any of its attendant parties. While Sokolova, Karsavina, Idzikowski, de Valois, Rambert, Markova and the Grigorievs were all gathered at an historic reunion dinner, Lydia was not among them; and when she did finally go to the exhibition, it was anonymously. Buckle spotted her 'queuing up at the gates before opening time, among a lot of boy scouts'.[35]

Lydia, who had once been the media's darling, now insisted that neither she nor her past were for public consumption.* Roy Harrod was both confused and disappointed when she refused to be consulted over Maynard's biography: 'She … does not want to pick over the old memories at all,' he said helplessly to Geoffrey Keynes, and Lydia would not even read the completed book. Importunate journalists who rang for a quote or an interview did not even merit a personal refusal as, pretending to be her own secretary and thickening her Russian accent, Lydia stated flatly down the telephone, 'Madam does not give interviews.'[36] Even Buckle felt that she was not entirely open with him. However generously she might gossip with him about the old days, she was suspicious of what he might put in print, and when he sent her a copy of his memoir, *Adventures of a Ballet Critic* (1953), he scented a note of reproach in Lydia's verdict: 'I should think most saleable with so much information.'[37]

Lydia would remain involved with ballet only on her own terms – which were essentially, and opportunistically, social. She liked to hold court in the Crush Bar at Covent Garden, where, escorted by Buckle, her nephews Stephen and Milo, or even Logan, she could gossip with former colleagues and fans. She liked to bring dancers and choreographers back to Gordon Square, where she once again began to hold her post-performance suppers and Russian lunches. But whilst Lydia felt energised by reconnecting with her profession, her protégées were now in positions of power, and she did not always feel comfortable with the change. De Valois, for instance, became less

*Lydia made a rare exception in the autumn of 1951 when she took part in a radio homage to Diaghilev, 'because I owe so much to him'.

dear to her. 'I don't like women in power,'[38] she generalised wildly to Buckle. And whilst she had grown fond of Fonteyn (their correspondence a flurry of 'Lydia Darlings' and 'Sweet Margots'), and Ashton was still her 'cronie', these stars of British ballet were far too busy for Lydia to see them regularly.

Her Russian friendships, with Karsavina, Larionov and Gontcharova, were distressing for other reasons.* Karsavina, now a widow too, was having to survive on a tiny pension, and Lydia was not only upset by her poverty, but moved by her refusal to complain. 'That woman touches me deeply. I rarely have seen such spiritual grandeur and modesty,'[39] she wrote to Florence, and whenever she visited she was careful to wear a hat, as a mark of respect. Guilty at her own relative luxury, Lydia set up a generous private covenant for Karsavina in 1952, which paid her £100 a year. For the two painters Larionov and Gontcharova, she established a public trust fund, sending out begging letters to everyone she knew and donating generously herself – despite warnings from Richard Kahn, who had been appointed the chief trustee of her finances and had little faith in her capacity to keep within her budget. Lydia rebuked him for his caution, telling him that she knew Maynard would have done something 'immediately' to help them.

An overture from Randolfo Barocchi received no such consideration. He wrote to Lydia from Rome in December 1950 in what may have been a genuine desire to renew contact, but may also have been a sly approach for money.

> I just happened to find out your address, and although you never answered any of my letters I sent to the old London address I still wish to write to you every happyness [sic] for the New Year. You needn't bother to reply to this letter, for, as long as I know that you are well and in good health I am perfectly content – although I don't wish to convey the thought that a few lines from you wouldn't bring me unspeakable happiness![40]

Those few lines were never written, although a few weeks previously,

*Lydia and Massine had lost all contact. She once told a journalist, 'We do not correspond, we were never intimate enough to afford the stamps and envelopes.'

Lydia had delighted in resuming contact with her old comrade Picasso. The painter had made a rare visit to England to attend a communist peace conference, and when that event had been suddenly cancelled, he had insisted that the one person he must see before leaving was Lydia. He came to her in Gordon Square and, as they embraced on the pavement outside number 46, Picasso demanded to know whether she still danced. When Lydia demonstrated some steps in the affirmative, he capered alongside her, the painter and the ballerina performing a historic duet for which only Milo Keynes, a wide-eyed observer, was the audience. Inside the house, the gossip was all of the old days and the break-up of Picasso's marriage to Olga ('She asked too much of me,'[41] the painter shrugged), and when they parted he promised to send Lydia the drawing that he had made long ago of her dancing the can-can with Massine. Later he claimed that he could not find it and sent her a photograph of the drawing, inscribed, 'pour Lydia en attendant l'original'. She kept this lovingly but the original never did arrive – Picasso having either lost it, or sold it long ago.

Happily as Lydia entertained her old friends, she did so haphazardly. She could afford only minimal staff at Gordon Square (her cook, Mrs Beaumont, left in 1949, although her cleaner, Mrs Turtle, stayed with her till she gave up the house); and although number 47 had been sublet, number 46 was a miserably inconvenient property to maintain. The house was riddled with dry rot and much of its plumbing was ancient, but Lydia was too daunted by the complication and the cost to get in any builders. She regularly complained, in fact, that she had barely enough money to keep herself warm, let alone pay for repairs, and for years Richard Kahn had to put up with her melodramatic campaign to wheedle more cash out of her trust fund. 'The big houses today are a liability and well off people like me live like paupers ... My teeth are troubling me, I get swollen cheeks, cold, I feel I cannot go out and I stay in without comforts except bed and electric fire.'[42]

Eventually Lydia figured out a strategy for surviving in number 46, which was simply to retreat into a smaller and smaller area of the house. She rented the basement to a Mr and Mrs Walker, who also acted as caretakers, and let the upper floors to a Christian Aid society, whom she found admirable, if mildly ridiculous tenants – any stranger ringing at Lydia's front door would be immediately quizzed as to whether they were 'a Christian'. All that was left to her was the ground floor, which acquired the stuffy and overstuffed atmosphere of a little nest. In the front room Lydia did her exercises and stared out of the window at 'the leaves whistling along' the square. It was here too that she slept, although not, as Buckle liked to fantasise, 'in a cupboard on top of a stove under ten eiderdowns, with Puskhin and Dostoievsky'.[43] The back room was reserved for eating and entertaining, with guests having to clear themselves a space in the sprawl of clutter. Lydia was a chronic and undiscriminating hoarder, and Buckle would write of how, 'among the piles of books and tins of food', one might casually come across 'a Cubist Picasso and a sketch by Delacroix'.[44]

Lydia's post-war style of catering was basic, and the years of fine linens were now ancient memory as she dined off a table covered in an oilcloth. The fish counter at Selfridges, where she dutifully used to pick out the catch of the day, also represented another era as she dreamed hopefully (and presciently) about a future in which one might just order 'pre cooked food from the library and it will take 35 seconds to heat a steak on a china plate'.[45] Stuck as she was in the pre-microwave 1950s, Lydia either fed herself out of tins that she had saved from her Washington trips, or served up chunks of cold chicken, or, for favoured guests, booked a table at Antoine's restaurant in Charlotte Street.

Expensive, understaffed and difficult as number 46 was to inhabit, when the lease came up for renewal in 1955 Lydia would not let it go. She still felt cravings for society and for shopping, which Sussex alone could not satisfy. 'I enjoy spending money,' she confessed to Florence, admitting that she suffered a 'complex of greed', which made her buy clothes and hats even when she knew she would never wear them.[46] On the other hand, making the transition to London was sometimes too 'feverish'. One hot July day in 1950 she wrote apologetically to Buckle that she could not bother to see the new ballets, because she was too happily stuck at Tilton – 'half naked creeping like a lizard (non poisonous) among cabbages and beans, I forget the world in "contemplative idleness'".[47]

The rural side of her life became more and more attractive. 'I am getting fat,' Lydia wrote comfortably, 'the middle aged spread is reaching down';[48] and she relished the lack of social complication. 'I find that I like myself when I do not talk ... Tilton community suits me, no diplomacy, gentleman's agreement, or prima donnas.'[49] The simple dramas of the farm increasingly absorbed her. 'We have a spiteful cockeral,' she reported to Florence in April 1952. 'I said why not eat him yet the female chickens like him so much if he is gone they will stop laying eggs,'[50] and her letters to Buckle hummed with the rhythm of long days in the garden, 'surrounded by broad beans, green peas and weeds'.[51]

Lydia was very much the rural aristocrat at Tilton, serenely caught up in her own world and grandly indifferent to what anyone else thought of her. Yet she was also reverting to the Russian peasant that she always claimed was embedded in her DNA. She took pleasure in the primitive household economies that were imposed by continuing rationing: eating squirrel, and gloating over her luck in finding a rabbit that had been killed by a stoat and could be put into the pot for supper. She also began to nest at Tilton just as she did at Gordon Square, moving into Maynard's former bedroom on the ground floor and letting a tide of clutter spread outwards in a mess of old snapshots, press cuttings, cans and pickle jars.

Within her Tilton hideaway, Lydia also began dressing like an elderly babushka. During winters, she wrapped herself up as thickly as if she were facing a Siberian freeze, swaddled in three overcoats as well as scarves, pullovers (usually old ones of Maynard's), woolly hats, and boots so 'huge', she boasted, that you 'could put rabbits into soles'.[52] Even in the summer she was wary of losing heat. When Cecil Beaton visited in August 1951, he was both unnerved and enchanted by the bundled figure who met him, wearing 'a mercerised silk skirt of cream leaf pattern, cocoa-coloured stockings, woollen socks, straw boots, an apron and about three different sweaters over a silk blouse. Her head was tied in a maize coloured handkerchief.'[53]

When the sun was shining hotly enough, however, Lydia ritually stripped off all her clothes, believing fervently, as many Russians did, in the health-giving effect of spreading 'a bit of sun on myself like butter'.[54] She would roam around Tilton's grounds reciting poetry to herself, stripped to the waist with her 'udders' (rubber gloves) kept handy in her pockets for pulling up thistles. She would also spend hours sunbathing naked, relishing the sensation of being baked into a stupefied unity with her surroundings: 'Life is wonderful in this weather I feel I love the world. 24 hours is just not enough to be happy. I wish for 48.'[55]

Lydia's favoured spot was among the redcurrant bushes, where she believed herself to be invisible – claiming that if anyone spotted her they just would not 'believe their eyes'. In fact a public footpath ran close by and Angelica Garnett's daughters, staying at Charleston one summer, were among several locals who had spied on Lydia's sun worship, crawling daringly through the bushes to see her wrinkled and freckled brown body stretched out beatifically in the heat.

Yet whilst Lydia was happy to pass days at a time lost in the rhythms of the countryside and gossiping with Logan or Ruby, throughout the 1950s she continued to make favoured guests welcome at Tilton, especially if they were male. As she wrote to Buckle, 'I like to be on my own yes I do, but I must have a man for Sunday lunch,'[56] and David Castilejo, a friend of Stephen Keynes, recorded how exuberantly she greeted those who obliged, gusting into their embrace, encouraging them to kiss her and swing her round in the air. Though Castilejo was much younger than Lydia, he found himself startled and aroused by her powerful femaleness, recalling how 'at times she could switch on a really powerful animal sexuality'.[57]

Other men friends were drawn by Lydia's eccentric style of pampering. E. M. Forster became an enthusiastic visitor to Tilton, seduced by Lydia's accumulated collection of electric blankets, whilst Jack Sheppard found himself being mothered in more intimate style, wrapped up solicitously against the cold in a shawl, extra blankets and even Maynard's old pants. The lengths to which Lydia would go to secure herself male company were, according to Stephen Keynes, occasionally outrageous, especially when she fancied seeing some nice young men in uniform. Once she ordered in a crate of beer and then rang up the local fire station to report a fire, exulting to Stephen afterwards that the firemen had forgiven her the prank and greatly 'enjoyed their beer'.[58]

But Lydia liked to have women around her too, especially old friends like Vera Bowen and Muriel Gore, and there were favoured couples on her guest list, including Noël Annan and his wife, and T. S. Eliot, who brought his second wife, Valerie, down to meet her. Whoever was staying, Lydia took her duties as a hostess seriously, considering them to be equivalent to giving a 'good performance' on stage. During the mornings, guests were expected to entertain themselves while she pottered through her chores, leafed through the newspapers and did a few perfunctory ballet exercises. Afternoons were devoted to serious reading and walks. But during the evening, Lydia's guests were treated to her most dedicated attentions. She wined and dined them liberally, and held court over long conversations in the drawing room. This room was, objectively, a hideous place to sit: painted apple green and furnished with bulky grey sofas, boxy occasional tables and thick beige curtains. Yet Lydia, wrapped up in rugs during the wintertime and always with a large box of cigarettes at her side, made her surroundings festive, reminiscing, joking and frequently jumping up to perform a few dance steps – the aura of her former ballerina graces suddenly present in the room.

Lydia was also framed by an astonishing collection of modern art: Maynard's astute buying had left her in charge of several Picassos, Braques and Cézannes, a Matisse, a Renoir and a Seurat, as well as many modern British works. She was merely curator to these treasures, as they would revert to King's after her death, and whilst she enjoyed the privilege of living among them, the responsibility of their keeping could at times infuriate her. Galleries regularly asked to borrow individual paintings, and even more disruptive was the crude burglar alarm system, which had been wired up around the most prized pieces in the collection and which was directly connected to the local police station. Every time a branch fell on the telephone line or someone accidentally touched one of the pictures, the alarm was set off and the police would come haring up the drive. Even Lydia, susceptible as she was to these uniformed young men being so 'very handsome and gallant and anxious for my safety', disliked the intrusion; and in desperation she took to hanging the pictures higher and higher up the wall, a lofty, lopsided collection that could not be touched, but also could not be properly seen.[59]

Whilst most of Lydia's guests came down to her from London, she also established her niche in local society, entertaining her GP and his wife, the Gage family, and other close neighbours. Every Christmas she had Logan and the 'sweet and noble' Leonard Woolf to help her to 'tackle' her turkey, and every Christmas Leonard brought her a pot of honey from Rodmell. (Although he knew that Lydia did not care for honey, it had been a favourite of Maynard's and she was touched by his constancy.)

At irregular intervals, too, Lydia braved the few hundred yards of flinty track that separated her from Charleston. After Maynard's death she worked quite hard to ingratiate herself with her Bloomsbury neighbours, using some of her diminishing cash to buy Vanessa's work, which she genuinely thought 'much improved from her earliest pictures', and being ready with compliments for the household's children and grandchildren – Quentin she thought 'brilliant with Clive's temperament and Vanessa's gifts'.[60] Yet the intimacy remained forced. Lydia was aware that Vanessa disliked visiting Tilton – frequently when Duncan or Clive came for supper the latter stayed behind – and Lydia herself was nervous of going over to Charleston. Duncan might be genuinely affectionate but Lydia never got over her ancient fear and resentment of Vanessa and had to nerve herself, every time, to see her.

The repressed tension between the two households puzzled Vanessa's observant granddaughter Henrietta. On several of her visits to Charleston, the little girl had encountered Lydia at the house and had found her a fascinating figure, 'sitting tiny and upright in the dining room and always muffled up in a great many clothes'. It was clear to Henrietta that this crinkly neighbour was an important figure, for Vanessa would tell stories of Lydia's ballerina past, recalling her 'ravishing' prettiness and talent. Yet Henrietta could not understand why Vanessa would always undercut this praise with a 'tolerant but superior laugh', making it clear that Lydia was not quite their 'type'. When she was ten she went alone to Tilton to try to unravel the mystery.[61]

It took her, as she later wrote, a great deal of courage. The drawing room where she had been asked to wait for Lydia was 'one of the strangest rooms' she had ever seen, in its ugly overheated stuffiness. And when Lydia walked in, she appeared to the little girl even stranger than the room, layered in woollens and looking 'rather like an old tea cosy except for her feet which were delicate and beautiful and for her hands which were very graceful'. Yet immediately Lydia set about charming away Henrietta's nerves and served her with a thrillingly sophisticated tea of sweet Sauternes and marrons glacés. At the end of the visit she covered Henrietta's face 'with short and dry little kisses' and told her to come again.

Back at Charleston, when Henrietta recounted her story, Duncan and even Vanessa seemed pleased that she had made this connection, and from then on whenever Henrietta came to stay it was understood that she would visit Tilton. As she now acknowledges, it became a magical place to her: 'Lydia skipped the commonplace. If she suddenly thought it would be a good idea to eat a bit of sausage at eleven o'clock that's exactly what you wanted to do.'[62] In return, Lydia found Henrietta 'a lovely creature, bright and lively',[63] and for several years encouraged their intimacy, even taking Henrietta to the theatre in Cambridge, where the little girl watched her new friend take ceremonial possession of her territory, 'sitting in her box like a little Empress'.[64]

But the most constant person in Lydia's life was Florence. Every week Lydia wrote to her mother-in-law, confiding both the trivia of her life and her most private feelings. So indomitably sprightly, so 'young in the mind' did Florence appear, even after Neville's death in 1949, that Lydia almost believed that she was immortal. Yet in February 1958 Florence died, slipping away suddenly and without any fuss, and her loss created a watershed in Lydia's life. Although she herself was only sixty-six, and thirty years Florence's junior, she had grown emotionally dependent on her mother-in-law, inspired by her vigour and relying on her meticulous memory for birthdays and anniversaries to maintain the structure of her own life. Without Florence's example, she began gradually to drift. Old friendships with the Bowens and Florrie became too much of a bother for her to sustain, and one by one her newer friends were discarded. Her last conversation with Richard Buckle was a brief telephone call, during which he invited himself down to Tilton and she rebuffed him almost as though he were a stranger.

After 1960, Lydia rarely stirred herself to leave Tilton. She found visits to London an upheaval and, and having resigned her trusteeship of the Arts Theatre, had little reason to go to Cambridge, beyond visiting her chiropodist – her dancer's bunions and corns required regular attention. She actively did not care to visit Geoffrey, who lived in a village close by the city, since she had formed a dislike of his wife, Margaret, and she wanted nothing more to do with the university. In 1967, when the newly constructed Keynes Building was unveiled (funded by Maynard's trust), she could not be persuaded to attend its opening.

Among the few people who knew of Lydia's fleeting appearances were a newly married couple who lived in the flat above hers in St Edward's Passage. One morning they met over the dustbins, where the young wife was searching for an accidentally discarded silver spoon, and the combination of this reassuring display of domestic ineptitude, plus the discovery that the husband spoke Russian, warmed Lydia out of her reclusiveness. Often in the evenings she would venture up the stairs to see them with a bottle of wine, although she would always hesitate anxiously outside the door until she was sure they did not have company.

It was a relief to Lydia when in 1965 she finally abandoned both St Edward's Passage and Gordon Square. She and Richard Kahn had always clashed over the costs of running three households as, pedantically loyal to the exact terms of Maynard's will, Kahn refused to raise Lydia's income to meet the rising costs of maintenance. According to her nephew, Richard Keynes, the trust could easily have spared her more, but Kahn never got over his anxiety that Lydia's spending might get out of control. If any large expense occurred, she was required to ask for a special handout, a process that she found demeaning. 'I have to ask the trustees for every half crown and for a hand basin for my bedroom,'[65] she complained once to Beaton, and often preferred to sell her possessions to avoid the humiliation. (Tilton's reroofing in 1955 was largely paid for by the cast of a Degas ballerina, which had once been given to her by Sam Courtauld.)

Fond as Lydia and Kahn were of each other – and mutually devoted to Maynard's memory – these financial clashes were inevitable. Kahn was a man of peculiarly precise habits, which grew more dogged with age, and it gave him almost physical pain to witness Lydia's approach to money. He was bewildered by her failure to fill in her cheque stubs and file away her chequebooks; he was bothered by her refusal to invest and dumbfounded by her dilatory attitude towards budgeting. She in return thought him over-controlling and timid.

In fact as Lydia grew older, most of her shopping demons ran out of energy, and she and Kahn had less reason to fight. She still retained a few pet charities (including annual subsidies to family members and lump sums given to the Royal Ballet Benevolent Fund) and she was still in thrall to shoes (partly because it was difficult to find styles that fitted her ballet-ravaged feet). Heat was also a major extravagance, and it was a point of pride to her that the 'house specialities' at Tilton should be 'well prepared electric blankets' and '80 degrees hot water', to ensure that there would 'not be a dull moment in the bathroom'.[66]

Otherwise she made a point of practising increasingly eccentric economies. She ate out of tins that were years past their sell-by date, she cut up newspapers for lavatory paper and she lost interest in doing anything to Tilton beyond essential repairs. Even by the late 1950s parts of the house had slipped towards dilapidation. Paint peeled, plaster cracked, and Maynard's cherished study lay empty and damp. Outside, the garden turned mournfully derelict as the driveway became pitted with holes and the flower beds reverted to grass. Logan also let the farm lapse. A lame foot made it difficult for him to do physical work, and without Maynard's chivvying he had fallen behind with the business side of the operations. It had been a torment to him when Kahn had arrived every year to go through the farm accounts and Lydia had regularly had to defend both him and his defective paperwork on the grounds that he was a farmer, not a bursar or civil servant.

If Tilton's decline was partly due to Lydia's shrinking dislike of having builders in the house, it was also because the sheer size of the property was too much for her to manage. After Maynard died, her landlord, Lord Gage, began to default on his contractual responsibilities for the house's upkeep, and Lydia did not have enough staff of her own to stem the decline. The post-war servant shortage had hit Tilton hard. After Maynard's death, Lydia had become very dependent on her live-in couple, Rosie and Leonard Carter, and had grown very fond of their three children, reporting on their doings and sayings with almost grandmotherly possessiveness in her letters to Florence. Crowing over the birth of the littlest, Gerald, 'adorable I watch him often in his bath',[67] was as close as Lydia came, in writing, to regretting her own lack of children, and when the Carters left in 1956 (Leonard having been offered better wages as a van driver) she felt abandoned. It took her months of disgruntled searching before she found a Mr and Mrs Taylor to replace them, but, having done so, she inflicted a new hardship on herself. Mrs Taylor also worked part time in a mental institution in Eastbourne and, to Lydia's extreme distress, began making it offensively apparent that she considered her new employer to be as batty as her other clients. During the Taylors' three-year stay, Lydia developed such a panicky hatred of them that she ordered the door to the servants' wing to be bricked up. In 1962 they were finally replaced by a more tactful Mr and Mrs Lessitor, but the couple stayed for only four years before emigrating to New Zealand. It was at this point that Logan moved in. Yet although he limped around the house looking after the fires and the boilers, and Ruby did what cleaning she could, Tilton slid inexorably towards chaos. By the time that Jean Whiter, a new housekeeper-companion, was hired in 1967, the house was not only dirty and dishevelled but, in view of the cigarette burns dotting Lydia's bedclothes, it may have narrowly escaped being burned down.

Given the decay of Lydia's surroundings as she entered her mid-seventies, it would have been easy to assume that she herself was becoming equally ramshackle. Yet whilst she occasionally liked to exaggerate her age and infirmity, either to gain Kahn's pity or to get out of doing something she disliked, she remained alert and independent. Apart from problems with her remaining teeth, which all had to be removed by 1965, she was also healthy. Sarah Walton (the daughter of some neighbours with whom Lydia became friendly) recalls Lydia flitting energetically through the landscape of her childhood – part lady of the manor, part lively, wrinkled sylphide. 'I used to see her walking through the woods and fields, and I remember once stopping and watching when I was playing in the garden with my parents. She smiled at us in this lovely way, with great respect and affection.' Even though Lydia struck her as an odd creature, who might even smell a little strongly if one got up close, she did not figure in Walton's imagination as an object of pity. 'She looked sun-burned and healthy and she seemed very comfortable in her own skin.'[68]

Lydia seemed equally vigorous to her Russian nephew, Vladimir Lopukhov, when he visited her in 1967 – the first and only member of her own family to make it to England. He had been born in 1947 to Fedor and his wife, Maya, and whilst Lydia had never felt any desire to brave the 'police state and spies'[69] of post-war Russia, she had enjoyed sending out clothes and sweets for the little boy, and treasured the photos and letters that she got in return, charting his progress from the Theatre School (now renamed the Vaganova) to the Kirov in 1965. Fedor himself had been restored to official favour after the war, creating only a few ballets but teaching choreography at the Vaganova School and at the Leningrad Conservatory. Among his pupils were the choreographers Yuri Grigorovich and Boris Eifmann, and according to the latter, Fedor had possessed for them an iconic status. 'He was highly intellectual and witty and he was in love with all the ballerinas – he used to look down on them from his apartment overlooking the Vaganova School, saying he could recognise them by their feet. But he had also lived through a history of terrible changes, and we knew how hard it was for him to be light and easy after what he had sacrificed.'[70]

There had been no obstacle when a family friend, the influential critic Yury Slonimsky, had asked permission for Vladimir to make a detour to Tilton while on a European tour with the Kirov, and Lydia had been ecstatic to greet her nephew: fêting his arrival, exclaiming over his family looks and revelling in the opportunity to speak Russian. Vladimir in turn was impressed by his aunt, captivated by the astonishing music of her laughter, stirred by her stoicism – 'she seemed not to miss her old life at all' – and surprised by her acuity. She was well informed about Russian politics, quick to deplore the 'loathsome' Brezhnev and very curious about ballet. 'She asked about everything I danced and she knew all the famous Russian dancers.' When Lydia took him out to Lewes, Vladimir was also struck by the extent of her local celebrity: 'She was like a rarity for people: a

Fedor, Vladimir and baby Lopukhov, circa 1972

Russian who became Lady Keynes. When we came to a restaurant everyone recognised and greeted her.'[71]

It surprised him, however, that Lydia did not live like a famous woman. The house, thanks to Jean Whiter's new regime, was tolerably clean but Vladimir was disappointed that Tilton was bare of 'any rich museum exhibits', and when he visited again with his wife, in 1969, the house seemed to him even more perplexing. By this time Lydia had sent the most valuable paintings up to King's, replacing only some of them with works by Vanessa, Duncan and Quentin. And if the walls had been partially stripped, the mess of clutter elsewhere had lapped higher and higher. The hallway and many of the rooms were now lined with dusty piles of papers, bottles of wine and tins of pet food to feed Lydia's expanding brood of cats. Over eighty pairs of Lydia's boots, slippers and shoes, some of them decades old, were stacked up along the walls.

In the midst of this accumulated flotsam and jetsam, Vladimir sensed a fundamental detachment in his aunt, noticing on his second visit that she 'communicated almost with no one, her circle was just two or three women'.[72] But Lydia was now seventy-eight and her world had been emptying steadily. Many of her neighbours were gone: Vanessa had died in 1961, Clive in 1964 and Leonard in 1969, and she barely had contact with Fedor, who would die in Leningrad in January 1973. Visitors were no longer allowed to stay unless they were close family. 'I do hope you will not think this very rude of me,' Lydia wrote to Kahn in 1967, 'but nowadays I enjoy people for few hours during the day, but hate to have them sitting on my door step. Forgive me.'[73]

Increasingly she preferred to be left alone, and from about 1970 her favourite spot in the house became the front hall. Having once roamed the world, Lydia liked to relax in an armchair, beside Logan, from which she could watch the changing weather from the open front door. Overhead was an electric heater towards whose heat the couple gently inclined their faces; behind them on the first landing was Vanessa's cartoon of Lydia and Maynard dancing the Keynes-Keynes – a snapshot from a different era.

From this point on, Lydia used to say, 'A little bit of me flies away like a bird',[74] and although she continued to leaf through the newspapers and welcome the occasional visitor, her thoughts and her conversation returned increasingly to her distant Russian past. Even though she had kept Maynard's letters, she rarely spoke of him, and it was on an outing to the opera at Glyndebourne that Richard and Anne Keynes realised just how vividly she now occupied her earliest memories. The performance (for which Lydia had dressed in a quilted Marks and Spencer's dressing gown, pinned at the chest with a gaudy brooch) had been *Eugene Onegin*, and throughout Act 1 Lydia had sung along loudly but fairly accurately with all the choruses. However, during the rest of the opera she had fallen silent, explaining afterwards that when she was a pupil she had been cast in one of the children's roles and had got to know the music well. She had only appeared in the first act and, having always been taken back to the school at the interval, she had never learned the rest.

But Lydia could still be roused to put on a performance of her own. Around 1971 the art critic Richard Cork visited Tilton to look at a painting by Frederick Etchells, which still hung in the living room. Cork and his wife were in their twenties and had expected to find Lady Keynes an ancient relic. Yet when Lydia came into the sitting room they were taken back by her extreme vitality. 'She was like a little imp,' remembers Cork,

> with sparkling, mischievous eyes and during our whole visit she hardly sat down. She didn't have much to say about Etchells but she was very keen to talk to us about Russia and her childhood, and she started showing us ballet steps, which she executed very beautifully. She was very vehement about what Stalinism had done to her country, very angry that they had dared to change all the names of the cities. But she wasn't bitter at all. We were completely bewitched. She made us feel as if she had known us all her life.[75]

In 1974, Lydia fell seriously ill with viral pneumonia and from then on her mind, according to Ruby, began to 'wander up and down'.[76] When Henrietta Garnett visited again, on 1 May 1975, Lydia and Logan were sitting as usual in their armchairs and it appeared that they now spent most of the day in silence, each lost in their scattered thoughts. Lydia's appearance had become, if possible, more peculiar, as she tried to keep herself warm. Around her head were wrapped the usual tangle of scarves, on her feet were short orange rubber boots and even indoors she wore a dark green nylon jacket that was fastened up tight to her chin. Yet this was not a desolate encounter. Garnett was offered her regular glass of Sauternes, and Lydia, enlivened by her presence, launched into something resembling her old chatter, fishing up dazzling if disconnected memories of her former profession, in whose company she now spent much of her time. 'Petipa had an old face, but his ankles continued to be interesting'; Diaghilev was 'a great man to work with ... a creator'; Nijinsky was 'potty. His soul had holes in it, but when he danced then his holes were healed, then he became alive and he was not unhappy any more.'[77]

Even after fifty years, Massine's 'twisted nature' still rankled, although Lydia paid tribute to his charisma on stage and his 'black eyes like a cat'. Karsavina she continued to revere – 'She had beauty and poetry' – whilst all that she recalled of Isadora Duncan were her hands: 'she used her hands like swans ... before her the Russians just had fists.' Looking at her own, Lydia warned Garnett that hands were the first to betray a dancer's age. 'Veins come between the fingers here and here. It is an insult to show veins in the theatre.'

Lydia had no illusions about the cruelty of a profession that retired its artists so early. 'After forty it is all over ... then only mime is left ... character parts ... Surgery exists for the face but that is vulgar. And in the theatre, there can be no lies.' Yet she was grandly pragmatic about her own old age. 'To have wrinkles is to be noble,' she instructed Garnett. 'We all of us grow old, what matters is how you age. We all grow old, very old and then we die.'

Apart from ballet, death now appeared to be Lydia's favourite topic. Garnett recalled that her conversation was punctuated with musings on mortality – 'We are none of us Christians. Soon we shall all be dead' – and that she was eager to be reminded which of her friends had already gone. She could not feign much sorrow for Vanessa: 'Ah well, she had to die', but was sad for Leonard: 'That is a pity. He was a good man', and relieved to hear that Duncan still survived: 'Dear Duncan, We all love him there is nothing more to be said about him.'

Yet according to Garnett this talk of death did nothing to diminish Lydia's 'irrepressible gaiety'. During that long afternoon, with the sun slowly sinking outside, she chatted and laughed as if she were a young girl, and when she fished a cigarette out of the enormous handbag that lay by her feet, Garnett marvelled at the 'extreme and touching grace' with which she slowly smoked it.

By the following September, however, Lydia had slipped deeper into senility. When Richard and Anne visited with their youngest son, Simon, she became very animated, embarking first on a ribald comparison of her and Anne's body shapes, then fretting suddenly that her guests must be hungry. Poignantly, she shuffled off to find a melon to feed them with, after which she attempted to lead them into the dining room, where, of course, no meal was waiting.

By 1976, Lydia was too frail, and too confused, to be left safely at Tilton, and the family found her a room at the Three Ways nursing home in nearby Seaford. Logan, too lame to look after himself, had to be moved into a separate home, where he would die only four years later. Yet if he suffered at this abrupt termination of their long, devoted friendship, Lydia herself had become too muddled to notice.

Lydia in old age, Seaford, 1980

She now found it hard to complete a sentence and reverted more and more frequently to her native language. When Milo gently reminded her that he could not understand Russian, she replied with devastating logic, 'But I do.'[78]

She still responded to visitors, however, reacting with childlike eagerness to physical affection and rarely appearing querulous. In some of the last pictures taken of her, a clear, steady energy was still in her eyes, and her hands, folded over the arm of her chair, were neither crabbed nor swollen. Lydia in old age looked noble, and at the age of eighty-nine, when the last little piece of her life 'flew away', her death was simple and peaceful. It was on 8 June 1981, and after a quiet cremation her ashes were taken to the top of Firle Beacon. They were scattered into the air, at exactly the same spot where Maynard's ashes had been cast thirty-five years earlier.

EPILOGUE

This tenderly symbolic reunion was all the ceremony that Lydia would have approved. Inevitably, however, her death caused a public stir. A memorial service, part-Russian Orthodox, part-Anglican, was sung in the chapel at King's (the spoken elegy, 'All joys go with you, let sweet pleasure attend you all the way', was from a poem by Henry King that Maynard had sent to Lydia years before from Cambridge). There were also a flurry of obituaries in the press, noting the passing of the former Lady Keynes and the loss of the once world-famous 'Bloomsbury ballerina'.

Yet whilst the newspapers might write about Lydia's extraordinary career, and the 'unequalled' ovations that she had received from her London fans, the long years that she had spent in seclusion reduced the impact of such notices. So little was left to measure Lydia's status by. She had choreographed no significant works, and she had only a small repertory created specifically for her. Even the style of her dancing was difficult to communicate. Nijinsky's legendary jump, Markova's uncanny virtuosity, the romantic beauty of Pavlova: all these were attributes that could be marvelled over posthumously. It was much harder for obituary writers to catch the slant of Lydia's wit and the luminous fizz of her energy. And she herself had deliberately accelerated the fading of her own image. Refusing to speak to the press, steering clear of public appearances, disdaining to sell her memoirs, she had guarded her privacy but also sealed her obscurity. Other great ballerinas might slip almost directly from celebrity to legend, like Pavlova, who died so tragically young, or Fonteyn, who perpetuated her career for so long. Lydia had simply shed her dancing past for a self-sufficient, anonymous old age.

After her death the Keynes family did what they could to keep her name in the public domain. In 1983, Milo published his lively biographical sketch of her, along with a series of commissioned essays from friends and colleagues; in 1989, Polly Hill and Richard Keynes published a scrupulously edited selection of Lydia and Maynard's early letters. Robert Skidelsky's masterly three-volume biography of Maynard added more pieces to the picture, giving a detailed assessment of his and Lydia's marriage and of Lydia's own contribution to Maynard's career. Best-selling biographies of Lytton Strachey, Virginia Woolf, Diaghilev and Nijinsky also featured tantalising snapshots of Lydia's life. From a very different angle, recent scholarly interest in Fedor has also brought revived interest in Lydia – the Lopukhov sister who got away.

Yet the fascination of Lydia and her story goes far beyond her contributions to ballet or economic history. Back in 1933, Virginia Woolf may have hated writing her 'tough little review' of *Twelfth Night*, yet it was she rather than the more pious legions of Lopokova fans who articulated the essential truth of Lydia's power. Beyond her talent, beyond her courage, beyond even her fabled charm, Lydia possessed something more compelling: 'that rare quality which is neither to be had for the asking nor to be subdued by the will – the genius of personality'.[1]

During her lifetime Lydia was admired as a darling soubrette, as a Russian exotic and as a drawing room eccentric; and as Diaghilev knew, the effects she created could not easily be replicated or analysed. Ultimately it was the force of her own character that made the comedy and poetry of her roles so brightly distinct. As Lydia danced out of the confines of the Imperial Ballet School and on to the international stage, as she graduated from the parties of Bloomsbury to the power centres of Washington, she did not simply figure as one of the great performers of the twentieth century. She was one of its true originals.

ROLES

Debuts in Dancing Roles

Cr. = roles created on L.L. Chor. = roles choreographed by L.L.

1903: Poupée de dentelles (cr.), *The Fairy Doll* (N. and S. Legat), Hermitage Theatre, St Petersburg.
1903–4: Marie (Clara), *The Nutcracker*, Mariinsky Theatre, St Petersburg.
1904: Pavot (Poppy), *The Blue Dahlia* (Petipa), Mariinsky Theatre, St Petersburg.
1905: Cupid (cr.), *Acis and Galatea* (Fokine), Theatre School, St Petersburg.
1906: Robin (cr.), *A Midsummer Night's Dream* (Fokine), Mariinsky Theatre, St Petersburg.
1908: Winter Snow Flake (cr.), *The Four Seasons* (Fokine), Theatre School, St Petersburg.
1909: Columbine, *The Nutcracker*, Mariinsky Theatre, St Petersburg.
1910: Miranda, *Le Pavillon d'Armide* (Fokine), Mariinsky Theatre, St Petersburg.
Bacchante (cr.), *Tannäuser* (Fokine), Mariinsky Theatre, St Petersburg.
Columbine, *Carnaval* (Fokine), Diaghilev's company, Berlin.
Prelude, *Les Sylphides* (arr. Fokine), Diaghilev's company, Berlin.
Enchanted Princess, *Festin* (Fokine), Diaghilev's company, Paris.
Polovtsian Maid, *The Polovtsian Dances* (Fokine), Diaghilev's company, Paris.
Peasant pas de deux, *Giselle*, Diaghilev's company, Paris.
Firebird, *L'Oiseau de feu* (Fokine), Diaghilev's company, Paris.
Dancer (cr.), *Czibulka Waltz* (Lopukhov), Imperial Russian Dancers, New York.
Waltz, *Les Sylphides* (Fokine), Chicago.
1911: Ta Hor, *Cléopâtre*, and Mazurka, *Les Sylphides* (after Fokine by Koslov and Hoffmann), Gertrude Hoffmann's Ballets Russes, New York.
Swan, *Dying Swan*, Mikhail Mordkin's staging of *Swan Lake*, Imperial Russian All-Star Ballet, autumn US tour.

1912: *Bacchanale* (Mordkin) and assorted cabaret numbers including *Xylophone Polka*, New York.
1915: Assorted cabaret numbers including *Pizzicato Solo* in 'Moment Musicale', New York; *In the Shadows*, *Blue Danube Waltz* and *Valse Triste* at 'Jardin de Danse', New York.
1916: Ballerina, *Petrushka* (Fokine), Diaghilev's Ballets Russes, New York.
Young Girl, *Le Spectre de la rose* (Fokine), Diaghilev's Ballets Russes, US Winter tour.
Bacchanale, *Cléopâtre* (Fokine), as above.
Young Girl, *Les Papillons* (Fokine), Diaghilev's Ballets Russes, New York.
1917: Mariuccia (cr.), *Les Femmes de bonne humeur* (Massine), Diaghilev's Ballets Russes, Rome.
Acrobat (cr.), *Parade* (Massine), Diaghilev's Ballets Russes, Paris.
1918: Snow Maiden (cr.), *Soleil de nuit* (Massine), Diaghilev's Ballets Russes, London.
1919: Can-Can dancer (cr.), *La Boutique fantasque* (Massine), Diaghilev's Ballets Russes, London.
1921: Ballerina (cr.), *Ballet of the Perfumes* (Fokine), in *The Rose Girl*, New York.
Pimpinella, *Pulcinella* (Massine), Diaghilev's Ballet Russes, London.
Lilac Fairy and Bluebird pas de deux, *The Sleeping Princess*, Diaghilev's Ballets Russes, London.
Princess Aurora, *The Sleeping Princess*, as above.
1922: Dancer, *Ragtime* (Massine), Wanger Covent Garden season, London. (Also during this season: Ballerina, *Fanatics of Pleasure*; Dancer, *Scotch Reel*; Lead Czardas dancer, *Lezghinka*; Ballerina, *La Cimarosiana*; also *Minuet*, *Arabella* and *Finale* in *The Cockatoo's Holiday* (all Massine).
Tarantella, *Variation*, *Minuet* and *Humming Bird* (all Massine), Coliseum, London.
Soloist (cr. and chor.) Chinese and Russian dances, Lopokova Company, London.
Lead Woman, *Les Élégants* (Vera Bowen), as above.
The Wife (cr.), *Masquerade* (L. Lopokova and Bowen), as above.
1923: Elaria de la Cueva (cr.), *Togo* (Massine) in *You'd Be Surprised*, London. (Also in the same production *An Incredible Polka* and *Trish Trash* [sic], (Massine).
1924: Grisette (cr.), *Soldier and Grisette* (N. Legat), Coliseum, London.
Dancing Girl (cr.), *Le Beau Danube* (Massine), Beaumont's Soirées de Paris, Paris. Also for the same season created roles in *Gigue*, *Les Roses*, *Premier Amour* (all Massine).
1925: The Maid (cr.), *The Postman* (N. Legat), Coliseum, London.
Lead Girl, *Les Matelots* (Massine), Diaghilev's Ballets Russes, London.

1927: The Princess (cr. and chor.) in Stravinsky's *The Soldiers Tale*, Arts Theatre Club, London.
1928: Dancer (cr. and chor.) in *Hiawatha*, Albert Hall, London.
1929: The Wife (cr.), *Jealousy*, Balanchine's ballet for *Dark Red Roses* (dir. Sinclair Hill), London.
1930: The Lassie (cr.), *Dances on a Scotch Theme* (Ashton), 'A Masque of Poetry and Music', Arts Theatre Club, London.
The Lady (cr.), *Follow Your Saint*: *The Passionate Pavane* (Ashton), as above.
1931: Milkmaid (cr.), *Jodelling Song* and Debutant (cr.), *Tango*, both in *Façade* (Ashton), Camargo Society, London.
Queen of the Port (cr.), *A Day in a Southern Port*, later *Rio Grande* (Ashton), Camargo Society, London.
Procris, *Cephalus and Procris* (de Valois), Vic–Wells Ballet, London.
1932: Dibutade (cr), *Origin of Design* (de Valois), Camargo Society, London.
1933: Swanilda, *Coppélia*, Vic–Wells Ballet, London.

Major Acting Roles

1901–2: Mamillius, *A Winter's Tale*, Alexandrinsky Theatre, St Petersburg.
1902–3: Peaseblossom, *A Midsummer Night's Dream*, Alexandrinsky Theatre, St Petersburg.
1913: Euphemia Kendal (cr.), *Just Herself*, originally *The Young Idea* (Henry Watts and Ethel Watts Mumford), Pittsfield, Mass.
1915: Julie Bonheur, *The Antick* (Percy MacKaye), Washington Players, New York.
Contesse de Chavigny, *Whims of Marianne* (Alfred de Musset), as above.
1928: The Afflicted Maid, *A Lover's Complaint*, Amateur Dramatic Club, Cambridge.
The Lady, *Comus* with George Rylands, King's College, Cambridge.
1929: Marie, *The Prisoners of War* (J. R. Ackerley), ADC, Cambridge.
Rosaura, *Life's a Dream* (Pedro Calderón de la Barca), ADC, Cambridge.
1933: Olivia, *Twelfth Night*, Old Vic, London.
1934: Nora Helmer, *A Doll's House*, Arts Theatre Club, London.
1936: Hilda Wangel, *The Master Builder*, Cambridge Arts Theatre.
1937: Célimène, *Le Misanthrope*, Cambridge Arts Theatre.
1938: Anna Vrodny (cr.), *On the Frontier* (W. H. Auden and Christopher Isherwood), Cambridge Arts Theatre.
1943: Female Narrator, *War and Peace*, BBC Radio, London.

NOTES

Introduction, pp. xv–xix

1 Letter from Lydia Lopokova (LL) to John Maynard Keynes (JMK), 18 April 1922. Kept among the Keynes Papers at King's College Archive, Cambridge (KCA). All letters between Lydia Lopokova and John Maynard Keynes are from the same source and are filed under JMK, PP/45/190. Other letters addressed to and from Lydia are also held in KCA in the Lydia Lopokova-Keynes Papers (LLK). Letters between Lydia and Maynard's mother, Florence Keynes, are filed under LLK/5/122. Most of the other correspondence and papers are also held in KCA, for which individual file references are given in the notes.
2 Austin Robinson, 'The Economist's Wife', Milo Keynes (ed.), *Lydia Lopokova*, Weidenfeld & Nicolson, London, 1983, p.166.
3 Patrick Hadley to LL, April 1946, LLK/5/229, also cited in Keynes (ed.), *Lydia Lopokova*, p.1.
4 LL to JMK, 23 November 1925.
5 Cited in Keynes (ed.), *Lydia Lopokova*, p.xiii.
6 This account is based on several contemporary press reports.
7 Marie Rambert, cited in Leo Kersley, 'Lopokova, Lydia', *International Dictionary of Ballet*, St James's Press, London, 1993, p.874.
8 From a collection of scripts drafted by Lydia for a series of BBC broadcasts on ballet music, held in LLK/3. There are several versions of these scripts, all undated, which were broadcast during the mid to late 1930s. Variations of individual anecdotes also appear in press interviews that Lydia gave during her career.

1 The Lopukhov Dynasty, pp. 1–14

1 BBC draft scripts, LLK/3.
2 Ibid.
3 LL to JMK, 14 May 1928.

4 Galina Doborovolskaya, *Fyodor Lopukhov*, Iskusstvo, Leningrad, 1976, p.22; unpublished trans. Geoff Whitlock.
5 Ibid.
6 BBC draft scripts, LLK/3.

2 Imperial Property, pp. 15–37

1 BBC draft scripts, LLK/3.
2 Ibid.
3 Tamara Karsavina, *Theatre Street*, revised edn, Constable & Co, London, 1948, p.102.
4 BBC draft scripts, LLK/3.
5 LL to JMK, 12 November 1926.
6 Lydia Lopokova, review of C. W. Beaumont's *Enrico Cecchetti* in *The Nation and Athenaeum*, 29 June 1929.
7 BBC draft scripts, LLK/3.
8 Ibid.
9 Ibid.
10 *Granta*, 9 November 1928.
11 Isadora Duncan, *The Dance of the Future* (1902–3), from Sheldon Cheney (ed.), *The Art of Dance*, New York, Theatre Arts Books, 1969.
12 BBC draft scripts, LLK/3.
13 Fyodor Lopukhov, 'Lydia Vasilievna Lopukhova', unpublished essay originally in Russian, translated and reprinted for Keynes (ed.), p.52.
14 BBC draft script, LLK/3.
15 F. Lopukhov, Keynes (ed.), p.52.
16 *St Petersburg Gazette*, 23 March 1909.
17 *St Petersburg Gazette*, 9 April 1909.
18 BBC draft scripts, LLK/3.
19 Ibid.
20 Ibid.
21 Ibid.
22 Cited in Orlando Figes, *Natasha's Dance: A Cultural History of Russia*, Penguin, Harmondsworth, 2003 (first published 2002), p.270.
23 Karsavina, *Theatre Street*, p.219.

3 Paris and Diaghilev, pp. 38–50

1 F. Lopukhov, Keynes (ed.), p.51.
2 BBC draft scripts, LLK/3.
3 Karsavina, *Theatre Street*, p.219.

4 Cyril Beaumont, *The Art of Lydia Lopokova*, Beaumont Press, London, 1920, p.3.
5 BBC draft scripts, LLK/3.
6 *Minneapolis Journal*, 12 February 1911.
7 *Figaro*, 19 June 1910.
8 BBC draft scripts, LLK/3.
9 S. L. Grigoriev, *The Diaghilev Ballet*, trans. Vera Bowen, Penguin, Harmondsworth, 1960 (first published 1953), p.51.
10 Ibid.
11 Alexander Benois, *Reminiscences of the Russian Ballet*, trans. Mary Britnieva, Putnam, London, 1941, p.308.
12 Letter from C. Ercole to A. Moul, quoted in Ivor Guest, 'The Alhambra Ballet', *Dance Perspectives*, Autumn 1959.
13 *St Petersburg Gazette*, 18 August 1910.
14 *Footlights and Life*, no.27, 1910.
15 Russian State Historical Archive, St Petersburg (trans. Olga Makarova).
16 Letter from V. Woolf to Barbara Bagenal, 24 June 1923.

4 The New World, pp. 51–74

1 Cited Keith Money, *Anna Pavlova: Her Life and Art*, Collins, London, 1982, p.91.
2 Money, p.111.
3 *New York Review*, 25 June 1911.
4 *New York Telegraph*, 23 July 1910.
5 *New York Telegraph*, 4 August 1910.
6 *America*, 4 August 1910.
7 *The Echo*, clippings file, undated, held at New York Public Library.
8 *New York Sun*, 18 August 1910.
9 *New York Tribune*, 18 August 1910.
10 *The Echo*, clippings file, undated, held at New York Public Library.
11 Fedor Lopukhov, *Sixty Years in the Ballet*, Iskusstvo, Moscow, 1966, p.156, unpublished trans. Geoff Whitlock.
12 *Chicago Tribune*, 26 October 1910.
13 *Sunday Times*, 17 July 1927.
14 State Historical Archive, St Petersburg (trans. Olga Makarova), filed 20 November, Old Style date.
15 Lopukhov, *Sixty Years in the Ballet*, p.160.
16 Ibid.
17 Lopukhov, *Sixty Years in the Ballet*, p.161.
18 *San Francisco Chronicle*, 22 November 1910.

19 2 January 1911 (OS date).
20 Lopukhov, *Sixty Years in the Ballet*, p.162.
21 Cited in Vera Krasovskaya, *Russian Ballet Theatre at the Beginning of the 20th Century*, Leningrad State Institute of Theatre, Music and Cinematography, 1972, p.140.
22 *New York Review*, 12 August 1911.
23 *New York Telegraph*, 19 August 1911.
24 *New York Review*, 12 August 1911.
25 *New York Review*, 5 August 1911.
26 *New York Times*, 25 June 1911.
27 Ibid.
28 The story was repeated by the *New York Star*, 6 January 1915.
29 *Montreal Herald*, 17 October 1911.
30 *Pittsburgh Dispatch*, 7 November 1911.
31 *Buffalo Times*, 11 November 1911.
32 *Buffalo Times*, 12 November 1911.
33 *New York Telegraph*, 20 December 1911.
34 *New York World*, 16 January 1912.
35 *New York Sun*, 16 January 1912.
36 *Variety*, undated, LL clippings file, New York Public Library.
37 *New York American*, 19 December 1912.
38 *Dramatic Review*, 25 December 1912.
39 *New York American*, 19 December 1912.
40 *Chicago News*, 5 November 1912.

5 American Projects, pp. 75–89

1 LL to Florence Keynes, 6 July 1944.
2 *Brooklyn Eagle*, 16 January 1914.
3 *New York Sun*, 6 January 1914.
4 *Des Moines Register*, 3 May 1914.
5 Undated, LL clippings file, New York Public Library.
6 *New York Tribune*, 20 March 1914.
7 *Christian Science Monitor*, 3 November 1914.
8 *New York Times*, 24 December 1914.
9 *New York Telegraph*, 24 December 1914.
10 *New York Herald*, 24 December 1914.
11 *Cleveland Leader*, 24 December 1914.
12 Ibid.
13 *New York Times*, 30 December 1914.
14 State Historical Archive, St Petersburg (unpublished trans. Olga Makarova).

15 *New York Herald*, 16 January 1915.
16 *New York Mail*, 31 July 1915.
17 *New York American*, January 1916.
18 Cited in Dale Kramer, *Heywood Broun*, Current Books Inc., New York, 1949, p.64.
19 *New York Mail*, 9 October 1915.
20 Kramer, pp.63–4.
21 Kramer, p.64.
22 Kramer, p.66.
23 Kramer, p.70.
24 Kramer, p.71.
25 Kramer, p.73.

6 The Reunion, pp. 90–116

1 Grigoriev, p.119.
2 Lydia Lopokova, review of C. W. Beaumont's *Enrico Cecchetti*, in *The Nation and Athenaeum*, 29 June 1929.
3 Lydia Sokolova, *Dancing for Diaghilev*, Mercury House edn, California, 1960, p.74.
4 Unsigned letter to Otto Kahn, 26 December 1915, Metropolitan Opera Archive, cited in Lynn Garafola, *Diaghilev's Ballets Russes*, Oxford University Press, New York and Oxford, 1989, p.449.
5 Vicente García-Márquez, *Massine*, Nick Hern Books, London, 1996, p.61.
6 *New York Tribune*, 18 January 1916.
7 Cited Richard Buckle, *Diaghilev*, Hamish Hamilton edn, London, 1979, p.306.
8 Sokolova, p.74.
9 *New York Post*, 20 January 1916.
10 Taruskin, Richard, *Stravinsky and the Russian Traditions*, Oxford University Press, 1996.
11 *Vogue*, British edn, August 1926.
12 Beaumont, *Diaghilev Ballet in London: A Personal Record*, Putnam, London, 1940, p.129.
13 F. Lopukhov, Keynes (ed.), p.53.
14 Barocchi to Diaghilev, April–May 1921, in the Kochno Collection, Bibliothèque Nationale, Opera, cited in Richard Buckle, *Diaghilev*, pp.380–1.
15 *Kansas City Star*, 4 March 1916.
16 Edward L. Bernays, *Biography of an Idea: Memoirs of Public Relations Counsel Edward L. Bernays*, Simon & Schuster, New York, 1965, cited in Garafola, pp.203–4.

17 These articles ran in the *Chicago Herald* in mid-February and were subsequently syndicated in the Milwaukee and Wisconsin press at the end of the month.
18 *Minneapolis Journal*, 2 March 1916.
19 Kramer, p.72.
20 *New York Times*, 15 April 1916.
21 Cited in Richard Buckle, *Nijinsky*, Weidenfeld & Nicolson, London, 1971, p.358.
22 M. Keynes, 'Lydia Lopokova', Keynes (ed.), p.2.
23 *New York Herald*, 13 April 1916.
24 *New York Dramatic Review*, 27 May 1916
25 *Daily News*, 29 July 1925.
26 Unidentified London press clipping, LLK/1.
27 Vera Stravinsky and Robert Craft, *Stravinsky in Pictures and Documents*, Simon & Schuster, New York, 1978, pp.141–2, cited in Stephen Walsh, *Stravinsky*, Alfred A. Knopf, New York, 1999, vol.1, p.265. Buckle also cites a conversation with Vera Stravinsky: Buckle, *Diaghilev*, p.313.
28 See Ernest Ansermet's delicate hint of 28 July 1918 that he had 'Plus de nouvelle de Lopokowa' to report, in Ernest Ansermet and Claude Tappolet (eds), *Correspondance Ansermet–Strawinsky*, Georg, Geneva, 1991, hereafter referred to as *Correspondance Ansermet–Strawinsky*.
29 Stravinsky and Craft, p.618.
30 *Boston Evening Transcript*, 10 November 1916.
31 Letter to Ernest Henkel, Metropolitan Opera Archives, cited in Garafola, p.208.
32 Sokolova, p.93.

7 Dancing through War, pp. 117–133

1 Sokolova, p.99.
2 BBC draft scripts, LLK, cited in Keynes (ed.), *Lydia Lopokova*, p.210.
3 Ibid.
4 Unidentified press clipping, May 1921, LLK/1.
5 *The Star*, 18 November 1926.
6 BBC draft scripts, LLK/3, cited Keynes (ed.), p.210.
7 BBC draft scripts, LLK/3, cited Keynes (ed.), p.25.
8 Ibid.
9 Cited in García-Márquez, p.103.
10 *Excelsior*, 11 May 1917, cited García-Márquez, p. 99.
11 Sokolova, p.104.
12 BBC draft scripts, LLK/3, cited Keynes (ed.), p.25.

13 BBC draft scripts, LLK/3, cited Keynes (ed.), p.206.
14 Ibid.
15 Randolfo Barrochi to Serge Diaghilev, 16 July 1919, in Kochno archives, cited in Keynes (ed.), *Lydia Lopokova*, p.4.
16 BBC draft scripts, LLK/3, cited Keynes (ed.), p.209.
17 Sokolova, p.120.
18 BBC draft scripts, LLK/3, cited Keynes (ed.), p.209.
19 Cited Buckle, *Diaghilev*, p.342.
20 BBC draft scripts, LLK/3.
21 García-Márquez, p.127.
22 From an interview titled 'How I am Hustled', undated clipping, LLK/1.

8 London, pp. 134–152

1 Osbert Sitwell, *Laughter in the Next Room*, London, Macmillan, 1949, cited Keynes (ed.), p.1.
2 *The Era*, 11 September 1918.
3 Cited Garafola, p.335.
4 Beaumont, *Diaghilev Ballet in London*, p.115.
5 Beaumont, *Diaghilev Ballet in London*, p.116.
6 Sokolova, p.133.
7 Cecil Beaton, *Ballet*, Doubleday, Garden City, NY, 1951, p.19.
8 Jill Sinclair to LL, 15 June 1922, LLK/5/194.
9 Ninette de Valois, *Come Dance with Me*, Lilliput Press, Dublin, 1992 (first published 1957), p.41.
10 Ibid.
11 BBC draft scripts, LLK/3.
12 Virginia Woolf, 12 October 1918, Anne Olivier Bell and Andrew McNeillie (eds), *The Diary of Virginia Woolf*, 5 vols, Hogarth Press, London, 1977–84, vol.1, p.202 (hereafter referred to as Diary).
13 JMK to Duncan Grant, 17 September 1918, British Library.
14 Cited Robert Skidelsky, *John Maynard Keynes*, 3 vols, Macmillan, London, 1983–2000, vol.1, p.352.
15 Duncan Grant to Vanessa Bell, 2 November 1918, Tate Gallery Archive.
16 JMK to Duncan Grant, 20 October 1918, British Library.
17 Ibid.
18 'A Letter from Quentin Bell', cited in Keynes (ed.), p.92.
19 LL to JMK, 29 December 1918.
20 Cited Keynes (ed.), p.2.
21 Beaumont, *Diaghilev Ballet in London*, p.141.
22 Beaumont, *Diaghilev Ballet in London*, p.139.

23 Beaumont, *The Art of Lydia Lopokova*, p.5.
24 BBC draft scripts, LLK/3.
25 Sokolova, p.143.
26 *Vogue*, London, August 1918.
27 Cited Garafola, p.336.
28 Clive Bell, 'The New Ballet', *The New Republic*, July 1919.
29 Ibid.
30 LL to JMK, 16 October 1926.
31 Beaumont, *Diaghilev Ballet in London*, pp.139–40.
32 Ibid.
33 See Ernest Ansermet to Igor Stravinsky, 1 June 1919, Ansermet and Tappolet (eds), *Correspondance Ansermet–Strawinsky*.
34 Unidentified press clipping, LLK/1.
35 Grigoriev, p.156.
36 Copy of letter in LLK/8.
37 Virginia Woolf to Vanessa Bell, 17 July 1919, in Nigel Nicolson and Joanne Trautmann (eds), *The Letters of Virginia Woolf*, 6 vols, Hogarth Press, London, 1975–80 (hereafter referred to as *Woolf Letters*).
38 *Observer*, 20 July 1919.
39 Copy of letter in LLK/5/231, trans. Loughlin.
40 Ibid.

9 Vanishing Secrets, pp. 153–160

1 Ernest Ansermet to Igor Stravinsky, 11 July 1919, *Correspondance Ansermet–Strawinsky*.
2 Sokolova, p.139.
3 Randolfo Barocchi to Serge Diaghilev, 16 July 1919, Kochno archives, copy in LLK/8.
4 LL to Barocchi, copy, LLK/8.
5 JMK to LL, 9 February 1931.
6 *New York World*, 20 September 1925.
7 Ernest Ansermet to Igor Stravinsky, 11 July 1919, *Correspondance Ansermet–Strawinsky*. See also see JMK to LL, 16 January 1925, referring to Barocchi's stealing.
8 LLto Richard Kahn, 25 September 1949, LLK/5/118.
9 Randolfo Barocchi to Serge Diaghilev, 16 July 1919, Kochno archives, translated copy in LLK/8.
10 Beaumont, *Diaghilev in London*, p.142.
11 Evgenia Lopukhova to LL, 8 May 1922, trans. Loughlin, LLK/5/231.
12 BBC draft scripts, LLK/3.

13 Randolfo Barocchi to Serge Diaghilev, 16 July 1919, see note 9.

10 A Prodigal Return, pp. 161–179

1 BBC draft scripts, LLK/3.
2 *Theater Magazine*, April 1921.
3 *New York Tribune*, 12 February 1921
4 *Globe*, 12 February 1921.
5 BBC draft scripts, LLK/3.
6 *New York Tribune*, 12 February 1921.
7 BBC draft scripts, LLK/3.
8 *London Evening News*, 4 June 1921.
9 LLK/5/105. The fan was Gertrude Holland, known to Lydia as Peter. They would become regular correspondents.
10 LL to unknown correspondents. The letter, undated, is in Russian, trans. Loughlin, LLK/5/23 I.
11 Cited Keynes (ed.), p.6.
12 Karsavina, pp.219–20.
13 Cited Keynes (ed.), p.6.
14 Unidentified press clipping, May 1921, LLK/1.
15 *Daily News*, 13 June 1921.
16 *Sunday Pictorial*, 30 May 1921.
17 *Vogue*, August 1926.
18 *Daily Telegraph*, 16 July 1921.
19 Cited in Skidelsky, vol.2, p.211.
20 Frederick Ashton, 'Lydia the Enchantress', cited Keynes (ed.), p.120.
21 Quentin Bell, 'Bloomsbury and Lydia', Keynes (ed.), p.85.
22 Sam Courtauld to LL, July 1921, LLK/5/57.
23 LLto JMK, 7 March 1925.
24 Cited Walsh, vol.1, p.343.
25 Sokolova, p.190.
26 BBC draft scripts, LLK/3.
27 Beaumont, *Diaghilev Ballet in London*, p.202.
28 Cited in Buckle, *Diaghilev*, p.392.
29 Raymond Mortimer, *Dial*, March 1922.
30 *The Times*, 3 November 1921.
31 Beaumont, *Diaghilev Ballet in London*, p.213.
32 Copy, in Maynard's handwriting, LLK/1; also cited in Keynes (ed.), p.78.
33 Copy in LLK/1.
34 Ibid.

11 Maynard, pp. 180–199

1 JMK to Vanessa Bell, 22 December 1921, Charleston Papers, KCA, CHA/1/341/3/2/.
2 JMK to Duncan Grant, 17 July 1919, British Library.
3 JMK to Lytton Strachey, 20 May 1920, JMK, PP/45/316/5.
4 David Garnett, diary, 28 May 1918, cited Skidelsky, vol.1, p.350.
5 Interview with JMK, *Pearson's Magazine*, 1922, also cited Skidelsky, vol.2, p.111.
6 G. E. Moore, *Principia Ethica*, Cambridge University Press, 1903, p.189.
7 J. M. Keynes, 'My Early Beliefs', in Keynes, *Collected Writings*, vol.10, 1972.
8 Virginia Woolf, *Moments of Being*, ed. Jeanne Schulkind, Sussex University Press, 1985 edn, p.201.
9 Lytton Strachey to Leonard Woolf, October 1905, cited Michael Holroyd, *Lytton Strachey*, Penguin, Harmondsworth, 1971 (first published 1967), p.292.
10 Lytton Strachey to James Strachey, 17 July 1908, British Library.
11 JMK to Florence Keynes, 23 December 1911, JMK, PP/45/168.
12 Vanessa Bell to JMK 16 [April] 1914, CHA/1/59/5/1.
13 JMK to Duncan Grant, 15 December 1917, British Library.
14 JMK to LL, 24 January 1926.
15 JMK to Margot Asquith, cited Skidelsky, vol.1, p.378.
16 John Maynard Keynes, *The Economic Consequences of the Peace*, *Collected Writings*, vol. 2, cited Skidelsky, vol.1, p.388.
17 JMK to Lytton Strachey, 23 December 1919, JMK, PP/45/316/5.
18 Lytton Strachey to JMK, 16 December 1919, JMK, PP/45/316/5.
19 LL to JMK, 28 December 1921.
20 LL to JMK, 12 November 1922.
21 Evgenia Lopukhova to LL, 8 May 1922, trans. Loughlin, LLK/5/231.
22 Vanessa Bell to JMK, 1 January 1922, CHA/1/59/5/3.
23 JMK to Vanessa Bell, 6 January 1922, CHA/1/341/3/3.
24 JMK to Vanessa Bell, 9 January 1922, CHA/1/341/3/3.
25 JMK to Duncan Grant, 26 July 1912, British Library.
26 Duncan Grant, unpublished diary, cited in Frances Spalding, *Duncan Grant*, Pimlico Press, London, 1998 (first published 1997), p.201.
27 Cited Holroyd, p.633.
28 Cited Skidelsky, vol.2, p.51.
29 John Maynard Keynes, 'My Early Beliefs', cited Skidelsky, vol.2, p.55.
30 Comment to Sarah Walton, interview with the author.
31 LL to JMK, 28 April 1922.
32 LL to JMK, 2 September 1922.

33 Cited Skidelsky, vol.3, p.156.
34 LL to JMK, 11 November 1922.
35 LL to JMK, 9 December 1922.
36 Ibid.
37 LL to JMK, 10 June 1922.
38 LL to JMK, 10 April 1922.
39 LL to JMK, 21 April 1922.
40 LL to JMK, 19 April 1922.
41 Vanessa Bell to JMK, 1 January 1922, CHA/1/59/5/3.
42 LL to JMK, 16 April 1922.

12 Cambridge and Bloomsbury Influences, pp. 200–217

1 Duncan Grant to Vanessa Bell, 25 January 1922, Tate Gallery Archive.
2 Unidentified press clipping, LLK/1.
3 JMK to Vanessa Bell, 9 February 1922, CHA/1/341/3/3.
4 LL to JMK, 24 April 1922.
5 Marie Stopes, *Married Love*, 1918, repr. Oxford University Press, 2004, Chapter 6 passim.
6 LL to JMK, 11 April 1922.
7 LL to JMK, 24 May 1923.
8 LL to JMK, 4 July 1922.
9 LL to JMK, 22 June 1922.
10 LL to JMK, 25 January 1923.
11 LL to JMK, 2 March 1923.
12 LL to JMK, 16 March 1923.
13 JMK to LL, 10 October 1924.
14 LL to JMK, 11 October 1923.
15 LL to JMK, 13 November 1925.
16 Quentin Bell, 'Bloomsbury and Lydia', Keynes (ed.), p.87.
17 Ibid.
18 Cited Keynes (ed.), p.15.
19 Polly Hill, '6 Harvey Road and 46 Gordon Square', Keynes (ed.), p.148.
20 Virginia Woolf to Barbara Bagenal, 23 December 1920, *Woolf Letters*.
21 LL to JMK, 20 April 1922.
22 LL to JMK, 23 April 1922.
23 LL to JMK, 11 April 1922.
24 LL to JMK, 15 April 1922.
25 LL to JMK, 21 April 1922.
26 Quentin Bell, Keynes (ed.), p.89.
27 Vanessa Bell to Roger Fry, 11 April 1922, cited Skidelsky, vol.2, p.111.

28 LL to JMK, 26 April 1922.
29 LL to JMK, 16 April 1922.
30 Cited Skidelsky, vol.2, p.112.
31 Vanessa Bell to JMK, 16 May 1922, CHA/1/59/5/3.
32 LL to JMK, 20 April 1922.
33 LLto JMK, 21 January 1923.
34 Vanessa Bell to Roger Fry, September 1917, CHA/1/59/4/9.
35 Virginia Woolf to Jacques Raverat, 8 June 1924, *Woolf Letters*.
36 Virginia Woolf to Vanessa Bell, April 1923, *Woolf Letters*.
37 Lydia Lopokova, 'We Russians – You English', *Daily Chronicle*, 13 March 1929.
38 Virginia Woolf to Jacques Raverat, September 1917, *Woolf Letters*.
39 Copy, LLK/8.
40 Lytton Strachey to James Strachey, 24 September 1911, British Library.
41 Cited Skidelsky, vol.1, p.352.
42 JMK to Vanessa Bell, 20 May 1922, CHA/l/341/3/3.
43 LL to JMK, 9 June 1922.
44 LL to JMK, 12 June 1922.
45 LL to JMK, 23 June 1922.
46 LL to JMK, 24 August 1922.
47 LL to JMK, 25 August 1922.
48 LL to JMK, 27 June 1922.
49 Denys Sutton (ed.), *The Letters of Roger Fry*, 2 vols, Chatto & Windus, London, 1972, vol.2, Roger Fry to H. Anrep, 23 December 1928.
50 Vanessa Bell to JMK, 22 August 1922, CHA/1/59/5/3.
51 LL to A. Genée, 22 September 1922, LLK/1.
52 Vanessa Bell to Roger Fry, 29 October 1922, CHA/1/59/4.

13 Private and Professional Skirmishes, pp. 218–245

1 Virginia Woolf to Jacques Raverat, 4 November 1923, *Woolf Letters*.
2 LL to JMK, 15 August 1922.
3 LL to JMK, 22 August 1922.
4 LL to JMK, 24 August 1922
5 LL to JMK, 14 August 1922.
6 Sokolova, p.142.
7 Marie Rambert, *Quicksilver: An Autobiography*, Macmillan, London, 1972, p.80.
8 LL to JMK, 9 June 1922.
9 LL to JMK, 11 June 1922.
10 LL to JMK, 16 October 1922.

11 Vera Bowen to LL, undated, trans. Loughlin, LLK/5/37.
12 LL to Vera Bowen, undated, LLK/5/37.
13 Vera Bowen to LL, undated, LLK/5/37.
14 LL to JMK, 29 September 1922.
15 *Dancing World*, November 1922.
16 LL to JMK, 20 October 1922.
17 LL to JMK, 23 October 1922.
18 LL to JMK, 11 November 1922
19 LL to JMK, 18 November 1922.
20 *The Era*, 21 November 1922.
21 LL to JMK, October 1922.
22 LL to JMK, 4 December 1922.
23 LL to JMK, 5 June 1925.
24 Sokolova, p.199.
25 *Dancing Times*, March 1923.
26 LL to JMK, 17 January 1923.
27 LL to JMK, 2 June 1923.
28 LL to JMK, 15 June 1923.
29 Ibid.
30 LL to JMK, 15 June 1923.
31 Ibid.
32 Evgenia Lopukhova to LL, trans. Loughlin, LLK/5/231.
33 Ibid.
34 Vanessa Bell to Roger Fry, undated, February 1923, cited in Skidelsky, vol.2, p.140.
35 Ibid.
36 Vanessa Bell to Duncan Grant, 27 April 1923, cited in Skidelsky, vol.2, p.141.
37 LL to JMK, 25 May 1923.
38 Ruby Weller, letter to Milo Keynes, 1981, LLK/8.
39 LL to JMK, 4 August 1923.
40 Harold Bowen, unpublished diary, 28 July 1923, 21 May 1924 and 13 October 1923, also cited in Skidelsky, vol.2, p.143.
41 Virginia Woolf to Vanessa Bell, 23 December 1922, *Woolf Letters*.
42 LL to JMK, 1 November 1925.
43 LL to JMK, 10 February 1929.
44 Virginia Woolf to Barbara Bagenal, 24 June 1923, *Woolf Letters*.
45 Virginia Woolf to Jacques Raverat, 4 November 1923, *Woolf Letters*.
46 Ibid.
47 Virginia Woolf, *Diary*, 9 August 1924.
48 Virginia Woolf, *Mrs Dalloway*, Penguin, Harmondsworth, 1992 (first published 1925), p.129.

49 Woolf, *Mrs Dalloway*, p.79.
50 Virginia Woolf, *Diary*, 15 August 1924.
51 Virginia Woolf, *Diary*, 11 September 1923.
52 Virginia Woolf to Vanessa Bell, 30 December 1929, *Woolf Letters*.
53 Virginia Woolf, *Diary*, 11 September 1923.
54 Virginia Woolf to Jacques Raverat, 4 November 1923, *Woolf Letters*.
55 Ibid.
56 Ibid.
57 LL to JMK, 14 September 1923.
58 JMK to LL, 20 September 1923.
59 Harold Bowen, unpublished diary, 22 November 1923.
60 JMK to LL, 21 and 20 September 1923.
61 JMK to LL, 28 October 1923.
62 Randolfo Barocchi to LL, 4 September 1923, copy LLK/8.
63 LL to JMK, 1 November 1923.
64 LL to JMK, 21 October 1923.
65 LL to JMK, 17 November 1923.
66 LL to JMK, 8 November 1923.
67 LL to JMK, 29 October 1923.
68 LL to JMK, 3 December 1923.
69 Harold Bowen, unpublished diary, 19 October 1923.
70 JMK to LL, 26 November 1923.
71 LL to JMK, 15 November 1923.
72 LL to JMK, 16 November 1923.
73 LL to JMK, 17 January 1924.
74 LL to JMK, 21 February 1924.
75 LL to JMK, 28 January 1924.
76 Vanessa Bell to Duncan Grant, 8 October 1923, cited Skidelsky, vol.2, p.146.
77 LL to JMK, 15 May 1924.
78 LL to JMK, 10 November 1924.
79 Quentin Bell, Keynes (ed.), p.90.
80 JMK to LL, 11 February 1924.
81 LL to JMK, 14 October 1925.

14 Anglo-Russian Treaties, pp. 246–269

1 LL to JMK, 3 February 1924.
2 LL to JMK, 14 January 1924.
3 LL to JMK, 29 February 1924.
4 LL to JMK, 26 January 1924.
5 LL to JMK, 20 February 1925.

6 *The Era*, undated clipping, LLK/1.
7 LL to JMK, 25 April 1924.
8 LL to JMK, 27 April 1924.
9 LL to JMK, 26 April 1924.
10 LL to JMK, 5 May 1924.
11 LL to JMK, 6 May 1924.
12 LL to JMK, 13 May 1924.
13 JMK to LL, 10 June 1924.
14 LL to JMK, 2 and 4 May 1924.
15 LL to JMK, 31 May 1924.
16 JMK to LL, 9 May 1924.
17 JMK to LL, 30 April 1924.
18 JMK to LL, 5 May 1924.
19 JMK to LL, 19 May 1924.
20 JMK to LL, 13 May 1924.
21 LL to JMK, 28 April 1924.
22 JMK to LL, 5 May 1924.
23 JMK to LL, 19 May 1924.
24 LL to JMK, 16 May 1924.
25 LL to JMK, 26 May 1924.
26 JMK to LL, 8 June 1924.
27 LL to JMK, 10 June 1924 and 13 May 1924.
28 *The Nation and Athenaeum*, 7 June 1924.
29 LL to JMK, 9 June 1924.
30 LL to JMK, 14 January 1924.
31 Cited García-Márquez, p.183.
32 LL to JMK, 27 May 1924
33 LL to JMK, 27 May 1924.
34 LL to JMK, 5 June 1924.
35 LL to JMK, 1 June 1924.
36 LL to JMK, 8 June 1924.
37 Ibid.
38 LL to JMK, 5 June 1924.
39 LL to JMK, 23 September 1924.
40 Duncan Grant to Vanessa Bell, 15 June 1924, cited Skidelsky, vol.2, p.179.
41 LL to JMK, 22 October 1924.
42 LL to JMK, 30 October 1924.
43 LL to JMK, 17 November 1924.
44 JMK to LL, 26 October 1924.

45 LL to Florence Keynes, 13 March 1936.
46 Alexandra Danilova, *Choura*, Knopf, New York, 1986, p.53.
47 LL to JMK, 25 October 1924.
48 LL to JMK, 12 October 1924.
49 LL to JMK, 1 December 1924.
50 Virginia Woolf to Vanessa Bell, 26 December 1924, *Woolf Letters*.
51 JMK to LL, 28 November 1924.
52 LL to JMK, 15 January 1925.
53 LL to Florence Keynes, 26 January 1925.
54 Virginia Woolf to Jacques Raverat, 4 November 1923, *Woolf Letters*.
55 LL to JMK, 19 January 1925.
56 JMK to LL, 25 January 1925.
57 LL to JMK, 16 May 1925.
58 *Weekly Dispatch*, 24 January 1926.
59 LL to JMK, 9 March 1925.
60 Ibid.
61 JMK to LL, 23 April 1925.
62 LL to JMK, 24 February 1925.
63 *Dancing Times*, May 1925.
64 LL to JMK, 31 January 1925.
65 LL to JMK, 26 April 1925.
66 Cited Spalding, *Duncan Grant*, p.263.
67 LL to JMK, 1 May 1925.
68 Virginia Woolf, *Diary*, 9 May 1925.
69 LL to JMK, 16 May 1925.
70 *Vogue*, November 1925.
71 *Daily News*, 5 August 1925.
72 Ibid.
73 Florence Keynes to Neville Keynes, 4 August 1925, cited Skidelsky, vol.2, p.208.
74 Ibid.
75 LL to JMK, 26 May 1929.
76 Cited Skidelsky, vol.2, p.209.
77 Ibid.
78 Cited Holroyd, pp. 516–17.
79 JMK to LL, 23 October 1925.

15 Marriage, pp. 270–294

1 JMK to LL, 1926.
2 Karlusha Lopukhova to LL, 11 April 1925, LLK/5.

3 Vladimir Lopukhov, interview with the author, trans. Makarova.
4 Karlusha Lopukhova to LL, 7 November 1925, LLK/5.
5 Karlusha Lopukhova to Florence Keynes, 17 September 1925, LLK/5.
6 Ibid.
7 Unidentified press clipping, 1925, LLK/1.
8 Virginia Woolf, *Diary*, 24 September 1925.
9 Virginia Woolf to Vanessa Bell, 20 March 1927, *Woolf Letters.*
10 LL to JMK, 14 October 1925.
11 LL to JMK, 7 October 1925.
12 Julie Kavanagh, *Secret Muses: The Life of Frederick Ashton*, Faber & Faber, London, 1996, p.116.
13 LL to JMK, 16 October 1926.
14 JMK to LL, 17 October 1926.
15 LL to JMK, 1 November 1936.
16 Ninette de Valois, *Come Dance with Me*, p.114.
17 LL to JMK, 26 November 1928.
18 LL to JMK, 28 February 1926.
19 LL, unpublished diary, 21 November 1926, LLK/6.
20 David Garnett, 'Lydia Lopokova', Keynes (ed.), p.154.
21 LL, unpublished diary, 29 March 1927, LLK/6.
22 LL to JMK, 20 November 1927.
23 Cited Skidelsky, vol.2, p.218.
24 LL, unpublished diary, 11 March and 14 April 1927, LLK/6.
25 LL to JMK, 21 February 1927.
26 Virginia Woolf to Vanessa Bell, 20 March 1927, *Woolf Letters.*
27 Cited in Spalding, *Vanessa Bell*, p.210.
28 D. Garnett, Keynes (ed.), p.154.
29 Virginia Woolf, *Diary*, 21 April 1928.
30 Virginia Woolf to Vanessa Bell, 30 December 1929, *Woolf Letters.*
31 Vanessa Bell to Duncan Grant, April 1926, cited Spalding, *Duncan Grant*, p.268.
32 Cited Skidelsky, vol.2, p.217.
33 Virginia Woolf to Margaret Llewelyn-Davies, 2 September 1926, *Woolf Letters.*
34 Duncan Grant to Vanessa Bell, 18 April 1926.
35 *Diary of Beatrice Webb*, N. MacKenzie and J. MacKenzie (eds), Virago, London, 1985, vol.4, pp. 93–4.
36 Cited Kavanagh, p.121.
37 Virginia Woolf to Lytton Strachey, 3 September 1927, *Woolf Letters.*
38 LL to JMK, 24 October 1925.

39 Milo Keynes, 'Lydia Lopokova', Keynes (ed.), p.34.
40 Ibid.
41 LLto JMK, 28 November 1925.
42 LL to Florence Keynes, 9 August 1936.
43 LL to Florence Keynes, 21 April 1929.
44 LL to Florence Keynes, 16 January and 3 May 1931.
45 LL to JMK, 16 January 1925.
46 LL to Florence Keynes, 5 January 1931.
47 LL to JMK, 2 November 1925.
48 LL to JMK, 4 February 1926.
49 LL to JMK, 4 December 1925.
50 *Vogue*, November 1925.
51 Cited Skidelsky, vol.2, p.211.
52 Cecil Beaton, 'A Visit to Lopokova', Keynes (ed.), p.184.
53 D. Garnett, Keynes (ed.), p.154.
54 LL to Florence Keynes, 17 June 1934.
55 LL to Florence Keynes, 1 October 1940.
56 LL to Florence Keynes, 8 June 1927.
57 LL to Florence Keynes, 16 October 1930.
58 *Daily Sketch*, 2 November 1926.
59 JMK to LL, 30 April 1926.
60 Vanessa Bell to Roger Fry, 29 October 1922, cited Skidelsky, vol.2, p.116.
61 JMK to LL, May 1926.
62 JMK to LL, 6 May 1927.
63 LL to JMK, 13 February 1927.
64 LL, unpublished diary, 19 May 1927, LLK/6.
65 Virginia Woolf to Vanessa Bell, 15 May 1927, *Woolf Letters*.
66 LL to JMK, 26 January 1928.
67 LL to JMK, 14 November 1927.
68 LL to JMK, 20 October 1928.
69 LL to JMK, 14 November 1927.
70 LL to JMK, 30 April 1928.
71 LL to JMK, 20 February 1927.
72 D. Garnett, Keynes (ed.), p.153.
73 *Daily Chronicle*, 13 March 1929.
74 LL to Florence Keynes, Good Friday, April 1928.
75 JMK to Ottoline Morrell, 2 May 1928, cited Skidelsky, vol.2, p.236.

16 Mrs Keynes on Stage, pp. 295–323

1 Annabel Farjeon, 'Lydia Lopokova and Serge Diaghilev', Keynes (ed.), p.81.
2 LL to JMK, 19 October 1925.

3 LL to JMK, 14 November 1925.
4 Frederick Ashton, 'Lydia, the Enchantress', Keynes (ed.), p.116.
5 LL to JMK, 14 November 1925.
6 LL to JMK, 12 November 1925.
7 LL to JMK, 9 November 1925.
8 JMK to LL, 23 November 1925.
9 LL to JMK, 4 February 1926.
10 LL to JMK, 30 April 1926.
11 LL to Florence Keynes, 6 June 1926.
12 LL to JMK, 29 May 1925.
13 LL to Florence Keynes, 29 June 1926.
14 LL to JMK, 31 May 1926.
15 LL to JMK, 30 May 1926.
16 LL to JMK, 29 May 1926.
17 LL to JMK, 14 June 1926.
18 Ashton, Keynes (ed.), p.116.
19 The *Star*, 18 November 1926.
20 LL to JMK, 14 November 1926.
21 LL to JMK, 15 and 19 November 1926.
22 LL, unpublished diary, 13 January 1927, LLK/6.
23 LL to JMK, 6 December 1926.
24 JMK to LL, 15 November 1926.
25 *Vogue*, August 1925.
26 Watson Lyle, untitled clipping from *Cassell's*, October 1928, LLK/1.
27 *Sunday Times*, 12 July 1926.
28 Farjeon, Keynes (ed.), p.82.
29 *The Nation and Athenaeum*, 20 July 1929.
30 BBC draft scripts, LLK/3, also cited in Keynes (ed.), p.23.
31 JMK to Florence Keynes, 20 September 1929, JMK, PP/45/168.
32 Anton Dolin, *Divertissement*, Sampson, Low & Marston, London, 1931.
33 *The Nation and Athenaeum*, 31 August 1929.
34 BBC draft scripts, LLK/3, also cited in Keynes (ed.), p.213.
35 LL to JMK, 16 October 1925.
36 Frederick Franklin, interview with the author.
37 LL to Florence Keynes, 18 June 1928.
38 LL to JMK, 30 April 1928.
39 Arnold Haskell, *Balletomania*, revised edn, Penguin, Harmondsworth, 1979, p.167.
40 Haskell, *Balletomania*, p.168.
41 LL to JMK, 30 January 1930.
42 *Daily Chronicle*, 18 February 1930.

43 LL to JMK, 30 April 1932.
44 Kavanagh, pp.117–18.
45 Kavanagh, p.144.
46 De Valois, p.102.
47 LL to Sam Courtauld, undated, LLK/5/57.
48 LL to JMK, 20 October 1930.
49 LL to JMK 19 January 1930.
50 LL to JMK, 26 October 1930.
51 Ashton, Keynes (ed.), p.118.
52 LL to JMK, 14 November 1930.
53 Ibid.
54 *Evening Standard*, 11 December 1930.
55 LL to JMK, 17 November 1930.
56 Ashton, Keynes (ed.), p.118.
57 *Manchester Guardian*, 27 April 1931.
58 LL to JMK, 29 April 1931.
59 LL to JMK, 7 June 1925.
60 LL to JMK, 14 November 1931.
61 Haskell, *Balletomania*, p.160.
62 R. Ellis Roberts, *New Statesman*, 5 March 1932.
63 LL to JMK, 5 March 1932.
64 Virginia Woolf to Ethel Sands, 18 August 1932, *Woolf Letters*.
65 Frederick Franklin, interview with the author.
66 Leo Kersley, interview with the author.
67 LL to JMK, 16 October 1932.
68 *Sunday Times*, 2 July 1933.
69 *Observer*, 2 July 1933.

17 Return to Acting, pp. 324–348

1 Lydia Lopokova, interview with Hubert Griffith, *Observer*, 26 March 1933.
2 Dennis Arundell, 'Lopokova as an Actress', Keynes (ed.), p.123.
3 JMK to LL, 19 October 1928.
4 Robert Helpmann, letter to Milo Keynes, 1978, LLK/8.
5 Arundell, Keynes (ed.), p.130.
6 JMK to LL, 22 October 1928.
7 *The Times*, 5 November 1929.
8 *The Times*, 11 December 1930.
9 *Standard*, 11 December 1930.
10 Vanessa Bell to Duncan Grant, 7 August 1930, cited Skidelsky, vol.2, p.433.
11 LL to Florence Keynes, 4 June 1931.

12 Vanessa Bell to Clive Bell, 10 October 1931, CHA, cited Skidelsky, vol.2, p.431.
13 JMK to James Strachey, 19 November 1933.
14 LL to JMK, 16 November 1931.
15 LL to JMK, 17 October 1932.
16 LL to JMK, 16 November 1932.
17 Ibid.
18 Ibid.
19 LL to Florence Keynes, 13 November 1932.
20 LL to JMK, 21 November 1932.
21 LL to Florence Keynes, 11 December 1932.
22 LL to JMK, 24 November 1932.
23 LL to JMK, 21 October 1933.
24 JMK to LL, 13 November 1931.
25 LL to JMK, 4 February 1933.
26 Vanessa Bell to Duncan Grant, August 1935.
27 LL to JMK, 20 February 1933.
28 Ibid.
29 LL to JMK, 28 February 1933.
30 JMK to LL, 1 March 1933.
31 LL to JMK , 20 April 1933.
32 *Observer*, 17 September 1933.
33 Letters to Milo Keynes, 1978 and 1979, LLK/8.
34 *Daily Express*, 19 September 1933.
35 *Daily Telegraph*, 19 September 1933.
36 Virginia Woolf, '*Twelfth Night* at the Old Vic', *New Statesman and Nation*, 30 September 1933, reprinted in Woolf, *The Death of the Moth and Other Essays*, Hogarth Press, London, 1945.
37 Ibid.
38 JMK to LL, 20 October 1933.
39 LL to JMK, 16–18 February 1934.
40 LLK.
41 *The Times*, 5 March 1934.
42 Virginia Woolf to Quentin Bell, 8 March 1934.
43 LL to JMK, 5 March 1934.
44 Cited Skidelsky, vol.2, p.503.
45 LL to Florence Keynes, 27 February 1933.
46 JMK to LL, 20 November 193
47 LL to JMK, 9 February 1936.
48 JMK to LL, 26 May 1935.
49 LL to JMK, 21 January 1935.

50 LL to JMK, 10 October 1935.
51 LL to JMK, 27 October and 10 November 1935.
52 Arundell, Keynes (ed.), *Lydia Lopokova*, p.131.
53 John Laurie, letter to Milo Keynes, 1979, also cited Arundell, Keynes (ed.), pp.132–3.
54 *Illustrated London News*, undated press cutting, LLK/1.
55 Kavanagh, p.219.
56 LL to JMK, 11 October 1951.
57 LL to JMK, 3 February 1935.
58 LL to JMK, 25 January 1937.
59 LL to JMK, 30 January 1937.
60 LL to JMK, 31 January 1937.
61 *Daily Telegraph*, 8 February 1937.
62 *Observer*, 14 February 1937.
63 LL to JMK, 1 March 1937.
64 Ibid.

18 Illness and Politics, pp. 349–365

1 LL to JMK, 29 April 1937.
2 Virginia Woolf, *Diary*, August 1934.
3 D. M. Bensusan-Butt, *On Economic Knowledge: A Sceptical Miscellany*, Australian National University, 1980, p.34, cited Skidelsky, vol.2, p.574.
4 Cited Skidelsky, vol.2, p.486.
5 Skidelsky, vol.2, p.515.
6 LL to JMK, 10 February 1935.
7 'Ballet Falsity', *Pravda*, 6 February 1936.
8 LL to JMK, 10 February 1935.
9 Lorie Tarshis, from an unpublished article, 'The Keynesian Revolution: What it Meant in the 1930s', cited Skidelsky, vol.2, p.574.
10 JMK to LL, 17 May 1936.
11 JMK to LL, 24 January 1937.
12 LL to Florence Keynes, 13 March 1937.
13 Ibid.
14 Cited in Skidelsky, vol.2, p.634.
15 LL to Florence Keynes, 12 February 1938.
16 LL to JMK, 28 June 1937.
17 JMK to LL, 29 June 1937.
18 LL to Florence Keynes, 19 July 1937.
19 LL to Florence Keynes, 22 July 1937.
20 LL to Florence Keynes, 13 September 1937.

21 Cited Skidelsky, vol.3, p.7.
22 LL to Florence Keynes, 5 February 1938.
23 Quentin Bell, quoted in Derek Crabtree and A. P. Thirlwall (eds), *Keynes and the Bloomsbury Group*, Macmillan, London, 1980, pp.82–3.
24 Ibid.
25 LL to Florence Keynes, 9 December 1937.
26 LL to Florence Keynes, 12 November 1937.
27 LL to Florence Keynes, 12 February 1938.
28 LL to Richard Kahn, 20 February 1938.
29 JMK to Vanessa Bell, 22 July 1937.
30 LL to Florence Keynes, 18 October 1937.
31 JMK to Margaret Keynes, 16 October 1937, JMK, PP/5.
32 LL to Richard Kahn, March 1938, LLK/5/118.
33 *Cambridge Review*, 22 April 1938.
34 LL to Florence Keynes, 10 June 1938.
35 LL to Florence Keynes, 25 September and 2 October 1938.
36 T. S. Eliot to JMK, 15 November 1938, JMK, PP/80.
37 *Manchester Guardian*, 15 November 1938.
38 LL to JMK, 10 February 1939.
39 *Observer*, 19 February 1939.
40 LL, unpublished diary, 1 March 1939, LLK/6.
41 JMK to Florence Keynes, 21 August 1939, JMK, PP/45.
42 JMK to Richard Kahn, 25 August 1939, RFK/13/57/433.
43 JMK to Florence Keynes, 27 August 1939, JMK, PP/45.

19 A Transatlantic War, pp. 366–399

1 *The Star*, 11 July 1942.
2 JMK to Florence Keynes, 21 October 1945, JMK, PP/45.
3 Virginia Woolf, *Diary*, 27 December 1939.
4 Ibid.
5 Bell, Keynes (ed.), p.91.
6 Ibid.
7 LL diary, 17 May 1940, LLK/6.
8 Ibid.
9 LL to Florence Keynes, 16 August 1940.
10 Ibid.
11 Cited in Skidelsky, vol.3, p.158.
12 JMK to Florence Keynes, 6 September 1940, JMK, PP/45.
13 Ibid.
14 JMK to Florence Keynes, 27 September 1940, JMK, PP/45.

15 LL to Florence Keynes, 31 December 1940.
16 LL to Florence Keynes, 21 March 1941.
17 LL to JMK, 30 April 1937.
18 LL to JMK, 28 June 1937.
19 Keynes (ed.), p.15.
20 LL to Florence Keynes, 3 April 1941.
21 Cited Hermione Lee, *Virginia Woolf*, pp.759–61.
22 Skidelsky, vol.3, p.90.
23 LL to Florence Keynes, 18 April 1941.
24 LL to Florence Keynes, 3 May 1941.
25 Ibid.
26 LL to Florence Keynes, 8 May 1941.
27 LL to Florence Keynes, 10 June 1941.
28 LLto Florence Keynes, 13 October 1944.
29 LLto Florence Keynes, 17 June 1941.
30 JMK to Florence Keynes, 28 June 1941, JMK, PP/45.
31 Cited Skidelsky, vol.3, p.118.
32 Skidelsky, vol.3, p.111.
33 Roy Harrod, *The Life of John Maynard Keynes*, Macmillan, London, 1951, p.556, also cited Keynes (ed.), p.16.
34 LL to Florence Keynes, 17 June 1941.
35 LL to Florence Keynes, 11 July 1941.
36 Wilfred Eady, *John Maynard Keynes*, cited Skidelsky, vol.3, p.148.
37 Cited Keynes (ed.), p.31.
38 Ibid.
39 Leo Kersley, interview with the author.
40 LL to Florence Keynes, 17 December 1942.
41 Mary Glasgow, *The Nineteen Hundreds*, Oxford University Press, 1986, pp.192–3.
42 Frances Partridge, *A Pacifist's War*, Hogarth Press, London, 1978, p.140.
43 JMK, *Collected Writings*, Cambridge University Press, vol.15, pp.363–4.
44 S. Howson and D. E. Moggridge (eds), *The Wartime Diaries of Robbins and Meades*, Macmillan, London, 1990, pp.97–100.
45 JMK to Florence Keynes, 9 October 1943, JMK, PP/45
46 LL to Florence Keynes, 12 July 1944.
47 Ibid.
48 Florence Keynes to LL, 17 July 1944.
49 Eady in *The Listener*, 7 June 1951.
50 Cited Skidelsky, vol.3, p.355.
51 LL to Florence Keynes, 10 August 1944.
52 Malcolm MacDonald, 'Lydia Keynes', Keynes (ed.), p.177.

53 Ibid, pp.178–9.
54 LL to Florence Keynes, 10 August 1944.
55 MacDonald, Keynes (ed.), p.179.
56 Isaiah Berlin, 'Maynard and Lydia Keynes', Keynes (ed.), p.173; also see version cited Skidelsky, vol.3, p.369.
57 Berlin, Keynes (ed.), pp.172–3.
58 R. Marler (ed.), *The Selected Letters of Vanessa Bell*, Bloomsbury, London, 1993, p.497.
59 JMK to Janos Plesch, 6 January 1946, JMK, PP/45.
60 Stephen Keynes, interview with the author.
61 JMK, *Collected Writings*, vol.28, pp.367–72, also published in *The Listener*, 12 July 1945.
62 Stephen Keynes, interview with the author.
63 Cited Skidelsky, vol.3, p.465.
64 Ibid.
65 Florence Keynes, 'In Memoriam', JMK, PP/45.
66 LLK/6.

20 After Maynard, pp. 400–426

1 Frederick Ashton to LL, cited Keynes (ed.), p.2.
2 These letters and the drafts of Lydia's replies are held in LLK/5/229.
3 Ibid.
4 Ibid.
5 LL to Florence Keynes, 17 January 1946.
6 LL to Florence Keynes, 20 February 1946.
7 LL to Florence Keynes, 7 December 1948.
8 LL to Florence Keynes, 20 December 1949.
9 LL to Florence Keynes, 1 May 1947.
10 Florence Keynes to LL, 20 May 1949.
11 Florence Keynes to LL, 26 April 1956.
12 A. A. Laanson to LL, undated, trans. Barbara Loughlin, LLK/5/231.
13 LL to Florence Keynes, 9 December 1947.
14 LL to Florence Keynes, 15 October 1951.
15 Logan Thomson to LL, 1 July 1956, LLK/5/209.
16 LL to Florence Keynes, 27 March 1956.
17 LL to Florence Keynes, 26 December 1957.
18 Leo Kersley, interview with the author.
19 Robert Helpmann to Milo Keynes, 1978, LLK/8.
20 LL to Florence Keynes, 5 January 1953.
21 LL to Florence Keynes, 9 September 1951 and Keynes (ed.), p.33.

22 LL to Richard Buckle, 8 May 1950, cited in Buckle, *In the Wake of Diaghilev*, Collins, London, 1982, p.105.
23 Buckle, *In the Wake of Diaghilev*, p.105.
24 Cited Kavanagh, p.366.
25 Cited Skidelsky, vol.3, p.483.
26 Stephen Keynes, interview with the author.
27 Robert Helpmann to Milo Keynes, 1978, LLK/8.
28 LL to Florence Keynes, 7 May 1954.
29 Beryl Grey, interview with the author.
30 LL to Florence Keynes, 26 November 1954.
31 LL to Florence Keynes, 9 August 1952.
32 LL to Florence Keynes, 5 March 1947.
33 LL to Florence Keynes, 3 October 1956.
34 LL to J. T. Sheppard, 1947, Sheppard Papers, KCA.
35 Buckle, *In the Wake of Diaghilev*, p.172.
36 Cited Skidelsky, vol.3, p.481.
37 Buckle, *In the Wake of Diaghilev*, p.109.
38 Ibid., p 104.
39 LL to Florence Keynes, 9 August 1952.
40 Randolfo Barocchi to LL, 27 December 1950, LLK/5/16.
41 Keynes (ed.), p.28.
42 LL to Richard Kahn, 23 October 1949, LLK/5/118.
43 Buckle, *In the Wake of Diaghilev*, p.105.
44 Ibid.
45 LL to Florence Keynes, 11 January 1950.
46 LL to Florence Keynes, 8 May 1956 and 7 May 1952.
47 Buckle, *In the Wake of Diaghilev*, p.106.
48 LL to Florence Keynes, 7 December 1948.
49 LL to Florence Keynes, 1 June 1949.
50 LL to Florence Keynes, 10 April 1952.
51 Buckle, *After the Wake*, p.106.
52 LL to Florence Keynes, 16 January 1950.
53 Beaton, 'A Visit to Lopokova', Keynes (ed.), p.185.
54 LL to Florence Keynes, 13 May 1957.
55 LL to Florence Keynes, 30 June 1951.
56 Buckle, *In the Wake of Diaghilev*, p.109.
57 David Castilejo to Milo Keynes, 1978, LLK/8.
58 Stephen Keynes, interview with the author.
59 LL to Geoffrey Keynes, September 1969, LLK/5/123.
60 LL to Florence Keynes, 7 May 1954.
61 Henrietta Garnett (Couper), 'Tea at Tilton', Keynes (ed.), pp.188–9.

62 Henrietta Garnett, interview with the author.
63 LL to Florence Keynes, 6 January 1957.
64 Henrietta Garnett, interview with the author.
65 Beaton, Keynes (ed.), pp.185–6.
66 LL to Richard Kahn, cited Skidelsky, vol.3, p.490.
67 LL to Florence Keynes, 3 November 1953.
68 Sarah Walton, interview with the author.
69 Vladimir Lopukhov, interview with the author, trans. Makarova.
70 Boris Eifmann, interview with the author.
71 Vladimir Lopukhov, interview with the author, trans. Makarova.
72 Ibid.
73 LL to Richard Kahn, 1967, LLK/5/118.
74 Cited in Keynes (ed.), p.37.
75 Richard Cork, interview with the author.
76 Henrietta Garnett (Couper), Keynes, (ed.), pp.192–4 and passim.
77 Ibid.
78 Keynes, (ed.), p 37.

Epilogue, pp. 427–428

1 Virginia Woolf, '*Twelfth Night* at the Old Vic', *New Statesman*, 30 September 1933.

SELECT BIBLIOGRAPHY

Anderson, Zoe, *The Royal Ballet*, London: Faber & Faber, 2006

Ansermet, Ernest, and Tappolet, Claude (eds), *Correspondance Ansermet-Strawinsky*, vol. 1, Geneva: Georg, 1991

Beaumont, Cyril W., *The Art of Lydia Lopokova*, London: Beaumont Press, 1920

Beaumont, Cyril W., *Diaghilev Ballet in London: A Personal Record*, London: Putnam, 1940

Benois, Alexander, *Reminiscences of the Russian Ballet*, trans. Mary Britnieva, London: Putnam, 1941

Bremser, Martha (ed.), *International Dictionary of Ballet*, Detroit and London: St James's Press, 1993

Buckle, Richard, *Nijinsky*, London: Weidenfeld & Nicolson, 1971

Buckle, Richard, *Diaghilev*, London: Hamish Hamilton, 1979

Buckle, Richard, *In the Wake of Diaghilev*, London: Collins, 1982

Buckle, Richard, with John Taras, *George Balanchine, Ballet Master*, New York: Random House, 1988

Crabtree, Derek, and Thirlwall, A. P. (eds), *Keynes and the Bloomsbury Group*, London: Macmillan, 1980

Daneman, Meredith, *Margot Fonteyn*, London: Viking, 2004

Danilova, Alexandra, *Choura*, New York: Knopf, 1986

Davis, Lee, *Scandals and Follies: The Rise and Fall of the Broadway Revue*, New York: Limelight Editions, 2000

Doborovolskaya, Galina, *Fyodor Lopukhov*, Leningrad: Iskusstvo, 1976

Dolin, Anton, *Autobiography*, London: Oldbourne, 1960

Drummond, John, *Speaking of Diaghilev*, London: Faber, 1997

Figes, Orlando, *Natasha's Dance: A Cultural History of Russia*, Harmondsworth: Penguin, 2003 (first published 2002)

Fokine, Michel, *Memoirs of a Ballet Master*, trans. V. Fokine, Boston: Little, Brown, 1961

Fonteyn, Margot, *Margot Fonteyn*, London: W. H. Allen, 1975

Garafola, Lynn, *Diaghilev's Ballets Russes*, New York and Oxford: Oxford University Press, 1989

Glendinning, Victoria, *Edith Sitwell: A Unicorn among Lions*, London: Weidenfeld & Nicolson, 1981

Glendinning, Victoria, *Leonard Woolf: A Life*, London: Simon & Schuster, 2006

Gottlieb, Robert, *Balanchine: The Ballet Maker*, London: Harper Press, 2006

Grigoriev, S. L., *The Diaghilev Ballet*, trans. Vera Bowen, Harmondsworth: Penguin, 1960 (first published 1953)

Hall, Coryne, *Imperial Dancer*, Stroud: Sutton Publishing, 2005

Harrod, Roy, *The Life of John Maynard Keynes*, London: Macmillan, 1951

Haskell, Arnold, *Balletomania*, revised edn, Harmondsworth: Penguin, 1979 (first published 1934)

Haskell, Arnold, with Walter Nuvel, *Diaghileff: His Artistic and Private Life*, London: Gollancz, 1935

Hill, Polly, and Keynes, Richard (eds), *Lydia and Maynard*, New York: Charles Scribners's Sons, 1989

Holroyd, Michael, *Lytton Strachey*, Harmondsworth: Penguin, 1971 (first published 1967)

Joffe, Lydia, 'The Lopukhov Dynasty', *Dance Magazine*, New York, January 1967

Karsavina, Tamara, *Theatre Street*, revised edn, London: Constable & Co., 1948 (first published 1930)

Kavanagh, Julie, *Secret Muses: The Lift of Frederick Ashton*, London: Faber & Faber, 1996

Keynes, Milo (ed.), *Essays on John Maynard Keynes*, Cambridge: Cambridge University Press, 1975

Keynes, Milo (ed.), *Lydia Lopokova*, London: Weidenfeld & Nicolson, 1983

Kramer, Dale, *Heywood Broun*, New York: Current Books, 1949

Kurth, Peter, *Isadora: The Sensational Life of Isadora Duncan*, London: Little, Brown, 2002

Lee, Hermione, *Virginia Woolf*, London: Chatto & Windus, 1996

Leonard, Maurice, *Markova: The Legend*, London: Hodder & Stoughton, 1995

Lopukhov, Fyodor, *Sixty Years in the Ballet*, Moscow: Iskusstvo, 1966

Markova, Alicia, *Markova Remembers*, Boston: Little, Brown, 1986

Marquez, Vicente Garcîa, *Massine*, London: Nick Hern Books, 1996

Massine, Léonide, Hartnoll, Phyllis, and Rubens, Robert (eds), *My Life in Ballet*, London: Macmillan, 1968

Moggridge, D. E., *Keynes*, London: Macmillan, 1976

Money, Keith, *Anna Pavlova: Her Life and Art*, London: Collins, 1982

Montefiore, Simon Sebag, *Stalin and the Court of the Red Tsar*, London: Weidenfeld & Nicolson, 2003

Motion, Andrew, *The Lamberts*, London: Chatto & Windus, 1986

Nicholson, Virginia, *Among the Bohemians*, Harmondsworth: Penguin, 2003

Nijinska, Bronislava, and Nijinska, I., *Early Memoirs*, trans. Jean Rawlinson, New York: Holt, Rinehart & Winston, 1981

O'Connor, Richard, *Heywood Broun*, New York: G. P. Putnam's Sons, 1975

Partridge, Frances, *Memories*, London: Victor Gollancz, 1981

Pritchard, Jane, 'London's Favourite Ballerina', *Dancing Times*, London, December 1989

Rambert, Marie, *Quicksilver: An Autobiography*, London: Macmillan, 1972

Seton-Watson, Hugh, *The Russian Empire 1801–1917*, Oxford: Oxford University Press, 1967

Sitwell, Osbert, *An Autobiography*, 5 vols, London: Macmillan, 1947–50

Skidelsky, Robert, *John Maynard Keynes*, 3 vols, London: Macmillan, 1983–2000 (editions used: 1984, 1994, 2000)

Sokolova, Lydia, *Dancing for Diaghilev*, London: John Murray; and California, Mercury House, 1960

Souritz, Elizabeth, *Soviet Choreographers in the 1920s*, Sally Banes (ed.), trans. Lynn Visson, London: Dance Books, 1990

Spalding, Frances, *Vanessa Bell*, London: Phoenix, 1996 (first published 1983)

Spalding, Frances, *Duncan Grant*, London: Pimlico, 1998 (first published 1997)

Stravinsky, Vera, and Craft, Robert, *Stravinsky in Pictures and Documents*, New York: Simon & Schuster, 1978

Taruskin, Richard, *Stravinsky and the Russian Traditions*, Oxford: Oxford University Press, 1996

Valois, Ninette de, *Come Dance with Me*, Dublin: Lilliput Press, 1992 (first published 1957)

Vaughan, David, *Frederick Ashton and His Ballets*, London: A & C Black, 1977

Walker, Kathrine Sorley, *Ninette de Valois*, London: Hamish Hamilton, 1987

Walsh, Stephen, *Stravinsky*, vol.1, New York: Alfred A. Knopf, 1999

Wiley, Roland John, *Tchaikovsky's Ballets*, Oxford: Oxford University Press, 1985

Woolf, Virginia, *Mrs Dalloway*, Harmondsworth: Penguin, 1992 (first published 1925)

Woolf, Virginia, *The Letters of Virginia Woolf*, Nigel Nicolson and Joanne Trautmann (eds), 6 vols, London: Hogarth Press, 1975–80

Woolf; Virgina, *The Diary of Virginia Woolf*, Anne Olivier Bell and Andrew McNeillie (eds), 5 vols, London: Hogarth Press, 1977–84

Main Archival Sources

John Maynard Keynes Papers, King's College Archive
Lydia Lopokova-Keynes Papers, King's College Archive
New York Public Library
Russian State Historical Archive, St Petersburg
Theatre Museum, London

INDEX

References to illustrations are indicated in *italics*.